Islamic Finance

"This book is a great addition to the growing literature on Islamic banking and finance. The chapters are sequenced well, beginning with a good introduction and followed by a discussion on the philosophy and basic principles of Islamic banking before embarking on the legal requirements of contracts and deposits. The authors then expound how these contracts are translated into practice by the contemporary Islamic banking industry and also compare the Islamic products with the prevailing conventional banking products. The book also covers the recent trends in technology and governance and complimenting markets like sukuk, takaful and wealth management. This book will be immensely useful for students of Islamic banking, as well as practitioners, academics, regulators and policy makers."
—Rafe Haneef, *CEO and Executive Director-CIMB Islamic Bank*

"This is an important book not just for students of Islamic finance but also for banking practitioners and consumers of banking products as it sets out the fundamental differences between Islamic finance and conventional banking and its importance in promoting a conscionable financial practice and sustainable economic development."
—Raja Teh Maimunah, *CEO, AmInvestment Bank*

Nafis Alam • Lokesh Gupta
Bala Shanmugam

Islamic Finance

A Practical Perspective

Nafis Alam
University of Reading Malaysia
Johor Bahru, Malaysia

Lokesh Gupta
RM Applications
Kuala Lumpur, Malaysia

Bala Shanmugam
Federation University Malaysia
Petaling Jaya, Malaysia

ISBN 978-3-319-88272-7   ISBN 978-3-319-66559-7 (eBook)
https://doi.org/10.1007/978-3-319-66559-7

© The Editor(s) (if applicable) and The Author(s) 2017
Softcover re-print of the Hardcover 1st edition 2017
This work is subject to copyright. All rights are solely and exclusively licensed by the Publisher, whether the whole or part of the material is concerned, specifically the rights of translation, reprinting, reuse of illustrations, recitation, broadcasting, reproduction on microfilms or in any other physical way, and transmission or information storage and retrieval, electronic adaptation, computer software, or by similar or dissimilar methodology now known or hereafter developed.
The use of general descriptive names, registered names, trademarks, service marks, etc. in this publication does not imply, even in the absence of a specific statement, that such names are exempt from the relevant protective laws and regulations and therefore free for general use.
The publisher, the authors and the editors are safe to assume that the advice and information in this book are believed to be true and accurate at the date of publication. Neither the publisher nor the authors or the editors give a warranty, express or implied, with respect to the material contained herein or for any errors or omissions that may have been made. The publisher remains neutral with regard to jurisdictional claims in published maps and institutional affiliations.

Cover designed by Jenny Vong
Cover illustration: © BornaMir / Getty Images

Printed on acid-free paper

This Palgrave Macmillan imprint is published by Springer Nature
The registered company is Springer International Publishing AG
The registered company address is: Gewerbestrasse 11, 6330 Cham, Switzerland

Foreword

Islamic banking and finance has emerged as a viable alternate finance stream and has lately gained a reputation as a full-fledged academic discipline knocking on doors of universities worldwide. Consequently there have been numerous books on the topic, but most of them are written exclusively for practitioners or for students only. This has inadvertently created a gap for readers who seek to comprehend both the theoretical underpinning and its applicability in the real world. *Islamic Finance- A Practical Perspective* provides a complete guide for the understanding of the theory and practices of Islamic finance. The book also highlights Islamic banking's suitability and its position in the world of finance.

By including chapters such as Information Technology in Islamic Banks and Islamic Wealth Management, the book provides another dimension of Islamic finance, which has not gained extensive support from researchers in this field. The use of simplistic language and day-to-day examples would assist readers in understanding key concepts easily.

The authors have also provided behind-the-scenes calculations done by Islamic banks for easy referencing when it comes to understanding the mechanics of profit loss sharing and financing charges.

The book will act as a good guide for students in both undergraduate and postgraduate programs in Islamic banking and finance, as well as Islamic banking practitioners and banking and finance researchers.

I wish to congratulate the authors for their exhaustive research and fluent exposition and wish the readers happy reading.

Asia e University
Kuala Lumpur, Malaysia

Prof. Dato' Dr Ansary Ahmed

Preface

Islamic banking as an industry has seen phenomenal growth since its rebirth in recent times, posting constant double-digit growth. It has not only transcended in Muslim world but has captured the attention of Western countries and global financial bodies such as World Bank and the International Monetary Fund. Many international banks now offer Sharia-compliant products and services, calling it 'Interest-free Banking', 'Socially Responsible Banking' or even 'Ethical Banking'—but the primary motive is to offer banking services with a big 'NO' to interest.

In these modern materialistic times, ethics and social objectives often take a back seat, but Islamic banking is one service where social motives and society welfare has been prioritized. This book is an attempt to create awareness of Islamic banking principles, and the development of its products and services by employing the profit computation method. While we wrote the book keeping bankers in mind, all concepts are presented in a simple and concise manner for easy comprehension.

We have tried to address the common questions about Islamic banking: What is Islamic banking? How is it different from conventional banking? How do Islamic banks generate profit? Is profit a substitute for interest in Islamic banking? How are Islamic banking products structured and applied for different banking needs? Why do Islamic banking practices differ from country to country? What is the role of information technology in Islamic banks and how can it leverage on Fintech? What kind of Corporate Governance model is practised by Islamic banks?

We wish to extend our appreciation to friends and family for their encouragement, patience and moral support. Special thanks to our banker friends who shared with us practical aspects of Islamic banking and to our publisher for their unending patience.

This book is our small contribution to society. We would be pleased to hear comments and constructive criticism from readers. While this book is the outcome of comprehensive research, errors nevertheless will exist, and for those we ask for your forgiveness.

Selangor, Malaysia   Nafis Alam

Kuala Lumpur, Malaysia   Lokesh Gupta

Petaling Jaya, Malaysia   Bala Shanmugam

The original version of this book was revised. Preface and Foreword are added to the front matter of this book.

Contents

1 Introduction to Islamic Banking — 1

2 The Religious Foundations of Islamic Banking — 17

3 Prohibition of Riba and Gharar in Islamic Banking — 35

4 Islamic Contracts — 55

5 Islamic Deposits in Practice — 79

6 Islamic Financing in Practice — 131

7 Comparative Analysis: Islamic Banking Products and Services in Different Countries — 245

8 IT in Islamic Banks — 307

9 Corporate Governance in Islamic Banks — 359

10	Islamic Capital Market	397
11	Takaful	431
12	Islamic Wealth Management	451

Index   475

List of Figures

Fig. 1.1	Historical developments in Islamic banking. Source: Author view	8
Fig. 2.1	Three Islamic faith foundations. Adapted from Haron and Shanmugam (2001)	18
Fig. 2.2	The Five Pillars of Islam	22
Fig. 2.3	Syariah overview	24
Fig. 2.4	Sources of Syariah	25
Fig. 2.5	Banking and finance needs of Muslims and non-Muslims. Source: Adapted from Khan (2007)	32
Fig. 3.1	Riba excesses	37
Fig. 3.2	Types of Riba	38
Fig. 3.3	Riba Qardh	39
Fig. 3.4	Riba Jahiliyyah	39
Fig. 3.5	Riba Fadhl	40
Fig. 3.6	Riba Nasiah	41
Fig. 3.7	Basis of Ribawi material	43
Fig. 3.8	Types of gharar	51
Fig. 4.1	Classification of contract according to nature of contract	60
Fig. 4.2	Classification of contract according to legal consequences	62
Fig. 4.3	Valid sale contract	69
Fig. 4.4	Islamic banking contracts	74
Fig. 5.1	Al-wadiah classification	84
Fig. 5.2	Mudharabah	86

List of Figures

Fig. 5.3	Saving Account based on the wadiah yad dhamanah principle	87
Fig. 5.4	Investment account based on the Mudharabah principle	103
Fig. 6.1	House Financing using BBA	138
Fig. 6.2	The modus operandi of umrah financing by using BBA	140
Fig. 6.3	Modus operandi of cash line financing by using BBA concept	142
Fig. 6.4	Instalment schedule inclusive of GPP	149
Fig. 6.5	*Modus operandi* of Murabahah financing	156
Fig. 6.6	Modus operandi of Murabahah financing for working capital	158
Fig. 6.7	*Modus operandi* of Ijarah financing	169
Fig. 6.8	*Modus operandi* of AITAB financing	179
Fig. 6.9	Musharakah classification. Source: Saiful Azhar Rosly (2005), "Critical Issues on Islamic Banking and Financial Market"	190
Fig. 6.10	*Modus operandi* of Musharakah financing	195
Fig. 6.11	*Modus operandi* of diminishing Musharakah for house financing	202
Fig. 6.12	*Modus operandi* of bai salam financing	221
Fig. 6.13	Structuring an Istisna financing transaction	224
Fig. 6.14	Bai al Inah financing mechanism	233
Fig. 8.1	Various key subsystems in core banking system	311
Fig. 10.1	Components of the ICM	399
Fig. 10.2	Working structure of Islamic unit trusts/mutual funds	408
Fig. 10.3	Structure of Sukuk Ijarah	419
Fig. 10.4	Illustration of a Sukuk mudarabah	420
Fig. 10.5	Sukuk Musharakah	422
Fig. 11.1	Comparison between Takaful and conventional insurance system	436
Fig. 11.2	Mudharabah model	437
Fig. 11.3	Wakalah model. Note: The surplus can also be shared with Takaful operators, as it depends on how the model is structured. The Wakalah model is the most recognized and accepted in the international Takaful market comprising 30 countries	439
Fig. 11.4	Wakalah with Waqf model	441
Fig. 12.1	Number of Islamic funds domiciled by country as on March 2017	466
Fig. 12.2	Global Islamic assets under management (AUM) by domicile as of Mar 2017. Source: www.mifc.com	466

List of Tables

Table 1.1	Differences between Islamic banking and conventional banking systems	12
Table 3.1	Rule matrix for ribawi materials	45
Table 3.2	Riba and profit	46
Table 5.1	Saving Account types	88
Table 5.2	Saving Account profit computation with 5% hibah rate	91
Table 5.3	Wadiah current account practice	94
Table 5.4	Mudharabah current account profit computation	100
Table 5.5	Mudharabah current account profit computation, dividend	101
Table 5.6	Mudharabah muthalaqah practice (general investment account)	105
Table 5.7	Mudharabah muthalaqah dividend computation	108
Table 5.8	Mudharabah Muqayyadah elements	110
Table 5.9	Mudharabah Muqayyadah (special investment account)	111
Table 5.10	Types of accounts offered by Islamic banks	128
Table 5.11	Types of deposit accounts	129
Table 6.1	Essential elements of BBA contract	135
Table 6.2	BBA financing practice	143
Table 6.3	Computation formula	146
Table 6.4	BBA financing instalment computation using Rule 78	150
Table 6.5	Murabahah financing practice	160
Table 6.6	Murabahah Financing Computation	161

Table 6.7	Comparison between BBA and Murabahah practice in Malaysia	166
Table 6.8	Essential elements of Ijarah contract	171
Table 6.9	Common features of product offered by banks	174
Table 6.10	Ijarah financing computation	175
Table 6.11	Comparison between Ijarah and conventional leasing	176
Table 6.12	Essential elements of AITAB	181
Table 6.13	AITAB financing computation	182
Table 6.14	Comparison between AIAB and conventional hire purchase	189
Table 6.15	Essential elements of Musharakah contract	193
Table 6.16	Diminishing Musharakah financing computation	204
Table 6.17	Shareholding	207
Table 6.18	Comparison between diminishing Musharakah and BBA financing	217
Table 6.19	Essential elements of bai salam contract	219
Table 7.1	Terminologies in practice for Islamic banking in ASEAN region	261
Table 7.2	Comparison of functions and principles	271
Table 7.3	Comparison of Islamic current account facilities	273
Table 7.4	Comparison of Islamic Saving Account facilities	274
Table 7.5	Comparison of Islamic investment facilities	279
Table 7.6	Comparison of Murabahah financing product	282
Table 7.7	Comparison of BBA financing products	286
Table 7.8	Comparison of Musharakah financing products	291
Table 7.9	Financial disclosure of Islamic banks of different countries	302
Table 8.1	Software companies currently providing Islamic banking solutions	347
Table 11.1	Number of Takaful operators/Takaful windows globally by category (2014)	445

1

Introduction to Islamic Banking

1   Introduction

Islamic banking is now a widely used term. Islamic banking has emerged in recent decades as one of the most important trends in the financial world. There has always been a demand for financial products and services that conform to the Syariah (Islamic law). With the development of viable Islamic alternatives to conventional banking, there are now Syariah-compliant banking products to meet the short-term and long-term banking needs of the customers.

Islamic banking is based on the principles of Syariah law. The Islamic banking system offers similar functions and services as the conventional banking system while abiding by Syariah principles.

There are two basic principles underlying Islamic banking:

1. The prohibition of riba (interest); and
2. The sharing of profit and loss between a bank and its customers.

The operations of Islamic financial institutions are based on a profit- and loss-sharing principle. An Islamic bank does not charge any interest for the financing offered to customers but rather participates in yield, resulting from the use of funds. On the other hand, depositors get their share from the bank's profit based on a predetermined ratio.

With the growth of Islamic finance, banks are now introducing various riba-free products and services to expand the banking scope and customer base.

1.1 Definition of Islamic Banking

An Islamic bank is a financial institution that operates with the objective to implement the economic and financial principles of Islam in the banking arena. Islamic banking has been defined in a number of ways.

The definition of an Islamic bank, as approved by the General Secretariat of the Organisation of the Islamic Conference (OIC), is stated in the following manner:

> An Islamic bank is a financial institution whose statutes, rules and procedures expressly state its commitment to the principle of Syariah and to the banning of the receipt and payment of interest on any of its operations.... (Ali and Sarkar 1995)

According to the Islamic Banking Act 1983, Malaysia, an Islamic bank is

> …a company which carries on Islamic banking business. Islamic banking business means banking business whose aims and operations do not involve any element which is not approved by the religion of Islam…. (Islamic Banking Act 1983)

The above definition was too generic and there was no exact definition of banking business. This is replaced by the new Islamic Financial Services Act (IFSA) 2013, and the revised definition under section 2 'Islamic banking business' means the business of:

(a) Accepting Islamic deposits on current account, deposit account, Saving Account, or other similar accounts, with or without the business of paying or collecting checks drawn by or paid in by customers; or
(b) Accepting money under an investment account;

(c) Provision of finance; and
(d) Such other business as prescribed under section 3; (http://www.bnm.gov.my/index.php?ch=en_legislation&pg=en_legislation_act&ac=1080)

This new Act has defined the Islamic banking business transactions thoroughly. From these definitions, we can summarize that Islamic financial institutions are institutions that are based on Syariah principles. This shall include but not be limited to the following Islamic principles:

1. The avoidance of riba (in the broad sense of unjustified increase or interest);
2. Prohibition of gharar (uncertainty, risk, speculation);
3. Focus on halal (religiously permissible) activities; and
4. More generally the quest for justice, and other ethical and religious goals.

In essence, Islamic banking operations are based on Islamic principles for financial transactions, that is, risk-sharing and prohibition of products and services having riba and profit- and loss-sharing are major features, ensuring justice and equity in the economy.

1.2 Islamic Banking Objectives

The primary objective of establishing Islamic banks is to spread economic prosperity within the framework of Islam by promoting and fostering Islamic principles in the business sector. Key objectives are listed below:

1. *Offer Financial Services*: Islamic banking statutes and laws are strictly in line with Syariah principles for financial transactions, where riba and gharar are all identified as un-Islamic. The thrust is toward financing on risk-sharing and strict focus on halal activities. The focus is on offering banking transactions adhering to Syariah principles and avoiding conventional interest-based banking transactions.
2. *Facilitate Stability in Money Value*: Islam recognizes money as a means of exchange and not as a commodity, where there should be a price for its use. Hence, riba-free system leads to stability in the value of money to enable the medium of exchange to be a reliable unit of account.

3. *Economic Development*: Islamic banking fosters economic development through utilities like Musharakah, Mudharabah, and so on, with a unique profit- and loss-sharing principle. This establishes a direct and close relationship between the bank's return on investment and the successful operation of the business by the entrepreneurs, which in turn leads to the economic development of the country.
4. *Optimum Resources Allocation*: Islamic banking optimizes allocation of scarce resources through investment of financial resources into projects that are considered to be the most profitable, religiously permissible, and are beneficial to the economy.
5. *Equitable Distribution of Resources*: Islamic banking ensures equitable distribution of income and resources among the participating parties—the bank, the depositors, and the entrepreneurs—with its profit-sharing approach which is one of a kind.
6. *Optimist Approach*: Profit-sharing principle encourages banks to go for projects with long-term gains instead of short-term gains. This leads the banks to conduct proper studies before getting into projects, which safeguards both the banks' and investors' interests in total. High returns distributed to shareholders maximize the social benefits and bring prosperity to the economy.

1.3 Islamic Banking Principles

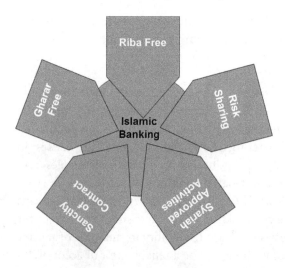

Islamic banking is the conduct of banking based on Syariah principles and does not allow the paying and receiving of interest while promoting profit-sharing. It has exactly the same purpose as conventional banking except that it operates under the Syariah law.

The best known feature of Islamic banking is fairness through the sharing of profit and loss and the prohibition of riba. The principles for Islamic banking are listed below:

- **Prohibition of Riba**
  Riba is strictly prohibited under Islam and is considered as haram (non-permissible). Islam prohibits Muslims from taking or giving riba regardless of the purpose for which such loans are made and regardless of the rates at which interest rate is charged. Islam allows only one kind of loan and that is Qardhul Hassan (benevolent loan) whereby the lender does not charge any interest or additional amount over the money lent. Traditional Muslim jurists have construed this principle so strictly that according to one commentator 'this prohibition applies to any advantage or benefits that the lender might secure out of the qard (loan) such as riding the borrower's mule, eating at his table, or even taking advantage of the shade of his wall'. The principle derived from the quotation emphasizes that direct or indirect benefits are prohibited.
- **Equity Participation**
  Riba is prohibited in Islam. Therefore, suppliers of funds become investors instead of creditors. The provider of financial capital and the entrepreneur share business risks in return for shares of the profits. Islam encourages Muslims to invest their money and to become partners in order to share profits and risks in the business instead of becoming creditors. In Islam, financing is based on the belief that the financier and borrower should equally share the risk of the business venture. The concept of sharing risk and rewards differentiates the Islamic banks from conventional banks, where all risks lie with the borrower and the customer has to pay the principal amount with interest, regardless of profit or loss from the venture. This provides stimulus to the economy and encourages entrepreneurs to maximize their efforts
- **Money as 'Potential Capital'**
  In Islam, money is only a medium of exchange. It is a way of defining the value of a thing. It has no value in itself and, therefore, should not

be allowed to give rise to more money, via fixed interest payments, simply by being put in a bank or when lent to someone. A mere postponement of consumption is no justification for reward. Money is treated as 'potential capital'. It becomes actual capital only when it combines with other resources to undertake productive activity. Islam recognizes the time value of money, but only when it acts as capital, not when it is 'potential capital'. This principle encourages Muslims to invest money into different ventures. Hoarding of money is considered haram. It is accepted that money represents purchasing power but only for the proper use of money. It cannot be used to increase purchasing power without any productive activity.

- **Prohibition of Gharar**

    An Islamic financial system discourages hoarding and prohibits transactions featuring extreme gharar (uncertainties) and maysir (gambling). Under this prohibition, any economic transaction entered into should be free from uncertainty, risk, and speculation. In business terms, gharar means to undertake a venture blindly without sufficient knowledge or to undertake excessively risky transactions. However, minor uncertainty can be permitted when it is deemed necessary. The prohibition applies even when the seller is not in a position to hand over the goods to the buyer or the subject matter of sale is incapable of acquisition, such as selling of fruit that are unripe or fish or bird not yet caught. As such contracting parties should have good knowledge of the products intended to be exchanged as a result of their transactions. Gharar is also applied to investments. This means that financial products such as options and futures are considered un-Islamic.

- **Sanctity of Contracts**

    Islam upholds contractual obligations and the disclosure of information as a sacred duty. This feature is intended to reduce the risk of asymmetric information and moral hazard. As such contracting parties should have good knowledge of the products intended to be exchanged as a result of their transactions. Furthermore, parties cannot predetermine a guaranteed profit. This is based on the principle of 'uncertain gains' which, on a strict interpretation, does not even allow an undertaking from the customer to repay the borrowed principal plus an amount to take into account for inflation. The rationale behind the prohibition is to protect the weak from exploitation.

- **Syariah-approved Activities**
  Islamic banks participate in business activities that do not violate the rules of Syariah. For example, any investment in businesses dealing with alcohol, gambling, and casinos would be strictly prohibited. As such, Islamic banks are expected to establish a Syariah Supervisory Board consisting of Syariah jurists who act as independent Syariah auditors and advisors to the banks. They will be responsible for ensuring that the practices and activities of Islamic banks do not contradict Islamic ethics.

1.4 Islamic Banking Evolution

Islamic banking was an abstract concept until the first half of the twentieth century. However, it has now developed into a full-fledged system and discipline. Islamic banking first started in Egypt at Mit Ghamr by Ahmad El Najjar in 1963. This bank neither paid nor charged any interest to investors and borrowers. It invested mainly in trade and industry. The profits made by the bank were paid to investors. The experiment, however, lasted only until 1967.

Islamic banking, with a very different approach to that in Egypt, also emerged in Malaysia. It was a financial institution developed for Malaysian Muslims undertaking the pilgrimage to Mecca and Medina. This institution called Lembaga Tabung Haji (Pilgrims Fund Board, Malaysia) was set up to help Muslims save for their pilgrimage expenses.

In 1971, the Naseer Social Bank was established in Egypt, and was declared an interest-free commercial bank, although its charter made no reference to Syariah. In the 1970s, changes took place in the political climate of many Muslim nations which facilitated the establishment of Islamic financial institutions. A number of Islamic banks came into existence in the Middle East during this period: the Islamic Development Bank (1975), the Dubai Islamic Bank (1975), the Faisal Islamic Bank of Sudan (1977), the Faisal Islamic Bank of Egypt (1977), and the Bahrain Islamic Bank (1979) to mention a few. Islamic banking made its debut in Malaysia in 1983 with the establishment of Bank Islam Malaysia Berhad (BIMB).

Since then, Islamic banks and financial houses have been established in Qatar, Sudan, Bahrain, Bangladesh, Indonesia, Senegal, Guinea, Denmark, Switzerland, Turkey, England, Jordan, Tunisia, and Mauritania.

Fig. 1.1 Historical developments in Islamic banking. Source: Author view

It is estimated that there are more than 250 Islamic banks now operating in over 75 countries. Even in countries with Muslim minorities, such as the USA, Australia, and Thailand, attempts are being made to set up Islamic financial institutions.

Figure 1.1 shows the important historical developments in Islamic banking. It demonstrates that Islamic banking operations are not limited to Arab soil, or Islamic countries, but are spread throughout the world. Many Muslim countries are taking their own initiatives to develop Islamic banking. Bank Negara Malaysia issued three new licenses exclusively for Islamic banking in 2006. Islamic finance is rapidly expanding in the global financial system with as many as 600 financial institutions across 75 countries offering Syariah-compliant products and services. Recent statistics published by Ernst & Young states that global Islamic banking assets reached US$1 trillion in 2015, and by 2020, the global Islamic banking industry profit pool is expected to reach US$30.3 billion.

1.5 Islamic Economics

Islamic banks are financial institutions established to promote Islamic economics. An Islamic economy is a market economy guided by moral values. Islam differs essentially from capitalism and socialism in the nature of ownership. Islam has given detailed regulations for economic life, which is balanced and fair. According to the Quran, everything on this earth belongs to Allah the Almighty. Man is a mere trustee and he is accountable to Him, in accordance with the rules laid down in the Syariah. As such, economic activities are based on the principles of cooperation and responsibility that are ethically guided, and aimed at establishing a just society wherein everyone will behave responsibly and honestly. The fundamental principles of an Islamic economic system are listed below.

- **Socio-economic Justice and Equitable Distribution**
  The essential feature of Islamic economics is that it is meant to establish socio-economic justice. Socio-economic justice comprises of two principles. The first principle is of general mutual responsibility and the second is about social balance. Islam encourages businesses to be carried out in an honest way that facilitates mutual benefit to the parties involved. Islam also encourages the practice of trade, just as it has denounced the injustices of interest. The focus is to achieve win/win outcomes while avoiding 'win/lose' or 'lose/lose' ones. This 'win/win' framework leads to better economic behavior and performance and thus promises a better future. The essence is the abolition of exploitation.
- **Trading of Forbidden Objects**
  Islam prohibits the trading of forbidden or unclean objects such as pigs; production, sale, and distribution of alcohol; fortune-telling, and so on. These activities are considered haram (non-permissible). In addition to these, certain objects are clean but not tradable, such as the soil of holy places. Haram is defined as 'not permitted, not allowed, unauthorised, unapproved, unsanctioned, unlawful, illegal, illegitimate or illicit;. As such, every Muslim has to ensure that any economic activity done by them should not involve any haram element.
- **Trusteeship**
  Islam has stressed that everything in this universe belongs to Allah the Almighty and He is the owner of everything. Allah has made man a trustee. Man is accountable to Allah the Almighty for the utilization of these resources. Realization of this dual ownership mitigates the selfish and dishonest tendencies that often crop up from the notion

of absolute ownership. The idea of trusteeship distinguishes the Islamic approach to economics from materialistic approaches like capitalism and socialism, and introduces a moral and spiritual element into business life. Absolute ownership by man is an alien concept in Islam. There are also definite obligations to be adhered to by man. An example is that it is forbidden to gain ownership of property or wealth by fraud, deceit, theft, or other falsehoods. Property can be acquired by combining one's labor with natural resources. Rights also can be transferred in exchange for a counter-value of the same worth or as a gift.

- **Prohibition of Hoarding**
  Islam prohibits hoarding of food, money, and other basic necessities as this practice is recognized as wasting of wealth. This principle rules out the seeking of economic gains at the cost of moral and spiritual values, both at the individual and the societal levels. It follows that savings (what is left after consumption and charitable giving) must be put to good use. Islam encourages investment in trade that in turn will generate revenue. This can be shared based on the profit- and loss-sharing concept, which will be productive for the community and can bring about economic prosperity. The important lesson is that Islam prohibits wealth hoarding and encourages investments that benefit the community.

- **Spirit of Cooperation**
  Islam requires that every man should give the needy a specified portion of his wealth. This contribution is called zakat which is a levy on certain categories of wealth. The importance of zakat is that it is one of the five pillars of Islam, the others being belief, prayers, fasting, and haj. Zakat is usually about 2.5% of personal wealth. Zakat is a means of narrowing the gap between the rich and the poor and to ensure that everyone's needs are met. A society can flourish only when its members do not spend all their wealth on satisfying their own desires but reserve a portion of it for their parents, relatives, neighbors, the poor, and the incapacitated. The principle of zakat is to take from those who have wealth and give it away to those who do not. This redistribution of wealth is a way to reduce social inequality.

- **The Duality of Risk**
  Islam has a dual conception of risk. On the one hand, it considers the partial acceptance of liability (for risk) in a productive venture as legitimate for a share in profit. On the other hand, risk should always be taken cautiously. Excessive and uncontrollable risks or obligations should be avoided as it leads to speculation. For example, the sale of an object which the seller does not yet possess is strictly prohibited. In addition, gambling and speculation are also forbidden. In business terms, the object of a contract must be known, ascertained, and in existence when the contract is concluded.
- **No Gain Without Either Effort or Liability**
  Islam recognizes money as a medium of exchange and not a commodity for exchange. Hence, any reward generated from the mere postponement of consumption, that is, savings, is not a justification for compensation, that is, riba or interest. Islam is not opposed to profit or financial gain, as long as:

(a) An effort is performed, or (partial) liability is accepted for the financial result of a venture.
(b) The effort or venture was productive, that is, it led to an increase of value.
(c) The profit was made in line with Syariah guidelines.

According to Islam, money is unproductive as long as it is not combined with labor. It follows that savings will produce additional value only when it is invested and the financial gain made from the investment can be shared with the investor. The rule here is that the reward of the investor should be tied to the result of the investment and is called 'profit- and loss-sharing'.

1.6 Islamic and Conventional Banking

Islamic banks, like conventional banks, are profit-making organizations. Their aim is to gain profit. However, they are prohibited to trade in riba or to engage in any business activity that is not in compliance with Syariah principles. In contrast, there are no such restrictions on conventional banks.

Islamic banking activities are based on the principle of buying and selling of assets. For example, in financing a home loan, the selling price (including the bank's profit margin) is fixed from the very beginning.

The differences between Islamic banking and conventional banking systems are listed in Table 1.1.

Table 1.1 Differences between Islamic banking and conventional banking systems

Characteristics	Islamic banking system	Conventional banking system (interest-based)
Business framework	Functions and operating modes are based on Syariah law Banks have to ensure that all business activities are in compliance with Syariah requirements	Functions and operating modes are based on secular principles and not based on any religious laws or guidelines
Prohibition of riba in financing	Financing is not interest-oriented and is based on the principle of buying and selling of assets, whereby the selling price includes a profit margin and is fixed from the beginning	Financing is interest-oriented and a fixed/floating interest is charged for the use of money
Prohibition of riba in deposits	Deposits are not interest-oriented but profit and loss-sharing-oriented whereby investors share a fixed percentage of profit when it occurs. Banks get back only a share of profit from the business to which it is a party, and in case of loss, the investor loses none in terms of money but foregoes the reward for its activities during that period	Deposits are interest-oriented and the investor is assured of a predetermined rate of interest with a guarantee of principal repayment
Equity financing with risk-sharing	Bank offers equity financing for a project or venture Losses are shared based on the equity participation while profit is shared based on the pre-agreed ratio	Not generally offered but available through venture capital companies and investment banks Normally they participate in management as well

(continued)

Table 1.1 (continued)

Characteristics	Islamic banking system	Conventional banking system (interest-based)
Restrictions	Islamic banks are restricted to participate in economic activities, which are not Syariah compliant	There are no such restrictions
Zakat (religious tax)	For example, banks cannot finance businesses involving pork, alcohol, and so on In the modern Islamic banking system, it has become one of the functions to collect and distribute zakat	Do not deal in zakat
Penalty on default	Have no provision to charge any extra money from the defaulters. Note: Some Muslim countries allow collecting of penalty, and the justification is the cost incurred on collecting the penalty, which is normally 1% of the instalment amount due	Normally charge additional money (compound rate of interest) in case of defaulters
Prohibition of gharar	Transactions with element of gambling and speculation are strictly forbidden For example, derivative trading is prohibited due to its speculative nature	Trading and dealing in any kind of derivative/futures involving speculation is allowed
Customer relation	The status of the bank, in relation to its clients, is that of partner/investor and entrepreneur.	The status of a bank, in relation to its clients, is that of creditor and debtors
Syariah Supervisory Board	Each bank should have a Syariah Supervisory Board to ensure that all business activities are in line with Syariah requirements	There is no such requirement necessary
Statutory requirement	Banks have to be in compliance with statutory requirement of Bank Negara Malaysia and also Syariah Guidelines	Has to be in compliance with the statutory requirements of the Bank Negara Malaysia only

1.7 Advantages of Islamic Banking

In the previous sections, we provided the definition, principles, and objective of Islamic banking along with the features that differentiate it from conventional banking. Here, we describe some of the major advantages of Islamic banking:

1. *Justice and Fairness*: The main feature of the Islamic model is that it is based on a profit-sharing principle, whereby the risk is shared by the bank and the customer. This system of financial intermediation will contribute to a more equitable distribution of income and wealth.
2. *Liquidity*: They follow the profit- and loss-sharing principle to mobilize resources and are less likely to face any sudden run on deposits. As such, they have a minimum need for maintaining high liquidity.
3. *Better Customer Relations*: Financing and deposits are extended under the profit- and loss-sharing arrangement. The banks are likely to know their fund users better in order to ensure that the funds are used for productive purposes, and *vice versa* for investors. In this way, it develops better relations between the financial intermediary and the fund providers or consumers. It will also promote productive economic activities and socio-economic justice.
4. *No Fixed Obligations*: Islamic banks do not have fixed obligations such as interest payments on deposits. Therefore, they are able to allocate resources to profitable and economically desirable activities. This also holds good for Islamic financing, as the payment obligations of the entrepreneur is associated with the revenue.
5. *Transparency*: They are transparent to the account holders on the investments made in different areas and the profits realized from these investments. The profit is then shared in the pre-agreed ratio.
6. *Ethical and Moral Dimensions*: Their strong ethical and moral dimensions of doing business and selecting business activities to be financed play an important role in promoting socially desirable investments and better individual/corporate behavior.
7. *Destabilizing Speculation*: Most of the non-Islamic institutions are trading heavily into financial markets and carrying out huge speculative

transactions. These transactions are sources of instability and the returns on investments are highly speculative. On the contrary, Islamic banks are prohibited from carrying out such activities. This destabilizes the speculation and is in the better interest of the depositors.
8. *Banking for All*: Although based on Syariah principles to meet the financial needs of Muslims, it is not restricted to Muslims only and is available to non-Muslims as well.

References

http://www.aibim.com.my/aibim/dsp_page.cfm?pageid=230
http://www.mymoneyskills.com/visa/my/en_US/banking_services/islamic.shtml
http://www.worldbank.org/fandd/english/0697/articles/0140697.htm
http://islam.about.com/library/weekly/aa022200a.htm
http://www.islamibankbd.com/page/ih_2.htm
Ali, M., & Sarkar, A. A. (1995, July–December). Islamic banking: Principles and operational methodology. *Thoughts on Economics, 5*(3 & 4.) Islamic Economics Research Bureau, Dhaka.
Ali, A. M. (2002, September 30). *The state and future of Islamic bank on the world economic scene*. Islamic Development Bank Staff Papers, Washington.
Ariff, M. (1988, September). Islamic banking. *Asian-Pacific Economic Literature, 2*(2), 46–62.
Lewis, M. K., & Algaoud, L. M. (2001). *Islamic banking*. Cheltenham, UK: Edward Elgar Publishing.
van Schaik, D. (2001, April). Islamic banking. *The Arab Bank Review, 3*(1), 45–52.

2

The Religious Foundations of Islamic Banking

1   Islam: An Overview

The word Islam, which originates from the Arabic word salaam, means submission or peace. Islam is a system of religious beliefs and an all-encompassing way of life. The person who believes in and consciously follows Islam is called a Muslim, also from the same root word.

Islam is a religion of laws—it is a legal code, not a theology, which establishes the criteria for right and wrong, proper and improper behavior. Muslims believe that Allah the Almighty revealed to Prophet Muhammad, the rules governing society and the proper conduct of the society's members. It is incumbent on the individual, therefore, to live in a manner prescribed by the revealed law, and on the community to build the perfect human society on Earth according to holy injunctions.

Islam is a complete religion, embracing all the facets of activities in this world and hereafter. In essence, it is a command of Allah the Almighty encompassing all aspects of human life including the essence of economic well-being and development of Muslims at the individual, family, community, society, and state levels. The three foundations that underlie the guidance contained in the Islamic faith are Aqidah, Akhlaq, and Syariah are illustrated in Fig. 2.1.

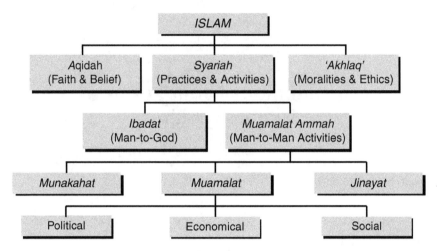

Fig. 2.1 Three Islamic faith foundations. Adapted from Haron and Shanmugam (2001)

We can gather from the chart in Fig. 2.1 that the economic and social transactions, as well as the educational and political systems, form part of the teachings of Islam. The chart can be explained as follows:

1. *Aqidah*: Aqidah governs the principles of faith and belief in Islam. It is derived from the word aqad, which means tie or knot. Aqidah from an Islamic point of view means strong beliefs in the heart of a person in Allah the Almighty and His Prophet, Muhammad.

Aqidah is the main foundation in Islam and a starting point in order to be a good Muslim. It is reflected in the activities conducted by the Prophet. Prophet Muhammad describes Islam as a building whereby its foundation is Aqidah. The foundation of Aqidah in Islam comprises six pillars:

(a) *Faith in God*: Muslims testify that 'there is no God except Allah the Almighty and that the Prophet Muhammad is His Messenger' with a belief in the oneness of God, and worship is to be directed to this one God.

(b) *Faith in the Angels*: In Islam, the Angels are the creatures whereby Allah the Almighty endorses his commandments on Earth. Their duties include maintaining a record of the actions, thoughts, and deeds of each human during his earthly life and protecting or taking life when commanded to do so by Allah the Almighty.

(c) *Faith in the Scriptures*: Muslims believe that the scriptures revealed by Allah the Almighty are for the guidance of mankind. The message of Allah the Almighty is the ultimate truth and guidance recorded in the Quran, Hadith (acts, deeds, and approval of Prophet Muhammad) is to be followed by Muslims. The point is man is not perfect; hence, his laws cannot be perfect either.

(d) *Faith in the Prophets*: Muslims believe that many individuals were called to prophethood prior to the advent of the Prophet Muhammad. Twenty-eight are mentioned in the Quran such as Abraham, Moses, and Jesus. The prophets are regarded as Allah's messengers to mankind and are equally deserving of respect.

(e) *Faith in the Day of Judgment*: Muslims believe that there is a Day of Judgment when all the people of the world throughout the history of mankind are to be brought for accounting, reward, and punishment. In this context, Allah the Almighty is the guarantor of ultimate justice in whom all earthly activity will be matched with the appropriate reward or punishment.

(f) *Faith in Destiny*: The Quran states that a man's fate is determined by his own actions.

2. *Akhlaq*: Akhlaq defines the Islamic ethical code as it relates to personal conduct. It covers all aspects of Muslim behavior, attitude, and work ethics by which he performs his practical actions. Akhlaq in Islam consists of the relationship between man and man, man and Allah, and man and others. In other words, Akhlaq is based on the submission of Muslims to Allah and the attitude of Prophet Muhammad as a role model to all Muslims.

To summarize, Akhlaq concerns the behavior, attitude, and work ethics by which a Muslim performs his practical actions.

3. *Syariah*: Syariah literally means 'way to water'—the source of all life—and signifies the way to Allah, as given by Allah. The literal meaning is to chalk out or march out a clear road to water. In the religious sense, it means the way which directs man's life to the right path.

The concept of Syariah is not only to govern man in the conduct of his life in order to realize the divine will, but it also covers all behavioral, spiritual, mental, and physical aspects. Therefore, Syariah principles are more than law, covering the total way of life that includes faith and practices, personal behavior, legal and social transactions, for a total way of life.

In short, Syariah governs all forms of practical action, comprising ibadat (the law pertaining to devotional matters) and muamalat (the law pertaining to activity in the political, economic, and social spheres):

(a) *Muamalat Ammah*: This presents a framework for conduct in the civil arena. It is concerned with the practicalities of a person's daily life, in the context of relationship between man and man, and other creatures, which include animal, plants, and non-living things. This can be further classified into three types:

  (i) *Munakahat*: This area deals with marriage, divorce, inheritance, guardianship, and related matters;
  (ii) *Jinayat*: Conduct related with offenses against the human body and torts are called jinayat. The term jinayat is also used for torts when the offense falls under ghasb (usurpation, misappropriation) and italf (destruction of property);
  (iii) *Muamalat*: Conduct that covers human activities related to business, trade, and efforts in accumulating wealth and means or activities related to economic development, in three areas:

    - *Political*—Conduct related to treasury/ministry of finance/government activities;
    - *Economic*—Public contract and Islamic finance fall under this category, such as the direct link of Islamic banking with Syariah;
    - *Social*—Conduct related to socio-economic justice and brotherhood, for example, zakat to be paid by Muslims.

4. *Ibadat*: The word ibadat is derived from abd which means 'servant and slave'. Therefore, the meaning of ibadat is servitude and slavery. It is concerned with the practicalities of worship to Allah, in the context of the relationship between man and his Creator. The rules of ritual purification, prayer, pilgrimage, fasting, war (jihad), and some other forms of worship are dealt with under this heading. Most of these rules deal with the rights owed to Allah by the individuals alone or by the community as a whole.

In essence, Islamic law prescribes Muslim behavior in every aspect of life from private matters between the individual and Allah, to relationships with others from the family to the widest community. Hence, Syariah covers not only religious rituals, but many aspects of day-to-day life. The Syariah contains categories and subjects of Islamic law, which includes Islamic worship, family relations, inheritance, commerce, property law, civil (tort) law, criminal law, administration, taxation, constitution, international relations, war and ethics, Islamic banking, and financing activities.

1.1 Pillars of Islam

In Islam, faith and good work go hand-in-hand. A mere verbal declaration of faith is not enough; only upon practice can one be a true Muslim as per Islam. The Five Pillars of Islam lay the foundation of Muslim life. The Five Pillars of Islam are the framework of Muslim life (Fig. 2.2).

1. Testimony of Faith

'There is none worthy of worship except Allah the Almighty and Muhammad is the Messenger of Allah.' This declaration of faith is called the shahadah, a simple formula that all the faithful pronounce. The significance of this declaration is the belief that the only purpose of life is to serve and obey Allah, and this is achieved through the teachings and practices of the last prophet, Muhammad. The testimony of faith is the most important pillar of Islam.

Fig. 2.2 The Five Pillars of Islam

2. Prayers

Formal prayer is the most important act of worship for Muslims. These are the obligatory prayers that are to be performed five times a day, and are a direct link between the worshipper and Allah. Prayers are said at dawn, mid-day, late afternoon, sunset, and nightfall, and thus determine the rhythm of the entire day. Prayers said in congregation bond Muslims together in love and brotherhood. Prayer also symbolizes the equality of believers; there is no hierarchy, and all stand side by side in rows and bow only to Allah.

3. Zakat

Paying zakat is considered as worshipping Allah. The original meaning of the word zakat is both 'purification' and 'growth'. Giving zakat means 'giving a specified percentage on certain properties to certain classes of needy people'. Paying of zakat leads to cleansing the heart from evil. This is a financial obligation for Muslims. The belief is that wealth is a gift from Allah; one has the duty to help his needy brethren when he is able.

4. Fasting

Muslims are required to fast during the holy month of Ramadan, the ninth month of the Islamic calendar. During Ramadan, all Muslims fast from dawn until sundown, abstaining from food, drink, and sexual relations.

Although the fast is beneficial to health, it is regarded principally as a method of spiritual self-purification. By cutting oneself off from worldly comforts, even for a short time, a fasting person gains true empathy with those who go hungry, as well as growth in his or her spiritual life.

5. Pilgrimage

The annual pilgrimage (Haj) to Mecca in Saudi Arabia is a once in a lifetime obligation for those who are physically and financially able to perform it. It was here that Abraham built the first house of worship (the Kaaba), toward which all Muslims stand in unity in their daily prayers. Pilgrimage to Mecca is worshipping of Allah by visiting the Holy House to perform the rituals of Haj. Haj trains the soul to devote time and physical effort in seeking to obey Allah.

Islam, as we explained before, is about faith and laws. The pillars are the basis of the Islamic law, which forms the foundation for Islamic banking.

2   Syariah Overview

Syariah is the 'centerpiece and backbone of the religion of Islam'. It is the source of all life—and signifies the way to Allah, as given by Allah. It is the way that encompasses the totality of man's life. The purpose of Syariah's legal code is to guide both individuals and society toward peace and justice, and to prevent crime and deter criminals.

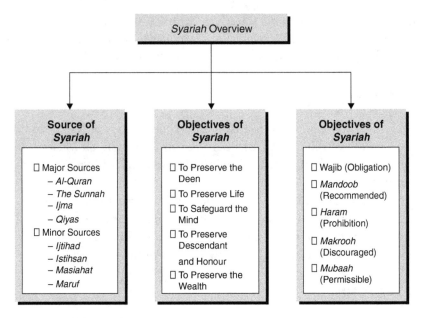

Fig. 2.3 Syariah overview

Syariah is not merely a collection of dos and don'ts, nor just a code of criminal laws prescribing punishments for certain crimes. Though it does contain both, its sweep is much broader and deeper, encompassing the totality of man's life. Syariah literally means a 'way to water'. It is the path that man, in Islam, must walk as he toils and strives to reach his Creator. It is the deep yearning to seek the Lord and the Master that Syariah translates into steps, concrete and specific, on the pathways of life. Syariah is the fulfillment of the total man—inner and outer, individual and corporate—as he seeks to live by the will of his one and only God.

The areas that will be covered under the Syariah overview are illustrated Fig. 2.3.

2.1 Sources of Syariah

Syariah is the comprehensive legal system for Muslims. Islamic law covers all aspects of life, which includes personal, civil, criminal, mercantile, constitutional, and international relations. Islamic law has been defined

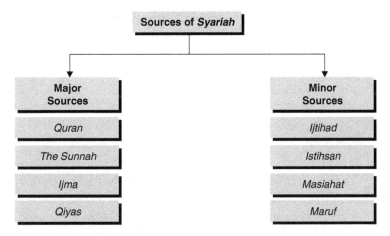

Fig. 2.4 Sources of Syariah

as the body of rules of conduct revealed by Allah to His Prophet, Muhammad, whereby the people are directed to lead their life in this world. The basic source of Islamic law is Divine Revelation, but there are other sources as well. For easy understanding, we have categorized the same under two broad headings as illustrated in Fig. 2.4.

1. **Major Sources**

   (a) *The Quran*: Quran is the foundation of Islam and is primarily a book of religious and moral principles. The Quran is a compilation of the word of God revealed to the Prophet Muhammad. It not only includes directives relating to individual conduct but also principles relating to all the aspects of social and cultural life. The Quran is the last and complete edition of Divine Guidance and is the only book of Allah which has not been distorted.

   The Quran was revealed between 611 AD and 632 AD, that is, during the period when the Prophet lived in Makkah and in Madinah, respectively. The Quran was memorized by the Prophet and many sahabas (companions). The Prophet chose scribes from among his companions to record the verses of the Quran on things such as wood, pieces of leather, flat pieces of stones, or flat bones. During the Caliphate of 'Othman Ibn 'Affan, a committee of four scribes including Zayd Ibn Thabit was formed to compile and bind the Quran in a single volume. These scribes wrote five copies of the original manuscript preserved by Hafsah binti Umar.

The features of Quran are listed below:

(i) Quran is the word of Allah revealed to the Prophet Muhammad in the Arabic language, conveyed by Angel Jibrail.
(ii) It consists of 114 chapters and 6235 verses.
(iii) The language in Quran is pure Arabic of the highest standard.
(iv) It contains information and stories about people of the past.
(v) It foretells future events, which really took place afterward.
(vi) It describes the realities of nature and the creation of a human life and the orbit of the Earth, the Sun, the Moon, and the stars.
(vii) It contains laws and rules on how to regulate political, legal, economic, social, and moral matters in society.

To summarize, the Quran's main emphasis is unquestionably on faith and the moral conduct of men and nations; however, it does lay down, both explicitly and implicitly, though with brevity, the principles, broad outlines, and necessary rules and regulations, which are essential for the formation of the community of Islam.

(b) *The Sunnah*: It is the second source of Islamic law. The Sunnah is an Arabic word, which means method. It was applied by the Prophet Muhammad as a legal term to represent what he said, did, and agreed to. The Sunnah consists of the sayings, deeds, and approval of the Prophet Muhammad. In other words, the Sunnah is the implementation and deliberation of the Quran. It is through the Sunnah, that the Quran was implemented and practiced.

The Quran and the Sunnah are the primary sources of Islamic law and are called as absolutely sure arguments or infallible proof. This is because these sources contain absolute truth and the undoubted fundamental doctrines of Islam.

(c) *Ijma*: Ijma is the verbal noun of the Arabic word ajma'a, which has two meanings: to determine and to agree upon something. The consensus of the jurists in understanding, interpreting, and applying the teachings of the Quran and the Sunnah forms the third basic source of the Syariah. Ijma or consensus is the agreement of qualified legal scholars in a given generation, and such consensus of opinion is deemed infallible.

In other words, ijma is the consensus of opinion of the qualified legal scholars among Muslims in a particular time after the death of the Prophet of God regarding the legal position of a matter or problem. As such, ijma is a unanimous consensus among jurists.

(d) *Qiyas*: Qiyas means analogy. Qiyas or analogy is resorted to in respect of problems about which there is no specific provision in the Quran or the Sunnah of the Prophet. In such issues, the scholars have derived law through analogical deduction on the basis of the provisions of the Quran and the Sunnah on some similar situation. The original case is regulated by a text of the Quran or the Sunnah, and qiyas seeks to extend the original ruling to the new case. The emphasis of qiyas is identification of a common cause between the original and new case. The ijma and qiyas are secondary sources of the Syariah and are known as arguments obtained by exertion.

2. Minor Sources

(a) *Ijtihad*: Ijtihad literally means 'striving or self-exertion'. Ijtihad consists of intellectual exertion. Ijtihad is a very broad source of Islamic law and comes after the Quran and the Sunnah. Ijtihad is the source or methodology which gives Islamic law its adaptability to new situations and capacity to tackle all new issues and problems. Propriety or justification of ijtihad is measured by its harmony with the Quran and the Sunnah.

(b) *Istihsan*: Istihsan literally means 'to deem something preferable in best of public interest'. In its juristic sense, istihsan is a method of exercising personal opinion (ray) in order to avoid any rigidity and unfairness that might result from literal application of law. Istihsan is not independent of Syariah; it is an integral part of Syariah. Istihsan as a concept is close to equity and plays a prominent role in adaptation of Islamic law to the changing needs of society.

(c) *Maslahat*: Maslahat literally means 'benefit or interest' and is referred to as unrestricted public interest. It consists of considerations which secure a benefit or prevent harm. Protection of life, religion, intellect, lineage, and property is Maslahat.

(d) *Maruf*: Maruf literally means 'well-known or customary'. It is defined as recurring practices, which are acceptable to people of sound nature. It is based on the principle: 'What is proven by custom is alike that proven by Syariah' given that custom is not in conflict with the rules, essence, and spirit of Syariah. This is mostly applicable in the case of a local or national practice.

2.2 Objectives of Syariah

The objectives (Maqasid) of Syariah are to protect the interest of people against harm. The Maqasid can be classified into three categories:

Objectives of Syariah

The Embellishments (Tahsiniyat)	
The Complementarities (Hajiyat)	
The Necessities	• Preserve the Deen or Religion • Preserve Life or Nafs • Safeguard the Mind or the Aql • Preserve Descendants and Honor • Preserve the Wealth
Sources of Syariah	• Major Sources (*The Quran, The Sunnah, Ijma, Qiyas*) • Minor Sources (*Ijtihad, Istihsan, Maslahat, Maruf*)

- *The Necessities (Daruriyyat)*: The following are the five basic and universal necessities for human existence:

  1. *To Preserve the Deen or Religion*: Deen means the totality of beliefs, practices, and laws by which Islam regulates the relationship between

man and his Creator, and between man and man. Preservation of deen is necessary for the welfare of individuals and society.
2. *To Preserve Life or Nafs*: This means measures to preserve the human species, and integrity of life is the second objective of Syariah. This includes protection of the human life, health, and integrity by establishing rules to preserve the human life and dignity, and punish those who transgress against it.
3. *To Safeguard the Mind or the Aql*: To preserve and protect the intellect, Syariah permits the right of promoting and attaining knowledge and prohibits things that demise the role of the intellect such as intoxicants and drugs. As such, Syariah forbids the consumption of alcohol and all intoxicating substances.
4. *To Preserve Descendants and Honor*: Syariah has to ensure the integrity and continuity of life. The goal of the Syariah law is to prohibit unlawful relationships between men and women and false accusations against people who are chaste.
5. *To Preserve the Wealth*: Wealth is the last objective because the intent of its acquisition is to serve the aforementioned four objectives. The rulings of Syariah came into being, to encourage people to work and earn a living lawfully and to prohibit exploitation and injustice.

- *The Complementarities (Hajiyat)*: The complementary things are matters that people need in order to facilitate practicing and applying the necessities. It intends to remove restrictions and hardship in applying the necessities as long as it does not pose a threat to the normal order defined by the essentials. For example, there are some concessions in cases of hardship such as sickness, and in traveling for performing prayers. Similarly, for people in other climates and cultures and those from different time zone, the divine law permits them to estimate what is similar to an average day time to break the fast.
- *The Embellishments (Tahsiniyat)*: The embellishments are intended to render human affairs or conditions more suited to the requirements of the highest standards of moral conduct. It facilitates enhancement and excellence in the conducts, customs, and practices to achieve the highest quality of the aforementioned objectives. For example, cleanliness of the body, good behavior, kindness, and elegance are some of the values promoted within this category.

2.3 Rulings of Syariah

Rules and regulations are very valuable for human being and are obeyed only once they are enforced. The enforcement of rules ensures discipline and is beneficial for everyone. The regulations and the ruling values in Islam are called Ahkam. However, if the rules are not enforced, they are seldom obeyed. The regulations and the ruling values in Islam are called Ahkam (Allaf n.d.). The rulings (Ahkam) of Syariah for the daily actions of Muslims are classified into five categories.

1. Wajib (obligation)
2. Mandoob (recommended)
3. Haram (prohibition)
4. Makrooh (discouraged or abominable)
5. Mubaah (permissible).

These five categories of Syariah rulings are legal and moral regulations. They are related to the behavior of Muslims in their relationship with Allah the Almighty. This gives the believer the freedom of choice in making a decision without giving specific preference to the choice made by the believer. The descriptions on the Syariah rulings are:

1. *Wajib (obligation)*: This type of required behavior is binding, and it is established by definitive proof in the Quran and Sunnah. The performance of wajib acts is rewarded. According to the Quran and Sunnah, if a Muslim neglects performing these required behaviors, they would be punished, both in this world and hereafter. This category would include obligations such as daily prayer and obligatory fasting.
2. *Mandoob (recommended)*: Mandoob is any act that is commendable but not required. While there is no punishment for the neglect of duties which are mandoob, there is reward for performing them. The mandoob or recommended acts include extra prayers, fasting on Mondays and Thursdays, praying, charitable acts, and remembrance of God and pious deeds of different kinds.
3. *Haram (prohibition)*: Haram is the opposite of an obligation. These are acts that are strictly prohibited by Islam. These acts are binding by definitive proof in the Quran and Sunnah. For the performance of haram,

there is punishment in this world or in the hereafter; for the avoidance of haram, there is reward. Some examples of haram are killing, theft, unlawful sexual activity or adultery, drinking alcohol, and gambling.

4. *Makrooh (discouraged or abominable)*: An act whereby avoiding its doing, is preferred to doing it. However, for acts of makrooh there is no punishment, and for the avoidance of these acts there is reward. Makrooh is the opposite of mandoob. The neglecting of a mandoob act is discouraged and leads to a makrooh. One such act would be divorce.
5. *Mubaah (permissible)*: Mubaah is any act that is left to the personal decision and to individual liberty. Muslims can make the decision whether or not to perform any act that is considered mubaah. Although there is neither reward for doing mubaah nor punishment for avoiding it, the intention might turn a mubaah act into a rewarding act. For example, eating with the sincere intention to strengthen your body so you can work more and help your parents is an act of reward because of the sincere intention toward the parents.

Rulings of Syariah					
Type	Wajib (obligatory)	Mandub (recommended)	Haram (forbidden)	Makruh (discouraged)	Mubaah (permissible)
Action	P: Rewarded NP: Punished	P: Rewarded NP: Not punished	P: Punished NP: Rewarded	P: Not punished NP: Rewarded	P: Not rewarded NP: Not punished
Example	Daily prayer/ fasting	Extra prayers/ charity	Drinking alcohol/ gambling	Divorce	Eating food

P = Performing of act; NP = Not performing of act
Reference: Khir, K., Gupta, L., & Shanmugam, B. (2007). *Islamic banking: A practical perspective*. Kuala Lumpur, Malaysia: Pearson-Longman

2.4 Banking for All

Islamic banking promises a positive role in stimulating economic development. This includes a vital contribution to the achievement of the socio-economic objective in the society. These objectives are elimination of poverty, equitable distribution of wealth, and sufficient opportunities for gainful employment. Hence, it is clear that Islamic banking is much more than just abstinence from interest. Islamic economic and financial system is based on a set of values, ideals, and morals, such as honesty, credibility, transparency, clear evidence, facilitation, cooperation, complementarily, and solidarity. These moral and ethical promises are also appealing to non-Muslims who find the practices of conventional financial institutions questionable on moral and ethical grounds as illustrated in Fig. 2.5.

There is an increase in demand for ethical investing among non-Muslims, and Islamic banking works on the same set of principles. Islamic banking is getting a firmer foothold in the market right now and is putting serious amount of efforts on establishing Islamic banking's image and performance, cost-competitive products, speed of transaction, channel of delivery system, banking convenience, and product diversity to attract Muslim and non-Muslim customers. In Malaysia, Islamic banking products such as home financing, hire purchase, and insurance (Takaful) have drawn considerable interest from Malaysia's ethnic Chinese and Indian minorities. Islamic banking is gaining grounds with non-Muslims in Malaysia, where it was reported that half of some of Islamic banks' customers in Malaysia are non-Muslims. Globally, Sukuk (Syariah bonds) are among the fastest growing Islamic finance instruments, and the issuers are coming from non-traditional Muslim markets such as Ireland, Luxembourg, and Japan. According to Ernst &

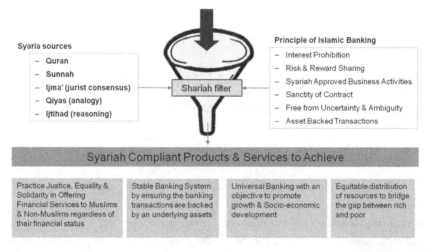

Fig. 2.5 Banking and finance needs of Muslims and non-Muslims. Source: Adapted from Khan (2007)

Young (Dec 2012), the value of Sharia-compliant assets worldwide stands at $1.8 trillion, up from $1.3 trillion in 2011, and the forecast is to grow beyond the milestone of $2 trillion by 2014. Islamic banking will grow further due to its emphasis on ethical and social or sustainable banking, which will be appealing to the wider segment of both Muslim and non-Muslim consumers.

3 Summary

Islamic banking is based on Syariah principles. To understand the essence of the Islamic banking, one must understand the relationship between Islamic banking and Syariah, which is explained under the 'Islam: An Overview' section.

As explained earlier, Islam means 'submission', and a 'Muslim', therefore, is one who submits to the will of Allah the Almighty. Syariah translated as 'Islamic law' is neither a document nor a code in the strict sense, but rather an amalgamation of scriptural (Quranic) injunctions, sayings of the Prophet Muhammad, juridical rulings, and legal commentaries dealing with all aspects of social, economic, and political life.

Syariah is not merely a collection of dos and don'ts nor is it just a code of criminal laws prescribing punishments for certain crimes. Though it does contain both, its coverage is much broader and deeper, encompassing the totality of man's life. Syariah includes both faith and practice. It embraces worship, individual attitude, and conduct, as well as social norms and laws, whether political, economic, familial, criminal, or civil. Islamic banking falls under economic activities.

References

http://www.ipislam.edu.my/index.php/artikel/read/1316/ISLAMIC-FACTS-Refuting-the-Allegations-against-Islam-P1
http://srikandeh.blogspot.my/2009/05/preservation-of-holy-quran.html
http://www.onislam.net/english/syariah/contemporary-issues/islamic-themes/459269-objectives-of-syariah.html

http://www.onislam.net/english/syariah/syariah-and-humanity/syariah-and-life/457642-islamic-syariah-bringing-value-to-our-lives.html?Life

http://www.muslimphilosophy.com/ma/works/maqasid.pdf

http://www.onislam.net/english/syariah/contemporary-issues/islamic-themes/459269-objectives-of-syariah.html

http://www.muslimphilosophy.com/ma/works/maqasid.pdf

http://kulsanofersyedthajudeen.blogspot.com/2012/11/maqasid-al-syariah-defined.html

http://www.islam4theworld.net/eBooks/IslamicFact/1_4.htm

http://www.bloomberg.com/news/2013-10-29/islamic-finance-can-save-the-world.html

Al-Allaf, M. (n.d.). *Islamic divine law (Syariah), the objectives (Maqasid) of the Islamic divine law or Maqasid theory*.

Ernst & Young. (2012, December). *World Islamic banking competitiveness report 2013 growing beyond DNA of successful transformation*.

Haron, S., & Shanmugam, B. (2001). *Islamic banking system: Concept & applications*. Petaling Jaya: Pelanduk Publications.

Khan, I. (2007, February). *Islamic finance: Relevance and growth in the modern financial age*. Founding ex-CEO, HSBC Amanah. London School of Economics.

3

Prohibition of Riba and Gharar in Islamic Banking

1 Introduction

Syariah-compliant financial institutions are those that do not contravene prohibitions against riba (interest) and gharar (speculation) in its business transactions. Prohibition of riba and gharar is the most significant principle of Islamic banking. The three broad Syariah precepts that distinguish Islamic banking from conventional style banking are:

1. The first is prohibition on riba or excessive profit, defined loosely as) 'interest';
2. The second is an injunction against gharar, or transactions involving uncertainty and/or speculation; and
3. The third is a prohibition against dealings with businesses involving forbidden products or activities (such as alcohol, pork, or gambling).

Most conventional banks offer deposit and financing products based on interest and not based on the profit-sharing principle. This list includes interest-bearing accounts and loans, which fall short of the strict riba rules, and most futures and options, which are considered speculative and gharar.

In this chapter, we review the two fundamental Syariah prohibitions, riba and gharar, and why are these intolerable by Syariah, whereas interest is the life blood of the conventional system. This chapter discusses the definition of riba, types of riba, and rulings for exchange of ribawi materials. The definition of gharar and its types will also be discussed.

1.1 Definitions of *Riba*

The basic principle of Islamic banking is the prohibition of riba. Riba translates literally from Arabic as 'an increase, growth, augmentation or accretion'. In Islam, lending money should not generate unjustified income. In the Islamic terminology, interest means "effortless profit or profit that increases the principal amount without putting any effort." Thus, riba, in general, is an unearned income, which comes as a growth or increase to the owner of money. Riba is seen as an unjustified earning where a person could receive a monetary advantage in a business transaction without giving a just counter-value.

As a Syariah term, it refers to the premium that must be paid by the borrower to the lender along with the principal amount, as a condition for the loan or for an extension in its maturity, which today is commonly referred to as 'interest'. Riba represents in the Islamic economic system, a prominent source of unjustified advantage. All Muslim scholars are adamant that this prohibition extends to any and all forms of interest and that there is no difference between interest-bearing funds for the purposes of consumption or investment, since Syariah does not consider money as a commodity for exchange. Instead, money is a medium of exchange and a store of value.

Abu al A'la al Mawdudi defined riba as 'a predetermined excess or surplus over and above the loan received by the creditor conditionally in relation to a specified period'. This definition entails that riba contains the following three elements:

1. Excess or surplus over and above the loan capital: Increase in terms of value, which comprises the quantity and quality, immaterial to minimum or maximum increase, fixed or variable increase.

2. Determination of this surplus in relation to time: Increase in terms of value upon extension at maturity.
3. Stipulation of this surplus in the loan agreement: The surplus condition over the principal is part of the agreement.

The explanation of the riba is illustrated in the chart below. We can conclude that there are actually two distinguishable types of excesses (Fig. 3.1):

1. The excess accruing from a financing transaction due to the postponement of time; and
2. The excess accruing in a sale or barter transaction.

To standardize the definition, riba is an increase or excess which accrues to the owner in an exchange or sale of a commodity or, by virtue of a loan arrangement, receives an increase or excess without giving an equivalent counter-value to the other party.

1.1.1 Types of Riba

Riba can be classified based on the excess accrued from the trading transactions and the excess accrued from the financing transaction. The classification of riba is illustrated (Fig. 3.2):

1. **Riba Duyun**

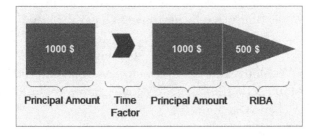

Fig. 3.1 Riba excesses

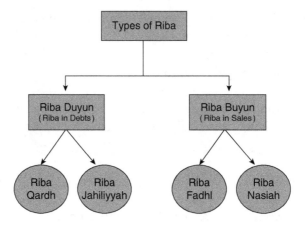

Fig. 3.2 Types of Riba

Riba duyun is debt usury that occurs in lending and borrowing. Any unjustified increment in borrowing or lending money, paid in kind or in money above the amount of loan, as a condition imposed by the lender or voluntarily by the borrower is defined as riba duyun.

This kind of riba is the extra amount of money over and above the principal of the loan and charge is either:

- Imposed by the lender or borrower in the contract; and/or
- Promised by the borrower in the contract.

To summarize, riba duyun is any conditioned increment in a loan and is strictly prohibited in Quran. Riba duyun can be further classified as:

(a) *Riba Qardh*: Riba is imposed from the beginning and will be proportionate to the time taken by borrower to repay the loan.
 For example:
 A borrowed RM1000 from B on 10% interest for one year. Upon maturity, A will pay RM1100 [Principal amount: RM1000; Interest: RM100 (1000×10/100×1)] to B. The example is illustrated in the following chart (Fig. 3.3):

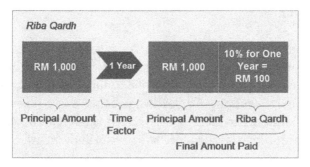

Fig. 3.3 Riba Qardh

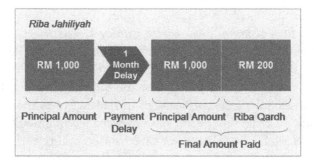

Fig. 3.4 Riba Jahiliyyah

(b) *Riba Jahiliyyah*: There is no riba at the beginning and riba is imposed upon default. This arises when the creditor in a deferred contract of exchange demands from the debtor an additional amount over and above that which was initially agreed to in the original contract. The creditor agrees to allow his debtor to delay payment of a matured debt in exchange for an increase in the indebtedness. Under riba jahiliyyah, charging constitutes an increase for further deferment of the payment of debt as a function of time (e.g. a late rental payment in a lease, or a late instalment payment in a credit sale).

For example:

A owes B RM1000 on 1/1. On 1/1, B is unable to pay A so A agrees not to collect his debt until 2/1 in exchange for B agreeing to pay him RM1200 instead of RM 1000. Syariah strictly prohibits this transaction. The example is illustrated below (Fig. 3.4).

2. Riba Buyun

Riba buyun occurs in trading transactions. A transaction (trading/sale) in which a commodity is exchanged for the same commodity but unequal in amount and the delivery of at least one commodity is postponed. This kind of riba may occur out of an exchange between two ribawi materials of the same kind, where the necessary rule(s) is (are) not observed. Riba buyun can be further classified into two as explained below:

(a) *Riba Fadhl*: The ribawi materials exchanged are of different weights, measurements, or numbers and are exchanged at the same time. This can be termed as riba of excess. It applies to the purchase and sale of homogenous commodities, where money is exchanged for money but in different quantities. This can occur when goods 'like for like and equal for equal' are exchanged in different amounts (e.g. number, weight, value, etc.). It is a dishonest and unjust exchange. Justice can be rendered only if the two scales of the balance carry the same value of goods. To avoid this, people have to exchange commodities equally such as dates for dates, silver for silver, and so on in equal amounts. For example:
Exchanging of 1 kg of dates for 2 kg of dates on December 10, 2004, at the same time. The excess of 1 kg dates is riba fadhl as illustrated in the following chart (Fig. 3.5):

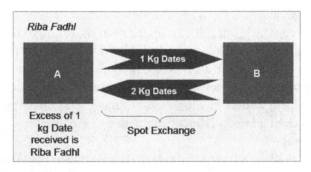

Fig. 3.5 Riba Fadhl

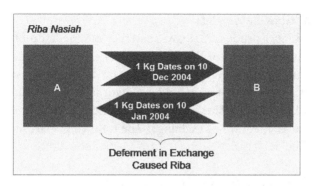

Fig. 3.6 Riba Nasiah

(b) *Riba Nasiah or Riba Yad*: Riba by virtue of deferment at the time of exchange is known as riba nasiah. Under this scenario, the ribawi materials exchanged are of equal weights, measurements or numbers but payment of the price and delivery of the goods are made at two different times. This can be termed as a sale transaction, which involves barter exchange of the homogenous commodity in equal amounts and postponement of delivery, by either or both parties (Fig. 3.6).

1.1.2 Ribawi Materials

Ribawi goods are subject to Syariah rules on riba in sales, variously defined by the schools of Islamic law: items sold by weight and by measure, foods, and so on. The Prophet Muhammad said:

> Sell gold in exchange of equivalent gold, sell silver in exchange of equivalent silver, sell dates in exchange of equivalent dates, sell wheat in exchange of equivalent wheat, sell salt in exchange of equivalent salt, sell barley in exchange of equivalent barley, but if a person transacts in excess, it will be usury (riba). If the exchange was between different kinds, you can buy and sell them any how you like, as long as it is immediate such as sell barley for dates anyway you please, on the condition it is hand-to-hand (on the spot).

1. **Basis of Ribawi Materials**

    In Islamic jurisprudence, ribawi materials are made up of two types. One is commodities and the other is the mode of price for exchanging commodities. Then every type has a class of varieties. For example, foodstuffs are a type of asset, and rice, wheat, and so on are its varieties. Similarly, silver, gold, and so on are varieties of the second type of asset, that is, medium of exchange. The following chart illustrates the above (Fig. 3.7):

2. **Rule of Exchange for Ribawi Materials**

    (a) *Ribawi material of the same basis and of the same kind*: Under this scenario we are exchanging gold with gold, that is, same basis (medium of exchange) and the same kind (gold). The exchange rule is:

    (i) Material must be of the same weight, measurement, or number of units.
    (ii) Exchange of goods must be done immediately, that is, on the spot, and cannot be deferred.
    Example:
    (i) USD100 exchanged with USD100 with payment and delivery made at the same time.
    (ii) A 10 kg of Basmati rice exchanged with 10 kg of ordinary rice whereby payment and delivery are made at the same time.

    (b) *Ribawi material of a different kind and of the same basis*: Under this scenario, we are exchanging gold with USD, that is, the same basis (medium of exchange) and a different kind (gold). The exchange rule is:

    (i) Difference in weight, measurement, or number of units allowed. As such, measurement or numbers of exchanged materials need not to be observed.

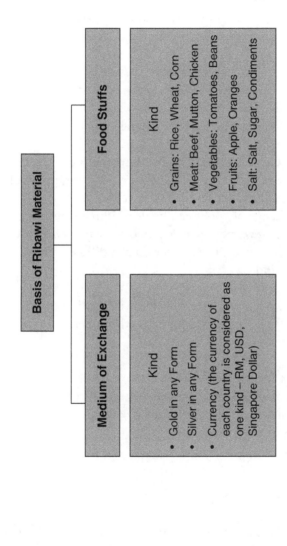

Fig. 3.7 Basis of Ribawi material

(ii) Exchange of goods must be done immediately, that is, on the spot, and cannot be deferred.
Example:
(i) A 5 kg of rice exchanged with 3 kg of apples whereby payment and delivery are made at the same time.
(ii) A 10 gram of gold exchanged with RM100 with payment and deliveries made at the same time.

(c) *Ribawi material of a different kind and a different basis*: Under this scenario, we are exchanging gold with wheat, that is, a different basis (gold, medium of exchange; wheat, foodstuff) and a different kind (gold and wheat). The exchange rule is:

(i) Difference in weight, measurement, or number of units allowed. Therefore, the measurement or number of materials exchanged needs not be observed.
(ii) Exchange of goods can be done immediately or deferred. To summarize, no rule is required to be observed in an exchange between two ribawi materials of a different basis and a different kind.
Example:
(i) A 5 kg of rice exchanged with RM10 on deferred payment terms.
(ii) A 10 kg of apples exchanged with USD1 on immediate payment terms.

3. Rule Matrix for Ribawi Materials

We have learned about the ribawi material, their types, rules of exchange, and other details. Table 3.1 will summarize all the rules discussed earlier for easy understanding.

1.1.3 Riba and Profit

There is a clear distinction between trade and riba under Syariah whereby trading is welcomed and riba is prohibited. Trade leads to profit and is totally different from riba as explained in Table 3.2.

Table 3.1 Rule matrix for ribawi materials

Basis of ribawi material	Kind of ribawi material	Quantity of ribawi material	Exchange of ribawi material (payment and delivery)	Riba type	Example
Same	Same	Equal	Immediate	No riba	10 kg of Basmati rice exchanged with 10 kg of ordinary rice, with payment and delivery made at the same time
Same	Same	Unequal	Immediate	Riba fadhl	10 kg of Basmati rice exchanged with 14 kg of ordinary rice, with payment and delivery made at the same time
Same	Same	Equal	Deferred	Riba nasiah	10 kg of Basmati rice exchanged with 10 kg of ordinary rice, with payment and delivery made after 20 days
Same	Same	Unequal	Deferred	Riba fadhl and riba nasiah	10 kg of Basmati rice exchanged with 14 kg of ordinary rice, with payment and delivery made after 20 days
Same	Different	Unequal/equal	Immediate	No riba	10 gram of gold for RM 1000 with payment and delivery made at the same time
Same	Different	Unequal/equal	Deferred	Riba nasiah	10 gram of gold for RM 1000 with payment and delivery made after 30 days
Different	Different	Unequal/equal	Immediate/deferred	No riba	5 kg of rice exchanged with RM 10 on deferred payment terms

Table 3.2 Riba and profit

Riba	Profit
Riba is the premium paid by the borrower to the lender along with the principal amount as a condition for the loan	Profit is the difference between the value of production and the cost of production
Riba is prefixed, and hence, there is no uncertainty on the part of either the givers or the takers of the loans	Profit is postdetermined, and hence, its amount is not known until the activity is done
Riba cannot be negative; it can at best be very low or zero	Profit can be positive, zero, or even negative
From the Syariah point of view, it is haram (forbidden)	From the Syariah point of view, it is halal (permissible) if all the Syariah rules are followed for trade

1.1.4 Why Riba Is Prohibited

The rationale behind prohibition of riba can be classified under two broad heading for easy understanding:

1. **Religious Perspective**

    The religious restriction on interest is quite explicit and unequivocal. All transactions based on riba are strictly prohibited in the Quran. Islam encourages businessmen to augment their capital through trade; it explicitly prohibits them from capital extension through lending or borrowing. The size of the rate of interest charged is immaterial; riba is absolutely prohibited. There is no opportunity cost of lending money in Islam. The lender is making money without any fear of loss.

    The strict prohibition of interest in Islam is a result of its deep concern for the moral, social, and economic welfare of mankind (see Box 3.1). This has played a very important role for Muslim thinkers to explore the ways of doing banking.

2. **Socio-economic Perspective**

    (a) The taking of interest implies appropriating another person's property without giving him anything in exchange, because one who lends RM1 for RM2 gets the extra RM1 for nothing. Now, a man's property is for fulfilling his needs and it has great sanctity, according to the Hadith, 'A man's property is as sacred as his blood'. This means that taking it from him without giving him something in exchange is haram.

(b) Riba makes the people lazy and prevents people from working to earn money, since the person with money can earn extra money through interest, either in advance or at a later date, without working for it.

Box 3.1 Prohibition of Riba

The prohibition of riba appears in the Quran in four different revelations. The first of these [30:39] in Mecca, emphasized deprivation of God's blessing for a man-making interest transaction and charity having the essence of manifold rise. The second revelation [4:161] concerning the subject took place in the early Madinah. It severely condemned interest—referring prohibitions taken place in the previous scriptures. The third revelation [3:130-2] enjoined Muslims to keep away from riba. The fourth revelation [2:275-81] reveals the completion of the Prophet's mission.

The prohibition of riba appears in the Quran in four different revelations. The first of these [30:39] in Mecca, emphasized deprivation of God's blessing for a man-making interest transaction and charity having the essence of manifold rise. The second revelation [4:161] concerning the subject took place in the early Madinah. It severely condemned interest- referring prohibitions taken place in the previous scriptures. The third revelation [3:130-2] enjoined Muslims to keep away from riba. The fourth revelation [2:275-81] reveals the completion of the Prophet's mission.

1st Stage	2nd Stage	3rd Stage	4th Stage
Moral Denunciation	Riba and the Jews	Categorical Prohibition	Al- Bay as the alternative to riba
Surah Al- Rum: 39	Surah al- Nisa: 161	Surah Al- Imran:130-2	Surah Al- Baqarah (275-278)
"That which you give riba to increase peoples' wealth increases not with God, but that which you give in charity, seeking the goodwill of God multiplies manifold."	"That they (Jews) took riba though they were forbidden and that they devoured the properties of people wrongfully."	"O ye who believes devour not riba doubled and multiplied But fear Allah that ye may prosper.."	"While God has permitted trade and forbidden riba.."

The verses giving strong verdict against *Riba* are as follows:

> Those who devour riba will not stand except as one whom the devil hath driven to madness by [his] touch [2:275].

Condemnation of the system of interest is so strong and without any doubt can be reflected in the following verse which imposes penalties on those who hesitate to observe the verdict:

> 'O ye who believe! Observe your duty to Allah and give up what remains (due to you) from Riba, if you are (in truth) believers. And if you do not, then be warned of war (against you) from Allah and His Messenger. And if you repent then you have your principal (without Riba). Wrong not, and you shall not be wronged' [2:278–9].

This is unacceptable under Islam and is termed as unjustified earning whereby there is an increase in the principal amount without putting any efforts.

(c) Permitting the taking of interest discourages people from doing good to one another, as is required by Islam. If interest is prohibited in a society, people will lend to each other based on goodwill, expecting back no more than what they have loaned, while if interest is made permissible, the needy person will be required to pay back more on loans, weakening his feelings of goodwill and friendliness toward the lender.

(d) The interest-based system is security-oriented rather than growth-oriented. Because of their commitment to pay a predetermined rate of interest to depositors, banks in their lending operations are most concerned about the safe return of the principal lent, along with the stipulated interest. This leads them to confine their lending to the already well-established big business houses or such parties that are in a position to pledge sufficient security. As such the small business with insufficient security to pledge cannot avail financing facility. Oversupply of credit to well-established parties and its denial to a large segment of the population also result in increasing inequalities of income and wealth.

(e) The interest-based system discourages innovation, particularly on the part of small-scale enterprises. Big industrial firms can afford to invest in research and development due to reserves and access to financing facilities. Small business house are hesitant to invest in Research and Development (R&D) due to fixed cost (interest) irrespective of the Research and Development outcome. This creates a barrier for economic growth but also leads to income inequalities.

In summary, the riba is prohibited but trade is encouraged; Muslims can neither receive nor give interest. Numerous Quranic verses indicate that Islam permits trade but forbids usury or riba. Islam encourages Muslims to invest their money and become partners in order to share the profits and risks in the business instead of becoming creditors. Riba leads to a manipulative and strained relationship between people, exacts another's property without counter-value, distracts and often prevents people from taking part in active professions for social well-being, and enables the rich to exploit those in financial need. As such, these factors drive the need to have an interest-free banking to meet the financing need of Muslims.

1.2   Gharar Definition

Gharar means 'uncertainty, hazard, chance or risk'. Islam prohibits uncontrollable risks or uncontrollable obligations as it leads to speculation. The definition of uncertainty in the muamalat transaction is 'Where there is a matter that is concealed by one party, where it (this concealment) can raise a sense of inequality as well as tyranny to another party'.

In business terms, gharar means to undertake a venture blindly without sufficient knowledge or to undertake an excessively risky transaction. However, minor uncertainties can be permitted when there is a necessity.

The risk pertaining to incomplete information in the contract such as consideration or measure of the object leads to speculation due to its inherent uncertainty. The presence of a gharar element in the contract makes the outcome not known or hidden and this is unacceptable under Syariah laws.

Contracting parties should have perfect knowledge of the countervalues intended to be exchanged as a result of their transactions. For example, if someone sells a car without informing the buyer about its faulty engine, the buyer is exposed to a risk. This is gharar. The unfair element of risk is the reason why gharar is disallowed. Islam lays down principles of fair and transparent business transactions. Contracts should be fair and transparent. Gharar extends to all forms of contract: employment, marriage, and so on. Some good examples of transactions which include gharar are:

1. Selling goods that the seller is unable to deliver;
2. Selling known or unknown goods against an unknown price, such as selling the contents of a sealed box;
3. Selling goods without proper description, such as a shop owner selling clothes with unspecified sizes;
4. Selling goods without specifying the price, such as selling at the 'going price';
5. Making a contract conditional on an unknown event that happens at an unspecified time;
6. Selling goods on the basis of false description; and
7. Selling goods without allowing the buyer to properly examine the goods.

A good interpretation of gharar is made by Professor Mustafa Al-Zarqa: 'gharar is the sale of probable items whose existence or characteristics are not certain, due to the risky nature which makes the trade similar to gambling…'.

The above definition states that the prohibition applies in a number of circumstances such as when the seller is not in a position to hand over the goods to the buyer or when the subject matter of the sale is incapable of acquisition. It includes the sale of fish in the sea, birds in the sky, an unborn calf in its mother's womb, runaway animal, fruit which has not ripened, and so on.

Gharar applies also for investments such as trading in futures on the stock market. According to the consensus of scholars, gharar is present in all future sales and is strictly prohibited.

1.2.1 Types of Gharar

Scholars accept that avoidance of gharar may not always be possible and the presence of gharar can be tolerated up to a certain degree. The reasoning is that every entrepreneur and every businessman takes risks as they deal with the unknown. They produce for the future and future is not known. Gharar can be classified under two broad headings based on the degree of uncertainty as explained in the following chart (Fig. 3.8):

1. *Gharar Fahish*: This can be called a major or serious gharar and is defined as:
   (a) An uncertainty which is so great that it becomes unacceptable; or
   (b) It is so vague that there is no means of quantifying it.

The presence of excessive gharar makes the contract null and void and is strictly prohibited under Syariah law. More specifically major gharar arise out of the following:
(a) Asset or merchandise does not exist;
(b) Asset or merchandise cannot be delivered;
(c) Asset or merchandise is not according to the specifications; and

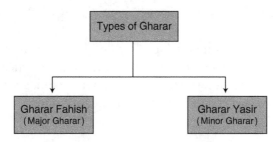

Fig. 3.8 Types of gharar

(d) Deferred sale in which the deferment period is unknown.

Excessive gharar may originate in ignorance and lack of information over the nature and attributes of an object, a doubt over its availability and existence, doubt over quantity, exact information concerning the price, and the unit of currency in which price is to be paid or the terms of payment. These are strictly forbidden because of the ignorance of the parties over the existence or the attributes, or both. There is a general consensus for these prohibitions. Some of the varieties of sale that are strictly prohibited are listed below:

(a) Sale of an unborn calf still in its mother's womb;
(b) Sale of a bird in the sky;
(c) Selling known or unknown goods against an unknown price, such as selling the contents of a sealed box where the contents are unknown; and
(d) Sale of a runaway camel.

2. *Gharar Yasir*: This is a minor gharar. It is found in nearly all contracts. The reasoning is if the ignorance is over an aspect of sale that is not likely to obstruct completion and delivery, the basic purpose of the sale is fulfilled and it remains valid. Knowledge of the specifics on sale is necessary because it is a prerequisite of consent, which cannot materialize without precise information. It is generally agreed that knowledge of the substance of the sale object and its price to an extent would preclude the prospect of arising of dispute among the parties. Hence, the sale is considered as valid. Some of the varieties of sale that are permissible are listed below:

(a) Purchase of fruits without peeling or cutting off the skin to see the inside;
(b) Charging a fix amount for a bus fare for a certain distance even though a passenger does not travel the whole distance; and
(c) Charging a fixed rate per night for a hotel room, even though different guests use the different number and quantities of the services in the room.

To conclude, gharar therefore, can be categorized into four categories based on the degree of:

(a) Uncertainty and risk pertaining to the existence of the subject matter;
(b) Uncertainty over its availability;
(c) Uncertainty over the quantities involved; and
(d) Uncertainty over timing of completion and delivery.

References

http://www.submission.org/islam/faq1.html
http://www.witness-pioneer.org/vil/Books/M_foi/ch3top12.html
http://www.jamaat.org/islam/sources.html
http://islamic-finance.net/research/riba-forum.html
Hannan, S. A. Usul al-Fiqh. Retrieved from http://www.ymofmd.com/books/uaf/
Harun, Z. Principles of Islamic finance, investment and banking.
Wisdom behind prohibition of riba. Retrieved from http://www.islamonline.com/cgi-bin/news_service/fatwah_story.asp?service_id=199

4

Islamic Contracts

1   Fundamentals of Islamic Contracts

In this chapter we will observe about Islamic contracts in general. In the previous chapter, we explored about riba and gharar; these two sets of rules and principles cut across all the contracts in Islamic law. Contract is the very essence of various transactions without which transactions are void of legal significance. Islam encourages trade and commerce and it is mentioned in many verses in the Quran. Islamic commercial law has laid down fairly detailed rules leading to the formation of contract, the guiding principle here is that there should not be any injustice to honest and legitimate trade and business. Islamic contract law is not expressed as a general theory of contract but states rules for various specific contracts such as law of sales, lease, pledge, and so forth.

Islamic commercial law is known as fiqh-al-muamalat in an Islamic legal term. It is an important law of branch, deals with issues of contract and the legal affect(s) arising from contracts; be it a valid, void or voidable contract respectively. Islamic contracts cover a variety of dealings and transactions to meet the needs of the society. The first article of the Majallah al-Ahkam al-'Adliyyah (the civil code of the Ottoman Empire) endorses the idea that man is social by nature and that social life is essential to him, stating that 'In view of the fact that man is social by nature, he cannot live in solitude like other animals, but is need of co-operation with his fellow men in order to promote an urban society. Every person, however, seeks the things, which suit him, and is vexed by any competition. As a result, it has been necessary to establish laws to maintain order and justice'. This approach of the Majallah is seldom found in the other compilations of law.

The Syariah law of contract is primarily based on three fundamental principles:

- The principle of justice to ensure neither party to a contract may exploit the other. Hence, the riba is strictly prohibited under the Quran.
- The principle of transparency. Those concerned must share all available information. Withholding crucial information bearing on the transaction could render the contract invalid. Also contracts involving a high degree of gharar are strictly prohibited. The objective is to prevent the transactions that lead to disputation and lack of trust.
- The principle of maslaha, meaning the common interest supported by the spirit of the Syariah and not by a specific text. On the basis of maslaha, a particular form of transaction may be exempted from a general rule because it has been shown in common practice to facilitate business.

1.1 Essential Elements of a Valid Contract

Contract (Aqd) in Syariah means a tie or knot binding two parties together. The contract is a declaration of offer and acceptance made at the same time. Islamic laws of contracts are developed through the work of Islamic jurists, based on the principles mentioned in the Quran and the narrations from the Prophet Muhammad. There are many verses in the Quran, which mentions of a number of contracts, and axioms of wide application in the area of a contractual relationship. These include various commercial contracts such as sale, hire, guarantee, security, and deposits.

Contracts are drawn to ensure the existence of clearly recognized guidelines for all parties involved. They state the standings of all those involved and the condition(s) of the transaction(s) that are to take place. A contract in Islamic law consists of an agreement made between two or more parties, and the basic elements are quite similar to those of English common law:

1.1.1   Offer and Acceptance

An offer is a proposal to make a deal, and an acceptance is an acknowledgment by the person to whom the offer was made that the offer is accepted. In other words, an offer is an agreement that is made by one of the parties to the contract, and acceptance is the statement that is made by second party in response to the offer. For example, if one of the parties says 'I want to sell this house to you for RM 150,000' and the other party says, 'I accept', then what has been said by the seller is offer and the statement made by the buyer is called acceptance.

The key conditions of offer and acceptance are listed below:

- It is necessary that the *acceptance conforms to the offer* in all its details. If the offer contains any material change in, or addition to, the terms of the original offer, it will not be accepted. A counteroffer is a new offer in Islamic law.
- The *offer and acceptance have to be executed in the same session*. In the event any party to the contract is missing, then the session lasts till the knowledge of it reaches to the party through messenger and he replies and communicates his acceptance to the offeror.
- *Assent must be genuine* as the person giving his consent may not be mentally competent or he may be a person subjected to coercion or under influence.
- *Existence of the offer till the issuance of acceptance*. An offer must remain open until it is accepted, rejected, retracted, or has expired. A counteroffer closes the original offer.

1.1.2 Contract Subject Matter

As the subject matter of the contract, both the item and consideration, Islamic law stresses on the following matters: lawfulness, existence, deliverability, and precise determination. The jurist lays down the following condition for subject matter:

- *Lawfulness*: The object must be lawful and should be permissible to trade. It must be of legal value, which means its subject matter and underlying clause must be lawful, and it must not be prohibited by Islamic law, neither a nuisance to public order or morality.
- *Existence*: The parties to a contract must legally own the object. The issue of existence presupposes that the object of a contract must be in existence at the time of a contract. For example, to sell a fetus.
- *Delivery*: The object should be potentially capable of certain delivery to the buyer at the time of the contract. Therefore, Syariah prohibits the sale of a camel which has fled, a bird in the air, or a fish in water.
- *Determination*: The object should be something known to the parties. It must be determined precisely as to its essence, its quantity, and its value to avoid any kind of exploitation and future disputes,

In addition, as per majority of jurists, the object should be clean and Halal. It should be permissible under Syariah.

1.1.3 Consideration

The consideration in the Islamic contract may consist of money, goods, or services. It must be something, which is capable of being given and, in the case of service, should be capable of being performed. It is the legal benefit received by one person and the legal detriment imposed on the other person. For example, the seller is selling a car for RM20,000. The seller gives up the car and gets RM20,000; the buyer gives RM20,000 and gets the car.

For price consideration, Islamic law does not restrict it to a monetary price, but it may be in the form of another commodity similar to barter trade. The Islamic prohibition against uncertainty requires that the price must be in existence and determined at the time of the contract. It must not be fixed at a later date with reference to the market price, nor can it be left open, whereby subject to determination by a third party. For example, in contract of money exchange, the rules of riba should be strictly adhered to avoid the contract being void.

1.1.4 Capacity of the Parties to Contract

The parties entering into a contract must be competent to make a contract means the legal capacity to make a contract. In Islamic law, no person can validly conclude a legal transaction without first having attained physical and intellectual maturity that being the equivalent of majority. To enjoy full capacity, a person, whether male or female, should attain physical puberty and enjoy sound judgment known also as prudence in his or her judgment. Islam does permit minors to get into agreement, which are beneficial, but with the approval of the guardian.

The underlying principle is that usually an incompetent person will make a contract without understanding that he is making a contract and without realizing the consequences of his action. In Islamic law, a minor, a person of unsound mind, an insolvent person, a person legally declared a prodigal, an intoxicated person, or a person suffering from an illness which leads to his or her death cannot enter into a binding contract.

1.1.5 Legality

Legal subject matter is required for a contract to be enforceable. The Islamic law does not enforce contracts based on illegal activity and are not permissible under Syariah. In other words, the purpose of the contract must be legal in terms of the Syariah. Some of the contracts that are strictly prohibited under Islamic legal provisions are listed below:

- Contracts in violation of the prohibition of Riba
- Contracts in violation of the prohibition of un-permissible good
- Contracts in violation of the prohibition of gharar, mayisir, and so on

For example, a contract to grow grapes for winemaking would be void because an element of un-permissible object (wine) exists in the contract and will make the contract null and void.

1.2 Classification Based on Nature of Contract

Classification of contract according to the nature of contract is conceptually divided into three main categories, namely, unilateral contract, bilateral contract, and quasi contract, as explained in the following picture (Fig. 4.1):

1.2.1 Unilateral Contract

A unilateral contract is a form of promise made by one with an intention and expectation that the other party to contract would accept it. This contract is gratuitous in character and does not require the consent of the recipient. In other words, a unilateral promise binds only the person who makes it until it is accepted by others, and once it is accepted, both parties are equally bound by the contract.

It is normally applicable in transaction like reward (Al-Jualah) in which someone offers a particular reward to the world at large in return for the delivery of a sought-after subject matter. In a contract of Al-Jualah, the offeror is bound by the offer unilaterally until other parties accept it. Once it is accepted, both parties are bound by their promises equally. Unilateral contract comprises of transactions in favor of the recipient such as gift (hibah), rebate on offset of the debt (Ibra), will (wasiyyat), qard Hassan loan, and so on.

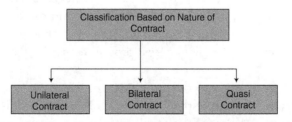

Fig. 4.1 Classification of contract according to nature of contract

In other words, unilateral contract is a binding promise that the offeror (a person who makes a proposal) makes and is conditional upon the performance by the offeree. For example, a person (offeror) approaches a real estate agent and asks him to find a house for him for which he will pay him one month's rent as commission. The broker finds a house which the person agrees to rent. The broker is entitled to his commission. The key here is that promise by the offeror, is one sided type of contract because only the offeror, who makes the promise, will be legally bound. The acceptance of the offer occurs through performance by offeree (real estate agent) i.e. upon renting the house.

1.2.2 Bilateral Contract

A bilateral contract requires at least two parties, formally in which one party should make a proposal and the other should accept. The mind of both parties must coincide and the declaration must relate to the same subject matter. The object of contract must be able to produce a legal and beneficial result for both the contracting parties. The dominant idea of a bilateral contract in Islamic law is that it establishes a legal relationship, arising from the mutual consent of the minds of at least two parties in dealing with each other, in respect of certain rights and obligations thereof.

For example, A sells his car to B for RM150,000 on cash basis. In this case the former consents to pass his car to the latter, who consents to take the car with an obligation to pay the price in cash.

The differentiation between bilateral or unilateral contract depends on what the offeree must do to accept the offer and to bind the offeror to a contract. If to bind the offeror, the offeree must only promise to perform, the contract is a bilateral contract. Hence the bilateral contract is a promise for a promise. The contract comes into existence the moment the promises are exchanged.

1.2.3 Quasi Contract

A quasi contract is not by nature a contract, but the implication gives rise to an obligation similar to that of contract. A quasi contract is an obligation, which does not originate from a proper verbal agreement, as in law of contract or tort. A quasi contract has little or no affinity with a contract, for example, an action to recover the money paid by mistake. If the innocent party mistakenly interprets the facts, pays to another party a sum of money which he does not really owe, the law being just will require the wrongful receiver of the money to restore it. However, his obligation is manifestly not based upon consent; therefore, this description of quasi contractual liability emphasizes its remoteness from any genuine concept of a contract.

To conclude here, in the quasi contract, the obligation is enforceable by the Syariah principle, since it is a matter of restoring the rights of others. The Islamic law sanctions this, because an appropriation could only be recognized if something is exacted through a proper transaction with a mutual consent.

1.3 Classification According to Legal Consequences

Classification of contract according to the legal consequences is illustrated in the following picture (Fig. 4.2):

1.3.1 Valid Contract (Sahih)

A valid contract is defined as a contract in which its essence and attributes are according to the Syariah and which subsequently has a legal effect of enforceability. In other words, a valid contract binds the contracting par-

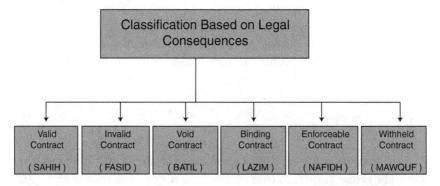

Fig. 4.2 Classification of contract according to legal consequences

ties equally. In a broader sense, a valid contract is one that is legal both as regards its asl and Waqf (origin and attributes) and is in compliance with the Syariah requirement. For a valid contract, the following three conditions should be met:

- All the elements required by law must be complete
- The additional conditions must be fulfilled
- The purpose of the contract and its subject matter must be in compliance with the Syariah.

The nature of a valid contract is that there must be contracting parties who have legal capacity and express their agreement in terms of a sound ijab (offer) and qabul (acceptance) on a particular subject matter recognized by the Syariah. In addition, for a contract to be valid, there must be an exchange of valuable consideration with a sincere intention, required from both parties, to create a legal relation.

To summarize a valid contract is when the offer and acceptance both are sound and the subject matter is in compliance with the Syariah requirement.

1.3.2 Invalid or Deficient Contract (Fasid)

An invalid contract is an agreement, which is lawful in its substance but unlawful in its description. The substance of an agreement refers to the offer, acceptance, and the subject matter. In other words, invalid contracts have the essential elements but doesn't fulfill all the necessary conditions, for example, price of the subject matter. If an agreement of sale for a definite article is concluded by proposal and acceptance but the price is not settled, the agreement would be fasid.

The object of a contract should be fit or suitable for carrying out a transaction, that is, it should be executable or doable within the normal business environment. The Syariah renders any such contract invalid in situations in which it will be impossible to achieve the consideration for which the contract was agreed. For example, If 'A' offers 'B' a certain amount of money to bring him the moon and 'B' accepts the offer, the Syariah rules it out as a valid contract since it will be impossible to carry it out.

1.3.3 Void Contract (Batil)

A void contract is an agreement in which both its substance and descriptions are not in compliance with Syariah. A void agreement is illegal in its origin and attributes; in other words, the necessary elements and necessary conditions are against the Islamic law. The Islamic jurists have a unanimous opinion that anything, which is forbidden by Syariah, is not tradable and hence cannot become the consideration or object of a contract. As such, the contract will be void if A and B agree on a liquor deal.

In the same manner, there can be no valid contract for the sale and purchase of stolen goods or delivery of inferior goods now at the promise of returning superior merchandise later as it will constitute one kind of riba or interest. Another example of a void contract is the agreement of sale concluded by a lunatic, a minor, or a prodigal. Such contract is void because it doesn't fulfill the required substance of an agreement, in which a sane, major, or sound-minded person must do the offer and acceptance. To conclude a contract is a void contract when it is not valid, effective, and enforceable, that is, opposite of valid contract.

1.3.4 Binding Contract (Lazim)

A binding contract is a sound contract without any defect either in its substance or descriptions. A lazim contract can be further classified into two based on the legal consequences:

- *Irrevocable Contracts*: An irrevocable lazim contracts are those where the parties shall not have any right to revoke in any stage of the contract, if such contract is concluded by mutual consent of the contracting parties, for example, a contract of marriage or any other bilateral contract. In the contract of a marriage, there is no revocation by either party once it is concluded, except by a 'Talaq' pronounced by the husband.
- *Revocable Contract*: Under revocable contract, the right to rescind can be exercised by either party without the consent of other party. There are two reasons due to which a contract becomes non-binding: nature

of contract and option. The nature of contract allows independence to both parties like agency (Wakalah), partnership (sharikah), and several others. Under option, an option is stipulated in the contract that prevents it from becoming binding.

1.3.5 Enforceable Contract (Nafidh)

A nafidh contract is an agreement, which does not involve any right of the third party. These contracts should not admit delays and must give rise to its effect immediately.

1.3.6 Withheld Contract (Mawquf)

A Mawquf contract is an agreement in which the substance and the description are lawful, but is concluded with the consent of a party who does not own the subject matter of the contract. A Mawkuf contract as a sale is dependent on the right of another like a contract of fuduli (fuduli means the catalyst or someone who makes the disposition of property without the consent of its owner or without the sanction of the Syariah). Thus, the legal consequence of a Mawquf contract is pending or hanging, until it is ratified by the owner on behalf of whom the fuduli concludes the contract.

1.4 Islamic Sale Contract

The main contract of exchange in Islamic commercial law is the contract of sale, and under this section, it will be covered in detail to understand the practical aspects of theory mentioned under above sections. Islamic banking activities are based on the trading principle of buying and selling of assets. As such contract of sale plays a pivotal role in the Islamic banking.

Sale (bai) is commonly defined in Syariah as 'the exchange of a thing of value by another thing of value with mutual consent'. In general sale involves an exchange of a commodity for another commodity (barter trading) or of a commodity for money (sale) or of money for money (sarf). The golden principle in trading is that the contract should not contain any element of riba, gharar, or maysir or else the contract is deemed void or voidable according to the condition.

1.4.1 Classification of Sale Based on the Things Sold

The classification of sale based upon the things sold is categorized as listed below:

- *Sale of property* to another person for a price and this is the most common category of sale.
- *Sale by exchange of money for money* is known as 'sarf' transaction, which consists of selling cash for cash.
- *Sale by barter*, that is, exchange of objects for object whereby no money is involved; each of the two commodities constitute both the price and the object.
- *Sale by immediate payment* against future delivery such as bay al-salam (forward sale) and bay al-istisna (advance payment may or may not applicable). The item of the sale is yet to exist in the future date. For both contracts there is an exemption from the rule about the prohibition of sale of non-existent goods.
  - *Bay al Salam*: This term refers to an advance payment for goods, which are to be delivered later. This is an exception to the rule that no sale can be affected unless the goods are in existence at the time of sale with a condition that goods are defined and the date of delivery is fixed, for example, RM10,000 paid in advance for a car to be delivered on the certain date.
  - *Bay al Istisna*: This is a kind of sale where a commodity is transacted before it comes into existence, in other words, to order a manufacturer to manufacture a specific commodity for the purchaser. The rules to be observed are that the price is fixed with the consent of the parties and that necessary specification of the commodity is fully settled between them.

1.4.2 Classification of Sale Based on the Nature of Profit-Sharing

Sale can be further classified based on the nature of profit agreed in the contract as mentioned below:

- *Musawamah*: This is the most common form and known as spot sale. The seller and buyer enter into an agreement for selling and buying of goods. The goods are delivered at once and the price is also paid. In other words, it is basically a sale by mutual consent completed and concluded through negotiations between the seller and buyer in which no reference is made to the original cost price. It is a 'profit sale' but the actual cost price and the amount of the profit is unknown to the buyer because the seller is not bound in musawamah sale to disclose the cost price.
- *Murabahah*: This is commonly known as cost-plus profit. This is a sale agreement whereby the seller purchases the goods desired by the buyer and sells them at an agreed marked up price, the payment being settled within an agreed time frame, either in installments or lump sum. The important thing in this contract is that the buyer knows the profit charged by the seller. In short, it is a cost-plus-profit sale in which the seller expressly discloses the profit to the buyer. Because of the sharing of cost and profit by the seller, the jurists have considered it as a sale based on trust (amanah).
- *Tawliyyah*: This is a sale at the cost price without any profit for the seller. This sale is again based on the principle of trust (amanah). The contract appears to be a form of substitution contract where one party who has bought goods no longer needs them and is willing to assign the right to a third party.
- *Wadiah*: This sale takes place when the seller agrees to sell a commodity at a lower price than that of the cost price. Since the seller is selling the commodity at a lower price, it is also a trust sale. This form of contract appears to be useful for a seller who is getting rid of his inventories to improve his liquidity position, for example, departmental store announcing sale based on wadiah for certain goods. It may serve as a sale gimmick to increase sales of other goods.

1.4.3 Possibilities of Payment Under Sales Contract

The possibilities of payment based on the sale contract are as mentioned below:

- *Cash Sale*: Under this sale the purchaser is under obligation to settle the purchase price agreed upon when concluding a contract. In the event the buyer is not able to settle the payment, the seller has a right to retain the goods sold until the buyer makes the payment.
- *Deferred Payment Sale*: Under this sale the amount is payable on installment basis. This is permissible provided the period thereof is definitely ascertained and fixed manner of payment is applicable to all types of sales except in the case of bay al-salam. This principle is normally followed for Bai Bithaman Ajil contracts.
- *Lump Sum Payment*: The lump sum amount is payable in the future. This manner of payment is also permissible provided the date of payment is fixed in advance. This manner of payment is also applicable on all the types of contract except bay al-salam.
- *Earnest Money (al-arabun)*: The advance payment of partial amount of total sale price is made to the seller which constitutes part of the purchase price should the buyer decides to buy the good. Otherwise, the seller forfeits the advance payment.

1.4.4 Essential Requirement for Sales Contract

In addition to the above general rules, the sales contract should have essential elements and the necessary conditions as illustrated in the following picture (Fig. 4.3):

Contract: Offer and Acceptance

The term 'offer' means that one person proposes to either sell his community to another person or buy from him, and 'acceptance' means that the person who has been offered gives his approval of the proposal.

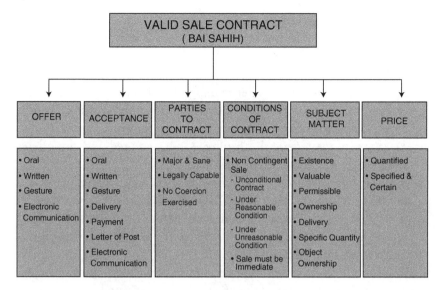

Fig. 4.3 Valid sale contract

Modes of Offer

(a) *Orally*: An offer can be made by words used for concluding a sale.
(b) *Written*: An offer could also be made by writing a deed, which will have equal legal effect as the one made verbally.
(c) *Gesture*: An offer by gesture is valid if a person who is incapable of making it either verbally or in writing makes it, for example, an offer made by a handicapped, dumb, or deaf person.
(d) *By post, telegram, telex, fax, phone, or by e-mail*. All these instruments convey offers made by words and writings.

Tense of Offer

An offer is generally made using past tense, but in some situations, an offer could also be made in other tenses and manners. The offer may be made by the aorist tense in which if it indicates a present tense then the sale is valid but if it indicates a future tense ('I will buy', 'I will sell') then the sale is invalid. In other words, an offer should be definite, absolute and have a decisive language.

Termination of an Offer

An offer could be terminated and will not have any legal effect under the following circumstances:

(a) *Revocation*: If the offeror after making the offer at any time before it is accepted changes his mind and revokes his offer, the latter will be effective and the offer will be treated as terminated.
(b) *Rejection by the Offeree*: If an offer is not accepted and the offeree rejects it, it will be treated as terminated.
(c) *Counter Offer*: An offer could also cease to have legal effect if it is neither rejected nor ignored by the offeree but the offeree may accept it with some additional condition in which the expression of the offeree would be treated as counteroffer and it will eventually terminate the original offer.
(d) *Absence of Acceptance*: An offer is made but no acceptance so far has been received to it; hence the offer will be terminated.
(e) *Death*: If death of either the offeror or the offeree occurs before it is accepted, the offer is terminated.
(f) *Lapse of Time*: An offer is made with a condition that it should be accepted within a specified period of time, and if the offeree fails to accept within the prescribed time limit, the offer is considered terminated.

Modes of Acceptance

An acceptance can be made in the following ways:

(a) *Oral Acceptance*: An acceptance may be made by words of mouth as long as the offeror could understand it.
(b) *Written*: An acceptance may be made in writing in the same way as it is made by words of mouth.
(c) *Gesture*: An agreement by implication or gesture is sufficient for the acceptance of the offer. For example, a sale is concluded by gestures, made by a dumb person.
(d) *Delivery*: A sale is concluded by an exchange being carried out, as that is evidence of the mutual agreement of the two parties.

(e) *Payment*: An acceptance in a contract of sale could be presumed by the payment made by the buyer in consideration of the subject matter.
(f) *Letter of Post*: A letter or message sent by post or messenger containing the message of acceptance may be substituted for a verbal and personal communication in the contract of sale.
(g) *Other Modes*: Telex, e-mail, telegram, phone, fax, and other instantaneous method of legal communications are recognized by Islamic jurisprudence as mode of acceptance to conclude a valid contract.

Tense of Acceptance

An acceptance must be either in past tense or present tense for a valid contract. In no situation, an acceptance can be made in future tense. This shall make the contract null and void.

Contract: Parties to the Contract

The parties to the contract are buyer and seller and both should meet the following eligibility criteria to get into a valid contract:

1. Parties to the contract must be sane and capable of taking responsibilities. They should be major, reasonable persons and who possess judgment.
2. The two parties to the contract must not be prohibited from dealing with their property, that is, they must not be bankrupt or prodigals.
3. There is no coercion or compulsion exerted on either of the two parties to the contract.

Contract: Conditions of Contract

- **Sale Must Be Non-contingent**

The delivery of the sold commodity to the buyer must be certain and should not depend on a contingency or chance. For example, 'A' sells his car stolen by some anonymous person to 'B' who purchases it in the hope that he will manage to recover it. This sale will be considered as void.

  (a) *Unconditional Contract*: The sale must be unconditional, for example, 'A' buys a car from 'B' with a condition that 'B' will employ his son in his firm. The sale is conditional and hence invalid.
  (b) *Under Reasonable Conditions*: I the conditions which do not go against the contract, for example, 'A' tells 'B' to deliver the goods within a month, the sale is valid.
  (c) *Under Unreasonable Condition But in Market Practice*: If a sale is under unreasonable condition but is in market practice, the sale is considered as valid. For example, 'A' buys refrigerator from 'B' with a condition that 'B' undertakes its service for one year. The condition being recognized as a part of the transaction is valid and the sale is lawful.

- **Sale Must Be Immediate**: The sale must be instant and absolute. Thus, a sale attributed to a future date or a sale contingent on a future event is void. If the parties wish to effect a valid sale, they will have to effect it afresh when the future date comes or the contingency actually occurs. For example, 'A' says to 'B' on January 1 that he will sell his car on February 1, the sale is void, because it is attributed to a future date.

Contract: The Subject Matter

The necessary conditions related with the subject matter to be taken care in the contract are listed below:

1. *Existence*: The subject matter of sale must exist at the time of sale. Thus, a thing, which does not exist, cannot be sold. If a non-existent thing has been sold, even with mutual consent, the sale is void according to the Syariah. For example, 'A' sells the unborn calf to 'B', the sale will be considered as void.

2. *Valuable*: The subject of sale must be a property of value. Thus, a thing having no value according to the usage of trade, for example, a leaf or a stone on roadside, cannot be sold or purchased.
3. *Permissible*: The subject of a sale should be permissible under the Syariah, for example, trading in pork or liquor.
4. *Ownership Can Be Transferred*: The subject matter should not be anything, which is not capable of ownership or title cannot be transferred, for example, sea or sky.
5. *Capable to Deliver*: The thing should be capable of being delivered and can be easily possessed. For example, an un-constructed building cannot be possessed since it is non-existent.
6. *Specific and Quantifies*: The subject of sale must be specifically known and identified either by pointing or by detailed specification that can distinguish it from other things, which are not sold. For example, if 'A' owns a building and offers 'B' to buy an apartment and 'B' accepts the offer, the sale is void unless the apartment is specifically identified and pointed out to the buyer.
7. *Object Ownership*: The subject matter of sale must be in the ownership of the seller at the time of sale. Thus, what the seller does not own cannot be sold. If he sells something before acquiring its ownership and risk, the sale is void. For example, 'A' sells a car to 'B', which is presently not owned by 'A'. The sale is void because at the time of the sale, 'A' did not own a car.

Contract: The Price

The necessary conditions related with price to be taken care in the contract are listed below:

- *Quantified*: The measuring unit of the pricing should be known, for example, currency and so on.
- *Specified and Certain*: A sale can be valid only if the price is ascertained and specified. If the price is uncertain, then the sale is void. In other words, currency and amount must be known and amount must be absolute.

1.5 Contracts in Islamic Banking

Islam permits trade and commerce and the contracts are applied thereto are termed muamalat in the Syariah. Muamalat are civil contracts and all civil contracts can be used in Islamic banking and finance. Thus, in the concept of Islamic banking, the mobilization of deposits is through contracts permissible by the Syariah, and the application of funds is also through contracts permissible by Syariah. This can be further classified into three broad categories as illustrated in the following picture (Fig. 4.4):

1.5.1 Trading Contracts

These contracts are based on the trading principle of buying and selling of assets and play a pivotal role in the Islamic banking. Islamic banking follows trading principle for financing the customer needs. The trading contract can be for goods, cash, and debt trading as explained in the

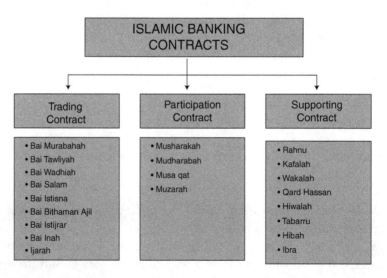

Fig. 4.4 Islamic banking contracts

Islamic sales contract. The most common trading contracts, which are followed by Islamic Banks, are listed below:

1. *Bai Murabahah (Cost Plus)*: It means a sale on mutually agreed profit. Technically, it is a contract of sale in which the seller declares his cost and the profit. Islamic banks have adopted this contract as a mode of financing.
2. *Bai Tawliyah*: It means a sale at cost without any profit for the seller. This sale is again based on the principle of trust (amanah).
3. *Bai Wadhiah*: This sale takes place when the seller agrees to sell a commodity at a lower price than that of the cost price. Since the seller is selling the commodity at a lower price, it is also a trust sale.
4. *Bai Salam*: *Salam* means a contract in which advance payment is made for goods to be delivered later on. The seller undertakes to supply some specific goods to the buyer at a future date in exchange of an advance price fully paid at the time of contract.
5. *Bai Istisna (Sale by Order)*: It is a contractual agreement for manufacturing goods and commodities, allowing cash payment in advance and future delivery or a future payment and future delivery. A manufacturer or builder agrees to produce or build a well-described good or building at a given price on a given date in the future.
6. *Bai Bithaman Ajil* (Deferred Payment Sale): It refers to the sale of goods on a deferred payment basis at a price that includes a profit margin agreed upon by both buyer and seller.
7. *Bai Istijrar* (Supply or Wholesale Financing): It refers to an agreement between the client and the supplier, whereby the supplier agrees to supply a particular product on an ongoing basis, for example, monthly, at an agreed price and on the basis of an agreed mode of payment.
8. *Bai Inah*: It refers to the selling of an asset by the bank to the customer through deferred payments. At a later date, the bank will repurchase the asset and pay the customer in cash terms. This is normally used for offering overdraft facility to the customers.
9. *Ijarah (Leasing)*: It refers to an arrangement under which the lessor leases an equipment, building or other facility to a client at an agreed rental against a fixed charge, as agreed by both parties.

1.5.2 Participation Contracts

Islam encourages equity-based participation where stress is more on profit- and loss-sharing. Bank/lender should invest their money to become partners in business instead of becoming creditors. This encourages entrepreneurship translated into banking terms; the depositor, the bank, and the borrower should all share the risks and the rewards of financing business ventures. The objective is that high-risk investments provide a stimulus to the economy and encourage entrepreneurs to maximize their efforts. The most common participation contracts, which are followed by Islamic banks are listed below:

1. *Musharakah*: Financing through equity participation is called Musharakah. Two or more partners contribute to the capital and expertise of an investment. Profits and losses are shared according to the amounts of capital invested. This type of transaction has traditionally been used to finance medium- and long-term investments. Banks have the legal authority to participate in the management of the project, including sitting on the board of directors.
2. *Mudharabah*: Under a Mudharabah contract, the bank provides the capital needed for a project, while the entrepreneur offers labor and expertise. The profits (or losses) from the project are shared between the bank and the entrepreneur at a fixed ratio. Financial losses are assumed entirely by the bank; the liability of entrepreneurs is limited to their time and effort. In cases of proven negligence or mismanagement by entrepreneurs, however, they may be held responsible for the financial losses.
3. *Musaqat*: It is a specific type of Musharakah contract for orchards. Musaqat is an arrangement between the farmer or garden owner and the worker who undertakes to water the garden and so on and do all such work, which would help the harvest or fruition. In this case the harvest is shared among all the equity partners according to their contributions.
4. *Muzarah*: It is essentially a Mudharabah contract in farming where the bank can provide land or funds in return for a share of the harvest.

1.5.3 Supporting Contracts

There are other contracts in compliance with the Syariah that support and facilitate trading and mobilization of capital. The most common supporting contracts practiced by banks are listed below:

1. *Rahnu (Mortgages)*: It is an activity whereby a valuable item is collateralized to a debt, which may be utilized as payment should the debt is not repaid within the agreed period. In the event the debtor is not able to repay the debt, the pawned asset will be sold off to settle the outstanding debt and any surplus will be given back to the owner of the asset.
2. *Kafalah (Guarantee)*: Under this contract a third party becomes surety for the payment of debt. It is a pledge given to a creditor that the debtor will pay the debt, fine, and so on.
3. *Wakalah (Agency)*: A contract of agency in which one person appoints someone else to perform a certain task on his behalf, usually against a certain fee.
4. *Qard Hassan (Benevolent Loan)*: This is an interest-free loan. The borrower is only required to repay the principal amount borrowed, but he may pay an additional amount at his absolute discretion, as a token of appreciation.
5. *Hiwalah (Transfer of Debt)*: It means transfer; legally, it is an agreement by which a debtor is freed from a debt by another becoming responsible for it, or the transfer of a claim of a debt by shifting the responsibility from one person to another—contract of assignment of debt. It also refers to the document by which the transfer takes place.
6. *Tabarru (Donation)*: It is a donation/gift, the purpose of which is not commercial but is for welfare or service in the name of God. Any benefit that is given by a person to other without getting anything in exchange is called Tabarru.
7. *Hibah (Gift)*: It is basically a gift; normally on Islamic Saving Account, the bank gives hibah as a token of appreciation to customers for keeping their money with the bank.

8. *Ibra' (Rebate)*: Ibra' is in the form of a reduction in the balance outstanding upon early settlement of financing amount and the computation will be based on the terms and condition agreed in the contract.

In the following chapters, we shall be discussing in detail the financing and investment contracts.

References

http://www.gulfnews.com/Articles/news.asp?ArticleID=101049
http://www.bnm.gov.my/index.php?ch=174&pg=469&ac=387
http://www.ambg.com.my/is_concepts.asp
Bakar, M. D. Contracts in Islamic commercial and their application in modern Islamic financial system.
Billah, M. M. Modern financial transactions under Syariah.
Islamic Law of Contract. Retrieved from http://islamic-finance.net/siber/lib2/law-2.html
Nyazee, I. A. K. *Outlines of Islamic jurisprudence*.
Sarker, M. A. A. Islamic business contracts, agency problem and the theory of the Islamic firm. *International Journal of Islamic Financial Services, 1*(2).
Usmani, M. I. A. *MEEZANBANK's guide to Islamic banking*.

5

Islamic Deposits in Practice

1 Introduction

Deposits are the main source of funds for commercial banks, merchant banks, finance companies, and discount houses based on the license granted by the Central Bank. These funds can be cash, claims, or money, like cheques placed in depositors' accounts, bank loans, or money from investments. Depositors are essentially the economic surplus units such as households, corporations, investors, and government. These deposits are collected for different time frames and are received in different accounts.

Without deposits, banks cannot survive and function as the funds collected in the form of deposits are used for lending. Deposits and savings play an important part in promoting economic stability. It also plays a vital role in the development of the country. It can indirectly help to increase the living standards of people.

The deposit collected from the economic surplus unit is used for the purpose of lending to economic deficit units. This function is known as financial intermediation, whereby banks collect funds from the community and extend credit (give loans) to people (borrowers) for useful purposes. Hence, bank deposits are the main source of money supply that can be mobilized to generate economic growth and wealth. By giving out loans to borrowers and investors, banks create credit. The ability of banks to create credit enables them to supply money to borrowers, suppliers, and investors to conduct economic activities such as opening up plants, funding their working capital requirements, financing business expansion, or increasing investments. Such economic activities create job opportunities, increasing productivity and income which leads to wealth creation in the economy.

Islamic financial institutions (IFIs) play the role of intermediaries where the flow of funds is indirect. They buy funds by offering a variety of deposit products such as wadiah- and/or qard-based current account deposits, Mudharabah-based Saving Account and investment account deposits, and the like. They then sell funds through a variety of other financing products which are either equity-based or debt-based.

- Islamic equity-based financing products comprise trustee partnership (Mudharabah) facility, joint-venture (Musharakah) facility, declining partnership (Musharakah) facility, and the like;
- Islamic debt-based financing products comprise cost-plus sale (Murabahah) with deferred payment (Bai Bithaman Ajil) facility, leasing (Ijarah) facility, deferred delivery sale (salam) facility, manufacture-sale (istisna) facility, recurring sale (istijrar) facility, benevolent loan (qard) facility, and the like.

The difference between the buy and sell of funds is the profit or loss earned by IFIs. In short, to a bank operating conventional banking or Islamic banking, deposits are the main source of funding which it uses to produce income. Recent studies indicate that Islamic banks' assets currently stand at US$1.48 trillion and Islamic banks' capital grew from US$200 billion in 2000 to close to US$3 trillion in 2016. Islamic banks have experienced average growth between 10 and 15% in the last decade. Considering the fact that there are only about 300 Islamic banks worldwide, their performance is exceptional.

In this chapter, we will discuss about Islamic deposits and the various types of deposits products offered in general by IFIs.

1.1 Modus Operandi of Islamic Banks

Islamic banks practice financial intermediation, whereby funds are mobilized from savers to fund seekers/entrepreneurs. Fixed pricing mechanism as practiced by conventional banks for intermediation is not permitted under Islamic banking. It is replaced by profit- and loss-sharing mechanism for both sides of intermediary functions that is deposits and funding. This could be a key driving force in accelerating the financial performance of Islamic banks. There is no fixed cost of funds attached and the returns to investors are based on the profit earned from investment, this lessens the heavy debt burden faced by conventional banks.

The Islamic finance is therefore a mix of commercial banks and investment banks. As with conventional banks, Islamic banks have to be viable to attract investors by generating an adequate rate of return. Like other financial intermediaries, Islamic banks have at one end the 'Source of Funds' and on the other 'Application of Funds'. In a nutshell, Islamic financial institutions intermediate the transference of excess funds of surplus units to deficit units in line with Syariah principles, the modus operandi of which is illustrated in the following diagram:

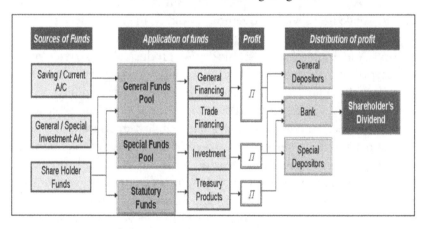

From the above diagram it is clear that Islamic banks make profits by putting the savings of investors at the services of borrowers. The sources of funds are mainly from funds deposited as savings, current, and investment accounts. The special investment account is related to investment accounts exclusively specified for projects preferred by individual corporate investor. Shareholder funds and deposits are channelled into general financing, trade financing (working capital, domestic and international import/export related financing etc.) and treasury products (Islamic Money Market Instruments) and services. Instead of charging fixed rates to borrowers, Islamic banks share in the profits and losses of the borrowers' business transactions, and divide their share of the profit with general and special investors who have deposited funds in the bank. Rates of return, calculated *ex post*, are variable, depending on entire business transactions rather than on any predetermined fixed rate, that would tantamount to interest. The profits earned by banks undergo further deduction for operating expenses, Zakat (Islamic welfare tax) and taxation before it is shared with shareholders as dividends.

1.2 Deposit Concept

Mobilization of funds from saving surplus units in the economy is an important task of financial intermediaries. A financial intermediary attempts to achieve this goal by creating and selling a variety of financial products that match the needs of the saving surplus units. A Muslim saver is in some ways different. While needs related to returns, liquidity, maturity, safety, stability, and the like are important to him/her, the Muslim saver has a unique concern—Syariah compliance. Islamic deposit products allow no trade-off in the matter of Syariah compliance. Islamic banks are engaged in mobilizing savings from this unique group of savers by offering Syariah-compliant products that also vary with respect to other dimensions of return (no existence of riba element), risk, liquidity, maturity, safety, stability, and the like.

In Islamic banking, deposits are backed by the motive of safe-keeping. Depository services facilitate deposit of goods or funds with the bank. Here the bank acts as a depository for safe-keeping. The relationship between depositor and the Islamic bank is different from the ordinary debtor-creditor relationship as is practiced in the Western banking system. In Islamic banks, it is seen as a partner relationship. The whole Islamic banking system is built on a partnership basis in which the depositors, investors, and borrowers participate.

1.3 Syariah Principle in Deposits

The deposit products are strictly governed by Syariah principles. The popular permissible contracts that can be utilized by IFIs for deposits are explained below:

1.3.1 Wadiah Principle

The term wadiah means 'deposit of money allowing somebody to claim the funds in the account'. The bank as trustee preserves and safe-keeps the funds deposited. Thus, depositors feel safe, keeping their money with the bank because the bank provides assurance of returning their money on demand.

Wadiah (deposit) is among the lawful muamalat (dealings) in Islam. It is defined as 'Any belongings left by the owner or his representative with somebody to take care of them'. Wadiah in the legal sense signifies a thing entrusted to the care of another. The proprietor of the thing is known as mudi (depositor). The person entrusted with it is known as wadi or mustawda (custodian) and the deposited asset is wadiah.

In wadiah, a bank is deemed as a keeper and trustee of funds. A person deposits funds in the bank and the bank guarantees refund of the entire amount of the deposit or any part of the outstanding amount, when the depositor demands it. The depositor, at the bank's discretion, may be rewarded with a hibah (gift) as a form of appreciation for the use of funds by the bank. In this case, the bank compensates the depositors for the time value of their money (i.e. pays interest) but refers to it as a 'gift' because it does not officially guarantee payment of the gift.

Wadiah is an aqad (contract) between two parties—the owner of the goods and the custodian of the goods. It is to ensure the safe custody of the goods. The goods are protected from being stolen, lost, destroyed, and so on. 'Goods' can refer to anything of value. Wadiah can be classified into types as illustrated below (Fig. 5.1):

1. *Wadiah Yad Amanah (Trustee Safe Custody)*: Bank acts as a trustee and takes care of the funds. There is no bank guarantee on return of the funds in the event of a loss due to theft, fire, flood, or other natural calamities provided that the bank has taken all necessary measures to safe-keep the funds. The custodian/bank has the duty to protect the property by:

    (a) Not mixing or pooling the properties (money) kept under custody;
    (b) Not using the property; and
    (c) Not charging any fees for safe custody;

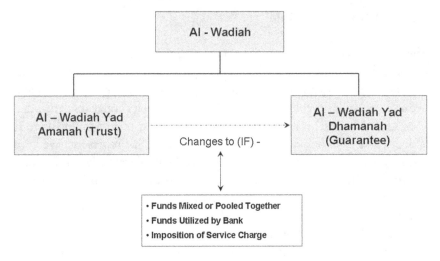

Fig. 5.1 Al-wadiah classification

The property must be taken care of in a manner that will not lead to it being lost or damaged. In this respect different kinds of items are kept differently. For instance, if the deposit is cash, it should be kept in a safe place such as in the banks. However, items such as gold or silver must be kept in a secured place such as in the house or other suitable places.

2. *Wadiah Yad Dhamanah (Guaranteed Safe Custody)*: Bank guarantees the refund of property kept with the bank or custodian. Hence, the bank returns (replaces) the properties to the owner if they were lost or destroyed. Under the agreement, the customer allows the bank to utilize its funds (limited to halal ventures and in compliance with Syariah), provided that all profits and losses resulting from use of the fund are the responsibility or property of the bank. The bank may provide incentives in the form of bonuses to the customer, provided that the amount is not agreed in advance and is granted voluntarily.

This principle can be observed in the contemporary practice applied in the Islamic banking system where the deposits are the source of funds for the bank. These funds are used for the bank's investment activities.

1.3.2 Mudharabah Principle

Mudharabah is an agreement between a capital provider (bank) and another party (entrepreneur), to enable the entrepreneur to carry out business projects. This is based on a profit-sharing basis at a pre-agreed ratio. In the case of losses, the losses are borne by the provider of the funds. The bank will not interfere with the business but rather give the partner the independence to run it.

Under deposits, the Mudharabah principle is defined as an agreement between a bank (as fund manager) and its customer which provides that the bank will manage the fund. According to this principle, the customer determines the amount of profit-sharing in advance and the details are agreed when opening the account. Here, the customer acts as a financing partner, while the bank is the managing partner. The bank pools all investment deposits and searches for suitable investment opportunities in compliance with Syariah. The bank does not guarantee the depositor that the investment will be profitable although the bank will conduct the investment on best-effort basis to ensure it is profitable. The return on investment (positive and negative) is then shared with the depositors, after the bank has deducted its own costs and a previously agreed fee for its efforts. In the event of a loss, the depositor only will bear the losses.

The type of investment account and the terms of the deposit determine a depositor's share in the investment's return. A higher share of profit is paid for deposits with a longer maturity. In the event the investment is not profitable, the depositors share the loss. Their maximum liability is the deposited sum. Investment deposits can only be withdrawn prematurely by paying a certain fine. The conditions of this account differ from those of the Saving Accounts by virtue of:

1. A higher fixed minimum amount;
2. A longer duration of deposits; and
3. The depositor may lose some of or all his funds in the event of the bank making losses (Fig. 5.2).

1. The Mudharabah muthalaqah principle is an agreement in which the owner of the account or fund (the customer) does not limit the

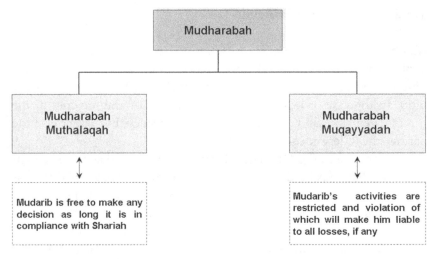

Fig. 5.2 Mudharabah

management of its fund in any way. The bank is given full power to manage the fund without limitations such as the period of time, types of business, business place, or types of services.

2. The Mudharabah muqayyadah principle is an agreement whereby the owner of the account or fund limits the management of its fund. The bank is only allowed to manage the fund within certain limitations as to time, types of business, business place, or types of services.

1.4 Saving Account

Under Saving Accounts, the bank accepts deposits from its customers looking for safe custody of their funds and a degree of convenience in their use together with the possibility of some profits in the form of Saving Accounts on the principle of wadiah. The bank requests permission to use these funds so long as these funds remain with the bank. The depositors can withdraw the balance at any time they so desire and the bank guarantees the refund of all such balances. All the profits generated by the bank from the use of such funds belong to the bank. However, in contrast with the current account, the bank may, at its absolute discretion, reward the customers by returning a portion of the profits generated from the use of their funds from time to time.

It must be pointed out that any return on capital is Islamically justified only if the capital is employed in such a way that it is exposed to a business risk. If saving depositors are guaranteed that their amounts will be refunded in full, if and when they want them, as is the case with traditional banks, then, they are not participating in a business risk. Under these circumstances, it has to be made clear that savings depositors are not Islamically entitled to any returns. If an Islamic bank refunds some portion of the profits generated from the use of savings deposits to the depositors, it is absolutely at the discretion of the bank concerned and it must be treated as a gift. The Islamic principle followed by banks for Saving Account is wadiah yad dhamanah.

The mechanism of Saving Account based on the wadiah yad dhamanah principle is illustrated in the following diagram (Fig. 5.3).

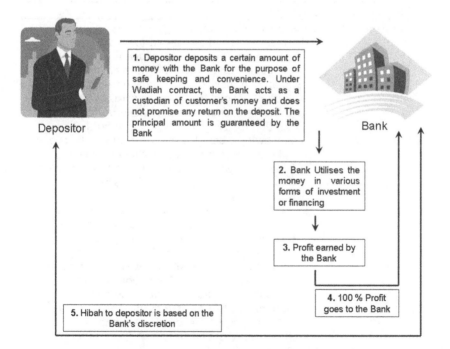

Fig. 5.3 Saving Account based on the wadiah yad dhamanah principle

1.4.1 Saving Account Practice

The common practice for the Saving Account is that depositors allow banks to use their money, but they obtain a guarantee of getting the full amount back from the bank. Banks adopt several methods of inducing their clients to deposit with them, but no profit is promised (Table 5.1).

1.4.2 Saving Account Profit Computation

Mohd. Shariff has opened a Saving-i account with XYZ on May 1, 2016. The balance maintained by him on daily basis is displayed in Table 5.2. The hibah rate is 5% and the computation of hibah to be credited to Mohd. Shariff's account is computed in Table 5.2.

Table 5.1 Saving Account types

Product feature	Description
Product name	Wadiah Saving Account
Definition	This is an account where the customers can deposit their savings. The depositor allows the bank to use this fund in business activities in compliance with Syariah principles. The bank guarantees their savings but is not obliged to pay any rewards to the savers. The bank may, however, pay hibah (profit) at its own discretion for using the customers' fund
Types of account holders	The following types of Saving Account may be opened: 1. Individual account: It is an account opened by individuals legally eligible to enter into a contract, that is, not a bankrupt, insane. or a minor 2. Minor account 3. Joint account: Two or more individuals may open a joint account, for example, husband and wife, parents and children. All account holders must be legally eligible individuals. The parties to a joint account must at the outset give clear instructions duly signed by all the account holders on the method of withdrawal from the account. A joint account may be operated by any one of the account holders, or a number, or all of them jointly 4. Clubs, societies, association 5. Trustee

(continued)

Table 5.1 (continued)

Product feature	Description
Minimum balance in account	The minimum balance in the account is to be maintained by the depositor
Return/profit	Hibah is at the discretion of the Islamic bank and is not pre-specified in the contract. All eligible depositors must get equal percentage of returns. The profit given to customers in the past is normally declared by the Islamic bank as percentage of returns per annum
Hibah calculation (option A)—Accumulated daily average method	Monthly Average Daily Balance in the Month (MADB) = $$\frac{\text{Total of End of Day Balances for the Entire Month}}{\text{No. of Days in the Month}}$$ Profit Amount for the Month $$= \frac{(\text{MADB} \times \text{Profit Rate} \times \text{No. of Days in the Month})}{(365)}$$ 1. MADB is the total balance for one month divided by the actual number of calendar days in the month of calculation, for example, for March, the number of days is 31 2. Profit rate is the rate derived by the bank for profit distribution 3. No. of days are the actual number of calendar days in the month of calculation The above calculation is based on the assumption that the profit is distributed monthly. The profit rate (hibah) is at the discretion of the bank and is not known at the time of deposit. Profit percentage can be derived based on the profit generated from deposits in the previous month The profit computation can be based on the average daily balance of the account and the crediting of profit can be monthly or half yearly basis. The crediting of profit varies from bank to bank
Hibah calculation (option B)—Daily balance method	Profit Amount = P × R × T • P = Principle, that is, end of the day balance • R = Profit rate is the rate derived by the bank for profit distribution • T = Number of days/365 The above calculation is normally practiced to compute the profit on daily basis and the crediting of profit can be monthly or half yearly basis. The crediting of profit varies from bank to bank

(continued)

Table 5.1 (continued)

Product feature	Description
Passbook facility	Normally passbook is providing to Saving Account holders
Withholding tax	Withholding tax is to be levied and deducted when dividend/hibah is credited to a customer's account or when an account is closed. Dividend earned on the *first RM100,000* is exempted from withholding tax. Any dividend amount earned over and above the RM100,000 exemption amount will be subject to 5% withholding tax
	Account holders who are exempted from paying withholding tax are:
	1. Clubs
	2. Associations
	3. Societies
	4. Non-Malaysian individuals with foreign addresses
Account statement facility	This facility is normally available on request basis. Bank may or may not charge for the same
Additional facilities	1. ATM card be issued to the depositor to withdraw money anytime even during off banking hours. The card can be used at any of the issuer's bank ATM or it can be used at other bank's ATM provided they are member of MEPS (Malaysian electronic payment system)
	2. Internet banking ID to perform banking transactions via Internet. The transactions that can be performed online are balance enquiry, utility payment, prepaid mobile top-up, account statement request, standing instruction, fund transfers, address update, and so on
	3. Phone banking: Customer can use the phone to perform banking transactions using the account number and TPIN (telephone personal identification number). Normally limited transactions can be performed including fund transfer, balance enquiry, other enquiries, and instalments payment
	4. Mobile banking: Mobile banking uses the mobile phones as the medium to perform limited transactions and enquiries into depositors' accounts. Normally limited transactions can be performed including fund transfer, balance enquiry, other enquiries, and instalment payment
Zakat	Zakat on the savings paid by the bank

(*continued*)

Table 5.1 (continued)

Product feature	Description
Dormant account/ unclaimed moneys	1. For inactive accounts, which have not been operated either by deposit (credit) or withdrawal (debit) for at least 6 months and more, the system will classify such accounts as 'dormant' accounts 2. Accounts not operated either by deposit or withdrawal for 84 months and more. If customers fail to respond by December 31 of the year, the accounts will be ultimately closed on January 1 of the following year and the amounts will be transferred to the registrar of unclaimed monies
Account closing	1. The account holder has to come in person to request closure of account. The request should be in writing and must be signed in accordance with the account operation authority 2. Force closure in the event 'NIL' balance is maintained by customer for 'X' months. The definition of 'X' month differs from bank to bank

Table 5.2 Saving Account profit computation with 5% hibah rate

Date	Daily balance (RM)	Date	Daily balance (RM)
1-May	10,000	17-May	6800
2-May	5000	18-May	6400
3-May	1000	19-May	1290
4-May	2000	20-May	8000
5-May	3000	21-May	2350
6-May	3000	22-May	3000
7-May	3000	23-May	4500
8-May	3000	24-May	4000
9-May	5,000	25-May	2000
10-May	5000	26-May	6000
11-May	5000	27-May	3000
12-May	5000	28-May	4500
13-May	7500	29-May	4000
14-May	2500	30-May	3000
15-May	3500	31-May	5000
16-May	4500	Total	131,840

Monthly Daily Average Balance = 131,840/31 = RM 4,252.90

$$Hibah = \frac{(Monthly\ Average\ Daily\ Balance \times Rate \times No.of\ Days)}{(365)}$$

$$Hibah = \frac{(4252.90 \times 5 \times 31)}{(365 \times 100)}$$

Hibah = RM 18.06

The hibah amount that will be credited to Mohd. Shariff's account on May 31 is RM18.06.

1.5 Current Account

Under current account, the deposits can be withdrawn on demand without any conditions and restrictions. The main motive for a customer to have a current account is to keep excess liquidity available on demand. The objective to earn profit is not the priority. The profit is paid to the account holder at the bank's discretion and is not promised by the bank. These accounts are operated for the safe custody of deposits and for the convenience of customers.

1. *Current Account based on Wadiah*: The wadiah yad dhamanah concept is utilized when the bank pools and utilizes the fund. The bank's responsibility is in the form of guarantee and therefore it is compulsory for the bank to return the fund as and when requested by the customer. If the bank gained high profit from their financing projects, the depositor will usually receive a good/ high hibah. On the contrary, in the event of a loss, the bank need not give any hibah to the customers. Furthermore, the depositors' money is still in custody and will not be reduced even though there is a loss. Wadiah yad dhamanah principle is widely used for current accounts by the Islamic banks in Malaysia.
2. *Current Account based on Qard Hassan*: Another view is to use Qard Hassan as an underlying principle for current accounts, whereby the deposits are treated as qardh or a benevolent loan by the depositor. This view has been adopted by Iranian Islamic banks which call the current account Qard Hassan current account. The bank is free to utilize these funds at its own risk. The depositor in its role as the lender is not entitled to any return as this would constitute riba. In fact, any kind of benefit passed on to the depositor that is a part of the agreement is deemed to be riba. Hence, the debtor owes the creditor only the principal amount

borrowed. The Qard Hassan model is less popular than the wadiah model among bankers for the simple reason that marketing considerations demand providing additional benefits to the depositor. In the Qard Hassan framework, benefits to a lender (the depositor in this case) are not attractive due to the modus operandi of Qard Hassan, whereby any profits cannot be shared with the lender. Hence, banks find it difficult to market such product as there is no return for account holder.

3. *Current Account based on Mudharabah*: Operations of this current account is based on an agreement between a customer, who will provide capital (deposits), and the bank. This is to enable the bank to carry out business projects, which will be on a profit-sharing basis, according to predetermined ratios agreed upon earlier. In the case of losses, the losses are to be borne by the customer. This concept is practiced by banks in Malaysia but it is not popular.

The main characteristics of current accounts utilizing the wadiah yad dhamanah concept, as operated by Islamic banks, are listed below:

1. Current account governs what is commonly known as call deposits or demand deposits. These accounts can be opened either by individuals or companies, in domestic currency or in foreign currency;
2. The bank guarantees the full return of these deposits on demand and the depositor is not paid any share of the profit or a return in any other form;
3. Depositors authorize the bank to utilize funds at the bank's own risk.
   Hence, if there is any profit resulting from the employment of these funds, it accrues to the bank, and if there is any loss, it is also borne by the bank;
4. There are no conditions with regard to deposits and withdrawals; and
5. Usually, account holders have a right to draw cheques on their accounts.

1.5.1 Wadiah Current Account Practice

The common practice for the current account is that the bank accepts deposits for the purpose of safe-keeping and the customer shall give permission to the bank to utilize all or any sum of the monies in the account based on Syariah law. As wadiah yad dhamanah is a trust, the bank becomes the guarantor and, therefore, guarantees payment of the whole sum or any part thereof of the account when demanded. The customer is not entitled to any share of the profits but the bank may provide returns to the customer as a hibah (gift). The common features of the product are explained in Table 5.3.

Profit computation method in Wadiah current account is similar to Wadiah Saving Account as explained under Section 1.4.2.

1.5.2 Mudharabah Current Account Practice

Banks also use Mudharabah as an underlying principle for the current account. The term Mudharabah refers to a form of business contract in which one party brings capital and the other a personal effort. The proportionate share in profit is determined by a mutual agreement. But the loss, if any, is borne only by the owner of the capital, in which case the

Table 5.3 Wadiah current account practice

Product feature	Description
Product name	Wadiah current account
Definition	A Wadiah current account is an agreement between customers and the bank to keep their deposits in the bank's custody. Under this scheme, the account holder enjoys interest-free safe-keeping services of money. The core of this arrangement is that the bank has the authority to use the deposits and gives a guarantee to return it to the account holder on needs basis. The portion of profit to be shared with customer is at the absolute discretion of the bank
Islamic principle utilized	Wadiah yad dhamanah
Types of account holders	The following entities can open a current account with Islamic Bank: 1. Individuals 2. Sole proprietors 3. Partners 4. Professionals 5. Companies 6. Clubs, societies, associations 7. Trustee
Minimum balance in account	The minimum balance in the account is to be maintained by the depositor

(continued)

Table 5.3 (continued)

Product feature	Description
Return/profit	Hibah is at the discretion of the Islamic bank and is not pre-specified in the contract. All eligible depositors must get equal percentage of returns. The profit given to customers in the past is normally declared by Islamic banks as percentage of returns per annum
Hibah calculation (option A)—Accumulated daily average method	Monthly Average Daily Balance in the Month (MADB) $$= \frac{\text{Total of End of Day Balances for the Entire Month}}{\text{No. of Days in the Month}}$$ Profit Amount for the Month $$= \frac{(\text{MADB} \times \text{Profit Rate} \times \text{No. of Days in the Month})}{(365)}$$ 1. MADB is the total balance for one month divided by the actual number of calendar days in the month of calculation, for example, for March, the number of days is 31 2. Profit rate is the rate derived by the bank for profit distribution 3. No. of days are the actual number of calendar days in the month of calculation The above calculation is based on the assumption that the profit is distributed monthly. The profit rate (hibah) is at the discretion of the bank and is not known at the time of deposit. Profit percentage can be derived based on the profit generated from deposits in the previous month. The profit computation can be based on the average daily balance of the account, and the crediting of profit can be monthly or half yearly basis. The crediting of profit varies from bank to bank
Hibah calculation (option B)—daily balance method	Profit Amount = P × R × T 1. P = Principle, that is, end of the day balance 2. R = Profit rate is the rate derived by the bank for profit distribution 3. T = Number of days/365 The above calculation is normally practiced to compute the profit on daily basis, and the crediting of profit can be monthly or half yearly basis. The crediting of profit varies from bank to bank
Hibah computation/ payment	The profit computation can be based on the daily balance or average daily balance of the account, and the crediting of profit can be monthly or half yearly basis. The crediting of profit varies from bank to bank

(continued)

Table 5.3 (continued)

Product feature	Description
Withholding tax	Withholding tax is to be levied and deducted when dividend/hibah is credited to a customer's account or when an account is closed. Dividend earned on the *first* RM100,000 is exempted from withholding tax. Any dividend amount earned over and above the RM100,000 exemption amount will be subject to 5% withholding tax
Account statement facility	A current account statement will be generated for all current accounts at the end of every month, irrespective of whether the account has zero transactions. In addition, the bank entertains customer's request to generate a current account statement on any other frequency such as daily, weekly, or monthly as well as supply statements via other media (diskette/e-mail/fax)
Additional facilities	1. ATM card is issued to the individual account holder only to withdraw money anytime, even during off banking hours. The card can be used at any of the issuer's bank ATM or it can be used at other bank's ATM provided they are member of MEPS (Malaysian electronic payment system) 2. Internet banking ID to the individual account holder to perform banking transactions via Internet. The transactions that can be performed online are balance enquiry, utility payment, prepaid mobile top-up, account statement request, standing instruction, fund transfers, address update, and so on 3. Phone banking: Individual customer can use the phone to perform banking transactions using the account number and TPIN (telephone personal identification number). Normally limited transactions can be performed that include fund transfer, balance enquiry, other enquiries, and instalment payment. 4. Mobile banking: Mobile banking uses the mobile phones as the medium to perform limited transactions and enquiries into depositors' accounts. Normally limited transactions can be performed that include fund transfer, balance enquiry, other enquiries, and instalment payment 5. Cash management: Corporates can use cash management solution normally known as corporate banking to perform banking transactions via Internet. It is different from Internet banking as it offers extra features such as bulk payments, fund sweeping, foreign exchange contract placement, trade finance, multi-level approval function, and so on

(continued)

Table 5.3 (continued)

Product feature	Description
Zakat	Zakat on the savings paid by the bank
Dormant account/ unclaimed moneys	1. For inactive accounts, which have not been operated either by deposit (credit) or withdrawal (debit) for at least 6 months and more, the system will classify such accounts as 'dormant' accounts 2. Accounts not operated either by deposit or withdrawal for 84 months and more. If customers fail to respond by December 31 of the year, the accounts will be ultimately closed on January 1 of the following year and the amounts will be transferred to the registrar of unclaimed monies
Cheque book	Current account customers are issued cheques which customer can draw to effect payment or withdrawal. A cheque is a bill of exchange drawn on a banker payable on demand A bill of exchange is an unconditional order in writing, addressed by one person to another, signed by the person giving it, requiring the person to whom it is addressed to pay on demand or at a fixed or determinable future time a sum certain in money to, or the order of, a specified person or to bearer Cheques are a useful and safe method of making payments. They also serve as evidence of payment of debt
Signatory(s)	Account holder has the option to define number of signatory(s) that should sign the payment cheques and for other account services. The signatory(s) can be changed after fulfilling the bank's prerequisites as per their policies
Biro Maklumat Cek (statutory requirement by central bank)	The Biro Maklumat Cek (BMC) is a central bureau set up by Bank Negara Malaysia (BNM) and the Association of Banks in Malaysia (ABM) to collect, monitor, and distribute information on and relating to the dishonor of cheques on account of insufficient funds in customers' accounts Through the bad cheque offenders' inquiry system, a bank's branch can make an inquiry to verify if a prospective customer has been reported in the previous bad cheque offenders' list and also if a new account opened is reported in the current bad cheque offenders' list

(*continued*)

Table 5.3 (continued)

Product feature	Description
	A bad cheque incident here refers to each occurrence when the branch, acting as paying bank, returns a cheque unpaid due to insufficient funds in the account on which cheque is drawn on. A customer will fall under BMC list upon issuance of three bad cheques within 12 months. The BMC operational process is to ensure that bad cheque offenders are successfully captured into the bad cheque tracking system and reported to Bank Negara Malaysia
	Note: Please refer to BMC guidelines issued by BNM for further details
Account closing	1. The account holder has to come in person to request closure of account. The request should be in writing and must be signed in accordance with the account operation authority
	2. Closure of current accounts falling under BMC (Biro Maklumat Cek) due to issuance of bad cheques

entrepreneur gets nothing for his labor. The provider of capital has no control over the management of the project. The financier is known as rab-al-maal and the entrepreneur or fund manager as mudarib. Under this concept, a customer provides funds for the bank to invest in permissible activities in accordance with the Syariah. In this case, the bank act as a mudarib (fund manager), whereas the client as rab-al-maal (fund owner). In the capacity of mudarib, the Islamic bank can undertake a variety of business activities that do not contradict with Syariah principles. This also includes other Mudharabah contract with other parties. The profits earned from the investment will be shared between customer and the bank; profit is shared as per pre-agreed ratios, and loss, if any, unless caused by negligence or violation of terms of the contract, is borne by the depositors.

The features of Mudharabah current accounts are similar to wadiah current account except for the profit distribution treatment. In wadiah current accounts, the customer is eligible for hibah based on the bank's discretion, but for Mudharabah, customers will earn dividends based on the profit made by the bank from the investment.

The formula followed for computation of dividend for Mudharabah account is as follows:

1. $$\text{Monthly Average Daily Balance in the Month (MADB)} = \frac{\text{Total of End of Day Balances for the Entire Month}}{\text{No. of Days in the Month}}$$

2. $$\text{Dividend} = \frac{\text{Number of Profit Sharing Days} \times \text{MADB} \times \text{DR}}{\text{Number of Calendar Days in a Year}}$$

(a) MADB is the total balance for one month divided by the actual number of calendar days in the month of calculation. For example, the number of days in the month of March is 31.
(b) Dividend rate (DR) is the rate derived by the bank for profit distribution.
(c) No. of days are the actual number of calendar days in the month of calculation.

1.5.3 Mudharabah Current Account Profit Computation

XYZ Bank has made a profit of RM20,000 from a pool of fund as mentioned in the Table A. Say Mr. Alam is holding a current account with XYZ Bank, and the balance maintained by him in the account is as per the Table B. The agreed profit-sharing ratio between Bank and Mr. Alam is 80:20. The profit earned by Mr. Alam is given in Table 5.4.

1. Funds pooled = Balance for all the products, used to form a pool of funds by the XYZ Bank.
2. Weight = The weight assigned by the Bank based on the usage of funds as the entire funds cannot be utilized by the Bank for investment. This also depends upon the Central Bank guidelines and the weights assigned differ from bank to bank.
3. Weighted balance = Funds pooled × Weight.
4. Income distribution = (Weighted balance for individual product/total weighted balance) × Total income earned.
5. Client ratio = The profit-sharing ratio as agreed with the client.
6. Profit for each product = Income distribution × Ratio.

Table 5.4 Mudharabah current account profit computation

Product type	Funds pooled	Weight	Weighted balance	Income distribution	Client ratio (%)	Profit for each product	Dividend rate %
Mudharabah current	2,000,000	0.95	1,900,000	3,864,734	20	772,947	4.64
Saving current	4,000,000	0.95	3,800,000	7,729,469	65	5,024,155	15.07
Mudharabah deposit (1 month)	2,500,000	0.95	2,375,000	4,830,918	70	3,381,643	16.23
Mudharabah deposit (3 month)	1,000,000	0.95	950,000	1,932,367	75	1,449,275	17.39
Mudharabah deposit (6 month)	800,000	0.95	760,000	1,545,894	80	1,236,715	18.55
Mudharabah deposit (12 month)	50,000	0.95	47,500	96,618	85	82,126	19.71
Total	10,350,000		9,832,500	20,000,000		11,946,860	

7. Rate % = (Profit for each product/funds pooled) × (Total number of month in a year/no. of profit calculation month) × 100%.

Following the above calculation, dividend rate for Mr. Alam is 20% and the dividend computation is as in Table 5.5.

Monthly Daily Average Balance = 150,200/31 = RM 4,845.16

$$Dividend = \frac{\text{Number of Profit Sharing Days} \times \text{MADB} \times \text{DR}}{(365)}$$

$$Dividend = \frac{(31 \times 4,845.16 \times 4)}{(365 \times 100)}$$

Dividend for the Month = RM 16.46

The dividend amount that will be credited to Mr. Alam's current account on May 31st is RM 6.46.

1.6 Investment Account

Investment accounts are also called participating accounts. They may be seen as an alternative to the fixed-term deposit accounts offered by conventional

Table 5.5 Mudharabah current account profit computation, dividend

Date	Daily balance (RM)	Date	Daily balance (RM)
1-May	10,000	17-May	7000
2-May	10,000	18-May	1000
3-May	10,000	19-May	1000
4-May	10,000	20-May	1000
5-May	5000	21-May	1000
6-May	5000	22-May	1000
7-May	5000	23-May	6000
8-May	2000	24-May	6000
9-May	2000	25-May	6000
10-May	2000	26-May	6000
11-May	1800	27-May	1800
12-May	1800	28-May	1800
13-May	7,000	29-May	6000
14-May	7000	30-May	6000
15-May	7000	31-May	6000
16-May	7000	Total	150,200

banks, except that the returns depend entirely on the result of the bank's dealings with various business projects. Mudharabah is a special type of investment contract. This contract is between two parties: a capital owner (called rab-al-maal) and an investment manager (called mudarib). Profit is distributed between two parties in accordance to the ratio that they agreed upon at the time of the contract. Financial loss is borne by the capital owner, the loss to the manager being the opportunity cost of his own labor, which failed to generate any income. Except for a violation of the agreement or negligence, the investment manager cannot guarantee either the capital extended to him or any profit generation (if profit is guaranteed, then it is considered as riba).

Under this concept, the bank will manage the customer's fund as mudarib. Normally, the bank uses the fund to make a sale or financing transaction with clients who wanted cash for their working capital, purchase asset for business, or might purchase an Islamic Sukuk from any Islamic issuer. Any profit attained from the business will be distributed based on the profit-sharing ratio between the bank and the customer. Profits are given away only when the investments are successful, while capital may depreciate or even diminish if the investment ends in losses.

Under the Islamic investment accounts, investors will have a better chance to gain higher profit because the profit will be distributed based on the profit-sharing ratio. The most important aspect that must be kept in mind is that the entire profit obtained through such contracts is halal. Mudharabah can be classified further based on the authority entrusted by the fund owners, that is, intended end-use of funds, and the degree of freedom accorded to the bank as explained in the following sections (Fig. 5.4).

1.6.1 Mudharabah Muthalaqah (General Investment Account)

Under this type of account, the investment account holder authorizes the Islamic bank to invest the account holder's funds in a manner which the Islamic bank deems appropriate without laying down any restrictions as to where, how, and for what purpose the funds should be invested. Under this arrangement, the Islamic bank can commingle the investment account holder's fund with its own funds or with other funds the Islamic bank has the right to use (e.g., Mudharabah current accounts). The

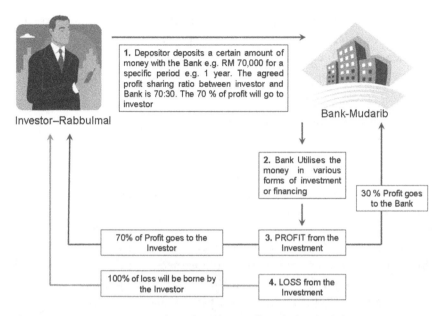

Fig. 5.4 Investment account based on the Mudharabah principle

investment account holders and the Islamic bank generally participate in the returns on the invested funds.

The capital is handed over to the mudarib without determination of the type of work that is to be done, the location, the time, method of payment from the client (cash or credit), the quality of work, the person with whom the mudarib may or have to trade, and so on. It is up to the discretion of the mudarib to run the business according to his expertise and experience. His authority is then absolute and he can use the capital in the manner he deems fit. In such a situation, he is permitted to undertake all transactions, which are normally allowed in commercial usage. Although the capital provider has no right to intervene, once he believes that the mudarib is not acting for the benefit of the venture, he may raise his dissatisfaction to that, even to the extent of requesting the court to prevent the mudarib from further usage of the capital.

In Malaysia, the Mudharabah muthalaqah principle is utilized for general investment accounts. Under Mudharabah muthalaqah, the bank acts as an investment manager, invests the money into permitted investments and Islamic financing activities, realizes profits, and shares the outcomes with depositors based on the ratio agreed. Therefore, for depositors, the actual return on deposits is known only upon maturity (or upon periodical payment of profit, e.g. monthly). The returns vary according to the actual outcome of investments, though some of them are relatively predictable.

1.6.2 Mudharabah Muthalaqah Practice (General Investment Account)

Mudharabah general investment account (MGIA) is a term deposit based on the concept of profit-sharing. The bank accepts the deposits based on the Islamic banking concepts of Mudharabah (trust profit-sharing). Under this concept, the customer will provide the capital for the bank to invest for a fixed duration with the intention of sharing the profit made from the utilization of funds. The profit earned from the investment will be shared as dividends between customer and the bank according to the predetermined profit-sharing ratio as per the aqad (contract).

In managing the Mudharabah funds, the bank covers the account's operational cost through the profit ratio it is entitled. In addition, the bank is not allowed to reduce the investor's profit rate without written consent. According to the prevailing income tax regulation, the tax imposed on profits earned from the Mudharabah investment is directly debited to the Mudharabah profit at the time of profit-sharing.

This is a popular deposit product of Islamic banks under which an investment pool is established. The pool includes investment deposits of different maturities. The funds are not tied to any specific investment project but are utilized in different and continuous financing operations of the bank. Profits are calculated and distributed at the end of the accounting period, which can be three months, six months, or one year.

The common features of the product are illustrated in Tables 5.6.

1.6.3 Mudharabah Muthalaqah Dividend Computation

Hashim has invested RM250,000 under MGIA for the period of one month. The weightage assigned to the investor's fund is 0.95. The total pool of funds invested by the bank is RM1,000,000 and the weightage assigned for rest of the funds is say 1. The total profit earned by the bank is RM150,000. The profit-sharing ratio agreed between Hashim and bank is 70:30. The dividend earned by Hashim is illustrated in Table 5.7.

1. Funds pooled = Balance for all the products, used to form a pool of funds by the XYZ Bank.
2. Weight = The weights assigned by the Bank based on the usage of funds as the entire funds cannot be utilized by the Bank for investment. This also depends upon the Central Bank guidelines and the weights assigned differ from bank to bank.
3. Weighted balance = Funds pooled × Weight.

Table 5.6 Mudharabah muthalaqah practice (general investment account)

Product feature	Description
Product name	Mudharabah general investment account.
Definition	This is an account where the customers can deposit their savings for short-, medium-, or long-term investment. The depositor allows the bank to use this fund in business activities in compliance with the Syariah principles The bank shares earned profit with the customer based on an agreed profit-sharing ratio; any losses will be borne by the customer
Types of account holders	The following entities are eligible for Mudharabah general investment account: 1. Individual account 2. Minor account 3. Joint account 4. Clubs, societies, association 5. Trustee
Minimum amount	The minimum amount for opening a Mudharabah general investment account.
Investment placement period	The periods for which deposits can be placed are one month and then multiple of one month and maximum up to a period of 60 months
Dividend	The profit earned from investment is distributed as per the proportionate share agreed between the bank and the customer based on the signed aqad The loss is only borne by the customer; unless caused by the negligence or violation of terms of contract, then it is borne by Islamic bank. The Mudharabah becomes void if the profit is fixed in any way

(continued)

Table 5.6 (continued)

Product feature	Description
Dividend calculation	The formula for computation of profit payable on maturity is as follows: Profit = (P × DR × T)/No. of days in year × 100 1. P = Principal amount 2. DR = Dividend rate is the rate derived by the bank for profit distribution 3. T = Duration of investment in number of calendar days in the month of calculation 4. No. of days = 365 for normal year and 366 for the leap year
Profit-sharing ratio	This might differ for each customer based on the bank's marketing strategies and internal policies. The PSR will be agreed upon by the investor and the bank at the time of deposit placement and it remains fixed until the time of the maturity
Investment certificate	An investment certificate with a unique number is issued to the investor acknowledging the receipt of funds with details on amount, tenure, and profit-sharing ratio. The customer has to present the certificate upon withdrawal, renewal, and upliftment
Withholding tax	Withholding tax is to be levied and deducted when dividend/hibah is credited to a customer's account or when an account is closed. Dividend earned on the RM100,000 with a tenure of less than 12 months is exempted from withholding tax. Any dividend amount earned over and above the RM100,000 exemption amount will be subject to 5% withholding tax
Additional facilities	Customer can view the profit accrued and earned via Internet banking, and they can also place the instruction for crediting the profit/principal upon maturity and can also place instruction for auto renewal
Upliftment before maturity	The normal practice for upliftment of deposits before maturity is as below: 1. No dividend will be paid on any one month, two months, or three months' investment that has not run the full period 2. No dividend will be paid on the investment of four months and above if uplifted before the completion of three months 3. Other than in the abovementioned circumstances, the rate payable for investment uplifted before maturity shall be based on the numbers of completed days Note: Partial withdrawal of investment before maturity is not practiced by any bank

(continued)

Table 5.6 (continued)

Product feature	Description
Renewal/rollover	Customer can place instruction for renewal/rollover of investment as explained: 1. Renewal refers to extension of the investment for the same period with or without dividend 2. Rollover refers to extension of the investment for a different period with or without dividend Instructions to renew/rollover may be given by the customer upfront or at any point of time before maturity. The normal practice is that the bank will automatically renew the general investment, in the event there is no instruction for renewal/rollover. The account holder is also given a grace period of 14 days to rollover for a different period. The grace period again differs from bank to bank
Mode of payment	The most common mode of payments for Mudharabah general investment account (principal + profit) are as below: 1. Cash 2. Transfer to savings, current account, or new investment account 3. Banker's cheque, demand draft, or funds transfer to other banks
Dormant account/ unclaimed moneys	1. For inactive accounts, which have not been operated either by deposit (credit) or withdrawal (debit) for at least 6 months and more, the system will classify such accounts as "dormant" accounts 2. Accounts not operated either by deposit or withdrawal for 84 months and more. If customers fail to respond by December 31 of the year, the accounts will be ultimately closed on January 1 of the following year and the amounts will be transferred to the registrar of unclaimed monies
Account closing	1. The investment account holder has to come in person to request closure of account. The request should be in writing and must be signed in accordance with the account operation authority 2. The investment account is to be closed when the customer has withdrawn all funds and the account has nil balance

4. Income distribution = (Weighted balance for individual product/total weighted balance) × Total income earned.
5. Client ratio = The profit-sharing ratio as agreed with the client.
6. Profit for each product = Income distribution × Ratio.

Table 5.7 Mudharabah muthalaqah dividend computation

Product type	Funds pooled	Weight	Weighted balance	Income distribution	Client ratio	Profit shared with client	Dividend rate %
Mudharabah investment	10,000,000	0.95	9,500,000	65,517	70%	45,862	5.5034
Saving current	5,000,000	1	5,000,000	34,483	65%	22,414	5.3793
Total	15,000,000		14,500,000	100,000		68,276	

7. Dividend rate % = (Profit for each product/funds pooled) × (Total number of month in a year/no. of profit calculation month) × 100%.

Dividend to be paid upon realization/liquidation/maturity is as below:
Dividend Computation : $P \times T \times DR/100$

- P = Principal amount invested by investor = RM 250,000
- T = actual number of days invested (tenure) = 1 month
- DR = 5.50

Dividend = $250,000 \times 1 \times 5.50/12 \times 100$
Dividend Paid to Mr. Hashim is RM 1,146

1.6.4 Mudharabah Muqayyadah (Special Investment Account)

This deposit account is similar in all respects to general investment deposit except that the depositor should meet the required minimum to invest in this product. For instance, the bank may selectively accept deposits from the government and/or the corporate customer. The modes of investment of the funds and the ratio of profit distribution may usually be individually negotiated. The product provides the bank with specific authorization to invest in a particular project or trade, and the profits of this particular project only are distributed between the bank and its customers according to mutually agreed terms and conditions.

Under this type of account, the investment account holder imposes certain restrictions as to where, how, and for what purpose his funds are to be invested. Further, the Islamic bank may be restricted from commingling its own funds with the restricted investment account funds for purposes of investment. In addition, there might be other restrictions which investment account holders may want to impose. For example, investment account holders may require the Islamic bank not to invest their funds in instalment sale transactions or without guarantor or collateral or require that the Islamic bank itself should carry out the investment rather than through a third party.

Mudharabah muqayyadah gives an opportunity to the investors to make sure that their funds are invested in companies, investments as per their preference. In addition, the profit-sharing ratio is negotiable, which makes it more attractive for investor, and the product principles are according to Syariah requirements. The main elements for special investment account are explained in Table 5.8.

1.6.5 Mudharabah Muqayyadah (Special Investment Account)

Mushir wants to invest RM100,000 in a special investment account whereby the funds are invested in rubber plantation. The whole investment collected from the investor in the scheme is around RM90 Million. The weightage assigned by the bank is 0.95 and the weightage assigned to bank's own fund for the same investment, that is, for RM14,500,000 is 1. The total profit made by the bank from the investment is RM1,020,000. The profit-sharing ratio agreed between the client and the bank is 70:30. The profit earned by Mushir is illustrated in Table 5.9.

1. Funds pooled = Balance for all the products, used to form a pool of funds by the XYZ Bank.

Table 5.8 Mudharabah Muqayyadah elements

No.	Mudharabah Muqayyadah elements	Details
1.	Rabbul mal	Customer
2.	Mudarib	Bank
3.	Capital	Fund deposit/placement
4.	Fund utilization	Bank utilizing/investing the deposit with in the restriction imposed by customer • Cluster pool of funds: The use of clustered funds is for several projects within the same type of industry • Specific project: The use of this fund is exclusively for specific project
5.	Profit	To be shared as per the agreed ratio
6.	Loss	To be borne by the customer
7.	Contract of offer and acceptance (ijab and qabul)	To be signed by the customer and bank officer

Islamic Deposits in Practice

Table 5.9 Mudharabah Muqayyadah (special investment account)

Product type	Funds pooled	Weight	Weighted balance	Income distribution	Client ratio	Profit shared with client	Dividend rate %
Mudharabah investment—investors	90,000,000	0.95	85,500,000	872,100	70%	610,470	8.1396
Mudharabah investment—bank	14,500,000	1	14,500,000	147,900	70%	103,530	8.5680
Total	104,500,000		100,000,000	1,020,000		714,000	

2. Weight = The weight assigned by the Bank based on the usage of funds as the entire funds cannot be utilized by the Bank for investment. This also depends upon the Central Bank guidelines and the weight assigned differs from bank to bank.
3. Weighted balance = Funds pooled × Weight.
4. Income distribution = (Weighted balance for individual product/total weighted balance) × Total income earned.
5. Client ratio = The profit-sharing ratio as agreed with the client.
6. Profit for each product = Income distribution × Ratio.
7. Dividend rate % = (Profit for each product/funds pooled) × (Total number of month in a year/no. of profit calculation month) × 100%.

Dividend to be paid upon realization/liquidation/maturity is as below:
Dividend Computation : P × T × DR/100

- P= Principal amount invested by Investor = RM 100,000
- T= actual number of days invested (tenure) = 1 month
- DR = 8.14

Dividend = 100 , 000 × 1 × 8.14/12 × 100
Dividend paid to Mr . Hashim is RM 678.33 ; *after rounding off*, *it will become RM 678.50*

1.7 Similarities and Differences of Deposits in Conventional and Islamic Bank

The traditional bank accepts deposits to supply money to income-generating activities of entrepreneurs. The major source of funds for traditional banks is customer deposit, on which the bank pays a fixed interest rate. This deposit is a form of debt given to the bank by a bank customer. The bank has to pay to the depositor the principal as well as interest. In case of a bad loan, the bank has to pay the depositor from its own resources. The depositor has not shared risk with the bank, but is getting paid for his debt to the bank. Islam views such transaction as unjust because it allows unequal treatment of creditor (depositors) compared to the debtor (the bank).

On the other hand, Islamic banks accept deposits with the condition that the money will be put to work combined with the skills and management expertise of banks. The depositor would get back his principal amount together with a share of profit after the expiry of the contract. In fact, the depositor agrees to put his money in the bank's investment account and to share profits with the bank. In this case, the depositor is the supplier of capital and the bank is the manager of capital. The depositor does not earn interest on a fixed rate in the Islamic banking system, but accepts some of the business risks and earns a share of the profit. The depositor is not guaranteed any predetermined return on the nominal value of his deposit like interest-bearing banks, but is treated as a shareholder of the bank and, as such, is entitled to a share of the profits made by the bank. Similarly, if the bank incurs losses, the depositor shares in these losses and the value of his deposit is reduced. Therefore, any shock to asset positions of Islamic banks is instantaneously reflected by changes in the values of shares (deposits) held by the public in the bank, and therefore, the real values of assets and liabilities of an Islamic bank would be equal at all times.

However, in the traditional banking system, because the nominal value of deposits is fixed, such a shock could cause a divergence between real assets and real liabilities. Since the bank engages in a two-way contract with both depositors and borrowers, the bank does not trade money for money, which is forbidden in Islam. Rather, the bank lends money, which is put to work by the borrower, and shares profit/loss of the invested capital. The Islamic equity system is proved to be a mechanism of efficiency, justice, welfare, and fair growth. Therefore, it may be concluded that although monetary benefits are paid to depositors in both Islamic and traditional banks, they are not the same. Payment to depositors by Islamic banks is variable, while payment to depositors by traditional banks is fixed.

1.8 Account Types

The credentials required for opening an account differs based on the type of applicant. Banks normally have different requirements for opening of accounts for minors, individuals, partnership firms, companies, and so on. Each entity has to sign the account opening form, which represents that applicant undertakes to comply with the bank's rules for the conduct of the account. In other words, both the bank and the application are getting into aqad (contract) based on the agreed terms and conditions between them. The following section will cover the various entities eligible for various types of savings, fixed deposit, and current accounts, and the general requirements for opening of the respective types of accounts:

1.8.1 Minor Accounts

Most of the Islamic banks in Malaysia allow minors to operate a savings or fixed deposit account only. Normally for minor accounts, the minimum age to open a wadiah Saving Account or Mudharabah deposits is 15 years old. The definition of 'major' according to the Majority Act, 1971 (Laws of Malaysia, Act 21), is all males and females, irrespective of religion who attain the age of majority at 18. Minors lack contractual capacity; therefore, they cannot be sued.

The Bills of Exchange Act 1949 does not prohibit minors to draw or endorse bills of exchange or cheques. Since minors can draw cheques, banks may open wadiah current accounts for minors. However, as a matter of practice, banks do not encourage the opening of current accounts for minors, as various complications could arise because minors have no capacity or power to incur liability on a bill.

Islamic banks also allow children below 12 years of age to have a Saving Account, that is, in a trust Saving Account but operated by a parent or guardian only.

1.8.2 Individual Accounts

The definition of an individual is one who has attained the age of majority and has contractual capacity. An individual may open any account with the bank based on the eligibility criteria set by the bank. The following information is generally required by an Islamic bank for opening of an account:

1. Name of the customer
2. Old and new identity card/passport particulars
3. Residential address;

4. Correspondence address
5. Contact details (telephone/fax/mobile/e-mail ID, etc.)/occupation/designation/nature of business
6. Name of employer
7. Photocopy of identity card/passport and work permit (if applicable—for foreigners)
8. Specimen signature and method of signing cheques where mandate to operate account is given to a third party
9. Name and signature of introducer
10. Married women are expected, in addition, to furnish the following information to the bank:

    (a) Name of husband
    (b) Husband's occupation and nature of business
    (c) Name of husband's employer or business

An undischarged bankrupt is stripped of his contractual capacity by operation of law. An undischarged bankrupt cannot operate an account whether personal, joint, or partnership unless acting as an agent. In addition, an individual with a criminal record indulging in subversive or illegal activities is not allowed to open any type of account with the bank.

1.8.3 Joint Accounts

Two or more individuals may open a joint account. Generally, joint accounts are opened between members of the family, for example, husband and wife or brothers. Professionals like lawyers, doctors, and accountants and businessmen may also open joint accounts. The parties to a joint account must, at the outset, give clear instructions duly signed by all the account holders on the method of signing or endorsing cheques and other operation of accounts. A joint account may be operated by any one of the account holders, or a number, or all of them jointly.

Most Islamic banks have a standard form which incorporates not only the method of operation of the account but also the survivorship clause and 'the joint account holder, the credit balance standing in the account will belong to the survivors'. However, in practice, the credit balance will still be subject to the provisions of the Estate Duty Act.

The 'joint and several' liability clause is for the protection of the bank. In the event of credit facility being given, the banker has legal remedy against all the joint account holders. The banker has the option of reverting to anyone or all of the joint account holders for the recovery of the outstanding debt, where necessary. The following information is generally required for the opening of a joint account:

1. Name of each joint account holder
2. Identity card/passport particulars of each account holder
3. Residential address
4. Correspondence address
5. Contact details (telephone/fax/mobile/e-mail ID, etc.)
6. Occupation/designation/nature of business of each account holder
7. Name of employer of each account holder
8. Mandate and method of signing cheques and other account operations
9. Specimen signature(s) of joint account holders authorized to sign
10. Name and signature of introducer

1.8.4 Sole Proprietorship Accounts

A sole proprietorship is a business owned by one individual and trading in his own name or under a trading name. A sole proprietorship business concern must be registered with the Registrar of Business as evidenced by a Registration of Business Certificate.

Upon registration, the sole proprietorship gains legal recognition. However, it has no legal entity of its own. The liability of the sole proprietorship firm is the personal liability of the sole proprietor. As such, most of the banking laws and practices relating to opening of individual accounts will apply to sole proprietorship.

For opening a sole proprietorship account, a bank, among other things, would require the following:

1. Names of firm and proprietor
2. Identity card/passport particulars
3. Residential address

4. Business address
5. Contact details (telephone/fax/mobile/e-mail ID, etc.)
6. Date of registration and certificate number
7. Photocopy of business registration certificate
8. Nature of business
9. Specimen signature and rubber stamp
10. Name and signature of introducer

Banks might require the original Certificate of Business Registration for verification. In view of the ever-increasing forgeries and frauds, banks also normally make a search at the Registrar of Business where the sole proprietor or his introducer is not well known to the bank.

1.8.5 Partnership Accounts

Partnership is the relationship between persons carrying on a business in common with a view to profit. Partnerships must be registered with the Registrar of Business under the Registration of Business Ordinance 1956. However, the legislation exempts those professions, which can be carried out only by any written law. Accordingly, professionals like lawyers, doctors, and so on who are governed by their respective professional legislation are not required to register their professional business though they may be running a partnership.

Upon registration, a Business Registration Certificate is issued by the Registrar of Business. An annual renewal certificate (Form D) is also issued. Changes in the particulars of the partnership (e.g. changes in partners) should be registered with the Registrar of Business using Form B. It is important for banks to know the changes in the partnership in view of the nature of the liability of partners. Under ordinary law, the partners are jointly liable. Where necessary, the bank can sue all the partners under one legal action for the recovery of any advances.

In view of this, a 'joint and several' liability clause is invariably incorporated in the current account application form. A partnership has no legal entity of its own. The liabilities of the firm are the liabilities of the partners jointly in their personal capacities. The partners of a firm would normally document their agreement on various matters, and particularly on profit-sharing. The written document is called the Partnership Agreement. As a general rule, the Partnership Agreement prevails in the event of a dispute. Partnership accounts are eligible only for Islamic current accounts and investment deposits but not for Saving Accounts. For opening a partnership account, a bank, among other things, would require the following:

1. Registered name and address of the firm
2. Names of partners
3. Business address
4. Contact details (telephone/fax/mobile/e-mail ID, etc.)
5. Identity card/passport particulars of all partners
6. Date of registration and certificate number
7. Photocopy of Business Registration Certificate
8. Nature of business
9. Mandate and method of signing or endorsing cheques
10. Partnership agreement, if any
11. Name and signature of introducer
12. Specimen signature(s) of the partner(s) duly authorized to sign or endorse cheques
13. Specimen of the rubber stamp to be used

Banks would generally require the original Business Registration Certificate for verification. Where necessary, banks may even conduct a search with the Registrar of Business to establish existence of the firm. The account should be in the name of the firm. In dealing with partnership accounts, banks are extra cautious in view of the many legal complications arising from various situations. Some common legal considerations are given below:

1. *Authority of any partner to countermand or stop payment*: Under the law, every partner has a right to take part in the management of a business. As such, any partner may request the bank to stop payment of a cheque signed by any other partner(s) though he himself may not be authorized to sign cheques under the mandate given to the bank;
2. *Collection of Cheques*: Any cheque favoring the partnership firm has to be paid into the account of the firm and should not be paid into the personal account of any partner;

3. *Bankruptcy of a Partner*: Bankruptcy of a partner does not necessarily involve the bankruptcy of the firm, but it does mean that the partnership is dissolved and the banker may not permit the account to be operated upon, especially if it is overdrawn;
4. *Bankruptcy of a Partnership*: The bankruptcy of the partnership firm means that every partner has become bankrupt. In such a case, the partnership account as well as the personal accounts of the partners would be frozen immediately; and
5. *Death of a Partner*: When a partner dies, the partnership is deemed to be dissolved. The remaining partners may be permitted to continue the business temporarily and to operate the account for the purpose of winding up the business of the firm on the condition that the account is conducted in credit balance. However, if there is a debt balance in the bank account, the bank may stop the account to be operated upon because of the legal case known as the 'Rule in Clayton's case'.

1.8.6 Professionals' Accounts

Professionals like solicitors, doctors, architects, and accountants need not register their professional business with the Registrar of Business. Their practice would be governed by the respective ordinances and the rules and regulations of their professional associations. Though professionals need not register the professional business with the Registrar of Business, they may operate their professional business and current account as a sole proprietorship or partnership as the case may be.

Partnership accounts are eligible only for Islamic current account and investment deposits but not for Saving Accounts. The following are generally required by banks for the opening of business account for professionals:

1. Names of firm and address
2. Nature of business/profession
3. Photocopy of certificates issued by relevant authorities (e.g. 'Practicing Certificate' issued by the High Court or 'Registration Certificate' issued to doctors by the Malaysian Medical Council). Banks would generally require the original certificates for verification

4. Name(s) of professional(s)
5. Identity card particulars
6. Correspondence address
7. Contact details (telephone/fax/mobile/e-mail ID, etc.)
8. Mandate (if applicable) and method of operation of account
9. Specimen signature(s) of authorized signatories and rubber stamp
10. Name and signature of introducer

1.8.7 Company Accounts

Unlike partnerships discussed earlier, a company is a separate legal entity. It has an existence distinct from that of its direction and members. A company may be:

1. *Limited by shares*: A company limited by shares is one in which the liability of each member is limited to the amount of unpaid shares. Once his shares are fully paid, he has no further liability.
2. *Limited by guarantee*: A company limited by guarantee is one, which is formed 'on the principle of having the liability of its members limited by the memorandum to such an amount as the members may respectively undertake to contribute to the adjusters (liquidators) of the company in the event of its being wound up' (Companies Act 1965). Non-profit making companies, professional bodies, or charitable organizations come under this category.
3. *Limited by both shares and guarantee*: It is a combination of above.
4. *Unlimited (i.e. with or without share capital)*: An unlimited company is one which is formed on the principle of having no limit placed on the liability of its members. Some stockbroking companies are unlimited companies.

In Malaysia, most companies are limited. There are two types of limited company:

1. Private limited company (Sendirian Berhad)
2. Public limited company (Berhad)

Limited companies are incorporated and registered with the Registrar of Companies under the Companies Act 1965. Both private and public limited companies are issued with a Certificate of Incorporation upon incorporation and registration with the Registrar of Companies. In addition, public limited companies are issued with a Certificate of Trading. According to the Companies Act 1965, a private limited company has the following attributes:

1. Restriction of the right to transfer its shares
2. Limitation in number of members to 50
3. Prohibition of any public offering of its shares and debentures
4. Prohibition of any invitation to the public to deposit money with the company

Both public and private limited companies may have a minimum membership of two. Private limited companies may commence business upon receiving its Certificate of Incorporation. However, public limited companies must, in addition, obtain the Certificate of Trading prior to commencement of business. The conduct of a limited company is governed by its Memorandum and Articles of Association. The Memorandum, among other things, provides the following information:

1. Name of the company
2. Address of registered office
3. Objectives of the company and
4. Amount of share capital and its division into shares of a fixed amount

The Articles of Association provides the following information:

1. Provision as to the operation of bank accounts
2. Powers of directors and extent of directors' borrowing powers
3. How the company's seal is to be affixed
4. Regulations governing the internal working and management of the company

Banks would normally require the following information, to open a current account for a limited company:

1. Name and address of the company
2. Photocopy of Certificate of Incorporation
3. Photocopy of Certificate of Trading (for public limited companies only)
4. Memorandum and Articles of Association duly certified by the company secretary and chairman
5. Form 24-Return of Allotment of Shares
6. Form 49-Particulars of Directors
7. Resolution of company's Board of Directors appointing the said bank and branch as bankers to the company

   (a) The appointment of various officers of the company to operate the account will normally be in the standard form of the respective banks. It will contain the names, designations, identity card particulars, and specimen signatures of the authorized signatories as well as the method of operation.
   (b) The copy of the resolution should be duly certified by the chairman and secretary of the company.

8. Specimen of the company rubber stamp
9. Correspondence address
10. Contact details (telephone/fax/mobile/e-mail ID. etc.) and
11. Name and signature of introducer

Banks normally require the original copies of the relevant certificates for verification. Where necessary, they would conduct a search with the Registrar of Companies to confirm genuineness and existence of the company.

1.8.8 Executor's and Administrators' Accounts

Upon the death of a customer, banks may open an Executor's Account or an Administrator's Account and discontinue or freeze the deceased customer's account based on the situation as explained below:

1. In the event a person has died testate (i.e. leaving a will), the court upon receiving an application issues a probate. A probate is a certificate under the court's seal accompanied by the will of the deceased, authorizing the executor(s) appointed under the will to administer the testator's estate. An executor's account may be opened immediately after the death of a customer-testator. However, banks would usually require the probate.
2. In the event a person dies interstate, that is, without leaving a will, the court upon receiving an application will appoints an administrator(s). Normally, the court will appoint member(s) of the family or next of kin of the deceased. The court will issue a Letter of Administration authorizing the person(s) appointed to administer the deceased customer's estate. Banks would open an Administrator's Account only upon receipt of the Letter of Administration.

Administrators and executors possess similar general powers. They are also considered as trustees. As various legal complications could arise from the operations of these accounts, banks are cautious and ensure compliance with the relevant provisions of the Probate and Administration Act 1959 and the Trustees Act 1949. Banks would generally require the following for opening an Executor's Account or Administrator's Account:

1. Photocopy of Probate or Letter of Administration.
2. Name of executor(s) or administrator(s) and address.
3. Identity card particulars of administrator(s) or executor(s).
4. Mandate (if applicable) and method of operation of account if there is more than one administrator or executor.
5. Specimen signature(s) of authorized signatories and rubber stamp.
6. Correspondence address.
7. Contact details (telephone/fax/mobile/e-mail ID, etc.).
8. Name and signature of introducer.
9. The original copy of the Probate or Letter of Administration would be generally required by the banks for verification. Banks normally endorse the original copy before returning it to the executors or administrators.

1.8.9 Trustee Account

Executors and administrators as mentioned earlier are in some ways trustees. Trustee may be appointed through a will or by a deed. However, sometimes there may not be a formal document. Where there is a Trust Deed, the powers of the trustees are normally clearly defined. Banks are very cautious in handing Trust Accounts as they could be implicated in the breach of trust by a trustee and be liable for abetment of that breach. Generally, banks require all trustees to jointly sign cheques drawn on the trust account. Banks normally require the following, among other things, for the opening of a trust current/saving/investment account:

1. Names of trust.
2. Trust Deed.
3. Names and addresses of trustees.
4. Identity card/passport particulars of trustees.
5. Specimen signature of all trustees.
6. Correspondence address.
7. Contact details (telephone/fax/mobile/email ID, etc.).
8. Name and signature of introducer.
9. The banks would sight the original Trust Deed for verification and retain a photocopy for their records and guidance.

1.8.10 Societies Clubs and Association Accounts

Under the Societies Act 1966, societies, clubs, and associations are required to be registered with the Registrar of Societies and must have their own set of rules. The rules must be approved by the Registrar of Societies. The conduct of the financial matters of societies, clubs, and associations is governed by these rules. Usually, the management committee of the societies, clubs, or associations decides on the opening and method of operation of accounts in concurrence with their rules. Banks would normally require the following, inter alia, for opening a current/savings/investment account for societies, clubs, and associations:

1. Name and address of society, club, or association
2. Photocopy of Certificate of Registration
3. Duly certified copy of the rules of the society, club, or association
4. Resolution passed by the management committee with regard to:

    (a) The opening of a current account with the said bank
    (b) Method of operation of the account

5. The following are to be furnished in the resolution:

    (a) Names, designation, and particulars of the authorized signatures
    (b) Specimen signature(s) of authorized signatories
    (c) Rubber stamp of the society, club, or association

6. Letter of undertaking to furnish the bank with certified copies of resolutions passed subsequently bringing about changes in the method of operation and authorized signatories
7. Photocopies of identity cards of all authorized signatories
8. Authority letter for clubs/societies
9. Rules and regulations of clubs/associations including by-laws
10. Correspondence address
11. Contact details (telephone/fax/mobile/e-mail ID, etc.)
12. Name and signature of introducer

1.8.11 Religious Bodies Accounts

Various religious bodies may operate savings/current/investment accounts with the Islamic bank. Religious bodies are not required to be registered with the Registrar of Societies. However, some religious bodies are registered as societies, while others are incorporated by Act of Parliament. Most established religious bodies have their own rules, regulations, and constitution. Generally, banks would require the Certificate of Registration (if applicable) and other details as in the case of societies.

1.8.12 Co-operative Societies

A co-operative society is defined under the Co-operative Society Ordinance as 'a society which has as its objective, the promotion of the economic interest of its members in accordance with co-operative principles'. All co-operative societies are required to be registered with the Registrar of Co-operative Societies. The operation of Co-operative Societies is governed by the Co-operative Societies Ordinance 1948. In order to open a current account for a co-operative society, banks would, among other things, generally require:

1. Photocopy of Certificate of Registration.
2. Certified copies of the by-laws of the co-operative society.
3. Co-operative society's application to open a current account with the said bank incorporating method of operation, duly certified by the Registrar of Co-operative Societies.
4. Copy of the resolution of the management committee of the co-operative society with respect to the opening of account with the said bank and the method of operation.
5. Specimen signature(s) of authorized signatories and rubber stamp.
6. Correspondence addresses.
7. Contact details (telephone/fax/mobile/e-mail ID, etc.).
8. Name and signature of introducer.
9. Banks do not permit cash line facility (overdraft) in accounts of co-operative societies unless such overdraft is authorized by the Registrar of Co-operative Societies.

1.8.13 Government Accounts

Bank Negara Malaysia, the Central Bank, is the government's bank. However, some local and state government bodies maintain current accounts with various commercial banks. To open such an account, banks would normally require a Letter of Introduction from the relevant financial authorities, for example, the Treasury or the State Financial Officer or the Municipal Treasurer. The Letter of Introduction should indicate the following:

1. Name and address of the government body
2. Names, designation, and identity card particulars of authorized signatories
3. Method of operation of account
4. Correspondence address
5. Contact details (telephone/fax/mobile/e-mail ID, etc.)
6. Specimen signature of authorized signatories and rubber stamp
7. Government accounts with commercial banks are normally conducted in credit

1.8.14 School Accounts

Applications to open a School Account should be approved by the Board of Governors and duly certified by the State Education Office. To open an account for a school, banks would generally require the following:

1. Application duly approved by the Board of Governors of the school and certified by the State Education Office
2. Request letter to open account issued by the State Education Department (exclusively for government schools)
3. Form 24-Return of Allotment of Shares
4. Form 49-Particulars of Directors
5. Memorandum and Articles of Association
6. Name and address of the school
7. Names, designation, and identity card particulars of authorized signatories
8. Method of operation of account
9. Correspondence address
10. Contact details (telephone/fax/mobile/e-mail ID, etc.)
11. Specimen signature of authorized signatories and the school rubber stamp

Government schools normally operate their current accounts on a credit balance. Private schools may have registered as a business enterprise and as such are to be treated as firm or company accounts as the case may be.

Table 5.10 Types of accounts offered by Islamic banks

Entity type	Islamic current account	Islamic Saving Account	Islamic investment account
Minor trust		✓	✓
Minor account		✓	
Individual (resident/foreigner)	✓	✓	✓
Joint accounts	✓	✓	✓
Partnership accounts	✓		✓
Professional accounts	✓		✓
Clubs, associations, societies	✓	✓	✓
Company accounts	✓		✓
Executors and administrators accounts	✓	✓ (individual A/c only)	✓
Trustees	✓	✓ (individual A/c only)	✓
Government departments	✓		✓
Professional accounts	✓		✓
Co-operative society	✓		✓
School accounts	✓		✓
Religious bodies accounts	✓	✓	✓

Sources: www.rhbislamicbank.com.my, www.muamalat.com.my, www.bankislam.com.my, www.bankinginfo.com.my

1.8.15 Eligible Account Holders

Table 5.10 summarizes the types of accounts offered by various Islamic banks and the entities eligible:

1.9 Deposit Products Summary

Deposits are the main source of funding, which is used to derive income. Deposits are the cheapest mode of funding compared to other financial components. The sources of funds of Islamic financial institutions as well as the types of financing proposed by Islamic financial institutions have evolved over time. The main sources of funds are classified broadly into current accounts, Saving Accounts, and investment accounts. Table 5.11 provides a summary of the various types of accounts:

The advantage to the investors are that investment/deposits with the banks are considered as low-risk investments and give secured returns for

Table 5.11 Types of deposit accounts

Source of funds	Purpose of investment/deposits	Use of funds by the bank
Wadiah current account	Safety and ready availability, transaction convenience	Short-term financing/investment
Mudharabah current account	Safety and ready availability, transaction convenience, sharing of profit based on pre-defined ratio	Short-term financing/investment
Wadiah Saving Account	Safety, easy availability; temporary holding and Hibah at the discretion of bank	Short- and medium-term financing/investment
Mudharabah—general investment account	Safety; investment for short-, medium-, and long-term; sharing of profit based on pre-defined ratio	Long- and medium-term financing/investment.
Mudharabah—special investment account	Safety; investment for short-, medium-, and long-term; sharing of profit based on pre-defined ratio	Long- and medium-term financing/investment with in the restriction imposed by investor

investors compared to other investments like unit trusts and stock market. Using the banks' management expertise, investors have indirect access to high-level investments with adequate risk management practiced by the Islamic banks.

References

http://www.takaful-malaysia.com/page.php?file=./Internet/mudh/index.htm
http://www.islamic-banking.com/shariah/sr_mudarabah.php
http://www.basis.wisc.edu/live/rfc/cs_06b.pdf
http://www.ruf.rice.edu/~elgamal/files/mutualize.pdf
http://imf.org/external/pubs/ft/mfs/manual/pdf/mmfsap2.pdf
http://www.iiff.com/index.cfm?page=news_details&category=1&id=163&menuid=2
http://www.southernbank.com.my/content/publish_frameset/en/main_pfs_ib_20040924174849.html
http://www.maybank2u.com.my/business/other_services/islamic_banking/maybank/mudharabah_rates.shtml
http://www.rhbislamicbank.com.my/rates_savings.html
http://www.hlib.com.my/

http://www.commerce-tijari.com.my/
http://www.muamalat.com.my/index.php?pg=consumer_deposits&ac=1
http://www.pbebank.com/en/en_content/personal/islamic/content.html
http://www.ambg.com.my/personal/rates/savingsacct.asp#SAV_Savings
http://www.affinbank.com.my/rates/ratesib.htm
http://www.bnm.gov.my/index.php?ch=116&pg=350&ac=1
/www.bankinginfo.com.my/
www.eoncap-islamicbank.com.my
http://www.malaysianislamicfinance.com/monthly/mifsupplement/article5.html

Abod, S. G. S., Agil, S. O. S., & Ghazali, A. H. (2005). *An introduction to Islamic economics & finance*. Kuala Lumpur: CERT Publications Sdn Bhd.

Agil, S. O. S., & Ghazali, A. H. (2005). *Readings in the concept and methodology of Islamic economics*. Kuala Lumpur: CERT Publications Sdn Bhd.

Bank Negara Malaysia. *Money and banking in Malaysia*. Silver anniversary edition 1959–1984.

Euromoney Books and AAOIFI. *Islamic finance innovation & growth*.

Haron, S., & Shanmugam, B. (2001). *Islamic banking system—Concept & applications*. Selangor, Malaysia: Pelanduk Publications.

Indian Institute of Banking & Finance. (2004). *Banking products & services*. New Delhi: Taxmann Publications Pvt Ltd.

Iqbal, Munawar, & Molyneux, Philip. *Thirty years of Islamic banking: History, performance and prospects*.

Pang, Johnson, & Savarimuthu, Nathaniel G. (1985). *Banking in Malaysia*. Heinemann Malaysia Sdn Bhd.

Shanmugam, Bala, Perumal, Vignesen, & Ridzwa, Alfieya Hanuum. *Islamic banking: An international perspective*.

Usmani, M. I. A. (2002a). *Meezanbank's guide to Islamic banking*. Karachi, Pakistan: Darul-Ishaat, Urdu Bazar.

Usmani, M. T. (2002b). *An introduction to Islamic finance*. Karachi: Maktaba Ma'ariful Quran.

6

Islamic Financing in Practice

1 Introduction

Islamic finance is developing at a remarkable pace. Since its inception three decades ago, the number of Islamic Financial Institutions (IFIs) worldwide has risen from 1 in 1975 to over 300 today in more than 75 countries. They are concentrated in the Middle East and Southeast Asia (with Bahrain and Malaysia the biggest hubs), but are also appearing in Europe and the USA. The volume of Islamic finance has now reached approximately $2.6 trillion and is witnessing an annual growth of about 10–15%. The products offered by these IFIs range from consumer credit to long-term finance for big investment projects using Islamic modes of financing such as Murabahah, Ijarah, salam, Musharakah, and Mudharabah.

In this chapter, we will discuss the various types of products offered in general by the IFIs.

1.1 Islamic Financing Concept

Islamic finance is in many aspects akin to socially conscious investing. It involves what may be called substantive principles that speak to the substance of the investment—in other words, the purpose for which the money will be utilized. In practice, substantive principles are applied to the target company's line of business and the specific activities that the money will advance. Industries such as gambling, pornography, alcohol, and tobacco are typically prohibited because they involve activities that Islamic law prohibits. Perhaps the most conspicuous feature of Islamic finance is that the mechanism of financing must also comply with what may be termed as procedural principles.

1.2 Key Features of Islamic Financing

Islamic financing involves the channeling of resources from wealth holders to deficit producing or consuming units. As such, financing enables deficit units to command a larger quantity of resources than they can command by internal means. According to prominent Muslim scholars, the need for financing arises because of the natural differences in resource endowments. For instance, in the case of Mudharabah, the necessity of matching financial resources with business skills may be the most important reason behind the need for financing. The first point derived from the above fact is that exchange or trade is indispensable for all societies. The financing is not only as a means of cooperation necessitated by the absence of compatibility in endowment distribution but also as a source of income, that is, an occupation of its own and is acceptable in Islam. The income-earning motive underlying financing is the most emphasized.

The second motive for financing is the human desire to make one's wealth grow. Ibn Qudamah argues that unlike certain forms of wealth such as plants, trees, and livestock which have a natural process of growth or certain assets whose value increases due to an increase in demand or to changes in other market conditions, money can only grow by means of exchange and turnover (Al Mughni, V. 5, p. 135). On the basis of this desire of growth, Ibn Qudamah validates a sort of financing in which an owner supplies a real productive asset instead of cash. He argues that although this kind of relationship is definitely not Mudharabah, it is very similar to Musharakah in which productive assets (capital goods) are furnished to the working party on the basis of gross output sharing.

Apparently, these two motives of financing along with the motive of matching resources with business skills portray productive financing, that is, the use of financing in the process of producing marketable goods and services. This process is always associated with the expectation of profits or returns which will be distributed between the financier and the entrepreneur according to an agreed formula. In addition, the social objective behind Islamic financing is to relieve and assist a person who is under pressure and is facing adversity.

Hence, Islamic financial products and services can be viewed as an element of the broad process of financial innovation and diversification of the financial landscape. IFIs are continuing to evolve in response to market demand and regulatory developments. Islamic banks are today offering a mature set of alternatives to conventional trade, asset, project, leasing, and many other financing needs.

1.3 Al Bai Bithaman Ajil

Bai Bithaman Ajil means sale of goods with deferred payments, that is, bai (sale), bithaman (price), Ajil (deferment). BBA is a sale with 'deferred payment' and is not a spot sale. It is a mode of Islamic financing used for property, vehicle, as well as financing of other consumer goods. Technically, this financing facility is based on the activities of buying and selling. The asset that the customer wishes to purchase, for example, is bought by the bank and sold to the customer at an agreed price after the bank and customer determine the tenure and the manner of the instalments. The price at which the bank sells the asset (house) to the customer will include the actual cost of the asset (house) and will also incorporate the bank's profit margin. The profit earned by the bank is legitimate from Syariah point of view since the transaction is based on a sale contract rather than a loan contract. The monthly instalments are determined by the selling price, repayment period, and the percentage margin of financing. One unique feature of the BBA facility is the selling price itself, which is fixed throughout the duration of the tenure. Any change in price will make the contract null and void. The bank must make sure that the selling price remains unchanged until the contract expires.

Practice in conventional banks is opposite of Islamic banks. The selling price of a BBA facility is similar to the nominal value of a loan plus the total interest payment. But interest rates vary from time to time, as dictated by market forces. Any variation in the profit portion of the selling price will cause the selling price to change as well. Interest rates on loans are adjustable to reflect changes in the cost of fund. But the same does not apply to BBA. The imputed profit rate must stay fixed even though cost of funds has changed. Therefore, when Islamic banks see higher interest rates on loans, there is nothing they can do to upgrade the BBA profit rate, as this will alter the existing BBA price. Conventional banks can revise interest rates upward, and customers may have to pay more monthly. This is not possible in Islamic banking because by taking a similar move, it will increase the contractual selling price, thus violating the BBA contract as the principle of aqad requires only one price in one sale.

Thus, BBA is a credit sale of goods by which ownership of the goods is transferred by the bank to the client, but the payment of sale price by the client is deferred for a fixed period.

1.3.1 Essential Elements of BBA Contract

The essential elements of a BBA contract with the necessary conditions for a valid contract are listed in Table 6.1:

1.3.2 Contracts in BBA

A BBA legal documentation must reflect the true nature of the sale (bai) contract. The terms and conditions of bai such as the purchase and selling prices, the rights and duties of a seller and buyer, consideration, and so on must be included. Any uncertainties and ambiguities about the principles of a sale contract can be tantamount to a contract being rendered null and void. Hence, the legal documentation in BBA plays a major role.

BBA financing documentation shall be prepared and executed prior to the disbursement of the financing amount and should reflect the buy and sell transactions. It must protect the bank's interest at all times under both Syariah and civil laws. For instance, when Munif purchased the

Table 6.1 Essential elements of BBA contract

Tenet	Mandatory characteristic/ conditions	Prohibited characteristic/ conditions
Buyer/seller	1. Must possess sound mind (aqil) 2. Must be at least 18 years old (attains the age of puberty—(baligh) 3. Must be intelligent	1. Forced to enter into a contract 2. He must not be prohibited from dealing: – not bankrupt – not prodigal
Asset/merchandise	1. Exist at the time of transaction 2. Bank must be the owner of the merchandise 3. Must be of pure substance (lawful) 4. Must be of some use or some value 5. Must be able to be delivered by seller to the buyer 6. Known to both the seller and buyer (i.e. full details of the goods is known to both parties)	
Price	1. Must be known to both the seller and the buyer 2. Must be with the quantum and type of the currency specified	
Contract (Aqad)—Offer and acceptance	1. Absolute and in definite and decisive language. – In the past or present tense. – Not in the future or imperative tense. – Not conditional – Not limited to a certain period. 2. The acceptance must agree with the offer. 3. The offer and acceptance must be made at the one and same meeting or session.	

house from XYZ Developer and the Sale and Purchase Agreement (SPA) between the two parties has been executed, the SPA requires Munif to pay 10% of the total selling price to XYZ Developer. Even though the bank has yet to be a party to the agreement, the SPA confers a beneficial right over the property to Munif which justifies him to sell the same to a bank. Syariah scholars have ruled that after paying 10% as down payment to the developer, Munif is in fact the beneficial owner. This opinion has been accepted by the Association of Islamic Banks Malaysia (AIBIM) and pursuant to that, Novation Agreement has been discontinued. Instead, Property Purchase Agreement (PPA) is now in place. A valid BBA sale consists of three contracts as explained below.

1. **Property Purchase Agreement (PPA)**

    PPA is the agreement between the customer and the bank wherein the bank purchases the property from the customer and immediately sells the same property to the customer on deferred terms under the Syariah principles of BBA. PPA provides that 'the customer is the beneficial owner of the property pursuant to the Sale and Purchase Agreement'. PPA further provides that 'In pursuance thereof the Bank agrees to sell and the customer agrees to purchase the property and subject to the terms and conditions herein contained'. So, at this juncture, there is a clear indication that the property which is purchased by the bank is intended to be resold to the customer immediately. PPA has passed greater responsibilities, thereby transferring responsibility and liability onto the customer as follows:

    (a) For securing the payment of sale price, the customer shall execute a registerable charge in favor of the bank;
    (b) The customer shall take Takaful Mortgage Plan as well as Takaful Fire Plan for the amount accepted by the bank;
    (c) The customer shall indemnify the bank against all loses that may be brought at any time by the vendor/proprietor or any party or parties;
    (d) The customer shall pay all quit rents, rates, taxes, assessments, and other charges imposed or to be imposed by the government or other competent authorities and other charges or levies in respect

of the property whether before or after the date of the execution of the agreement; and

(e) All stamp duties, taxes, fares, fees, expenses, and other charges in connection with PPA as well as litigation cost and solicitor costs, and so on shall be borne entirely by the customer.

2. **Property Sale Agreements (PSA)**

This agreement reflects the act of reselling the same to the customer upon deferred payment which includes the bank's profit margin. The agreement also states: 'Beneficial ownership of land rights of the property shall pass to the customer upon the execution of this agreement'" In addition, under PSA the bank adds more responsibilities on the customer to the extent that the bank is free from all risks whatsoever. This is to ensure that the bank is fully covered and in a much more secures position.

3. **Charge Document (Form 16A and Annexure) or Deed of Assignment**

This is an agreement made between the bank and the customer whereby the latter agrees to assign all his rights and interest over the property to the former as security for the financing granted. Charge Document will be used when the IDT (Issue Document of Title) has been issued, while Deed of Assignment is used when the IDT is yet to be issued. The issue at hand is khiyar al-ayb or option of defect. It is about the option given to the customer to cancel or annul the BBA contract when a defect on the goods sold is evident. To ensure that the contract remains valid, the bank is expected to deal directly with the developer to ensure that the defects are removed and the ensuring damages rectified. It will be a violation of Syariah law when the bank forcefully imposes a condition that can alter the right of option of defect in its favor.

1.3.3 Modus Operandi of House Financing

BBA is a type of sales contract, to make provisions for an immediate delivery of goods while postponing the payment of the price to a later date.

Step 1: The client approaches the housing developer and identifies the house he wishes to buy. He signs a Sale and Purchase Agreement with the housing developer.

Step 2: The bank determines the requirements of the customer in relation to the financing period and nature of repayment. The bank then purchases the house at a purchase price of, say, RM40,000, and signs Property Purchase Agreement with the customer. The bank pays the RM40,000 to the housing developer or the bank pays the money to the customer and then the customer pays to the developer.

Step 3: The bank subsequently sells the relevant asset/property to the customer and signs a Property Sale Agreement at an agreed price, which consists of the actual cost of the asset to the bank, that is, financing amount and the bank's profit margin (the selling price comes to RM60,000 after including the profit margin).

Step 4: The customer is to settle the payment of RM60,000 by equal or staggered instalment payments throughout the financing period (Fig. 6.1).

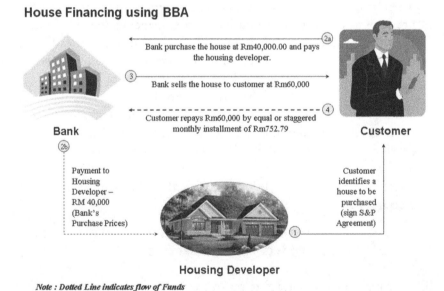

Fig. 6.1 House Financing using BBA

Step 1: The customer owns the asset and he needs funds for renovation.

The bank determines the requirements of the customer in relation to the financing period and nature of repayment. The bank then purchases the house at a purchase price, say RM50,000, and signs a Property Purchase Agreement with the customer.

Step 2: The bank subsequently sells the relevant asset/property to the customer and signs a Property Sale Agreement at an agreed price, which consists of the actual cost of the asset to the bank, that is, financing amount and the bank's profit margin (the selling price becomes RM75,000 after including the profit margin).

Step 3: The bank disburses the RM50,000 to the customer based on the agreed disbursement schedule.

Step 4: The customer is to settle the payment of RM75,000 by equal or staggered installment payments throughout the financing period.

1.3.4   Modus Operandi of Umrah Financing

The modus operandi of umrah financing by using BBA concept is illustrated below.

Step 1: The customer identifies the preferred umrah package from a travel agent and collects all the necessary information.

Step 2: The client approaches the bank for BBA financing and submits the quotation and relevant information to the bank. He also promises to buy the umrah package from the bank upon resale at the marked-up price.

Step 3: The bank makes payment of the base price to the vendor (e.g. purchase price of the travel package is, say, RM5000).

Step 4: The travel agent transfers the ownership of the travel package to the bank.

Step 5: The bank sells the package to the customer at a marked-up price including profit margin of, say, RM6000. The ownership is transferred to the customer by signing a Property Sale Agreement.

Step 6: Client pays the marked-up price RM6000 in full or in parts over future (known) time period(s) (Fig. 6.2).

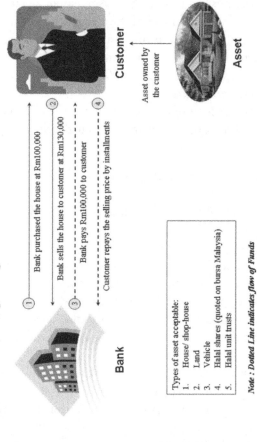

Fig. 6.2 The modus operandi of umrah financing by using BBA

1.3.5 Modus Operandi of Cash Line Facility

The modus operandi of cash line financing by using BBA concept is illustrated in Fig. 6.3.

Step 1: In this scenario, the customer owns the asset. As per above illustration, the customer owns the house.
Step 2: The customer approaches the bank to apply for a cash line facility and submits the relevant documents to assess his credit worthiness.
Step 3: Based upon the customer's credit worthiness, the bank will purchase the house from the customer at a purchase price.
Step 4: The bank pays to the customer in the form of cash limit (overdraft) which will be tagged to the customer's wadiah account.
Step 5: Subsequently, the bank sells the house to the customer at a selling price, which comprises the purchase price and profit.
Step 6: The customer may utilize the cash line according to his requirement and make payment on profit based on the actual amount of utilization of facility. Ibra' (rebate) on profit will be given for unutilized amount of facility.

Normally for cash line facility, there will be no commitment fee charged on the unutilized portion of the line. Settlement of the line will be based on the yearly reducing limit or on a lump sum payment at the end of the financing period. Usually this facility is suitable for financing general administrative cost such as payment of salary. It can also be used for general purposes as long as it is operated within the prescribed limit.

1.3.6 BBA Financing Practice

This is the selling of goods on a deferred payment basis at a price, which includes a profit margin agreed to by the bank and customer. Under conventional banking, Bai' Bithaman Ajil is applicable to a negotiable debt certificate, home or property financing, share or unit trust financing, umrah (Muslim pilgrimage to Mecca), and visitation financing.

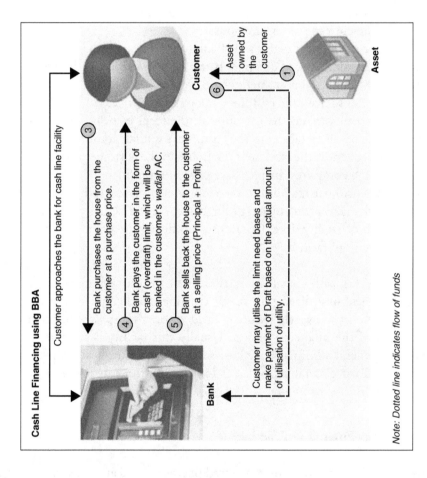

Fig. 6.3 Modus operandi of cash line financing by using BBA concept

The common features of the product offered by banks are illustrated in Table 6.2.

Table 6.2 BBA financing practice

Product feature	Description
Product name	BBA financing
Definition	THE BBA house financing is an Islamic financing facility, which is based on the Syariah concept of Al Bai' Bithaman Ajil (BBA). It is a contract of deferred payment sale, that is, the sale of goods on deferred payment basis at an agreed selling price, which includes a profit margin agreed by both parties. Profit in this context is justified since it is derived from the buying and selling transaction as opposed to interests accruing from the principal lent out

Scope of financing	1. Land/property financing:
	  (a) House/shop-house
	  (b) Land
	  (c) Apartment/condo
	  (d) Factory
	2. Vehicle financing
	3. Consumer financing
	  (a) Computer
	  (b) Umrah package
	  (c) Education package
	3. Refinancing of assets
	  (a) Working capital
	  (b) Renovation and so on

Types of account holders	The following types of Saving Account may be opened: 1. Individual account 2. Joint account 3. Clubs, societies, association 4. Trustee
Legal documents	1. Letter of offer 2. Property sale agreement 3. Property purchase agreement 4. Legal charge or, 5. Assignment and power of attorney 6. Or any other Islamic financing documents that are required for the house financing
Margin of financing	The margin of financing differs from one bank to another. Generally, the margin ranges from 100% against the sales and purchase value or the current market value of the asset. Again, the customer's repayment capacity will also affect the margin of financing that the bank can offer

(continued)

Table 6.2 (continued)

Product feature	Description
Security/collateral requirement	The property financed by the bank will be used as the security/collateral for the financing facility under the BBA house financing. The property is usually secured by way of first party charge
	The purpose of charging the financing assets as collateral is to minimize the credit risk faced by the Islamic bank should the financing customer fail to pay monthly instalments as agreed upon under the contract of sale
Takaful (insurance)	Takaful is the equivalent of the Mortgage Reducing Term Assurance (MRTA), whereby a protection on the financing amount will be given, in case any untoward incidents were to befall the customer. Even though it is not compulsory, most banks are making it a financing condition to encourage the mortgage. Takaful protection is beneficial to the customers and their next of kin. Most banks provide financing assistance for the Takaful premium. Normally, the mortgage Takaful premium will be included in the financing amount and will be subjected to the agreed margin of financing
Security deposit	In view of the fact that no charges may be imposed for late payments, the customer is to place at least 6 to 12 monthly instalments as security deposit with the bank. The security deposit will be invested by the bank in the general investment account (al-Mudharabah) or al-wadiah Saving Account on behalf of the customer. The profit from investment will be returned to the customer, while the principal will keep on renewing based on the financing tenure. In the event of a default in repayments, the security deposit can be utilized by the bank to settle the repayment
Rebate on early redemption	BBA customers who request for full redemption may be entitled to rebate (muqasah) which shall be equivalent to the amount of the unearned income
Benefits of BBA financing to the customer	1. The total cost of the property purchased is determined at the time of contract or aqad 2. There is no additional or 'hidden' cost that will change the price of the property purchased 3. The transaction is transparent 4. There is no element of uncertainties or gharar 5. Customers will know exactly when the financing will end 6. There will be no compounding of arrears and outstanding penalty charges 7. Unlike conventional loan, repayment is not subjected to fluctuation of the base lending rate 8. Allows better financial planning

(continued)

Table 6.2 (continued)

Product feature	Description
Restriction	Bank is prohibited to offer financing for haram (forbidden) activities such as casino, disco, factory operating liquor business, and so on
Bank's purchase price	The 'bank's purchase price' or 'cost of financing' is equivalent to the amount of financing provided by the bank based on the bank's policy for margin of financing. Normally the contribution for Takaful and/or legal fees may be financed by the bank and could be included in the bank's purchase price
Bank selling price	The bank's selling price is equivalent to the amount of financing provided by the bank plus the amount of profit margin, and grace period profit margin, if any. The important feature to note here is that the bank's selling price, which has been entered into a contract, will be maintained throughout the financing tenure. The total selling price represents the maximum ceiling price to be paid by the financing customer to the Islamic bank, that is, on agreed monthly instalments. Any additional amount against the total selling price may lead to the contract of sale between the financing customer and the Islamic bank being declared null and void.
	The calculation of profit and selling price can be done in any manner such as method of constant rate of return (monthly, quarterly, half yearly, or yearly rest). The practice differs from bank to bank.
Grace period of profit	Grace period profit is charged when bank is financing property under construction. As such, during the construction period, customer will pay the grace period profit only. During this grace period, the bank may charge a grace period profit to avoid loss of income pending the completion of the dwelling
Account statement facility	This facility is normally available on request basis.
Penalty	In an interest-based system, the seller would impose penalties (interest) on the buyer in case of a late payment. Such would not be permissible under Islam. However, the scholars agree that the seller may impose penalties for late payment in the form of mandatory charity (e.g. in the event of late payment, the buyer would pay $X per day to a specified charitable organization).
	This must act solely as an incentive for the buyer to settle the account in a timely fashion. The seller must not benefit from the penalties paid by the buyer.

1.3.7 BBA Financing Instalment Computation Using CRR

Most of the banks currently follow the Constant Rate of Return (CRR) and monthly rest for the computation of profit. The computation formula is mentioned in Table 6.3.

Table 6.3 Computation formula

Component	Computation formula	Details
Annuity factor (AF)	$\dfrac{i(1+i)^n}{(1+i)^n - 1}$	i = Periodic profit rate p.a. or CRR rate n = Total number of periodic payments
Periodic repayment	AF × Purchase price	AF = Annuity factor Purchase price = Financing amount
Selling price	PR × n	PR = Periodic repayment n = Total number of periodic payments
Profit amount	Selling price − Purchase price	

Example A (BBA Financing Without Grace Period Profit)

Ali approaches the Islamic bank and applies for financing under the concept of

Bai Bithaman Ajil. Let us say the purchase price for the house is RM700,000 and profit rate is 8%. The period of financing is 20 years and Ali has to repay the selling price in 240 instalments. The computation of selling price and monthly instalment based on the constant rate of return method is as below:

Step 1: Computation of annuity factor

Annuity factor (AF)	$\dfrac{i(1+i)^n}{(1+i)^n - 1}$	$i = 8/(100 \times 12) = 0.006667$ n = 240 instalments
	$0.006667(1+0.006667)^{240}/(1+0.006667)^{240} - 1 = 0.00836423$	

Step 2: Computation of periodic repayment

Periodic repayment	AF × Purchase price	AF = 0.00836423
		Purchase price = RM 700,000
	0.00836423 × 700,000 = 5854.96	

Step 3: Computation of selling price

Selling price	PR × n	PR = 5854.96
		n = 240 instalments
	5854.96 × 240 = 1,405,190	

Step 4: Computation of profit

Profit amount	Selling price−Purchase price
	1,405,190−700,000 = 705,190

Example B (BBA Financing with Grace Period Profit)

Ali approaches the Islamic bank and applies for financing under the concept of Bai Bithaman Ajil. Assume that the purchase price for the house is RM1,000,000 and profit rate is 10%. The period of financing is 17 years and inclusive of 2 years as grace period. The profit rate for the grace period is 5%. Ali wants to repay the selling price in 204 instalments. The computation of selling price and monthly instalment based on the constant rate of return method with grace period profit is as below:

Step 1: Computation of annuity factor

Annuity factor (AF)	$\dfrac{i(1+i)^n}{(1+i)^n - 1}$	$i = 10/(100 \times 12) = 0.008333$
		n = 180 instalments
	0.008333(1+0.008333)^{180}/(1+0.008333)^{180}−1 = 0.01074606	

Step 2: Computation of periodic repayment

Periodic repayment	AF × Purchase price	AF = 0.00836423 Purchase price = RM1,000,000
	0.01074606 × 1,000,000 = 10746.06	

Step 3: Computation of original selling price

Original selling price	PR × n	PR = 10746.06 n = 180 instalments
	10746.06 × 180 = 1,934,291	

Step 4: Computation of grace period profit

Grace period profit	$\dfrac{\text{GPPR} \times \text{PP} \times \text{GP}}{2}$	GPR = Gross period profit rate PP = Purchase price GP = Grace period in years
	$(5 \times 1,000,000 \times 2)/(2 \times 100) = 50,000$	

Step 5: Instalment amount during grace period

Instalment during grace period	$\dfrac{\text{Grace period profit}}{\text{Grace period}}$	GPP = Gross period profit rate Grace period = duration in months = 24
	$50,000/24 = 2083.33$	

Step 6: Selling price inclusive of GPP

Selling price	Original selling price + GPP
	1,934,291+50,000=1,984,291

The customer's instalment schedule is illustrated in Fig. 6.4:

1.3.8 BBA Financing Instalment Computation Using Rule 78

Few banks follow Rule 78. It is also known as a flat rate or a sum of digits for the computation of profit. The computation formula is shown in Table 6.4:

Example

Hisham approaches the Islamic bank and applies for financing under the concept of Bai Bithaman Ajil. Assume that the purchase price for the house is RM1,000,000 and the profit rate is 10%. The period of financing is 10 years. The profit rate for the grace period is 5%. The customer wants to repay the selling price in 120 instalments. The computation of selling price and monthly instalment based on Rule 78 is as below:

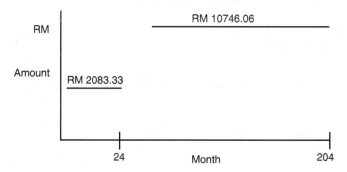

Fig. 6.4 Instalment schedule inclusive of GPP

Table 6.4 BBA financing instalment computation using Rule 78

Component	Computation formula	Details
Selling price (SP)	$CF + (CF \times i \times n)$	CF = Cost of financing (purchase price) i = Rate of return per annum n = Period of financing in years
Monthly repayment	$SP/(n \times 12)$	SP = Selling price n = Total number of periodic payments
Total profit	$SP - CF$	SP = Selling price CF = Cost of financing

Step 1: Computation of selling price

Selling price (SP)	$CF + (CF \times i \times n)$	CF = 1,000,000 i = 10% n = 10
	$= 1,000,000 + (1,000,000 \times 10 \times 10 / 100)$ $= 1,000,000 + (1,000,000)$ $= 2,000,000$	

Step 2: Computation of monthly repayment

Monthly repayment	$SP/(n \times 12)$	SP = 2,000,000 $n = 10 \times 12 = 120$
	$2,000,000/120 = 16666.67$	

Step 3: Total profit earned by bank

Total profit	$SP - CF$	SP = 2,000,000 CF = 1,000,000
	$2,000,000 - 1,000,000 = 1,000,000$	

1.3.9 BBA with Floating Rate

A variable rate financing product under the concept of Bai Bithaman Ajil (deferred payment sale) was introduced in 2003 as an instrument to diversify the financing portfolio of IFIs from over-reliance on fixed-rate financing as well as to mitigate the risk associated with funding mismatch. This fixed-rate regime has resulted in a funding mismatch to the Islamic financial institutions because their long-term financing was funded by short-term bank deposits, which can give variable returns. As the banks had locked in their profit rates for the financing over a long period, any upward movement in the market rates, therefore, may result in the Islamic banking institutions finding it difficult to give a satisfactory return to their depositors. This is because the constant income stream from the financing is tied to a fixed profit rate, which is relatively lower when compared to a conventional floating rate loan whose rate has risen. Inevitably, this situation would cause a switching of Islamic funds to conventional funds.

The variable rate of financing is designed to mitigate the mismatched risk currently faced by the Islamic financial institutions by allowing them to vary the profit rate for the financing in order to raise the deposit rates. As a result, the depositors will obtain satisfactory returns *vis-à-vis* that in the conventional banking market, and hence, would not switch their deposits which otherwise could adversely affect the Islamic banking operation. This new option reduces the vulnerabilities of the Islamic financial institutions to exposure in market risk in a banking environment, where the Islamic banking system and conventional banking system operate side by side.

The variable rate of financing is an innovation to the existing BBA financing concept, which is a fixed rate in nature. Under the BBA, the selling price of the asset sold to the customer on deferred terms would be fixed at a profit rate known as the ceiling profit rate which is higher than the profit rate under the fixed-rate BBA financing where, in principle, the contractual selling price and installments would be higher. However, rebate known as ibra (a waiver of right to claim unearned profit) is required to be granted at every installment, for example, on a monthly basis, in order to reduce the monthly installments to match that of the current market level.

The financing is created upon the bank purchasing the asset from the customer for cash, which will be immediately sold back on deferred terms. Computed at a ceiling rate of 12% per annum as in the example, the selling price (which is higher than under the BBA fixed financing) will be agreed upon and the contractual repayment is to be made in equal monthly installments of RM2000 over the agreed period. If the Base Lending Rate (BLR) plus margin used as a benchmark in the pricing calculation is 10% per annum for the first month, the bank would give a monthly rebate of RM500, which represents the difference between the ceiling profit rate of 12% per annum and the effective profit rate of 10% per annum. If in the fourth month, the market rate rises to 11% per annum, the bank would then only grant a monthly rebate of RM300.

In practice, the rebate would be varied so that the effective profit rate (ceiling profit rate less rebate) reflects the fluctuating market financing rate. Accordingly, the bank would be able to raise the financing rate when there is a rise in market rate. Hence, it can give better returns to its depositors. As such, this justifies the setting of a high ceiling profit rate to buffer any rise in the market rate. However, if the market rate rises beyond 12% per annum, the effective profit rate would remain at the ceiling rate. The ceiling rate would provide some comfort to the customer that the effective profit rate is capped.

To govern this mode of financing, such rates are subject to a ceiling profit rate of 4 percentage points above the market's BLR unless supported by findings that the market rate is forecasted to be volatile and escalating. In setting the effective profit rate, the banks are required to observe the maximum profit spread of 2.5 percentage point above the BLR. However, as a matter of policy, the effective profit rate cannot transgress the ceiling profit rate even if the market rate rises above the latter, while any change to the effective profit rate would have to be communicated to the customer prior to the change.

At maturity, any difference in the amount between the selling price and the total repayments plus the monthly rebates granted, would be rebated. In addition to the rebates on installments and at maturity, which have been made mandatory to be included in the financing agreement, rebates must also be granted in the event of early settlement or redemption, or termination of contract. Bank Negara Malaysia has allowed rescheduling of the financing (where the period of financing can be extended) if the bank wishes to grant the option that the effective monthly installment need not be increased if the effective profit rate rises, on the condition that the financing agreement contains a rescheduling clause and the total repayments are not in excess of the original selling price. The computation of capital adequacy for the BBA variable rate financing will be accorded the same risk weight as under the BBA fixed-rate financing.

Currently, this new mode of financing is applicable to house, property, and term financing only and would be extended to other types of financing in due course. Undoubtedly, this new product is expected to grow significantly as it is a natural hedging product, particularly in view of the risk exposure issues prevalent in Islamic banking today.

1.4   Murabahah

Murabahah refers to a particular kind of sale and has nothing to do with financing in its original sense. If a seller agrees with his purchaser to provide him a specific commodity on a certain profit added to his cost, it is called a Murabahah transaction. The basic ingredient of Murabahah is that the seller discloses the actual cost he has incurred in acquiring the commodity, and then adds some profit thereon. This profit may be in a lump sum or based on a percentage.

According to Tarek al-Diwany, Murabahah is a form of trust sale since the buyer must trust that the seller is disclosing his true costs. After discussing the true costs, a profit margin may be agreed either on a percentage of cost basis or as a fixed amount. It is very important to remember that the amount of profit earned in this transaction is not a reward for the use of the financier's money. In other words, a financier cannot take the money if he does not perform any services other than the use of his money for the transaction. Such an occurrence would cause this type of deal to resemble the charging of interest.

Islamic principles of finance are based on a well-established rule that '"the benefit of a thing is a return of the liability for loss from that thing'. Hence, in a Murabahah transaction, the bank or financier assumes the risk of purchasing the commodity before he sells it at a mark-up. This mark-up is considered as the reward of the risk the financier assumes. In other words, the bank is really engaged in buying and selling that entail certain risks. This lends the profit that the bank derived and the transaction legitimacy. The payment in the case of Murabahah may be at spot and may be on a subsequent date agreed upon by the parties.

Murabahah is often referred to as 'cost-plus financing'. In its simplest form, this contract involves the sale of an item on a deferred basis. The item is delivered immediately, and the price to be paid for the item includes a mutually agreed margin of profit payable to the seller. In this contract, the market cost price (true cost) of the item is shared with the buyer at the time of concluding the sale. The only feature distinguishing it from other kinds of sale is that the seller in Murabahah expressly tells the buyer how much cost he has incurred and how much profit he is going to charge in addition to the cost.

1.4.1 Essential Elements of Murabahah Contract

The essential elements of Murabahah contract with the necessary conditions for a valid contract are similar to the Bai Bithaman Ajil (BBA) explained in the earlier section. The conditions, which are different from the BBA contract, are explained below:

1. Buyer should be aware of the cost price of the goods. Murabahah is a particular kind of sale where the seller expressly mentions the cost of the sold commodity he has incurred, and sells it to another person by adding some profit or mark-up thereon. For example, the bank purchased machinery for RM100,000 and sold it to the customer (buyer) on Murabahah with 10% mark-up. The exact cost is known and the Murabahah sale is valid.
2. Buyer should be aware of the profit margin used for mark-up. The profit in Murabahah can be determined by mutual consent, either in a lump sum or through an agreed ratio of profit to be charged over the cost.
3. All the expenses incurred by the seller in acquiring the commodity like freight, custom duty, and so on shall be included in the cost price and

the mark-up can be applied on the aggregate cost. However, recurring expenses of the business like salaries of the staff, the rent of the premises, and so on cannot be included in the cost of an individual transaction. In fact, the profit claimed over the cost takes care of these expenses.

4. Murabahah is valid only where the exact cost of a commodity can be ascertained. If the exact cost cannot be ascertained, the commodity cannot be sold on a Murabahah basis. In this case, the commodity must be sold on a musawamah (bargaining) basis, that is, without any reference to the cost or to the ratio of profit/mark-up. The price of the commodity in such cases shall be determined in a lump sum by mutual consent. For example, the bank has purchased a notebook and printer in a single transaction for a lump sum price of RM5000. The bank can sell the notebook and printer together under Murabahah. But the bank cannot sell the notebook separately on Murabahah, because the individual cost of the notebook is not known. If the bank wants to sell the notebook separately, then it should be sold at a lump sum price without reference to the cost or the mark-up.

5. Murabahah is a form of sale and Syariah also instructs the ethics of buying and selling beyond informing the formality of transacting. The five options of sale as formalized in classical fiqh are:

   (a) *Buyer's option to rescind*: time-limited seller has similar option, but ceases before execution of contract;
   (b) *Option of inspection*: the right to see and verify the object of the sale;
   (c) *Option of defect*: right to return if defective;
   (d) *Option of quality*: right to specified quality; and
   (e) *Option of price*: right to fair price within market range.

Hence, Murabahah contract is an unconditional contract of sale between the buyer and seller, where the goods, cost price, mark-up, and payment date are clearly defined, agreed, and documented. The important element is price, in a Murabahah contract, and it should be set by mutual consent as Murabahah is all about price deferment.

1.4.2 Modus Operandi of Murabahah Financing

There are three parties involved in Murabahah financing. The seller, the buyer, and the bank act as intermediary traders between the buyer and the seller (Fig. 6.5).

Step 1: The client approaches the housing developer and identifies the house or asset he wishes to buy. He requests the seller to provide a price quotation and other relevant details.
Step 2: The seller provides the price quotation, brochure, terms and condition and other relevant details requested by the customer.
Step 3: The customer approaches the bank for financing and both agree on the financing using Murabahah as an underlying contract. The customer promises to buy the commodity from the bank upon resale at a marked-up price.
Step 4: The bank purchases the commodity from the seller based on the asset details provided by the customer. The bank will purchase it via cash payment at a purchase price.
Step 5a: The seller transfers the ownership of the asset to the bank.

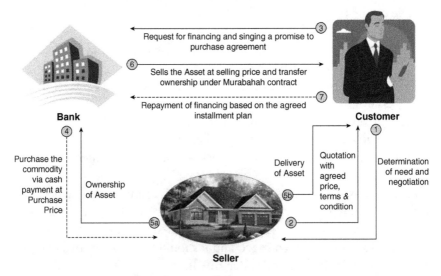

Fig. 6.5 *Modus operandi* of Murabahah financing

Step 5b: The seller delivers the asset to the customer based on the agreed terms and conditions and submits a proof of delivery with the customer's acceptance to the bank.

Step 6: The bank sells the asset to the customer at an agreed selling price, that is, purchase price + marked-up profit.

Step 7: The customer pays the agreed selling price in a lump sum or staggered payments based on the agreed installment plan.

1.4.3 Modus Operandi of Murabahah Financing for Working Capital

The best way for Murabahah, according to Syariah, is that the financier himself purchases the commodity and keeps it in his own possession, or purchases the commodity through a third person appointed by him as the agent before he sells it to the customer. However, in exceptional cases, the bank may appoint the customer as an agent and the payment to supplier is based on the purchase order and other necessary documentations. The transaction structure for financing working capital is illustrated below:

Step 1: The client approaches the housing developer/seller and identifies the house or asset he wishes to buy. He requests the seller to provide a price quotation and other relevant details.

Step 2: Seller provides the price quotation, brochure, terms and conditions, and other relevant details requested by the customer.

Step 3: The customer approaches the bank along with the necessary supportive documents on asset for financing and both agree on financing using Murabahah as an underlying contract. The customer promises to buy the commodity from the bank upon resale at a marked-up price, whereby the cost is known to the customer.

Step 4: The bank appoints the client as its agent and allows him to buy the asset on behalf of the bank directly from the seller and an agreement of agency is signed by both parties (Fig. 6.6).

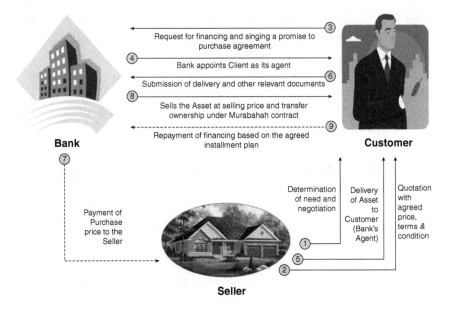

Fig. 6.6 Modus operandi of Murabahah financing for working capital

Step 5: The seller delivers the asset to the customer (bank's agent) based on the agreed terms and conditions. It is advisable that the bank should oversee the process of the customer taking physical possession of the goods.

Step 6: The customer submits the proof of delivery, invoice, and other respective documents to the bank for processing of payment to supplier.

Step 7: The bank does the necessary to make payment of purchase price to the seller/vendor.

Step 8: The bank sells the asset to the customer at an agreed selling price, that is, purchase price + marked-up profit. The ownership as well as the risk of the commodity is transferred to the customer.

Step 9: The customer pays the agreed selling price via a lump sum or staggered payments based on the agreed installment plan under the Murabahah contract.

In the above case, the client first purchases the commodity on behalf of the bank and takes its possession as such. Thereafter, he purchases the commodity from the bank at a deferred price. His possession over the commodity in the first instance is in the capacity of an agent of his financier. In this capacity, he is only a trustee, while the ownership rests with the financier, and the risk of the commodity is also borne by him as a logical consequence of the ownership. But when the client purchases the commodity from his financier, the ownership, as well as the risk, is transferred to the client.

Hence, the buyer is not able to reject the goods and escape contractual payment obligations except in extraordinary circumstances.

The above transaction structure is followed by banks to mitigate the delivery risk. The most frequent means protecting the bank from buyer (customer) rejection is to appoint the buyer as an agent for the bank to order the desired goods. As an agent, the buyer will be responsible for defining the specifications, executing the order and then inspecting the delivery of goods.

1.4.4 Murabahah Financing Practice

Originally, Murabahah is a particular type of sale and not a mode of financing but now it has been accepted by Syariah subject to conditions that all essential elements have been fulfilled in the contract. The common features of the product offered by banks are illustrated in Table 6.5.

1.4.5 Murabahah Financing Computation

The method used for the computation of selling price is a lump sum, whereby the customer has to make full repayment upon maturity. The formula used for computation is in Table 6.6.

Example

Akram approaches the Islamic bank and applies for financing under the concept of Bai Bithaman Ajil. He wants to buy a machine for his factory. He cannot make the cash payment to buy the machine. Let us say

Table 6.5 Murabahah financing practice

Product feature	Description
Product name	Murabahah financing
Definition	Murabahah refers to the sale of goods at a price, which includes profit margin as agreed by both the seller and buyer. Such sales contract is valid on condition that the cost and profit are made known by the seller and agreed by the buyer
Scope of financing	1. Short-term consumer financing 2. Working capital financing 3. Vehicle financing 4. Trade finance products including imports, exports, and alternative to bill purchase
Types of account holders	The following types of Saving Account may be opened: 1. Individual account 2. Joint account 3. Clubs, societies, association 4. Companies 5. Sole proprietorships
Legal documents	1. Master Murabahah financing agreement 2. Agency agreement 3. Order form/draw down notice 4. Declaration 5. Purchase evidences 6. Demand promissory note 7. Payment schedule
Selling price	Purchase price (cost of funds) + profit margin (as agreed between both parties)
Payment structure	1. On spot 2. In installments 3. In lump sum after a certain time
Financing tenor	Tenor ranges from 1 month to 6 months as the financing is for short-term only
Charges	Expenses incurred such as Takaful Insurance, legal fees, and other incidental cost are normally borne by client and are included in the selling price
Rebate on early redemption	This is normally prohibited by Syariah Board since it can make the Murabahah transaction similar to conventional debt
Penalty on late payments	In Malaysia, the Central Bank Negara has agreed that the bank can charge 1% from the total outstanding amount or the actual loss as the compensation for default of payment and it shall only be charged once and should not be compounding

Islamic Financing in Practice

Table 6.6 Murabahah Financing Computation

Component	Computation formula	Details
Selling price (SP)	CF + (CF × I × n/360)	CF = Cost of financing (purchase price)
		i = Rate of return per annum
		n = Period of financing in days
		360 is total number of days in a year and some banks follow 365 days
Total profit	SP – CF	SP = Selling price
		CF = Cost of financing

that the purchase price for the machine is RM50,000 and the profit rate the bank wants to charge is 10%. The period of financing is 6 months. Akram is willing to make a lump sum payment upon expiry of 6 months. The computation of the selling price is as below:

Step 1: Computation of selling price

Selling price (SP)	CF + (CF × I × n/365)	CF = 50,000
		i = 10%
		n = 180

$$= 50{,}000 + (50{,}000 \times 0.10 \times 180 / 360)$$
$$= 50{,}000 + (2{,}500)$$
$$= 52{,}500$$

Step 2: Total profit earned by bank

Total profit (RM)	SP – CF	SP = 52,500
		CF = 50,000
	52,500 – 50,000 = 2500	

1.4.6 Challenges in Murabahah Financing

Special care is required when implementing the Murabahah and the underlying Islamic principles. Usmani (2002) has highlighted some challenges in his book, *Meezan Bank's Guide to Islamic Banking*. This should help in conceptualizing the practical aspects of the transaction structure and designing product features and functions.

1. *Interest as Benchmark Rate*: Many institutions determined that the profit rate for Murabahah computation is based on LIBOR (Inter-Bank Offered Rate in London). For example, if LIBOR is 10% per cent, they determine their mark-up on Murabahah equal to LIBOR or some percentage above LIBOR. This practice is often criticized on the grounds that profit based on a rate of interest should be as prohibited as interest itself.
2. *Security*: Under Murabahah financing, the selling price is payable at a later date. For the bank to ensure that the price will be paid on the due date, normally, the customer has to furnish a security for risk mitigation. The security may be in the form of a mortgage, a hypothecation, or some kind of lien or charge. In such an event, the basic rules for security must be followed by the bank are as follows:

    (a) The first is that the security can be claimed rightfully where the transaction has created a liability or a debt. No security can be asked from a person who has not incurred a liability or debt. As highlighted earlier, there are different stages involved in Murabahah financing and, rightfully, the bank should ask for a security, once the asset is sold to the customer. This is the stage where the client incurs a debt and is more appropriate for the bank to request that the customer furnishes a security. The bank may request the customer to produce security at the earlier stages, but only after the Murabahah price is determined. In this case, if the security is possessed by the bank, it will remain at its risk, meaning any damage caused due to negligence or misconduct, the bank will have to bear the market price of the mortgaged asset, and cancel the agreement of Murabahah, or sell the commodity required by the client

and deduct the market price of the mortgaged asset from the price of the sold property.
(b) The second rule pertaining to securities is that it is permissible that the sold commodity itself is given to the seller as a security.

3. *Guarantee*: Under the Murabahah financing, the bank may ask the purchaser to furnish a guarantee from a third party. In the event of a default, the bank can recover the money from the guarantor. The bank has to be cautious of the following:

   (a) Under conventional banking, the guarantor will not guarantee a payment until a fee is paid by the original debtor. The classical fiqh literature is almost unanimous on the point that the guarantee is a voluntary transaction and no fee can be charged on a guarantee. However, it is permissible for the guarantor to recover his actual secretarial expenses incurred in offering a guarantee, but the key point here is that the guarantee should be free of charge. The explanation here is that the guarantor is not advancing anymore and any fee charged for advancing a loan falls under the definition of riba.
   (b) However, some contemporary scholars are considering the problem from a different angle. They feel that guarantee has become a necessity, especially in international trade where the sellers and the buyers do not know each other, and the payment of the price by the purchaser cannot be simultaneous with the supply of the goods. There has to be an intermediary who can guarantee the payment. It is difficult to find the guarantors who can provide this service free of charge in required numbers. Keeping these realities in view, some Syariah scholars of our time are adopting a different approach. They say the prohibition of guarantee fee is not based on any specific injunction of the Quran or the Sunnah of the Holy Prophet. It has been deducted from the prohibition of riba as one of its ancillary consequences. Moreover, guarantees in the past were of a simple nature. In today's commercial activities, the guarantor sometimes needs a number of studies and a lot of secretarial work. Therefore, they opine, the prohibition of the guarantee

fee should be reviewed in this perspective. The question still needs further research and should be placed before a larger forum of scholars. However, unless a definite ruling is given by such a forum, no guarantee fee should be charged or paid by an Islamic financial institution. Instead they can charge or pay a fee to cover expenses incurred in the process of issuing a guarantee.

4. *Rebate on Early Repayment*: This is normally prohibited by the Syariah Board since it can make the Murabahah transaction similar to conventional debt. However, if the rebate is not taken to be a condition for earlier payment, and the bank gives a rebate voluntarily on its own, it is permissible. Hence, in a Murabahah transaction no rebate can be stipulated in the agreement and nor can the client claim it as his right. However, if the bank or a financial institution gives customer a rebate on its own, it is not objectionable, especially where he is a needy person.
5. *Roll over in Murabahah*: Murabahah is the sale of a commodity with a deferred price to predefined future date. Once the commodity is sold, its ownership is passed onto the client. It is no more the property of the seller. Hence, roll over in Murabahah is not possible since each Murabahah transaction is for the purchase of a particular asset. The roll over in Murabahah is nothing but an agreement to charge an additional amount on the debt created by the Murabahah sale. However, a new Murabahah can only be executed for the purchase of new assets. It is advisable that there must be a gap of 1–2 days between maturity of the previous Murabahah and disbursement of the new one.
6. *Penalty on Late Payments*: Upon signing of a Murabahah agreement between the bank and the customer, selling price becomes a receivable (dayn) for the bank. According to the rules of Islamic fiqh, any amount charged over and above the dayn amount will be considered as riba. Hence, the bank cannot impose any late payment charges. The bank may, however, ask the customer to pay a forced charity in case of overdue so as to create a disincentive for him to delay the payment. In Malaysia, Bank Negara has agreed that the bank can charge 1% from the total outstanding amount or the actual loss as compensation for default of payment and it shall only be charged once and should not be compounded.

7. *Rescheduling of Payments*: In the event the customer is unable to meet the agreed payment dates in the Murabahah contract, then the bank can reschedule the instalments. The important point to note here is upon rescheduling of the instalments, no additional amount can be charged for rescheduling. The amount of the Murabahah price will remain the same in the same currency.

1.4.7 Comparison Between BBA and Murabahah Practice in Malaysia

Murabahah and Bai Bithaman Ajil (BBA) financing are modes of Islamic financing offered by both Islamic banks and conventional banks in Malaysia. Syed Musa Syed Jaafar Alhabshi from Universiti Tun Abdul Razak, Malaysia, conducted a survey to explore the nature and types of financing activities in relation to Murabahah and BBA contracts and reporting of such activities in the financial statements of IFIs. Specifically, it identified the recognition, measurement, presentation, and disclosure practices of IFIs on Murabahah and BBA financing activities. The findings from the survey are reflected in Table 6.7.

Distinguishing characteristics between Murabahah- and bai bithaman ajil-reported practices are that Murabahah refers to a lump sum repayment and is meant for short-term financing, while BBA is an instalment payment for long-term financing. Both contracts disclose the cost of financing which is a requirement for Murabahah.

1.5   Ijarah

The Islamic alternative to conventional leasing is Ijarah. Ijarah is an Arabic term with origins in Islamic fiqh, meaning to give something on a rental basis or wages. Under Islamic jurisprudence, the term Ijarah is used for two different situations as explained in the following chart.

1. *Ijarah 'Amal*: It means to employ the services of a person and wages are paid as a consideration for the services rendered (Maulana Taqi Usmani). The employer is called mustajir while the employee is called ajir, and

Table 6.7 Comparison between BBA and Murabahah practice in Malaysia

Financing contracts			
Features	Murabahah	Bai Bithaman Ajil	Comments
Types and purpose	Acquisition and refinancing working capital and trade.	Acquisition and refinancing property	More acquisition financing is applied for both. Product financing type varies with financing contract
Disclosure of cost of financing	Cost disclosure	Cost disclosure	No distinction
Existence of goods at POS	Most goods exist	Most goods exist except for property financing	Goods exist for both
Repayment mode	Lump sum	Deferred instalment	Different mode of payment typifies the contract
Average period of financing	Short-term	Long-term	Murabahah is short while BBA is long term
Asset recognition	Full or part disbursement basis	Full or part disbursement basis	Similar basis preferred and applied
Asset measurement	Mark-up value	Market value	Need to clarify further on nature of market value
Payment amount	Include both principal and income portion	Include both principal and income portion	Similar basis preferred and applied
Deferral profit	Majority recognize in the balance sheet, while others disclose in notes	Majority recognize in the balance sheet, while others disclose in notes	Similar basis preferred and applied
Segmental information	Disclosure by product type, industry, and general pool fund	Disclosure by product type, industry, and general pool fund	Similar basis preferred and applied
Disclosure of profit rate	None	None	Not disclosed

(continued)

Table 6.7 (continued)

Financing contracts			
Features	Murabahah	Bai Bithaman Ajil	Comments
Early settlement	Granted but not prevalent	Granted but not prevalent	Similar response
Accrued income and classification	Most accrue in Murabahah receivables, while some classify as other receivables	Most accrue in BBA receivables, while some classify as other receivables	Tendency to accrue income in principal amount. May have difficult implications in refinancing
Security investment deposit	Treated as investment deposits and separate disclosures vary from balance sheet to notes	Treated as investment deposits and separate disclosures vary from balance sheet to notes	Similar disclosure practices. But lack information whether such disclosure referred to as security deposit
Recognition of accrued income	Most accrue income	Most accrue income	Similar basis
Income recognition method	47% Lump sum 40% CRR	96% CRR	Varying methods employed
Early settlement	Majority (69%) requires full settlement with rebate	Majority (79%) requires full settlement with rebate	Preference for early settlement with rebate

Source: Hassan Vaseehar, Shanmugam Bala, Perumal Vignesan, (2005) "Corporate Governance: An Islamic Paradigm", published by Universiti Putra Malaysia Press

wages paid to the ajir are known as ujrah. For example, ABC Islamic Bank hires Encik Mustafa Mansor as a product manager on a monthly salary of RM7000. In this case ABC Islamic Bank is mustajir, Encik Mustafa Mansor is ajir, and RM7000 is ujrah. This is a typical example of Ijarah amal. This type of Ijarah includes every transaction where the services of a person are hired by someone else and the compensation is for effort expended of skill used (by an employee or a contractor).

2. *Ijarah 'Ain*: This type relates to the hiring of any assets or properties in order to reap its benefits without the transfer of ownership, or better known in English as usufruct. The price or consideration of this is the

rent. In this case, the term Ijarah is analogous to the English term leasing. Here the lessor is called mujir, the lessee is called mustajir, and the rent payable to the lessor is called ujrah. Under this contract, there is no element of interest involved and the title of asset remains with the lessor and there is no option for the lessee to buy the asset during or upon expiry of the contract. Hence, Ijarah ain is a true leasing and does not involve sales of tangible object, but rather sales of intangibles known as usufruct or manfaah.

It is the second type of Ijarah, which is the subject matter in the following subsection as it is generally used as a form of investment and also as a means of finance. Hence, Ijarah has been conceptually understood as a contract of exchange in which one party enjoys the benefit arising from employment by another party, in return for a consideration for the services rendered and from the use of an asset.

To summarize, Ijarah is defined as the sale of manfaah (the right to use assets) for a specific period of time to another party. Unlike the conventional lease, Ijarah is a contract under which an Islamic bank or business unit purchases and leases out an asset required by its client in return for a rental fee not related to interest. Under an Ijarah contract, the ownership remains with the lessor who also enjoys the right to negotiate the lease payments at various agreed intervals to ensure that the payment is equal with the residual balance value of the assets and the cost for the lessor in relinquishing its right to use the assets. On the contrary, the lessee holds the right to use the property but not to sell it. Ijarah is for a known time period called Ijarah period, whereby risks associated with ownership of the asset remain with the bank and the asset is supposed to revert to the bank at the end of the Ijarah period.

1.5.1 Modus Operandi of Ijarah Financing

From the above definition, we can say that Ijarah concept is very much similar to the rules of sale, because in both cases something is transferred to another person for a valuable consideration. Hence, it is correct to say that Ijarah is not a means of finance as originally envisaged. It is simply a transaction much as a sale/purchase. Ijarah differs from sale only insomuch as not transferring the corpus or ownership of the property which remains with the lessor. In addition, Ijarah differs from sales due to the time limitation involved, which is not practiced under sales contract. As such in Syariah, a lease transaction is governed by a separate set of rules, which we shall outline in the following paragraphs.

Ijarah is a true example of operation lease under Islamic context. It is a transaction whereby the bank acquires different assets that are in demand in the market. Then, it leases such assets to the customers against a fixed rent for a certain period of time according to the terms of the contract. Upon the expiry of the lease, the property in question is returned to the bank. Such Ijarah is useful for helping to meet certain requirements and achieving objectives at reasonable prices (Fig. 6.7).

Step 1: The client approaches the seller/vendor and identifies the house or asset he wishes to lease. He requests the seller to provide a price quotation and other relevant details.
Step 2: The seller provides the price quotation, brochure, terms and conditions, and other relevant details requested by the customer.
Step 3: The customer approaches the bank for financing and both agree on financing using Ijarah as an underlying contract. The customer

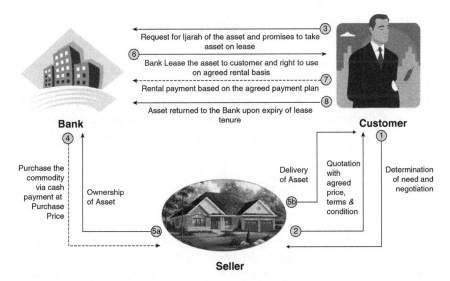

Fig. 6.7 *Modus operandi* of Ijarah financing

promises to take the asset on lease for an agreed time period and rental from the bank upon purchase.

Step 4: The bank purchases the commodity from the seller based on the asset details provided by the customer. The bank will purchase it via cash payment at a purchase price.

Step 5a: The seller transfers the ownership of the asset to the bank.

Step 5b: The seller delivers the asset to the customer based on the agreed terms and conditions and submits a proof of delivery with the customer's acceptance to the bank.

Step 6: The bank leases the asset and transfers possession and right of specified use to the lessor. The bank enters into a Ijarah contract, whereby the object, benefit, rental, and period are clearly defined.

Step 7: Customer pays the agreed rental based on the agreed payment plan and time period.

Step 8: Once the Ijarah time period expires, the customer returns the object of Ijarah to the bank.

Note: The bank can also appoint the customer as an agent to take the delivery of asset to mitigate the delivery risk as explained under the *Modus Operandi* of Murabahah Financing for Working Capital.

1.5.2 Essential Elements of Ijarah Contract

Ijarah contract is where the bank buys and leases equipment or other assets to the business owner (lessee) for a fee or commonly known as rental income. The duration of the lease as well as the fee must be set in advance and mutually agreed. To be acceptable as an Islamic financial product, the leasing contract must meet the following conditions (Table 6.8):

1.5.3 Ijarah Financing Practice

Ijarah transaction is based upon the transfer of benefits, rather than the ownership of goods. Hence, Ijarah can be defined as the right to utilize a product or service by means of paying a certain compensation. In this light, there is no transfer of ownership under an Ijarah contract, except a mere transfer of benefit from the lessor to the lessee (Table 6.9).

Table 6.8 Essential elements of Ijarah contract

Tenet	Mandatory characteristic/conditions	Prohibited characteristic/conditions

Lessor (mujir)/lessee (*mustajir*)	1. Must possess sound mind (aqil)
	2. Must be at least 18 years old (attains the age of puberty—baligh)
	3. Must be intelligent
		1. Forced to enter into a contract
		2. He must not be prohibited from dealing:
		  – not bankrupt
		  – not prodigal

Asset/merchandise	1. Exist at the time of transaction 2. Bank must be the owner of the merchandise 3. Must be of pure substance (lawful) 4. Must be of some use or some value 5. Must be able to be delivered by seller to the buyer 6. Known to both the seller and buyer (i.e. full details of the goods is known to both parties) 7. The risk always remains with the lessor throughout the lease period. Any harm or loss caused by the factors beyond the control of the lessee shall be borne by the lessor	
Benefit (usufruct)	1. It can be fixed in value 2. The lessor has the power and capacity to use and lease the asset 3. It must be permissible 4. The purpose for which the asset is used must be known 5. The period of lease must be determined in clear terms	1. It must not be any material part of the asset 2. In the event, the purpose of lease is not specified in the agreement and then the lessee can use it for whatever purpose it is used in the normal course

(continued)

Table 6.8 (continued)

Tenet	Mandatory characteristic/conditions	Prohibited characteristic/conditions
Rental	1. Must be known to both the lessor and the lessee 2. Must be known in currency and absolute amount 3. It is permissible that different amounts of rent are fixed for different phases during the lease period, provided that the amount of rent for each phase is specifically agreed upon at the time of affecting a lease 4. The lease period and rental shall commence from the date on which the leased asset has been delivered to the lessee, no matter whether the lessee has started using it or not	5. The lessor cannot increase the rent unilaterally, and any agreement to this effect is void

Contract (aqad)—Offer and acceptance	1. Absolute and in definite and decisive language
	  – In the past or present tense
	  – Not in the future or imperative tense
	  – Not conditional
	  – Not limited to a certain period.
	2. The acceptance must agree with the offer.
	3. The offer and acceptance must be made at the one and same meeting or session.	

Source:
- Adapted from 'Certification in Introduction to Syariah Concept' tutorial notes from Islamic Banking Financing Institute Malaysia
- Taqi Usmani

1.5.4 Ijarah Financing Computation

The method used for computation of rental price is flat rate, whereby the customer has to pay rental on a monthly basis or on an agreed time period. The formula used for computation is stated in Table 6.10.

Example

Nafis approaches the Islamic bank and applies for leasing a bottle packaging machine for a period of 5 years. The cost of financing a machine is RM100,000 and Nafis is willing to pay the lease in monthly instalments. Let us say that the profit rate the bank wants to charge is 10%. The computation of the selling price is as below:

Step 1: Computation of profit

Profit (P)	CF × I × D	CF = 100,000 I = 10% D = 5 years
	$= (100,000 \times 10 \times 5)/100$ $= (5,000,000)/100$ $= 50,000$	

Step 2: Total lease rental computation

Total lease rental (TLR)	CF + P	CF = 100,000 P = 50,000
	100,000 + 50,000 = 150,000	

Step 3: Monthly rental computation

Monthly rental	TLR/n	TLR = 150,000 n = 60, that is, (5 years × 12 months)
	150,000/60 = 2500	

Table 6.9 Common features of product offered by banks

Product feature	Description
Product name	Ijarah financing.
Definition	It is a leasing contract whereby the benefits/use of an asset is transferred by the owner (lessor) to the lessee at an agreed price/rental amount for an agreed period of time or lease period. The total lease rental, which is fixed throughout the tenure, comprises the original cost of equipment and the bank's profit margin. The lessor retains ownership of the equipment and seeks to recover the capital cost of the equipment plus a profit margin out of the lease rentals receivable during the period of the lease
Scope of financing	1. Capital goods: Fixed assets, buildings, offices, and so on 2. Production goods: machinery, equipment 3. Consumer goods 4. Computers 5. Motor vehicles 6. Other suitable and acceptable assets
Eligible entities	The following entities can be 1. Individual account 2. Joint account 3. Clubs, societies, association 4. Companies 5. Sole proprietorships
Legal documents	1. Undertaking to Ijarah 2. Ijarah agreement • Description of the Ijarah asset • Schedule of Ijarah rentals • Receipt of asset
Rental	Lease rentals can be fixed or floating. Normally the banks design *Ijarah* contract in such a way that rental will increase by a certain percentage after a certain period. Another option exercised by the bank or financial institution is that contract is for a short-term *Ijarah* with a renewable option
Payment structure	Normally on equal instalments basis
Financing tenor	Tenor can be up to 7 years as the financing is for long-term and differs from bank to bank
Charges	Expenses incurred such as legal fees and other incidental cost are normally borne by the lessee
Rebate on early redemption	This is normally prohibited by Syariah Board since it can make the Murabahah transaction similar to conventional debt

(*continued*)

Table 6.9 (continued)

Product feature	Description
Termination	If the lessee contravenes any term of the agreement, the lessor has a right to terminate the lease contract unilaterally. However, if there is no contravention on the part of the lessee, the lease cannot be terminated without mutual consent
Penalty for the late payment	To compensate the actual loss, the bank can charge 1% on outstanding instalment amount or Islamic Money Market rate. The lessor must not benefit from the penalties paid by the lessee

1.5.5 Comparison Between Ijarah and Conventional Leasing

The comparison between conventional leasing and Ijarah is explained in Table 6.11:

1.6 AITAB Financing

The Islamic concept of Al-Ijarah Thumma Al-Bai (AITAB) refers to lease or hire or rent ending with purchase. It is a type of lease which concludes with an option to buy-back in which the legal title of the leased asset will be passed to the lessee at the end of the lease period. It is one of the contemporary innovative products which are designed to meet the public

Table 6.10 Ijarah financing computation

Component	Computation formula	Details
Profit (P)	CF × I × D	CF= Cost of financing (purchase price)
		i = Rate of return per annum
		D = Period of financing in years
Total lease rental (TLR)	CF + P	CF= Cost of financing (purchase price)
		P = Profit
Monthly rental	TLR/n	TLR = Total lease rental
		n = Number of months

Table 6.11 Comparison between Ijarah and conventional leasing

Conventional lease	Ijarah
Commencement of the lease	
In most cases the customer (lessee) purchases the asset on behalf of the bank (lessor) who pays its price to the supplier, either directly or through the lessee. In some lease agreements, the lease commences on the very day on which the price is paid by the lessor, irrespective of whether the lessee has effected payment to the supplier and taken delivery of the asset or not. It may mean that the lessee's liability for the rent starts before the lessee takes delivery of the asset	According to Syariah, the procedure is that rent will be charged after the lessee has taken the delivery of the asset, and not from the day the price has been paid. In the event the supplier has delayed the delivery after receiving the full price, the lessee should not be liable for the rent during the period of delay
Expenses consequent to ownership	
In most scenarios, all the expenses incurred in the process of purchasing the asset—registration charges, import expenses, freight, and customs duty—are all borne by the lessee	Lessor is liable to bear all the expenses incurred in the process of purchasing the asset. Lessor is allowed to factor in all his cost while calculating the rental amount
Liability of the parties in case of loss	
Lease agreement generally does not differentiate between (a) natural wear and tear, (b) expenses caused by misuse or negligence of the lessee, and (c) situations that are out of the control of the lessee. The lessee is not liable for costs incurred due to events that are out of his control, such as theft of the asset or damage in the event of a natural disaster	The lessee is responsible for any loss caused to asset by misuse or negligence. The important point to note here is that he cannot be made liable for a loss caused by factors beyond his control
Penalty for late payment of rent	
Extra monetary amount is charged normally based on compounding interest, in the event rent is not paid as per the agreed schedule. The extra payment paid by the lessee is treated as income	The lessee is charged 1% or Islamic money market rate on the outstanding instalment and it is to cover the cost incurred by the lessor on administration due to late payment. The lessor must not benefit from the penalties paid by the lessee

(*continued*)

Table 6.11 (continued)

Conventional lease	Ijarah
Termination of the Lease	
The lessor usually has an unrestricted power to terminate the lease unilaterally whenever desired	In the event the lessee contravenes on any term in the agreement, the lessor has a right to terminate the lease contract unilaterally However, if there is no contravention on the part of the lessee, the lease cannot be terminated without mutual consent
Insurance	
The cost incurred on getting the asset insured is borne by the lessee.	The leased asset insured under the Islamic 'Takaful' model will be borne by the lessor

demand at the same time, securing long-term competitiveness in the financial market. AITAB comprises two contracts, that is, al-Ijarah (leasing/renting) contract and which is followed by al-bai (sale) contract:

1. *Al-Ijarah*: A contract whereby the lessor (Islamic bank) will rent the asset(s) to the lessee (customer) over a certain period and at a monthly rental amount as agreed by both parties.
2. *Al-bai*: Upon completion of the rental period or upon early settlement, the lessor will then enter into the sale contract with the lessee to sell the asset at a pre-agreed selling price.

Al-Ijarah and al-bai are both categorized under the contract of exchange. The former relate to the exchange of usufruct for money, while latter involves the exchange of goods for money. In AITAB, the contract of al-Ijarah runs separately from the contract of al-bai. Since both contracts are executed in a sequence, a new contract AITAB can be used to describe the process of converting an Ijarah into a sale contract.

AITAB is one of the contemporary innovative approaches in the Islamic hire purchase instrument which is an alternative product to conventional hire purchase. The significant difference between the two is that, Islamic hire purchase is a unique contract involving a combination of two different contracts, thus invoking a number of legal and Syariah issues. It calls for special rules on leasing and sale at different stages of the transaction in the light of Syariah.

In Malaysia, Islamic hire purchase has evolved in various stages. The concept of Islamic hire purchase came into reality when the Syariah scholars introduced a new product via reasoning (ijtihad) based on the Islamic traditional contract of Ijarah and al-bai. Consequently, two major contracts of Islamic hire purchase were formed as new modes of financing, namely, Al-Ijarah Thumma al Bai (a contract of leasing ending with sale) or Al-Ijarah Muntahiya Bittamlik (a contract of leasing ending with ownership). While the former (famously known as AITAB) is widely adopted as an instrument to be used in motor vehicles financing, the latter is applied by some banks in corporate financing. Bank Islam Malaysia Berhad was the first bank to launch AITAB in Malaysia, and since then, it has grown in popularity and is the most preferred product among the Malaysian customers.

1.6.1 Modus Operandi of AITAB Financing

Al-Ijarah Thumma Al-Bai incorporates the Syariah principles of Ijarah (lease) and bai (sale). In essence, the bank will buy the vehicle based on the customer's requirement from the dealer or third party and then lease it back to the customer for an agreed period and rental rate. At the end of the lease period, the bank will sell the asset back to the customer at an agreed price (Fig. 6.8).

Step 1: The client approaches the seller/vendor and identifies the house or asset he wishes to buy. He requests the seller to provide a price quotation and other relevant details.
Step 2: The seller provides the price quotation, brochure, terms and conditions, and other relevant details requested by customer.
Step 3: The customer approaches the bank for financing and both agree on financing using AITAB as an underlying principle. The customer promises to take the asset on lease and buy-back for an agreed time period and rental from the bank upon purchase.

Islamic Financing in Practice 179

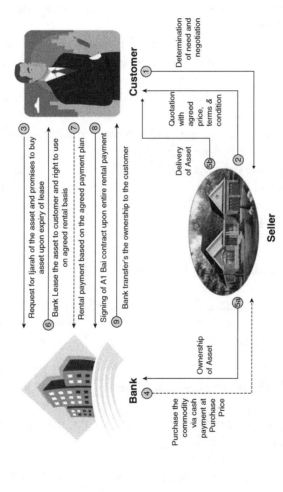

Fig. 6.8 *Modus operandi* of AITAB financing

Step 4: Bank purchases the asset from the seller based on the asset details provided by customer. Bank will purchase it via cash payment at a purchase price.

Step 5a: The seller transfers the ownership of the asset to the bank.

Step 5b: The seller delivers the asset to the customer based on the agreed terms and conditions and submits a proof of delivery with customer's acceptance to the bank.

Step 6: The bank leases the asset and transfers possession and right of specified use to the lessor. Bank enters into a Ijarah contract, whereby the object, benefit, rental, and period are clearly defined.

Step 7: The customer pays the agreed rental based on the agreed payment plan and time period.

Step 8: Once the Ijarah time period expires, the bank signs the al-bai agreement with the customer to sell the asset.

Step 9: Bank transfers the ownership of asset to the client at the end of the Ijarah period based on al-bai contract either through a gift or sale based on the terms agreed. In Malaysia, final rental payment is taken as the agreed selling price

1.6.2 Essential Elements of AITAB

AITAB comprises Ijarah and bai contracts. The essential elements for Ijarah have been discussed in the earlier section. Under AITAB, the bai contract must meet the following conditions (Table 6.12):

1.6.3 AITAB Financing Computation

Most of the banks currently follow a flat rate for the computation of profit (Table 6.13).

Example

Nafis approaches an Islamic bank and applies for an AITAB financing for a new Honda City car. Nafis agrees to a financing tenure of 5 years. The cost of financing the vehicle is RM150,000; Nafis is willing to pay the rental in monthly instalments and the last instalment will be treated as a selling price. Let us say the profit rate the bank wants to charge is 10%. The computation of various components under AITAB is as below:

Table 6.12 Essential elements of AITAB

Tenet	Mandatory characteristic/ conditions	Prohibited characteristic/ conditions

Seller/buyer	1. Must possess sound mind (aqil)
	2. Must be at least 18 years old (attains the age of puberty—baligh)
	3. Must be intelligent
		1. Forced to enter into a contract
		2. He must not be prohibited from dealing:
		  (a) not bankrupt
		  (b) not prodigal

Asset/merchandise	1. Exist at the time of transaction 2. Bank must be the owner of the merchandise 3. Must be of pure substance (lawful) 4. Must be of some use or some value 5. Must be able to be delivered by seller to the buyer 6. Known to both the seller and buyer (i.e. full details of the goods is known to both parties)	
Price	1. Must be known to both the seller and the buyer. 2. Must be known in currency and absolute amount.	

Contract (aqad)—Offer and acceptance	1. Absolute and in definite and decisive language:
	  (a) In the past or present tense
	  (b) Not in the future or imperative tense
	  (c) Not conditional
	  (d) Not limited to a certain period.
	2. The acceptance must agree with the offer.
	3. The offer and acceptance must be made at the one and same meeting or session.	

Source:
- Adapted from 'Certification in Introduction to Syariah Concept' tutorial notes from Islamic Banking Financing Institute Malaysia
- Taqi Usmani

Table 6.13 AITAB financing computation

Component	Computation formula	Details
Profit (P)	$CF \times I \times T/12$	CF= Cost of financing (purchase price) i = Rate of return per annum T= Time period (years)
Instalment amount	$\dfrac{CF + P}{N}$	CF= Cost of financing (purchase price) P= Profit N= Total number of periodic payments
Income recognition	$P - \dfrac{n(n+1)}{T(T+1)} \times P$	P = Profit n = The number of months remaining N = Total number of periodic payments
Penalty in the event of default	$UIA \times PR \times OP/365$	UIA = Unpaid installment amount PR = Penalty rate OP= Outstanding period in days

Step 1: Computation of profit

Profit (P)	$CF \times I \times T/12$	CF= 150,000 I = 10% T = 5 Years
	= (150,000 × 10 × 5) /100 = (7,500,000)/100 = 75,000	

Step 2: Monthly instalment amount computation

Monthly instalment amount (MIA)	$\dfrac{CF + P}{N}$	CF= 150,000 P = 75,000 N = 60 Months (12 × 5)
	$= \dfrac{(150,000 + 75,000)}{60}$ $= (225,000)/60$ $= 3750$	

Islamic Financing in Practice

Step 3: Final instalment amount computation

Final instalment amount (FIA)	$CF + P - [MIA \times (N-1)]$	CF = 150,000 P = 75,000 MIA = 3750 N = 60
	= 150,000 + 75,000 − [3750 × (60−1)] = 225,000 − [3750 × 59] = 225,000 − 221,250 = 3,750 Note: Normally the final instalment amount will be lower if the MIA has got decimal value and it is rounded off to the next higher RM.	

Step 4: Income recognition under AITAB for first month

Profit in the first instalment amount	$P - \dfrac{n(n+1)}{T(T+1)} \times P$	P = 75,000 n = 59 T = 60

$$= 75,000 - \frac{59(59+1)}{60(60+1)} \times 75,000$$

$$= 75,000 - \frac{59(60)}{60(61)} \times 75,000$$

$$= 75,000 - \frac{3540}{3660} \times 75,000$$

$$= 75,000 - 0.967 \times 75,000$$

$$= 75,000 - 72,525$$

$$= 2,475$$

Step 5: Penalty in the event of default, say Mr. Sajjad did not pay his instalment for two consecutive months

Penalty amount for the first month	$UIA \times PR \times OP/365$	UIA= 3750 PR = 1% OP = 30
	$= 3{,}750 \times 0.01 \times 30 / 365$	
	$= 3{,}750 \times 0.01 \times 0.0821$	
	$= 3{,}750 \times 0.000821$	
	$= 3.08$	
Penalty amount for the second month	$UIA \times PR \times OP/365$	UIA= 7500 (first and second month) PR = 1% OP = 31
	$= 7{,}500 \times 0.01 \times 31 / 365$	
	$= 7{,}500 \times 0.01 \times 0.0849$	
	$= 3{,}750 \times 0.000849$	
	$= 6.37$	
Total penalty amount payable	$= 3.08 + 6.37 = 9.45$	

1.6.4 Challenges in Implementing AITAB

A number of issues pertaining to the operation of AITAB as highlighted by Abdullah and Dusuki based on their research findings via a survey in Malaysia are listed below:

1. Customer awareness

    One of the problems faced in offering AITAB facility is the customer's awareness toward the product. The research findings are that, at large, customers do not really understand the basic differences between AITAB and conventional hire purchase facility. This is mainly due to their perception that AITAB resembles conventional hire purchase, especially in their operations, documentations, and legal prescriptions. Customers are not aware on the distinction of AITAB as a Syariah-compliant product and in what way it would provide them with a better scheme and prospect.

2. Lack of experience among bank officers

    The misleading view of AITAB among the customers is partly due to the lack of experience and knowledge among bank officers in giving correct and satisfactory explanations about AITAB. Some of these bank officers do not even understand the distinction between AITAB and conventional hire purchase. Many proclaim that both products are similar, especially with regard to its documents, procedures, and governance. Hence, they are unable to highlight the advantages and benefits of AITAB to customers as compared to conventional hire purchase.

3. Lacks of awareness and cooperation among dealers

    A dealer acts as a middleman between a financial institution and a customer. In the Malaysian context, the customer usually approaches the dealer first for the purpose of purchasing a particular vehicle before applying for a hire purchase facility from a financial institution. The customer's choice between conventional and Islamic financing facility depends mostly on the dealer's explanation and recommendation. Ideally, a dealer with proper understanding of Islamic financial products will propose AITAB. However, not all dealers are knowledgeable about the AITAB facility. They are unable to inform and educate their customers accordingly. Quite often, dealers would propose conventional facility because their understanding of AITAB is limited or they do not want to be embroiled in any complications.

4. Documentation

    The documentation processing for AITAB may seem more complicated than that of conventional facility, because it involves additional document: acceptance (aqad) letter. Documents must be presented before the customer in sequence: first, leasing (Ijarah) agreement, and second, sale and purchase agreement. The bank officers must explain the terms, conditions, rights, and liabilities in the agreement, the commencement and expiry of agreement. The customer must also be made aware of the consequences of signing every document to have a clear understanding of rights and obligations. Some banks even require a customer to complete a bulk of documents relating to the facility, and in the event of any errors, it delays the processing of the application. Hence, the dealer and the customers perceive that availing conventional hire purchase financing facility is faster and convenient in comparison to AITAB.

5. Competitions in the market

   Another pertinent challenge faced by AITAB facility is in the issue of competition vis-à-vis conventional hire purchase. The main issue here is how to penetrate into a market which has long been occupied by a more established conventional hire purchase product. Naturally, as a relatively new product, AITAB faced a challenge on how it can be offered at a lower cost compared to its counterpart since AITAB requires more documents and paper works to be filled by both parties. Hence, a lack of customer awareness on the difference between AITAB and conventional hire purchase and cost benefits are the main challenges faced by the banks in pushing AITAB into the market.

6. Syariah

   Despite being one of the most demanding facilities of Islamic bank, AITAB is unfortunately lacking in Syariah regulatory framework. Thus, any disputes arising from the transaction will be referred to the conventional regulations. The visible inclination of AITAB operation to conventional concepts is due to several factors including the following:

   (a) Absence of proper and standard Islamic hire purchase regulation; thus, practitioners in AITAB transaction have no other legal recourse except the conventional hire purchase law: Hire Purchase Act 1967 (HPA).
   (b) The basic operation of AITAB in effect is similar to conventional hire purchase; the only difference is in the issue of interest (riba)

and issuance of acceptance (aqad) letter. As regards to determination of fixed rate, standard documentation, and formation of agreement, AITAB transactions follows the same spirit of HPA.
(c) Conventional hire purchase business has been in the market for quite a long time and has established its rules and policy; thus, its operation appears to be much easier in practice.
(d) Legal institutions (civil court) that handle commercial and mercantile matters will decide a case based on the existing rules of law. Jurisdiction of civil courts also covers Islamic banking transactions. Since there is no legal authority for the AITAB transaction, any case connected to it will be referred to the HPA.
(e) As stated in the earlier part, motor vehicles are the most demanding goods under the AITAB facility, and consumer goods are also in demand. Both types of goods are bound by the HPA. Thus, any institution offering these goods must abide to this law.
(f) Full understanding of the Islamic law among the practitioners has not been attained yet.
Currently, AITAB is operated on the basis of conventional concepts because, presently, there is no written Syariah law which specifically regulates the operation of AITAB. The only existing regulatory Syariah rules on the facility can be found in Syariah rules for investment and financing instruments, the Accounting and Auditing Organisation for Islamic Financial Institutions of Bahrain (AAOIFI). In Malaysia, because there is no specific regulations governing AITAB, institutions offering this facility tend to impose rules in the spirit of Hire Purchase Act 1967 and Contract Act 1950.

7. Other operational challenges

(a) Bank as a true lessor will have to maintain the rental asset and fulfill other obligations. In this manner, for vehicle financing the bank must pay for the insurance, road tax, and car maintenance. The cost has to be borne by the bank, which at times eats up their profits.
(b) Customer cannot be forced to pay the outstanding balance, if he fails to pay rentals. The customer needs to inform his intention to

the bank to terminate the contract and he is not liable to pay any sum of money. This is not in favor of the bank but it is done to conform to the true concept of leasing.

Hence, AITAB involves more risk to an Islamic financial institution than a conventional hire purchase offered by a conventional bank.

1.6.5 Comparison Between AIAB and Conventional Hire Purchase

The general perception among the customer is that AITAB is really no different from the conventional product except in their use of religious or Arabic names to disguise the current established practice. In real fact, both products are different as explained in Table 6.14:

1.7 Musharakah

In Islamic jurisprudence, the term shirkah is used to denote Musharakah, which literally means 'sharing'. It is a form of partnership where two or more persons combine either their capital or labor to take on a business venture and share the profits and enjoy similar rights and liabilities. Under this principle, all partners share the profit according to a specific ratio, while the loss is shared according to the ratio of capital contribution. It is an agreement whereby the customer and the bank agree to combine financial resources to undertake any type of business venture and agree to manage the same according to the terms of the agreement.

Historically, Musharakah was practiced by the Arabs long before the advent of Islam (*The Halal Journal*, 2006). The system was permitted to continue after Islam, and many scholars considered it to be the most authentic form of Islamic contract. There is a consensus of opinion among all the jurists from different schools of thought (including Hanafi, Maliki, Shafi'i, Hanbali, and Shia) that Musharakah is a valid and legitimate contract in Islam. However, the jurists do differ on terms, conditions, and other details.

Table 6.14 Comparison between AIAB and conventional hire purchase

Hire purchase	AITAB
Number of contracts	
Hire purchase uses single contract covering both rental and sale aspects	AITAB comprises two separate contracts, that is, 'Ijarah' and 'al-bai'
Contract terms	
1. Hire purchase is considered as a loan to the customer
2. The bank charges interest on the financing amount to procure the asset
3. The charges on purchase are borne by the customer
4. Late payment interest is charged in the event customer doesn't pay the instalment on time	1. Hire purchase is considered as a financing to the customer
2. The bank charges fixed profit rate on the cost of financing
3. The charges on purchase are borne by the bank
4. Late payment charges, that is, maximum 1% on the unpaid instalment
Source of funds	
There is no such restriction on sourcing of funds to offer hire purchase facility.	The financing for AITAB is sourced from *Halal* funds
Acceptance letter	
There is no such agreement.	Under AITAB, the customer has to sign the *aqad* letter (acceptance letter) to denote the offer and acceptance of transactions
Eligible goods/assets	
At large it is limited to consumer goods, motor vehicles and non-act goods (corporate)	It is open to all types of goods as long as it is in compliance with Syariah
Purchase price	
It is floating based on the annual rate and is decided upfront.	It is determined at the end of Ijarah contract based on the existing market value of asset
Responsibility	
The customer bears all costs of maintenance and expenses incurred on the purchasing of asset	The bank bears all basic and structural maintenance expenses including the expenses incurred on the purchasing of asset
Insurance	
The goods are insured by using conventional insurance.	The goods are insured using Takaful.

(continued)

Table 6.14 (continued)

Hire purchase	AITAB
Penalty	
Normally customer is charged a fee of 8.00% p.a. of the instalment due and on compounding basis in the event of late payment	A minimal late payment fee of 1.00% p.a. of the instalment due will be charged to customer in the event of late payment

Source: Bank Negara Website

The Islamic banks use the mode of partnership in many projects. They finance their customers with part of the capital in exchange for a share of the output as they may agree upon. Mostly, they leave the responsibility of management to the customer partner and retain the right of supervision and follow-up.

1.7.1 Musharakah Classification

Musharakah can be split further as illustrated in the Fig. 6.9.

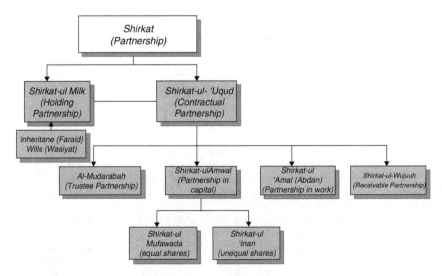

Fig. 6.9 Musharakah classification. Source: Saiful Azhar Rosly (2005), "Critical Issues on Islamic Banking and Financial Market"

Shirkat-ul-Milk

Shirkat-ul-milk implies co-ownership and comes into existence when two or more persons happen to obtain a joint ownership of some asset without having to enter into a formal partnership agreement, for example, two persons receiving an inheritance or a gift of land or property which may or may not be divisible. The partners have to share the gift or inherited property or its income, in accordance with their share in it until they decide on how to divide it. If the property is divisible and the partners still decide to stick together, the shirkat-ul-milk is termed ikhtiyariyyah (voluntary). However, if it is indivisible and they are constrained to stay together, the shirkat al-milk is characterized as jabriyyah (involuntary).

Shirkat-ul-Aqd

Shirkat-ul-Aqd is a partnership affected by a mutual contract, which can be translated as a 'joint commercial enterprise'. This is considered a proper partnership because the parties concerned have willingly entered into a contractual agreement for joint investment and the sharing of profit and risks. The agreement need not necessarily be formal and written; it could be informal and oral. This has been further divided into four types as mentioned below:

1. *Shirkat-ul-amal*: It can be translated as a 'Partnership in Services', where all the parties jointly undertake to render some service for their customers, and the fee charged from them is distributed among them according to an agreed ratio. For example, two workers agreed to undertake carpeting services for their customers on the condition that the wages so earned will go to a joint pool. This pool shall be distributed between them, irrespective of the effort contributed by each partner. This partnership will be known as shirkat-ul-aamal, shirkat-ul-taqabbul, shirkat-ul-sunai, or shirkat-ul-abdan.
2. *Shirkat-ul-wujooh*: It can be translated as a 'Partnership in Goodwill'. The wujooh has its root in the Arabic word wajahat, which means 'goodwill'. Under this principle, there is no investment needed from partners. They purchase the commodity on a deferred price by getting

capital on loan due to their goodwill and sell it for cash on spot. The profit so earned is distributed between them at an agreed ratio.
3. *Shirkat-ul-amwal*: It can be translated as 'Partnership in Capital'. In this financial contract, all partners invest some capital as well as expertise into the new business. This can be further subclassified as below:

   (a) *Shirkat-ul-mufawada*: In this financial contract, capital and labor contributed are at par. The contributions from partners in terms of share capital, management, profit, and risk are equal. It is a necessary condition that all four categories to be shared equally among the partners; in the event any one category is not equally shared, then it falls under shirkat-ul-ainan. Hence, under this partnership, each partner enjoys full and equal share and authority to transact with the partnership capital.
   (b) *Shirkat-ul-ainan*: Under this partnership model, there might be equality in capital, management or liability might be equal in one case but not equal in all the areas. For example, the sharing ratio is equal for profit but not for capital. Hence, it is not a must to have equal proportion in investment amount whereby all the parties may hold unequal shares in the partnership.

In this type of Musharakah, each one of the partners is considered as an agent or representative of the other(s) in acting on things concerning the capital of the company and trade transactions. However, the right to transact with the partnership capital is very much based on the partnership agreement and should be in the best interest of the company. In addition, any of the partners will not guarantee the liabilities of the other partners. The contract of this company, though legal, is not binding. This means that anyone of the partners is within his right to cancel the contract whenever he wishes. This is because this contract is based on each one of the partners being a representative or agent of his partner.

1.7.2 Essential Elements of Musharakah Contract

The essential elements of BBA contract with the necessary conditions for a valid contract are listed in Table 6.15:

Table 6.15 Essential elements of Musharakah contract

Tenet	Mandatory characteristic/conditions	Prohibited characteristic/conditions
Partners	1. Must possess sound mind (aqil) 2. Must be at least 18 years old (attains the age of puberty—baligh) 3. Must be intelligent 4. Partner can opt to be a sleeping partner	1. Forced to enter into a contract 2. He must not be prohibited from dealing: – not bankrupt – not prodigal
Capital	1. In the event capital is in the form of asset, then it should be valued in money, and the value agreed upon by all partners. 2. It should be in specific amount 3. It should be existent and easily accessible 4. The capital contributed by partners should be put into capital fund 5. It is permissible for partners to have unequal ownership in the company/venture	1. Establishing a company with borrowed money is not permitted
Business	1. The business carried out by partners should be permissible and in compliance with Syariah 2. All partners have right to manage 3. Each partner implicitly permits and gives power of attorney to the other partner(s) to dispose of and work with capital as is deemed necessary to conduct business	1. To impose a condition forbidding one of the partners from work 2. Non-halal business such as gambling, dealing in alcohol, or interest-based activities
Profit sharing	1. Profit-sharing percentage to be known to all partners to avoid any uncertainty 2. Profit-sharing has to be determined in ratio 3. Loss has to borne by partners according to the proportion of shares (ownership) 4. It is permissible to have profit-sharing not according to the proportion of shares (ownership) 5. Liability of partners is limited to the capital contribution	1. Fixed lump sum amount for profit-sharing

(continued)

Table 6.15 (continued)

Tenet	Mandatory characteristic/conditions	Prohibited characteristic/conditions

Contract (aqad)—offer and acceptance	1. Absolute and in definite and decisive language
	   (a) In the past or present tense
	   (b) Not in the future or imperative tense
	   (c) Not conditional
	   (d) Not limited to a certain period
	2. The acceptance must agree with the offer
	3. The offer and acceptance must be made at the one and same meeting or session
	4. In principle, a partnership is a permissible and non-binding contract. But some of the jurists take the view that the partnership contract is binding up to the liquidation of capital or the accomplishment of the job accepted at the contract
	5. Termination of partnership:
	   (a) At any time upon consensus agreement
	   (b) In the event an partner dies/incapacitated/insane/insolvent and so on	

1.7.3 *Modus Operandi* of Musharakah Financing

Musharakah involves a partnership in which both the bank and its customer-client contribute to entrepreneurship and capital. Under this model, the bank participates in the equity of a company (customer) and receives an annual share of the profits on an agreed profit-sharing ratio basis (Fig. 6.10).

Step 1: The client approaches the bank with a detailed business plan, roles and responsibilities, profit- and loss-sharing percentage, and so forth to start a new business venture.

Islamic Financing in Practice 195

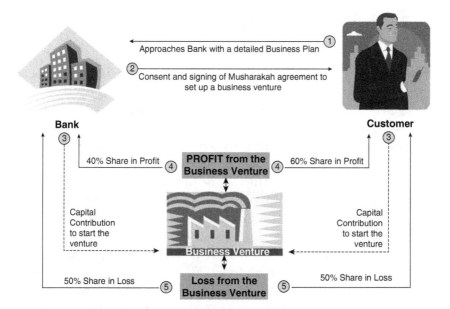

Fig. 6.10 *Modus operandi* of Musharakah financing

Step 2: The bank will do the necessary valuation based on the documentation and other necessary information provided by the customer. Upon successful review, the customer and the bank will sign a Musharakah agreement to set up a business venture.

Step 3: The customer and the bank will contribute the capital (50:50 ratio) to set up the business venture and manage its operations, sharing the responsibilities as the pre-agreed terms in the contract.

Step 4: In the event there is profit from the business venture, the profit is divided between the two parties in accordance with the agreement. For above scenario the profit-sharing ratio between the bank and the customer is, say, 40:60.

Step 5: In the event there is loss from the business venture, the loss is divided between the two parties in proportion to its share in the capital. For above scenario, the loss-sharing ratio between the bank and the customer will be 50:50.

1.7.4 Musharakah Financing Practice

Musharakah is helpful in providing financing for large investments in modern economic activities. Islamic banks can engage in Musharakah partnerships for new or established companies and activities. Islamic banks may become active partners in determining the methods of production cost control, marketing, and other day-to-day operations of a company to ensure that the objectives of the company are met. On the other hand, they can also choose to either directly supervise or simply follow up on the overall activities of the firm. As part of the agreement, Islamic banks will share in both profits and losses with its partners or clients in the operations of the business.

Musharakah is currently not that actively practiced in Malaysia. However, it is seen as one of the most effective way, to help in driving the 'Halal Goods' industry in Malaysia. In this regard, the Malaysian Government is pushing banks to finance viable projects involving the halal business. This includes various business segments such as real estate, construction, manufacturing, plantations, halal food, automotive, and oil and gas. Hence, it is an ideal alternative for the interest-based financing with far-reaching effects on both production and distribution.

1.7.5 Musharakah in Venture Financing

From an Islamic point of view, venture capital is based on Musharakah, and it falls within the framework of Islamic finance. It, therefore, combines economic viability and Islamic compliance and makes it a promising option for Islamic financial institutions. Venture capitalists normally provide financing to small start-up companies, which are expected to go for listing within a year. The financing process is done in stages, and the amount of capital given at each stage is sufficient only to reach the next stage. Venture capitalists do take an active role in the recipient companies through membership on boards of directors. Both parties share profits on a pre-agreed ratio, but losses are shared on the basis of equity participation.

Example

XYZ Islamic Bank injected RM 1 Million in a new start-up company ABC Sdn. Bhd. The percentage of ownership held by the bank is, say,

50%, and the rest is owned by the director of ABC. Let us assume that at the time of exiting, the company's value is RM 10 Million. Hence, the bank will earn RM 5 Million (i.e. 50% of RM 10 Million) as revenue. The actual profit earned by the bank will be RM 4 Million (i.e. RM 5 Million—RM 1 Million).

Under Musharakah venture, the Islamic bank does not intend to own the business on a permanent basis. Normally, the stages for investment could be as follows:

1. *Seed Stage*: Under this stage, the Islamic bank provides seed capital, which is used to purchase equity-based interest in a new or existing company. This seed capital is usually quite small because the venture is still in the idea or conceptual stage. The financing at this stage is considered extremely risky.
2. *Expansion Stage*: Under this stage, the Islamic bank offers an additional capital to expand marketing and to meet growing working capital needs of an enterprise that has commenced production but does not have positive cash flows sufficient to take care of its growing needs. Usually at this stage, the company has started turning profitable.
3. *Mezzanine Level*: At mezzanine level, a company is somewhere between start-up and Initial Public Offering (IPO) stage. An Islamic bank committed at mezzanine level usually has less risk but less potential appreciation than at the start-up level, and more risk but more potential appreciation than in an IPO.

Normally for a successful venture capital financing, the Islamic bank has to do the initial screening of the business plan and ensure that the business is in line with Syariah requirements. This is followed by detailed due diligence checks on the entrepreneur to measure the level of trustworthiness and individual credibility based on industry studies, study of financial statements, research on business viability and demand, visits to firm, and discussions with key employees, customers, suppliers, and creditors. This helps the banks in mitigating the risk prior to signing an agreement with the entrepreneur, and the rest can be covered under the agreement as explained under 'Essential Elements of Musharakah Contract' with a clear term, profit- and loss-sharing, and exit plan as well.

1.7.6 Challenges in Implementing Musharakah

Banks do face challenges in implementing Musharakah as a mode of financing although it is the most desired form of financing in the eyes of Syariah. It is sometimes presumed that Musharakah is an old instrument which cannot keep pace with the ever advancing need for speedy transactions. However, this presumption is due to the lack of proper knowledge concerning the principles of Musharakah. In fact, Islam has not prescribed a specific form or procedure for Musharakah. Rather, it has set some broad principles which can accommodate numerous forms and procedures. A new form or procedure in Musharakah cannot be rejected merely because it has no precedent in the past. In fact, every new form can be acceptable to Syariah insofar as it does not violate any basic principle laid down by the Quran, the Sunnah or the consensus of the Muslim jurists. Therefore, it is not necessary that Musharakah be implemented only in its traditional form.

The profit- and loss-financing techniques are extremely vulnerable to the problems of moral hazard. Information uncertainty may lead the bank to choose weak and dishonest enterprise. It may be difficult to review the actual working results of the firm because of the widespread malpractice of defaulting profits and losses. The bank normally finds lack of honesty and trustworthiness among entrepreneurs. Some of them did not declare their profits while others did not possess the skill to engage in business. This can be eliminated by performing detailed due diligence and by frequent management and performance reviews by participating in board meetings or other regular meetings. To do this, the bank needs to have skilled resources with good operational and management skill to protect the bank's interest.

Musharakah financing is normally for long-term financing and it involves higher risks and there is a lack of qualified personnel to undertake the operation. To overcome this problem, the bank can set up an Islamic investment company with professional consultants. This company will firstly identify the potential sectors such as manufacturing, agriculture, services, and small- and medium-sized industries. They will then evaluate each project based on its economic and financial viability, and propose it to the bank for funds. The final decision for approval will rest with the Islamic bank.

Lack of strong, reliable, and efficient project appraisal mechanisms is also a hindrance in extending finance on the basis of profit- and loss-sharing. This is the main reason why the Islamic banks are relying more on mark-up-based financing techniques as compared to profit- and loss-sharing financing techniques. This could be overcome by setting up a specialized Islamic investment company. It all boils down to the bank's ambition and aggressiveness: there are means to address the mentioned challenges.

The fact is that the Islamic banks should advance toward practicing Musharakah in gradual phases and should head toward increasing the size of Musharakah financing. No doubt challenges are there, but at the same point it can be addressed as well. Some Islamic banks in Malaysia are using Musharakah for project financing.

1.7.7 Comparison Between Mudharabah and Musharakah

It has to be noted that there are huge differences between Musharakah and Mudharabah contracts, and they are summarized in the following points:

1. *Investment*: The investment under Musharakah comes from all the partners, while under Mudharabah, investment is the sole responsibility of the rabbul-maal (investor) and the mudarib (entrepreneur) only offers his skill to run the business.
2. *Participation in Management*: In Musharakah, all the partners can participate in the management of the business and can work for it, while in Mudharabah, the rabbul-maal has no right to participate in the management which is carried out by the mudarib only.
3. *Profit and Loss-Sharing*: In Musharakah, all the partners share the loss to the extent of the ratio of their investment, while in Mudharabah, the loss if any, is suffered by the rabbul-maal only, because the mudarib does not invest anything. His loss is restricted to the fact that his labor has gone in vain and his work has not bore any fruits for him. However, this principle is subject to a condition that the mudarib has worked with due diligence which is normally required for the business of that type. If he has worked with negligence or has committed dishonesty, he shall be liable for the loss caused by his negligence or misconduct.

4. *Partner's Liability*: The liability of the partners in Musharakah is normally unlimited. Therefore, if the liabilities of the business exceed its assets and the business goes into liquidation, all the exceeding liabilities shall be borne pro rata by all the partners. However, if all the partners have agreed that no partner shall incur any debts during the course of business, then the exceeding liabilities shall be borne by that partner alone who has incurred a debt on the business in violation of the aforesaid condition. Contrary to this is the case of Mudharabah. Here the liability of rabbul-maal is limited to his investment, unless he has permitted the mudarib to incur debts on his behalf.
5. *Ownership of Assets*: In Musharakah, as soon as the partners mix up their capital in a joint pool, all the assets of the Musharakah become jointly owned by all of them according to the proportion of their respective investment. Therefore, each one of them can benefit from the appreciation in the value of the assets, even if profit has not accrued through sales. The case of Mudharabah is different. Here all the goods purchased by the mudarib are solely owned by the rabbul-maal, and the mudarib can earn his share in the profit only in case he sells the goods profitably. Therefore, he is not entitled to claim his share in the assets themselves, even if the value has increased.

1.8 Diminishing Musharakah

Digressive or diminishing Musharakah is a special form of Musharakah which ultimately culminates in the ownership of the asset or the project by the client. Under this concept, normally the bank participates as a financial partner, in full or in part, for a project or business venture. The agreement clearly stipulates profit-sharing ratio among the partners and also a clear definition of the portion of profit to be paid by partner to the bank as a repayment of the funds provided by the bank. In this way, the bank's share of the equity is progressively reduced and the partner eventually becomes the full owner. Under this partnership model, the bank agrees to accept payment on an instalment basis or in one lump sum from the partner to sell the bank's partnership interest. In this way, as the bank receives payments over and above its share in partnership profits, its partnership interest reduces until it is completely bought out of the partnership. After the discharge, the bank withdraws its claims from the firm and the partner (customer) becomes the sole proprietor or owner of the property.

Diminishing Musharakah utilizes Musharakah mutanaqisah as an underlying financing principle. It is an innovative and flexible tool for Islamic financing in the area of business working capital, asset acquisition, and property venture.

1.8.1 *Modus Operandi* of Diminishing Musharakah

Diminishing Musharakah process is more complex in comparison with the permanent Musharakah. Under this contract, the bank does not intend to remain associated with the client indefinitely. Instead, the Islamic bank offers its partner the right to repurchase its share in the capital of partnership in accordance with the agreement. This model is very much practiced for house financing. Under Musharakah mutanaqisah, there are two portions of the contract, that is, shirkat-al-milk (joint ownership of the asset) of the house. Then the house is leased to the customer under the concept of Ijarah (leasing) and the rental income earned is shared between the bank and the customer based on an agreed ratio. In addition to rental, the customer will pay a fixed payment to buy the bank's capital portion.

The *modus operandi* of diminishing Musharakah for house financing is illustrated in the following picture (Fig. 6.11):

Step 1: The client approaches the housing developer/seller and identifies the house or asset he wishes to buy. He requests the seller to provide a price quotation and other relevant details.
Step 2: The seller provides the price quotation, brochure, terms and conditions, and other relevant details requested by the customer.
Step 3: The customer approaches the bank along with the necessary supportive documents on the asset for financing using diminishing Musharakah as an underlying contract. The customer promises to take the house on lease and the payment of capital portion to own the house.

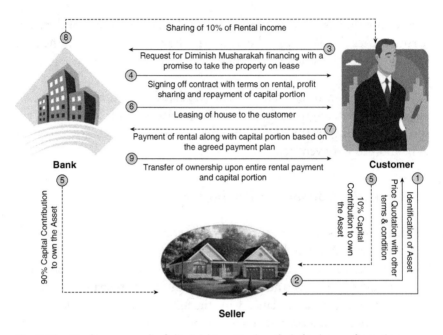

Fig. 6.11 *Modus operandi* of diminishing Musharakah for house financing

Step 4: Based upon the customer's credit worthiness, the bank will sign a diminishing Musharakah contract with clear terms on profit-sharing, loss-sharing, monthly rental payment, and repayment of capital portion, tenure, and other necessary conditions.

Step 5: The customer and the bank contribute the capital (90:10 ratio) to own the house and share the responsibilities as per the pre-agreed terms in the contract.

Step 6: The house is leased to the customer by the bank based on the agreed rental terms in the contract.

Step 7: The customer pays the rental along with the fixed capital portion based on the agreed payment plan.

Step 8: The periodic rental amount will be jointly shared between the customer and the bank according to the percentage share-holding at the particular time, because it keeps on changing as the customer redeems the bank's capital portion. The customer's sharing ratio will increase after each rental payment.

Step 9: The transfer of ownership of the house is upon the entire payment of rental and the bank's capital portion. Eventually, the house is fully owned by the customer.

1.8.2   Diminishing Musharakah in Financing Practice

The decreasing Musharakah is suitable for the finance of industrial establishments, house financing, farms, hospitals, and every project capable of producing regular income. The scholars agreed that it is best to implement diminishing Musharakah partnership for house financing or machinery financing whereby both assets can be leased out according to agreed rental. Joint ownership of a house or machinery is accepted by all schools of Islamic jurisprudence since the financier sells its shares to the customer (Usmani, 2002). The concept of diminishing Musharakah is not confined to home ownership only. It can also be applied to other forms of acquiring assets such as buying a car or a taxi to earn an income by using it as a hired vehicle creating joint ownership in the form of shirkah al-milk as allowed in Syariah.

These days, diminishing Musharakah is considered to be an appropriate mode to finance collective investment due to the benefits to the respective parties as mentioned below:

1. *The Bank's Perspective*: It earns periodical profit all the year round.
2. *The Partner's Perspective*: It encourages the partner to participate in halal investment. It realizes the customer's ambition to individually own the asset/project in the short run when the bank withdraws gradually.
3. *The Society's Perspective*: It corrects the course of the economy by developing the mode of positive partnership instead of the negative relationship of indebtedness. By doing so, it achieves equity in distributing the results.

This product is currently not offered by any of the Malaysian banks but few banks are in the process of implementation. The concepts have been adopted and practiced by other Islamic financial services providers worldwide. Successful cooperative-type models include the Islamic Housing Co-operative (Canada), Ansar Co-operative Housing (Canada), and the

Ansar Housing Limited (UK). In Pakistan, Meezan Bank's Easy Home scheme was the first diminishing Musharakah-based home financing facility. In addition, there are two financial institutions that have adopted the Musharakah mutanaqisah model in the UK and Ireland: Lloyds TSB and Bristol & West (in partnership with Arab Banking Corporation).

1.8.3 Diminishing Musharakah Financing Computation

This product is currently not offered in Malaysia. Based on our research and various papers published by authors on the practice of diminishing Musharakah in other countries, the popular computation logic is illustrated in Table 6.16:

Example

Munif wishes to buy a house priced at RM500,000 and he is willing to pay 10% of the price as part of his capital. He is also willing to opt for the leasing. The Islamic bank agrees to fund the 90%, that is, remaining RM450,000, and the current prevailing rent for similar houses in the locality is RM2,500. Munif wants to buy-back capital portion of the bank in 20 years. The computation of various components is as below:

Table 6.16 Diminishing Musharakah financing computation

Component	Computation formula	Details
Annual rate of return (P %)	$\dfrac{R \times 100 \times T}{TE}$	R = Monthly rental T = Time period can be month or year TE = Total equity
Monthly periodic capital payment (PCP)	$\dfrac{i\left[TE - (1+i)^n CE\right]}{(1+i)^n - 1}$	i = Periodic profit rate p.a. or CRR rate TE = Total equity CE_0 = Customer's initial equity n = Total number of periodic payments
Customer's present investment CE_n	$CE_{n-1} + CSR + PCP$	CSR = Customer's share in rent CE_{n-1} = Customer's equity as of last month PCP = Monthly periodic capital payment
Revenue sharing	$CE_n \times R/TE$	CE_n = Customer's investment as of date R = Monthly rental TE = Total equity

Step 1: Computation of annual rate of return

Annual rate of return (P%)	$\dfrac{R \times 100 \times T}{TE}$	R = 2500 T = 12 months TE = 500,000
	$= (2{,}500 \times 100 \times 12) / 500{,}000$	
	$= (3{,}000{,}000) / 500{,}000$	
	$= 6\%$	

Step 2: Computation of monthly periodic capital payment (PCP)

Monthly periodic capital payment (PCP)	$\dfrac{i\left[TE - (1+i)^n\, CE\right]}{(1+i)^n - 1}$	$i = 6/1200 = 0.005$ TE = 500,000 n = 20 years × 12 months = 240 CE = 50,000

$$= \dfrac{0.005\left[500{,}000 - (1+0.005)^{240} \times 50{,}000\right]}{(1+0.005)^{240} - 1}$$

$$= \dfrac{0.005\left[500{,}000 - 3.3102 \times 50{,}000\right]}{3.3102 - 1}$$

$$= \dfrac{0.005\left[500{,}000 - 3.3102 \times 50{,}000\right]}{3.3102 - 1}$$

$$= \dfrac{0.005\left[500{,}000 - 165{,}510\right]}{2.3102}$$

$$= \dfrac{0.005\left[334{,}490\right]}{2.3102}$$

$$= \dfrac{1672.45}{2.3102}$$

$$= 723.94$$

Step 3: Computation of customer's present investment (for the first month)

Customer's present investment (CE_1)	$CE_{n-1} + CSR + PCP$	$CE_{n-1} = 50,000$ CSR = RM 250 (10% of RM 2500) PCP = 723.94
	= 50,000 + 250 + 723.94	
	= 50,000 + 973.94	
	= 50,973.94	

Step 4: Payment schedule for diminishing Musharakah (Table 6.17)

From the above payment schedule, it is clear that at the end of the tenure, the customer owns 100% and bank ownership is 0%.

1.8.4 Comparison Between Diminishing Musharakah and BBA Financing

In Malaysia, BBA is heavily used for house financing. The main differences between the joint ownership (diminishing Musharakah) and the debt-type (BBA) financing are listed in Table 6.18.

1.9 Bai Salam Financing

Bai salam is a deferred delivery contract, whereby the seller undertakes to supply some specific goods to the buyer at a future date in exchange for an advanced price fully paid on the spot. It is normally used as the underlying principle for agriculture financing, whereby small farmers need money to grow their crops and to feed their family up to the time of harvest. Under this contract, the farmer will undertake to supply crops of a specific quality and quantity to the bank at a future date in exchange of an advance price fully paid at the time of contract. It is necessary that the quality of the commodity intended to be purchased is fully specified leaving no room for ambiguity. The bank will then sell the crops and the

Table 6.17 Shareholding

No.	TI	Shareholding customer %	customer RM	Bank %	Bank RM	Rental	PCP	Sharing of rent Cust.	Sharing of rent Bank	Total Pymnt
0	500,000	10	50,000	90	450,000	2500.00	723.94	250	2,250.00	3,223.94
1	500,000	10.195	50,974	89.805	449,026	2500.00	723.94	254.870	2,245.13	3,223.94
2	500,000	10.391	51,953	89.609	448,047	2500.00	723.94	259.764	2,240.24	3,223.94
3	500,000	10.587	52,936	89.413	447,064	2500.00	723.94	264.682	2,235.32	3,223.94
4	500,000	10.785	53,925	89.215	446,075	2500.00	723.94	269.625	2230.37	3,223.94
5	500,000	10.984	54,919	89.016	445,081	2500.00	723.94	274.593	2,225.41	3,223.94
6	500,000	11.183	55,917	88.817	444,083	2500.00	723.94	279.586	2,220.41	3,223.94
7	500,000	11.384	56,921	88.616	443,079	2500.00	723.94	284.604	2,215.40	3,223.94
8	500,000	11.586	57,929	88.414	442,071	2500.00	723.94	289.646	2,210.35	3,223.94
9	500,000	11.789	58,943	88.211	441,057	2500.00	723.94	294.714	2,205.29	3,223.94
10	500,000	11.992	59,961	88.008	440,039	2500.00	723.94	299.807	2,200.19	3,223.94
11	500,000	12.197	60,985	87.803	439,015	2500.00	723.94	304.926	2,195.07	3,223.94
12	500,000	12.403	62,014	87.597	437,986	2500.00	723.94	310.070	2,189.93	3,223.94
13	500,000	12.610	63,048	87.390	436,952	2500.00	723.94	315.241	2,184.76	3,223.94
14	500,000	12.817	64,087	87.183	435,913	2500.00	723.94	320.436	2,179.56	3,223.94
15	500,000	13.026	65,132	86.974	434,868	2500.00	723.94	325.658	2,174.34	3,223.94
16	500,000	13.236	66,181	86.764	433,819	2500.00	723.94	330.906	2,169.09	3,223.94
17	500,000	13.447	67,236	86.553	432,764	2500.00	723.94	336.181	2,163.82	3,223.94
18	500,000	13.659	68,296	86.341	431,704	2500.00	723.94	341.481	2,158.52	3,223.94
19	500,000	13.872	69,362	86.128	430,638	2500.00	723.94	346.808	2,153.19	3,223.94
20	500,000	14.086	70,432	85.914	429,568	2500.00	723.94	352.162	2,147.84	3,223.94
21	500,000	14.302	71,509	85.698	428,491	2500.00	723.94			

(continued)

Table 6.17 (continued)

No.	TI	Shareholding				Rental	PCP	Sharing of rent			Total Pymnt
		customer		Bank							
		%	RM	%	RM			Cust.	Bank		
22	500,000	14.518	72,590	85.482	427,410	2500.00	723.94	357.543	2,142.46		3,223.94
23	500,000	14.735	73,677	85.265	426,323	2500.00	723.94	362.950	2,137.05		3,223.94
24	500,000	14.954	74,769	85.046	425,231	2500.00	723.94	368.384	2,131.62		3,223.94
25	500,000	15.173	75,867	84.827	424,133	2500.00	723.94	373.846	2,126.15		3,223.94
26	500,000	15.394	76,970	84.606	423,030	2500.00	723.94	379.335	2,120.67		3,223.94
27	500,000	15.616	78,079	84.384	421,921	2500.00	723.94	384.851	2,115.15		3,223.94
28	500,000	15.839	79,193	84.161	420,807	2500.00	723.94	390.395	2,109.60		3,223.94
29	500,000	16.063	80,313	83.937	419,687	2500.00	723.94	395.967	2,104.03		3,223.94
30	500,000	16.288	81,439	83.712	418,561	2500.00	723.94	401.566	2,098.43		3,223.94
31	500,000	16.514	82,570	83.486	417,430	2500.00	723.94	407.194	2,092.81		3,223.94
32	500,000	16.741	83,707	83.259	416,293	2500.00	723.94	412.850	2,087.15		3,223.94
33	500,000	16.970	84,849	83.030	415,151	2500.00	723.94	418.534	2,081.47		3,223.94
34	500,000	17.199	85,997	82.801	414,003	2500.00	723.94	424.246	2,075.75		3,223.94
35	500,000	17.430	87,151	82.570	412,849	2500.00	723.94	429.987	2,070.01		3,223.94
36	500,000	17.662	88,311	82.338	411,689	2500.00	723.94	435.757	2,064.24		3,223.94
37	500,000	17.895	89,477	82.105	410,523	2500.00	723.94	441.555	2,058.44		3,223.94
38	500,000	18.130	90,648	81.870	409,352	2500.00	723.94	447.383	2,052.62		3,223.94
39	500,000	18.365	91,825	81.635	408,175	2500.00	723.94	453.239	2,046.76		3,223.94
40	500,000	18.602	93,008	81.398	406,992	2500.00	723.94	459.125	2,040.87		3,223.94
41	500,000	18.839	94,197	81.161	405,803	2500.00	723.94	465.040	2,034.96		3,223.94
42	500,000	19.078	95,392	80.922	404,608	2500.00	723.94	470.985	2,029.01		3,223.94
43	500,000	19.319	96,593	80.681	403,407	2500.00	723.94	476.960	2,023.04		3,223.94
44	500,000	19.560	97,800	80.440	402,200	2500.00	723.94	482.964	2,017.04		3,223.94
45	500,000	19.803	99,013	80.197	400,987	2500.00	723.94	488.999	2,011.00		3,223.94
46	500,000	20.046	100,232	79.954	399,768	2500.00	723.94	495.064	2,004.94		3,223.94

(continued)

Table 6.17 (continued)

No.	TI	Shareholding customer %	Shareholding customer RM	Shareholding Bank %	Shareholding Bank RM	Rental	PCP	Sharing of rent Cust.	Sharing of rent Bank	Total Pymnt
47	500,000	20.291	101,457	79.709	398,543	2500.00	723.94	501.159	1,998.84	3,223.94
48	500,000	20.538	102,688	79.462	397,312	2500.00	723.94	507.284	1,992.72	3,223.94
49	500,000	20.785	103,925	79.215	396,075	2500.00	723.94	513.440	1,986.56	3,223.94
50	500,000	21.034	105,169	78.966	394,831	2500.00	723.94	519.627	1,980.37	3,223.94
51	500,000	21.284	106,419	78.716	393,581	2500.00	723.94	525.845	1,974.16	3,223.94
52	500,000	21.535	107,675	78.465	392,325	2500.00	723.94	532.094	1,967.91	3,223.94
53	500,000	21.787	108,937	78.213	391,063	2500.00	723.94	538.374	1,961.63	3,223.94
54	500,000	22.041	110,206	77.959	389,794	2500.00	723.94	544.686	1,955.31	3,223.94
55	500,000	22.296	111,481	77.704	388,519	2500.00	723.94	551.029	1,948.97	3,223.94
56	500,000	22.552	112,762	77.448	387,238	2500.00	723.94	557.404	1,942.60	3,223.94
57	500,000	22.810	114,050	77.190	385,950	2500.00	723.94	563.810	1,936.19	3,223.94
58	500,000	23.069	115,344	76.931	384,656	2500.00	723.94	570.249	1,929.75	3,223.94
59	500,000	23.329	116,645	76.671	383,355	2500.00	723.94	576.720	1,923.28	3,223.94
60	500,000	23.590	117,952	76.410	382,048	2500.00	723.94	583.223	1,916.78	3,223.94
61	500,000	23.853	119,266	76.147	380,734	2500.00	723.94	589.759	1,910.24	3,223.94
62	500,000	24.117	120,586	75.883	379,414	2500.00	723.94	596.328	1,903.67	3,223.94
63	500,000	24.383	121,913	75.617	378,087	2500.00	723.94	602.929	1,897.07	3,223.94
64	500,000	24.649	123,246	75.351	376,754	2500.00	723.94	609.563	1,890.44	3,223.94
65	500,000	24.917	124,586	75.083	375,414	2500.00	723.94	616.231	1,883.77	3,223.94
66	500,000	25.187	125,933	74.813	374,067	2500.00	723.94	622.932	1,877.07	3,223.94
67	500,000	25.457	127,287	74.543	372,713	2500.00	723.94	629.666	1,870.33	3,223.94
68	500,000	25.729	128,647	74.271	371,353	2500.00	723.94	636.434	1,863.57	3,223.94
69	500,000	26.003	130,014	73.997	369,986	2500.00	723.94	643.236	1,856.76	3,223.94
70	500,000	26.278	131,388	73.722	368,612	2500.00	723.94	650.072	1,849.93	3,223.94

(continued)

Table 6.17 (continued)

No.	TI	Shareholding customer %	Shareholding customer RM	Shareholding Bank %	Shareholding Bank RM	Rental	PCP	Sharing of rent Cust.	Sharing of rent Bank	Total Pymnt
71	500,000	26.554	132,769	73.446	367,231	2500.00	723.94	656.942	1,843.06	3,223.94
72	500,000	26.831	134,157	73.169	365,843	2500.00	723.94	663.846	1,836.15	3,223.94
73	500,000	27.110	135,552	72.890	364,448	2500.00	723.94	670.785	1,829.21	3,223.94
74	500,000	27.391	136,953	72.609	363,047	2500.00	723.94	677.759	1,822.24	3,223.94
75	500,000	27.672	138,362	72.328	361,638	2500.00	723.94	684.767	1,815.23	3,223.94
76	500,000	27.956	139,778	72.044	360,222	2500.00	723.94	691.811	1,808.19	3,223.94
77	500,000	28.240	141,201	71.760	358,799	2500.00	723.94	698.890	1,801.11	3,223.94
78	500,000	28.526	142,631	71.474	357,369	2500.00	723.94	706.004	1,794.00	3,223.94
79	500,000	28.814	144,068	71.186	355,932	2500.00	723.94	713.153	1,786.85	3,223.94
80	500,000	29.102	145,512	70.898	354,488	2500.00	723.94	720.339	1,779.66	3,223.94
81	500,000	29.393	146,964	70.607	353,036	2500.00	723.94	727.560	1,772.44	3,223.94
82	500,000	29.684	148,422	70.316	351,578	2500.00	723.94	734.818	1,765.18	3,223.94
83	500,000	29.978	149,888	70.022	350,112	2500.00	723.94	742.112	1,757.89	3,223.94
84	500,000	30.272	151,362	69.728	348,638	2500.00	723.94	749.442	1,750.56	3,223.94
85	500,000	30.569	152,843	69.431	347,157	2500.00	723.94	756.809	1,743.19	3,223.94
86	500,000	30.866	154,331	69.134	345,669	2500.00	723.94	764.213	1,735.79	3,223.94
87	500,000	31.165	155,826	68.835	344,174	2,500.00	723.94	771.653	1,728.35	3,223.94
88	500,000	31.466	157,329	68.534	342,671	2,500.00	723.94	779.131	1,720.87	3,223.94
89	500,000	31.768	158,840	68.232	341,160	2500.00	723.94	786.647	1,713.35	3,223.94
90	500,000	32.072	160,358	67.928	339,642	2500.00	723.94	794.200	1,705.80	3,223.94
91	500,000	32.377	161,884	67.623	338,116	2500.00	723.94	801.790	1,698.21	3,223.94
92	500,000	32.683	163,417	67.317	336,583	2500.00	723.94	809.419	1,690.58	3,223.94
93	500,000	32.992	164,958	67.008	335,042	2500.00	723.94	817.086	1,682.91	3,223.94
94	500,000	33.301	166,507	66.699	333,493	2500.00	723.94	824.791	1,675.21	3,223.94
95	500,000	33.613	168,063	66.387	331,937	2500.00	723.94	832.534	1,667.47	3,223.94

(continued)

Table 6.17 (continued)

No.	TI	Shareholding customer %	Shareholding customer RM	Shareholding Bank %	Shareholding Bank RM	Rental	PCP	Sharing of rent Cust.	Sharing of rent Bank	Total Pymnt
96	500,000	33.926	169,628	66.074	330,372	2500.00	723.94	840.317	1,659.68	3,223.94
97	500,000	34.240	171,200	65.760	328,800	2500.00	723.94	848.138	1,651.86	3,223.94
98	500,000	34.556	172,780	65.444	327,220	2500.00	723.94	855.999	1,644.00	3,223.94
99	500,000	34.873	174,367	65.127	325,633	2500.00	723.94	863.898	1,636.10	3,223.94
100	500,000	35.193	175,963	64.807	324,037	2500.00	723.94	871.837	1,628.16	3,223.94
101	500,000	35.513	177,567	64.487	322,433	2500.00	723.94	879.816	1,620.18	3,223.94
102	500,000	35.836	179,179	64.164	320,821	2500.00	723.94	887.835	1,612.16	3,223.94
103	500,000	36.160	180,799	63.840	319,201	2500.00	723.94	895.894	1,604.11	3,223.94
104	500,000	36.485	182,427	63.515	317,573	2500.00	723.94	903.993	1,596.01	3,223.94
105	500,000	36.813	184,063	63.187	315,937	2500.00	723.94	912.133	1,587.87	3,223.94
106	500,000	37.141	185,707	62.859	314,293	2500.00	723.94	920.313	1,579.69	3,223.94
107	500,000	37.472	187,359	62.528	312,641	2500.00	723.94	928.534	1,571.47	3,223.94
108	500,000	37.804	189,020	62.196	310,980	2500.00	723.94	936.797	1,563.20	3,223.94
109	500,000	38.138	190,689	61.862	309,311	2500.00	723.94	945.100	1,554.90	3,223.94
110	500,000	38.473	192,367	61.527	307,633	2500.00	723.94	953.446	1,546.55	3,223.94
111	500,000	38.810	194,052	61.190	305,948	2500.00	723.94	961.833	1,538.17	3,223.94
112	500,000	39.149	195,746	60.851	304,254	2500.00	723.94	970.261	1,529.74	3,223.94
113	500,000	39.490	197,449	60.510	302,551	2500.00	723.94	978.732	1,521.27	3,223.94
114	500,000	39.832	199,160	60.168	300,840	2500.00	723.94	987.246	1,512.75	3,223.94
115	500,000	40.176	200,880	59.824	299,120	2500.00	723.94	995.802	1,504.20	3,223.94
116	500,000	40.522	202,608	59.478	297,392	2500.00	723.94	1004.400	1,495.60	3,223.94
117	500,000	40.869	204,345	59.131	295,655	2500.00	723.94	1013.042	1,486.96	3,223.94
118	500,000	41.218	206,091	58.782	293,909	2500.00	723.94	1021.727	1,478.27	3,223.94
119	500,000	41.569	207,845	58.431	292,155	2500.00	723.94	1030.455	1,469.54	3,223.94

(continued)

Table 6.17 (continued)

No.	TI	Shareholding customer %	Shareholding customer RM	Shareholding Bank %	Shareholding Bank RM	Rental	PCP	Sharing of rent Cust.	Sharing of rent Bank	Total Pymnt
120	500,000	41.922	209,609	58.078	290,391	2500.00	723.94	1039.227	1,460.77	3,223.94
121	500,000	42.276	211,381	57.724	288,619	2500.00	723.94	1048.043	1,451.96	3,223.94
122	500,000	42.632	213,161	57.368	286,839	2500.00	723.94	1056.903	1,443.10	3,223.94
123	500,000	42.990	214,951	57.010	285,049	2500.00	723.94	1065.807	1,434.19	3,223.94
124	500,000	43.350	216,750	56.650	283,250	2500.00	723.94	1074.756	1,425.24	3,223.94
125	500,000	43.712	218,558	56.288	281,442	2500.00	723.94	1083.750	1,416.25	3,223.94
126	500,000	44.075	220,374	55.925	279,626	2500.00	723.94	1092.788	1,407.21	3,223.94
127	500,000	44.440	222,200	55.560	277,800	2500.00	723.94	1101.872	1,398.13	3,223.94
128	500,000	44.807	224,035	55.193	275,965	2500.00	723.94	1111.001	1,389.00	3,223.94
129	500,000	45.176	225,879	54.824	274,121	2500.00	723.94	1120.175	1,379.82	3,223.94
130	500,000	45.547	227,733	54.453	272,267	2500.00	723.94	1129.396	1,370.60	3,223.94
131	500,000	45.919	229,595	54.081	270,405	2500.00	723.94	1138.663	1,361.34	3,223.94
132	500,000	46.293	231,467	53.707	268,533	2500.00	723.94	1147.976	1,352.02	3,223.94
133	500,000	46.670	233,348	53.330	266,652	2500.00	723.94	1157.335	1,342.66	3,223.94
134	500,000	47.048	235,239	52.952	264,761	2500.00	723.94	1166.742	1,333.26	3,223.94
135	500,000	47.428	237,139	52.572	262,861	2500.00	723.94	1176.195	1,323.80	3,223.94
136	500,000	47.810	239,049	52.190	260,951	2500.00	723.94	1185.696	1,314.30	3,223.94
137	500,000	48.194	240,968	51.806	259,032	2500.00	723.94	1195.244	1,304.76	3,223.94
138	500,000	48.579	242,897	51.421	257,103	2500.00	723.94	1204.840	1,295.16	3,223.94
139	500,000	48.967	244,835	51.033	255,165	2500.00	723.94	1214.484	1,285.52	3,223.94
140	500,000	49.357	246,783	50.643	253,217	2500.00	723.94	1224.176	1,275.82	3,223.94
141	500,000	49.748	248,741	50.252	251,259	2500.00	723.94	1233.916	1,266.08	3,223.94
142	500,000	50.142	250,709	49.858	249,291	2500.00	723.94	1243.706	1,256.29	3,223.94
143	500,000	50.537	252,686	49.463	247,314	2500.00	723.94	1253.544	1,246.46	3,223.94
144	500,000	50.935	254,674	49.065	245,326	2500.00	723.94	1263.431	1,236.57	3,223.94

(continued)

Table 6.17 (continued)

No.	TI	Shareholding customer %	Shareholding customer RM	Shareholding Bank %	Shareholding Bank RM	Rental	PCP	Sharing of rent Cust.	Sharing of rent Bank	Total Pymnt
145	500,000	51.334	256,671	48.666	243,329	2500.00	723.94	1273.368	1,226.63	3,223.94
146	500,000	51.736	258,678	48.264	241,322	2500.00	723.94	1283.355	1,216.65	3,223.94
147	500,000	52.139	260,696	47.861	239,304	2500.00	723.94	1293.391	1,206.61	3,223.94
148	500,000	52.545	262,723	47.455	237,277	2500.00	723.94	1303.478	1,196.52	3,223.94
149	500,000	52.952	264,761	47.048	235,239	2500.00	723.94	1313.615	1,186.38	3,223.94
150	500,000	53.362	266,808	46.638	233,192	2500.00	723.94	1323.803	1,176.20	3,223.94
151	500,000	53.773	268,866	46.227	231,134	2500.00	723.94	1334.041	1,165.96	3,223.94
152	500,000	54.187	270,935	45.813	229,065	2500.00	723.94	1344.331	1,155.67	3,223.94
153	500,000	54.603	273,013	45.397	226,987	2500.00	723.94	1354.673	1,145.33	3,223.94
154	500,000	55.020	275,102	44.980	224,898	2500.00	723.94	1365.066	1,134.93	3,223.94
155	500,000	55.440	277,202	44.560	222,798	2500.00	723.94	1375.511	1,124.49	3,223.94
156	500,000	55.862	279,312	44.138	220,688	2500.00	723.94	1386.008	1,113.99	3,223.94
157	500,000	56.286	281,432	43.714	218,568	2500.00	723.94	1396.558	1,103.44	3,223.94
158	500,000	56.713	283,563	43.287	216,437	2500.00	723.94	1407.160	1,092.84	3,223.94
159	500,000	57.141	285,705	42.859	214,295	2500.00	723.94	1417.816	1,082.18	3,223.94
160	500,000	57.571	287,857	42.429	212,143	2500.00	723.94	1428.525	1,071.48	3,223.94
161	500,000	58.004	290,021	41.996	209,979	2500.00	723.94	1439.287	1,060.71	3,223.94
162	500,000	58.439	292,195	41.561	207,805	2500.00	723.94	1450.103	1,049.90	3,223.94
163	500,000	58.876	294,380	41.124	205,620	2500.00	723.94	1460.973	1,039.03	3,223.94
164	500,000	59.315	296,575	40.685	203,425	2500.00	723.94	1471.898	1,028.10	3,223.94
165	500,000	59.756	298,782	40.244	201,218	2500.00	723.94	1482.877	1,017.12	3,223.94
166	500,000	60.200	301,000	39.800	199,000	2500.00	723.94	1493.911	1,006.09	3,223.94
167	500,000	60.646	303,229	39.354	196,771	2500.00	723.94	1505.000	995.00	3,223.94
168	500,000	61.094	305,469	38.906	194,531	2500.00	723.94	1516.145	983.85	3,223.94

(continued)

Table 6.17 (continued)

No.	TI	Shareholding customer %	Shareholding customer RM	Shareholding Bank %	Shareholding Bank RM	Rental	PCP	Sharing of rent Cust.	Sharing of rent Bank	Total Pymnt
169	500,000	61.544	307,720	38.456	192,280	2500.00	723.94	1527.346	972.65	3,223.94
170	500,000	61.997	309,983	38.003	190,017	2500.00	723.94	1538.602	961.40	3,223.94
171	500,000	62.451	312,257	37.549	187,743	2500.00	723.94	1549.915	950.09	3,223.94
172	500,000	62.908	314,542	37.092	185,458	2500.00	723.94	1561.284	938.72	3,223.94
173	500,000	63.368	316,839	36.632	183,161	2500.00	723.94	1572.710	927.29	3,223.94
174	500,000	63.829	319,147	36.171	180,853	2500.00	723.94	1584.193	915.81	3,223.94
175	500,000	64.293	321,466	35.707	178,534	2500.00	723.94	1595.734	904.27	3,223.94
176	500,000	64.760	323,798	35.240	176,202	2500.00	723.94	1607.332	892.67	3,223.94
177	500,000	65.228	326,141	34.772	173,859	2500.00	723.94	1618.989	881.01	3,223.94
178	500,000	65.699	328,495	34.301	171,505	2500.00	723.94	1630.703	869.30	3,223.94
179	500,000	66.172	330,862	33.828	169,138	2500.00	723.94	1642.477	857.52	3,223.94
180	500,000	66.648	333,240	33.352	166,760	2500.00	723.94	1654.309	845.69	3,223.94
181	500,000	67.126	335,630	32.874	164,370	2500.00	723.94	1666.200	833.80	3,223.94
182	500,000	67.606	338,032	32.394	161,968	2500.00	723.94	1678.151	821.85	3,223.94
183	500,000	68.089	340,446	31.911	159,554	2500.00	723.94	1690.161	809.84	3,223.94
184	500,000	68.574	342,872	31.426	157,128	2500.00	723.94	1702.232	797.77	3,223.94
185	500,000	69.062	345,311	30.938	154,689	2500.00	723.94	1714.362	785.64	3,223.94
186	500,000	69.552	347,761	30.448	152,239	2500.00	723.94	1726.554	773.45	3,223.94
187	500,000	70.045	350,224	29.955	149,776	2500.00	723.94	1738.806	761.19	3,223.94
188	500,000	70.540	352,699	29.460	147,301	2500.00	723.94	1751.120	748.88	3,223.94
189	500,000	71.037	355,187	28.963	144,813	2500.00	723.94	1763.495	736.50	3,223.94
190	500,000	71.537	357,686	28.463	142,314	2500.00	723.94	1775.933	724.07	3,223.94
191	500,000	72.040	360,199	27.960	139,801	2500.00	723.94	1788.432	711.57	3,223.94
192	500,000	72.545	362,724	27.455	137,276	2500.00	723.94	1800.994	699.01	3,223.94
193	500,000	73.052	365,261	26.948	134,739	2500.00	723.94	1813.618	686.38	3,223.94

(continued)

Table 6.17 (continued)

No.	TI	Shareholding customer %	Shareholding customer RM	Shareholding Bank %	Shareholding Bank RM	Rental	PCP	Sharing of rent Cust.	Sharing of rent Bank	Total Pymnt
194	500,000	73.562	367,812	26.438	132,188	2500.00	723.94	1826.306	673.69	3,223.94
195	500,000	74.075	370,374	25.925	129,626	2500.00	723.94	1839.058	660.94	3,223.94
196	500,000	74.590	372,950	25.410	127,050	2500.00	723.94	1851.872	648.13	3,223.94
197	500,000	75.108	375,539	24.892	124,461	2500.00	723.94	1864.752	635.25	3,223.94
198	500,000	75.628	378,141	24.372	121,859	2500.00	723.94	1877.695	622.30	3,223.94
199	500,000	76.151	380,755	23.849	119,245	2500.00	723.94	1890.703	609.30	3,223.94
200	500,000	76.677	383,383	23.323	116,617	2500.00	723.94	1903.776	596.22	3,223.94
201	500,000	77.205	386,024	22.795	113,976	2500.00	723.94	1916.915	583.09	3,223.94
202	500,000	77.736	388,678	22.264	111,322	2500.00	723.94	1930.119	569.88	3,223.94
203	500,000	78.269	391,345	21.731	108,655	2500.00	723.94	1943.390	556.61	3,223.94
204	500,000	78.805	394,026	21.195	105,974	2500.00	723.94	1956.726	543.27	3,223.94
205	500,000	79.344	396,720	20.656	103,280	2500.00	723.94	1970.130	529.87	3,223.94
206	500,000	79.886	399,428	20.114	100,572	2500.00	723.94	1983.600	516.40	3,223.94
207	500,000	80.430	402,149	19.570	97,851	2500.00	723.94	1997.138	502.86	3,223.94
208	500,000	80.977	404,883	19.023	95,117	2500.00	723.94	2010.743	489.26	3,223.94
209	500,000	81.526	407,632	18.474	92,368	2500.00	723.94	2024.416	475.58	3,223.94
210	500,000	82.079	410,394	17.921	89,606	2500.00	723.94	2038.158	461.84	3,223.94
211	500,000	82.634	413,170	17.366	86,830	2500.00	723.94	2051.969	448.03	3,223.94
212	500,000	83.192	415,959	16.808	84,041	2500.00	723.94	2065.848	434.15	3,223.94
213	500,000	83.753	418,763	16.247	81,237	2500.00	723.94	2079.797	420.20	3,223.94
214	500,000	84.316	421,581	15.684	78,419	2500.00	723.94	2093.816	406.18	3,223.94
215	500,000	84.883	424,413	15.117	75,587	2500.00	723.94	2107.905	392.10	3,223.94
216	500,000	85.452	427,259	14.548	72,741	2500.00	723.94	2122.064	377.94	3,223.94
217	500,000	86.024	430,119	13.976	69,881	2500.00	723.94	2136.294	363.71	3,223.94
218	500,000	86.599	432,994	13.401	67,006	2500.00	723.94	2150.595	349.40	3,223.94

(continued)

Table 6.17 (continued)

No.	TI	Shareholding customer %	Shareholding customer RM	Shareholding Bank %	Shareholding Bank RM	Rental	PCP	Sharing of rent Cust.	Sharing of rent Bank	Total Pymnt
219	500,000	87.176	435,882	12.824	64,118	2500.00	723.94	2164.968	335.03	3,223.94
220	500,000	87.757	438,786	12.243	61,214	2500.00	723.94	2179.412	320.59	3,223.94
221	500,000	88.341	441,704	11.659	58,296	2500.00	723.94	2193.929	306.07	3,223.94
222	500,000	88.927	444,636	11.073	55,364	2500.00	723.94	2208.518	291.48	3,223.94
223	500,000	89.517	447,583	10.483	52,417	2500.00	723.94	2223.181	276.82	3,223.94
224	500,000	90.109	450,545	9.891	49,455	2500.00	723.94	2237.916	262.08	3,223.94
225	500,000	90.704	453,522	9.296	46,478	2500.00	723.94	2252.726	247.27	3,223.94
226	500,000	91.303	456,513	8.697	43,487	2500.00	723.94	2267.609	232.39	3,223.94
227	500,000	91.904	459,520	8.096	40,480	2500.00	723.94	2282.567	217.43	3,223.94
228	500,000	92.508	462,541	7.492	37,459	2500.00	723.94	2297.599	202.40	3,223.94
229	500,000	93.116	465,578	6.884	34,422	2500.00	723.94	2312.707	187.29	3,223.94
230	500,000	93.726	468,630	6.274	31,370	2500.00	723.94	2327.890	172.11	3,223.94
231	500,000	94.339	471,697	5.661	28,303	2,500.00	723.94	2343.149	156.85	3,223.94
232	500,000	94.956	474,779	5.044	25,221	2,500.00	723.94	2358.485	141.52	3,223.94
233	500,000	95.575	477,877	4.425	22,123	2,500.00	723.94	2373.897	126.10	3,223.94
234	500,000	96.198	480,991	3.802	19,009	2,500.00	723.94	2389.386	110.61	3,223.94
235	500,000	96.824	484,119	3.176	15,881	2500.00	723.94	2404.953	95.05	3,223.94
236	500,000	97.453	487,264	2.547	12,736	2500.00	723.94	2420.597	79.40	3,223.94
237	500,000	98.085	490,424	1.915	9,576	2500.00	723.94	2436.320	63.68	3,223.94
238	500,000	98.720	493,600	1.280	6,400	2500.00	723.94	2452.121	47.88	3,223.94
239	500,000	99.358	496,792	0.642	3,208	2500.00	723.94	2468.001	32.00	3,223.94
240	500,000	100.000	500,000	0.000	0	2500.00	723.94	2483.961	16.04	3,223.94

Table 6.18 Comparison between diminishing Musharakah and BBA financing

Bai Bithaman Ajil (BBA)	Diminishing Musharakah (DM)
Number of contracts	
The BBA follows the Murabahah concept of buying and selling of property	There are two separate contracts under the MMP method. The first is a *Musharakah mutanaqisah* where the bank and the client enter into a joint partnership to own the house. The second contract is *Ijarah* which involves the leasing of the property to the partner
Reflection of market value	
Under BBA, the selling price of the house does not reflect the market value since the mark-up for the deferred payment is quite substantial	On the contrary, the value of the house under DM always reflects the market price and the rental is determined by the market rental values
Returns	
The return to the BBA is based on a fixed selling price	Under DM, the financer is not tied to a fixed profit rate throughout the financing tenor. This is because the rental rate can be revised periodically to reflect current market conditions. Indeed, the rental can be tied to some economic variables like Rental Index, House Price Index, and so on
Penalty	
In the event of payment defaults, the penalty charges under BBA can be challenged	Under DM, defaults will cause the equity of financier to remain constant and therefore entitled to higher rental portions when payments are made later
Product recognition	
The BBA is recognized predominantly in the east, that is, in Malaysia, Indonesia, Brunei, and so on	The DM is accepted globally as a *Syariah* compliant
Early settlement	
Customer is entitled for rebate in the event of early settlement	The DM is a more flexible financing structure as the customer can own the property earlier by redeeming faster the principal sum of the financier, without the need to compute rebates

(continued)

Table 6.18 (continued)

Bai Bithaman Ajil (BBA)	Diminishing Musharakah (DM)
Liquidity risk	
This is not possible under the fixed-rate BBA as the profit rate is constant throughout the entire tenor of financing	The financier can manage the liquidity risks better as rental payments can be adjusted at the end of each subcontract period

Source: Ahamed Kameel Mydin Meera & Dzuljastri Abdul Razak (2009), "Islamic Home Financing through Musharakah Mutanaqisah and al-Bay' Bithaman Ajil Contracts: A Comparative Analysis"

difference between the selling price and the purchase price is, therefore, the bank's profit. In essence, bai salam is a pre-payment sale, that is, contract of sale whereby payment is made today by the bank and goods are delivered in the future. Such an agreement benefits both parties:

1. The seller receives advance payment in exchange for the obligation to deliver the commodity at some later date. He benefits from the salam sale by locking in a price for his commodity, thereby allowing him to cover his financial needs whether they are personal expenses, family expenses, or business expenses.
2. The purchaser benefits because he receives delivery of the commodity when it is needed to fulfil some other agreement, without incurring storage costs. Second, a bai salam sale is usually less expensive than a cash sale. Finally, a bai salam agreement allows the purchase to lock in a price, thus protecting him from price fluctuation.

This is the only contract with an exception that the asset is sold before it exists and is in compliance with Syariah requirements.

1.9.1 Essential Elements of Bai Salam Contract

Bai salam is the sale of a deferred item in exchange for an immediate price. The permissibility of salam is an exception to the general rule that prohibits forward sale, and therefore, it is subject to the following strict conditions for a valid contract (Table 6.19).

Table 6.19 Essential elements of bai salam contract

Tenet	Mandatory characteristic/conditions	Prohibited characteristic/conditions
Buyer/seller	1. Must possess sound mind (aqil) 2. Must be at least 18 years old (attains the age of puberty—baligh) 3. Must be intelligent	1. Forced to enter into a contract 2. He must not be prohibited from dealing: (a) not bankrupt (b) not prodigal
Asset/merchandise	1. The commodity should not yet exist when the finance is provided 2. Must be of pure substance (lawful) 3. Must be of some use or some value 4. Must be able to be delivered by seller to the buyer 5. The object type, volume, weight, number, and size must be known to both the seller and buyer (i.e. full details of the goods is known to both parties)	1. Precious stones cannot be sold on the basis of salam because each stone differs in quality, size, and weight, and their exact specification is not possible 2. Salam cannot be affected on a particular commodity or on a product of a particular field or farm 3. Salam cannot be affected in respect of those things that must be delivered at the spot. For example, if gold is purchased in exchange of silver, it is necessary, according to Syariah, that the delivery of both be simultaneous. Here, Salam cannot work
Price	1. Spot settlement price must be known to both the seller and the buyer 2. Must be with the quantum and type of the currency specified 3. The price has to be paid in full to the seller at the time of effecting the sale	

(continued)

Table 6.19 (continued)

Tenet	Mandatory characteristic/conditions	Prohibited characteristic/conditions

Contract (aqad)—Offer and acceptance	1. Absolute and in definite and decisive language
	  (a) In the past or present tense
	  (b) Not in the future or imperative tense
	  (c) Not conditional
	  (d) Not limited to a certain period
	2. The acceptance must agree with the offer
	3. The offer and acceptance must be made at the one and same meeting or session
	4. The exact date and place of delivery must be specified in the contract	

1.9.2 *Modus Operandi* of Bai Salam Financing

Bai salam is a pre-payment sale and the *modus operandi* is as follows (Fig. 6.12):

Step 1: Submission of application form with necessary documents (identification credential, land ownership, other sources of income, past production volume) to the bank for credit screening.

Step 2: The bank will offer a purchase price to the farmer based on the credit worthiness evaluation, crop quality, delivery date, and so forth.

Step 3: The farmer accepts the offer and signs a bai salam contract stating predefined crop delivery date/crop quality between the farmer and the bank.

Step 4: The bank pays the settlement price on the spot as defined in the contract.

Step 5: The farmer delivers the crop to the bank based on the agreed specification and pre-defined' delivery date and venue.

Step 6: The bank sells the crop/object in the market at a selling price. The selling price will be higher than the purchase price (cash advanced to farmer under bai salam) and the difference will be the bank's profit.

1.9.3 Bai Salam Financing Practice

Bai salam is frequently used to finance the agricultural industry. Banks advance cash to the farmers today for delivery of the crop during the harvest season (future date). This helps farmers in meeting their working capital requirement for production and personal needs. It is a structured financing that can help farmers to move away from informal financing means such as money lenders, whereby they are charged a heavy interest on a compounding basis. To mitigate their risk at times, the bank also gets into parallel salam contract with the merchant for the same object/crop. Upon purchasing a commodity by way of bai salam, the banks may sell it through a parallel contract of bai salam for the same date of delivery. The period of bai salam in the second (parallel) transaction being

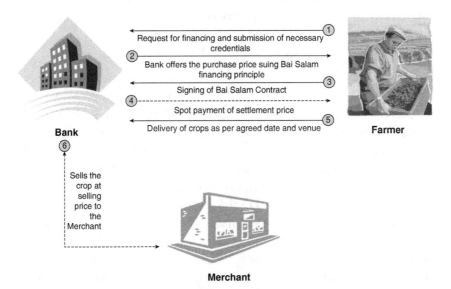

Fig. 6.12 *Modus operandi* of bai salam financing

shorter, the price may be a little higher than the price of the first transaction, and the difference between the two prices shall be the profit earned by the institution. The shorter the period of salam, the higher the price, and the greater the profit. The institutions may manage their short-term financing portfolios in this way. In an arrangement of a parallel salam, there must be two different but independent contracts; one where the bank is a buyer (i.e. between the farmer and the bank) and the other in which it is a seller (i.e. between the bank and the merchant). These two contracts cannot be tied together and the performance of one should not be contingent on the other (Usmani, 2002).

Bai salam is also used to finance commercial and industrial activities. Here again, the bank advances cash to the corporate customer to finance the cost of production, operations, and expenses in exchange for future delivery of the end product. In the meantime, the bank is able to market the product to other merchants at lucrative prices to earn profit. In addition, the salam sale is used by banks to finance craftsmen and small producers, by supplying them with the capital necessary to finance the inputs to production in exchange for the delivery of products at some future date. In addition, scholars are also working on using bai salam contract for derivatives and it is still at the research stage.

1.10 Istisna Financing

After bai salam, istisna is the second sale contract approved by Syariah whereby a commodity is transacted before it comes into existence. It means to order a manufacturer to manufacture a specific commodity for the purchaser. If the manufacture undertakes to manufacture the goods for him, the transaction of istisna comes into existence. It is necessary for the validity of istisna that the price is fixed with the consent of the parties and that necessary specification of the commodity (intended to be manufactured) is fully settled between them. The contract of istisna creates a moral obligation on the manufacturer to manufacture the goods, but before he starts the work, any one of the parties may cancel the contract after giving a notice to the other. But after the manufacturer has started the work, the contract cannot be cancelled unilaterally.

Under istisna, the work is not conditioned to be accomplished by the undertaking party, and this work or part of it can be done by others under his control and responsibility. The unique feature of istisna is that nothing is exchanged on the spot or at the time of contracting. It is a pure and perhaps the only forward contract where the obligations of both parties relate to the future. The buyer makes payment of price in parts over the agreed time period or in full at the end of the time period.

Hence, it is a contract to purchase for a definite price, something that may be manufactured later on according to agreed specifications between the parties. In other words, it is a contract of sale of specified items to be manufactured or constructed with an obligation on the part of the manufacturer or contractor to deliver them to the customer upon completion. Basically, istisna financing is also a transaction of sale and purchase in instalments, much like a Bai Bithaman Ajil (BBA) financing, but the only difference is that the asset is delivered in advance of the instalment under BBA, while in istisna, the goods are deferred although the payment is also made in instalment. The only difference here is the time of delivery.

1.10.1 Structuring an Istisna Financing Transaction

Step 1: The client approaches the housing developer/seller and identifies the house or asset he wishes to buy. He requests the seller to provide a price quotation and other relevant details.

Step 2: The seller provides the price quotation, brochure, terms and conditions and other relevant details requested by the customer.

Step 3: The customer approaches the bank along with the necessary supportive documents on the asset for financing of the house purchasing. The customer provides the detailed house specification and delivery date.

Step 4: Based upon screening of customer's credit worthiness, the bank will sign an istisna contract with clear terms on price, delivery date, specification, payment plan, and other necessary conditions.

Step 5: The bank enters into a parallel istisna contract with the constructor, stating the specification, price, and delivery date based on the first 'istisna contract' with the customer.

Step 6: The constructor will sign the agreement as an acceptance with agreed terms and conditions.

Step 7: The constructor develops or constructs the house and receives progress payments from the bank as per agreed terms during different stages of construction.

Step 8: The contractor constructs the house and hands over the completed house directly to the customer.

Step 9: The customer will pay the monthly instalments for the cost of the house and profit to the bank as per the agreed payment plan (Fig. 6.13).

1.10.2 Istisna Financing in Practice

The contracts in the nature of BOT (build, operate, and transfer) can be categorized as istisna transactions. It widens the financing scope as mentioned:

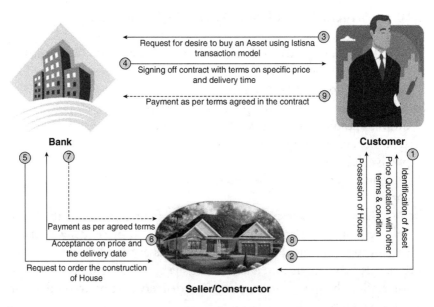

Fig. 6.13 Structuring an Istisna financing transaction

1. Istisna contract opens wide the fields of application for Islamic banks to finance public interest projects;
2. Istisna contract is applied in high-technology industries such as aircraft industry, locomotive and ship-building industries, in addition to other capital goods; and
3. Istisna contract is also applied in the construction industry such as apartments, hospitals, schools, and universities, and so on

Currently, istisna is widely used in the Gulf countries for home financing, commercial projects, and construction of industrial or commercial buildings.

1.10.3 Comparison between Istisna and Bai Salam

Keeping in view this nature of istisna, there are several points of difference between istisna and salam, which are summarized below:

1. The subject of istisna is always a thing that needs manufacturing, while bai salam is usually for agricultural product;
2. It is necessary for bai salam that the settlement price is paid on the spot, while it is not necessary in the case of istisna. Normally for istisna, the price is paid in cash or by instalments (progress payment) as per agreed terms during the different stages of construction;
3. The contract of bai salam, once agreed upon, cannot be cancelled unilaterally, while the contract of istisna can be cancelled before the manufacturer starts the work.
4. The time of delivery is an essential part of the sale in salam, while it is not necessary in istisna that the time of the delivery is fixed.

1.11 Qard Hassan Financing

The word qardh is derived from the Arabic word qirad which means 'to cut'. It is called qardh, as it cuts a certain part of the lender's property by giving a loan to the borrower. Hassan, an Arabic word, originates from ihsan, which means kindness to others. So, hassan is an act which benefits persons other than those from whom the act proceeds without any obligation. The term Qard Hassan means beneficial loan or benevolent loan. It is a kind of gratuitous loan given to the needy people for a fixed period without requiring the payment of interest or profit. The receiver of Qard Hassan is only required to repay the original amount of the loan. In other words, it is a debt given in the form of money or borrowed items like a car or hand phone to another on condition that it is returned to the owner the way it was, without anything removed from it or anything added to it.

This financing is extended on a goodwill basis, and the debtor is only required to repay the amount borrowed. However, the debtor may, at his or her discretion, pay an extra amount beyond the principal amount of the loan (without promising it) as a token of appreciation to the creditor. Some Muslims consider this to be the only type of loan that does not violate the prohibition on riba, since it is the one type of loan that truly does not compensate the creditor for the time value of money.

For example, a sum of RM10,000 borrowed by the customer must be returned to the bank in the same amount, that is, RM10,000, without any additional amount or benefits being charged. However, the administrative cost and management fee charged for the financing granted under Qard Hassan has been widely questioned by Islamic scholars. As per standards published by the Accounting and Auditing Organization for Islamic Financial Institutions (AAOFI), the charging of service cost is allowable with a strict condition that it is an actual cost. It has mentioned further that the charge in excess of the actual cost is prohibited and thus the Islamic jurists have unanimously agreed in the assembly that the formula used to calculate the cost must be appropriate, exact, and accurate. Moreover, indirect costs, such as employment expenditure, office rental and expenses, and other liabilities, are not included in the actual cost financing.

Hence, the banks are allowed to charge the borrower actual administrative expenses incurred in its operations. Normally, Qard Hassan is offered by banks to small producers, farmers, and entrepreneurs who are unable to get financing from other sources. Bank Islam Malaysia also uses qardh financing for its Islamic card, in the event of over-limit usage of cash by the cardholder. The cardholder here is not levied with extra charges or fees, but is required to repay the over-limit amount used.

1.12 Ar-Rahnu Financing

Rahnu principle is mainly used for Islamic pawn-broking services in Malaysia. Under rahnu, a valuable item is collateralized to a debt which may be utilized as payment if the debt is not repaid within the agreed period. In the event the debtor is not able to repay the debt, the pawned asset will be sold off to settle the outstanding debt and any surplus will be given back to the owner of the asset. However, if the owner of the asset could not be traced, it is the responsibility of the Islamic pawn-broker to place the fund in the Baitulmal account for future savings should any claims be made for the surplus by the owner or his heir.

Rahnu is a means of providing short-term financing to the public by pawning his/her jewelery to banks or pawnshops as a security. It is one of the microcredit and financial instruments for low-income earners seeking financial assistance to meet their fast working capital needs. It is a combination of three concepts applied to short-term financing under Islamic pawn-broking: Qard Hassan (benevolent loan), rahnu, and wadiah (custodian).

1. *Qard Hassan*: A bank will grant a benevolent loan to the applicant who wishes to pawn his valuable item. The loan will be issued under the concept of Qard Hassan, whereby the customer is only required to pay the amount borrowed;
2. *Rahnu*: Prior to the disbursement of cash to the applicant, the applicant is required to place a valuable asset as collateral for the loan extended by the bank;
3. *Wadiah*: The bank accepts custody of the valuable asset on a wadiah concept whereby the bank promises to keep the valuable asset in a safe place. The bank will need to take precautionary measure such as providing security and insurance to ensure its safe returns once the customer pays his debt. Under the wadiah concept, the bank will charge the customer for the services rendered in keeping the valuable asset.

Rahnu is relatively a new concept in Malaysia even though pawn-broking dates back to ancient times and is one of the earliest recorded lending transactions in financial history. In Malaysia, the first Islamic pawn-broking institution was Mu'assasah Gadaian Islam Terengganu (MGIT) in Terengganu which was created by the Majlis Agama Islam dan Adat Istiadat Terengganu in January 1992. This was followed in March 1992 by Kelantan State Economic Development Corporation's Permodalan Kelantan Berhad (PKB) which opened the Kedai Ar-Rahnu in Kelantan. On August 21, 1993, the Minister of Finance announced the introduction of a scheme, known as Skim Ar-Rahnu (SAR) through the collaboration of three institutions, namely, Bank Negara Malaysia, Yayasan Pembangunan Ekonomi Islam Malaysia, and Bank Kerjasama Rakyat Malaysia Berhad. On October 27, 1993, the first phase of SAR was launched at the six branches of Bank Rakyat. It was introduced later by other banks such as EON Bank, Bank Pertanian Malaysia, Bank Islam Malaysia, Bank Muamalat, and other financial institutions.

1.12.1 Objective of Ar-Rahnu Scheme

Rahnu is a quick and easy access to short-term financing for lower-income group. The prime objectives of this scheme are as below:

1. To provide a fast, hassle-free, and riba-free (interest-free) microcredit financing facilities to the small traders to meet their working capital needs.
2. To provide an alternative source of financing from the conventional pawning scheme.
3. To allow individuals to fulfill their financing needs without having to resort to other more expensive means such as loan sharks, money lenders, and interest-based loans.
4. To act as a means of fast and less cumbersome financing.
5. To develop the socio-economic well-being of the poor, by acting as a source of

(a) Capital to the small business
(b) Financing educational needs
(c) Development of agricultural and village Industries

6. To increase the number of financial instruments under Islamic banking and finance in line with the government aspiration for a complete and comprehensive Islamic financial system in Malaysia.

1.12.2 Rahnu Financing Mechanism

The Malaysian Pawn-brokers Act 1972 (Act 81) defines a pawn-broker as:

'A person, who purchases, receives or takes in articles and pays, advances or lends thereon any sum or sums of money not exceeding RM10,000 with or under an agreement, understanding expressed, implied or to be from the nature and character of the dealing reasonably inferred that those articles may afterwards be redeemed or repurchased on any items'.

Loans are typically small, averaging between RM100 and RM500—or as high as several thousand ringgits depending on the value of the collateral. In conventional pawn-broking, when a customer pawns an item, a ticket stating the customer's identification, amount borrowed, maturity date, interest rate, and amount needed to redeem the item is given to him. If the customer defaults on his loan, the collateral becomes the property of the pawn shop and is put up for sale after the loan is delinquent for a specific period of time.

Rahnu does not contain any elements of usury. The mechanism behind an Islamic pawn-broking is simple. Instead of interest, there is a 'storage cost'—the same concept when keeping one's luggage at the airport or bus terminal. The computation of safe-keeping as per Ustaz Hj Zaharuddin Hj Abd Rahman is as below:

1. *Margin of Financing*: For gold, the margin of financing ranges from 50% to 70% against the market value of gold item pawned. Usually, financing will be given based on the value of the gold item and the client's background (e.g. whether regular wage earner or business owner). The valuation is based also on the purity of the gold item (no comparison).

2. *Safe-keeping Rate*: For safe-keeping, charges are based on the value of the collateral. Most banks follow tier rate, whereby the charge keeps on increasing with the high value of the collateral item as illustrated in the following table:

Collateral item value (RM)	Safe keeping rate (% per month)
1–199	1.65
200–999	1.85
1000 and above	2.05

Example:

Akram approaches a bank to pawn his gold ring worth RM5000. The bank offers him a margin of 50%, that is, RM2500. As such the safe-keeping charges for 6 months would be RM615 (2.05% × RM5000 × 6 months). At the end of the sixth month, the customer has to pay back RM3115 (financing amount + safe-keeping fee).

1. *Safe-keeping Fee*: Few of the scholars say that the delayed amount is a safe-keeping fee but in the actual fact, when the safe-keeping fees are linked by percentage to the marhun value (gold and silver), it is considered as a trading transaction for businesses and no longer a safe-keeping fee based on rahnu. As an alternative, the permissible safe-keeping fee may be based on the fee charged for use of safe deposit boxes. It can be as follows:

Collateral item value (RM)	Safe keeping fee (RM per month)
1–499	5.00
500–1,999	10.00
2000 and above	30.00

Example:

Akram approaches a bank to pawn his gold ring worth RM5000. Bank offers him a margin of 50%, that is, RM2500. As such the safe-keeping charges for 6 months would be RM180 (RM 30 × 6 months). At the end of the sixth month, the customer has to pay back RM2680 (financing amount + safe-keeping fee).

1.12.3 Implementation of Ar-Rahnu

Rahnu is a new Islamic financial product with the potential of achieving social welfare objectives. As a catalyst for further promoting the growth of Islamic pawn-broking in Malaysia, the following criteria should be taken into account:

1. The product should always comply with its mission and objective, that is, take it as a social obligation for the benefit of the needy;
2. The financing amount disbursed to customer shall be based on Qard Hassan at all time, and the safe-keeping fee cannot be related to the Qard Hassan amount;
3. The safe-keeping fees should be much lower than conventional pawn-broking fees. Therefore, it is not advisable for Islamic pawn-broking entrepreneurs and financial institutions to impose high safe-keeping fee. It must be understood that by linking the safe-keeping fee to the marhun value by percentage, typically the fee would be higher. In the end, it will not be suitable for microcredit financing;
4. In case of failure to return the murtahin bih (financing amount) and the rahin (customer) cannot be contacted, the marhun can be sold, and if there is any surplus, it shall be placed in a separate account should any claims be made by the owner or his heir. It is very important that the financial institution does not use that balance amount for any other purposes; and
5. If the customer (rahin) requests for the extension of the maturity period, it must be negotiable, and the rahnu company must not impose any extra charges except for the storage fee.

1.13 Bai al Inah Financing

Bai inah is a contract, which involves the sale and buy-back transaction of assets by a seller. Under this contract, the bank first sells an asset to the customer at a price comprising the financing amount plus the bank's profit margin, whereby the payment by the customer is on deferred payment term (first contract). The bank will, subsequently, buy-back the asset from the customer on cash basis which is equivalent to the financing amount (second contract). It can also be applied *vice versa* where a financier buys an asset from a customer on cash terms. Immediately after, the financier sells back the same asset to the customer on deferred payment terms at a price higher than that of the cash sale.

This is also called 'two-party inah' because the whole transaction takes place between two parties. The contracts in this case are independent, each being a complete and full-fledged contract not made conditional to the other, which results in the creation of legal consequences in the form of rights and obligations on the parties, and is carried out to its end through formal and unconditional transfer of possession of the traded asset. Jurists of the Shafi'i School hold this type of transaction reprehensible, however, valid, while some others hold it invalid.

1.13.1 Bai al Inah Financing Mechanism

Bai inah is currently practiced in Malaysia for personal and education financing, Islamic credit card, and so on. whereby the customer pays the selling price in instalments as per the agreed payment schedule. The *modus operandi* of bai inah financing is as below:

Step 1: The customer approaches the bank for personal financing and submits an application form with necessary documents (identification credential, collateral, other income source, etc.) to the bank for credit screening.

Step 2: The bank and the customer agree on bai inah as an underlying financing principle. Bank identifies the asset that will be traded under bai inah contract (Fig. 6.14).

Step 3: The bank will sign a first contract with the customer, whereby it sells the asset at a selling price (financing amount + profit margin) on deferred terms and the ownership is transferred to the customer.

Step 4: The bank will sign a second contract with the customer, whereby it buys back the asset sold to the customer at a price equivalent to financing amount, that is, the purchase price.

Step 5: The bank pays to the customer the financing amount on cash basis.

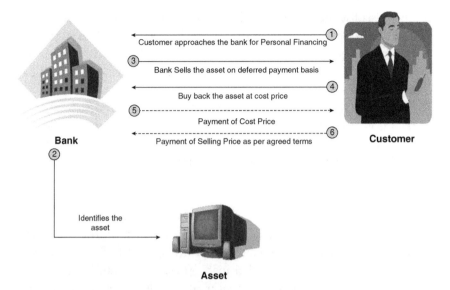

Fig. 6.14 Bai al Inah financing mechanism

Step 6: The customer pays the selling price to the customer as per agreed payment schedule.

1.13.2 Permissibility of Bai al Inah Financing Mechanism

Islamic jurists have different views on the permissibility of using bai inah as a mode of financing. The following are their views:

1. The majority are of the opinion that bai inah is not permissible because it is the zariah (way) or hilah (legal excuse) to legitimize riba (usury);
2. The Hanafi hashab is of the opinions that bai inah is permissible only if it involves a third party, which acts as an intermediary between the seller (creditor) and buyer (debtor);
3. The Maliki and Hanbali mazhab, on the other hand, rejected bai inah and considered it invalid. Their opinion is based on the opinion of Sadd Zariah that is aimed at preventing practices that could lead to forbidden acts, in this case, riba;

4. The basis for the opinion of the majority of the Islamic jurists is the hadith dialogue between Aishah and the slave Zaid bin al-Arqam which showed the prohibition of bai inah. They also held to the hadith of the Prophet in which he warned that those who practiced bai inah would suffer scorn;
5. The Shafi'i and Zahiri mazhab viewed bai inah as permissible. A contract is valued by what is disclosed and one's niyyah (intention) was up to Allah to judge. They criticized the hadith used by the majority of the Islamic jurists as the basis for their argument, saying that the hadith was weak, and therefore could not be used as a basis for the hukum.

From the study done on the opinions of past Islamic jurists on the issue of bai inah, the SAC (Syariah Advisory Council of The Malaysian Securities Commission) decided to accept the opinions of the Shafi'i and Zahiri mazhab who permitted bai inah. Therefore, it can be developed into a product for the Islamic capital market in Malaysia. Furthermore, when institutions or individuals are in need of capital for a specific purpose, they can use this method of payment, using their assets as mortgage. As they will still require the assets, this method allows them to liquidate without losing the asset. ((INFAD- www.infad.kuim.edu.my).

1.14 Two-Tier Mudharabah Model

Under a two-tier Mudharabah model, both funds mobilization and funds utilization are based on profit-sharing among the three parties: investor, the bank, and the entrepreneur. A single-tier Mudharabah is based on profit-sharing between the investor and the bank only where the investors are suppliers of the funds and the bank acts as a mudarib. Here the funds are placed with the bank in an investment account. Such investments based on profit-sharing are not liabilities but considered a variant of limited term non-voting equity.

In the two-tier model, the investors deposit their money in the bank. The bank supplies these funds to the entrepreneurs who agree to share profits according to a fixed percentage stipulated in the contract and the bank shares these profits with the investors. In addition to investment deposits, the bank accepts demand deposits that yield no returns and are repayable on demand at par value and are treated as liabilities. There is no reserve requirement on the demand deposits. A unique feature of the two-tier model is that the assets and liabilities of a bank's balance sheet are fully integrated and thus minimize the need for active asset/liability management that would provide stability against economic shocks.

In short, the bank funds could comprise share capital, demand deposits, and various types of investment deposit. The main feature of the model described above is that it replaces interest by profit-sharing on both the liabilities and the assets side of the bank's balance sheet. This change brings about a number of positive effects on the efficiency, equity, and stability of the banking system.

1.15 Challenges in Financing

The emergence and growth of the Islamic finance industry is a phenomenon that has generated considerable interest in the financial world in recent years. Given its ability to offer innovative financial solutions to an under-served market, it is seen as a community banking niche with considerable growth potentials. In spite of the growth potential in Islamic banking, there are several challenges facing Islamic financial institutions.

- *Uniform Regulatory Framework*: A uniform regulatory and legal framework supportive of an Islamic financial system has not yet been developed. Existing banking regulations in Islamic countries are based on the Western banking model. Similarly, Islamic financial institutions face difficulties operating in non-Islamic countries owing to the absence of a regulatory body that operates in accordance with Islamic principles. The development of a regulatory and supervisory framework that would address the issues specific to Islamic institutions would further enhance the integration of Islamic markets and international financial markets.

- *Innovation*: The pace of innovation is slow. For years, the market has offered the same traditional instruments geared toward short- and medium-term maturities, but it has not yet come up with the necessary instruments to handle maturities at the extremes. There is a need for risk-management tools to equip clients with instruments to hedge against the high volatility in currency and commodities markets. In addition, the market lacks the necessary instruments to provide viable alternatives for public debt financing.
- *Standardized Accounting Standards*: An Islamic financial system needs a sound accounting procedures and standards. Western accounting procedures are not adequate because of the different nature and treatment of financial instruments. Well-defined procedures and standards are crucial for information disclosure, building investors' confidence, and monitoring and surveillance. AAOIFI (Accounting and Auditing Organization for Islamic Financial Institution) is one such organization working on standardization of accounting standards. Proper standards will also help the integration of Islamic financial markets with international markets.
- *Skill-set Shortage*: Islamic institutions have a shortage of trained personnel who can analyze and manage portfolios and develop innovative products according to Islamic financial principles. Only a limited number of Islamic institutions can afford to train their staffs and deploy resources in product development. The supply of trained or experienced bankers has lagged behind the expansion of Islamic banking.
- *Credit Analysis*: Islamic banks have no appropriate standard of credit analysis, which differs from conventional loans as it is based on profit- and loss-sharing principle. Similarly, there is a widespread training need involving related aspects such as financial feasibility studies, monitoring of ventures, and portfolio evaluation.
- *Short term Investment Instruments*: One of the biggest challenges facing institutions is the provision of short-term investment instruments. Several institutions have tried to develop high-quality short-term instruments, but have been hampered by their ability to generate assets, by their credit ratings, and by liquidity.

- *Standardization of Religious Principles*: There is lack of uniformity in the religious principles applied in Islamic countries. In the absence of a universally accepted central religious authority, Islamic banks have formed their own religious boards for guidance. Islamic banks have to consult their respective religious boards, or Syariah advisors, to seek approval for each new instrument. Differences in interpretation of Islamic principles by different schools of thought may mean that identical financial instruments are rejected by one board but accepted by another. Thus, the same instrument may not be acceptable in all countries. This problem can be addressed by forming a uniform council representing different schools of thought to define cohesive rules and to expedite the process of introducing new products.

1.16 Comparison Between Islamic and Conventional Financing

Interpreting the system as 'interest-free' tends to create confusion. The philosophical foundation of an Islamic financial system goes beyond the interaction of factors of production and economic behavior. Whereas the conventional financial system focuses primarily on the economic and financial aspects of transactions, the Islamic system places equal emphasis on the ethical, moral, social, and religious dimensions, to enhance equality and fairness for the good of society as a whole. The system can be fully appreciated only in the context of Islam's teachings on the work ethic, wealth distribution, social and economic justice, and the role of the state.

There are at least three characteristics which makes it different from the conventional debt finance. First, it prohibits *riba* or interest, or in other words a fixed and predetermined rate of return to be paid on the deposits or to be received from the borrowers. The rate of return is variable and determined by the profit and loss that the bank makes during a given period and the returns on assets depend on the particular mode and purpose of financing, that is, *Murabahah* (trade finance), *Mudharabah* (profit sharing), *Musharakah* (partnership), *Ijarah* (leasing), and so on.

Second, Islamic finance does not allow undertaking or financing the anti-social and unethical businesses such as gambling, prostitution, alcoholic liquor, nightclubs, and narcotics. These are the main channels used for money laundering, terrorism financing, and organized crimes, etc. Islamic banks are prohibited from opening accounts or providing financing to persons or institutions involved in such activities. In this respect, it is clearly ahead of the recent surge in ethical finance and socially responsible finance that are becoming quite popular in the Western world. Islamic financial institutions, because of their active involvement and knowledge of the nature of businesses of their clients, are in a better position to detect and prevent the channeling of depositors' money for financing highly risky but equally remunerative anti-social activities. The financing it provides is mostly asset-based, whereby the Islamic bank knows the actual utilization of its funds.

Third, Islamic finance has to be compliant with the basic percepts of Syariah, the legal code of Islam which is based on the principles of justice, fair dealings, and harmony through equitable distribution of wealth. Islam is deadly opposed to exploitation of an individual or institution by the other for self-aggrandizement. Riba or usury is considered exploitative by its construct and is therefore prohibited. The equitable distribution dimension of Islamic finance is therefore an add-on that is clearly absent from the conventional modes of financing. Thus, all dealings, transactions, business approaches, product features, investment focus, and responsibilities are derived from Syariah law, leading to a significant difference in many parts of the operations compared to conventional banking.

In addition, a fundamental distinction of an Islamic Bank is the lack of deposit insurance common in conventional banks. The PLS structure permits receipt of money by depositors where deposits invested have incurred a profit, but they must incur losses in situations where deposit investments incur losses to comply with Syariah. Deposit insurance defeats the purpose of PLS because the depositor does not incur any risk. In other words, there should not be any reward without taking a risk. This principle is applicable to both labor and capital. As no payment is allowed for labor, unless it is applied to work, there is no reward for capital unless it is exposed to business risk. This very fundamental aspect of an Islamic bank runs contrary to the standards of Western banking regulations.

1.17 Regulating and Supervising Islamic Financing

Undoubtedly, one of the biggest challenges is developing a framework for governing, supervising, and regulating Islamic banks. To begin with, there is no common approach among countries where Islamic banking exists. One of the two main views—held by regulators in Malaysia and Yemen, for example—is that Islamic banks should be subject to a supervisory and regulatory regime of central banks that is entirely different from that of conventional banks. The second main view recognizes the uniqueness of Islamic banks' activities, but favors putting them under the same central bank supervision and regulatory regime as that for conventional banks, with slight modifications and special guidelines that are usually formalized in occasional central bank circulars. Bahrain and Qatar are examples of countries that practice this latter form of central bank supervision and regulation.

Since the late 1990s, however, the Islamic banking world has stepped up efforts to standardize regulation and supervision. The Islamic Development Bank is playing a key role in developing internationally acceptable standards and procedures and strengthening the sector's architecture in different countries. Several other international institutions are working to set Syariah-compliant standards and harmonize them across countries. These include the Accounting and Auditing Organization for Islamic Financial Institutions (AAOIFI), the Islamic Finance Service Board (IFSB), the International Islamic Financial Market, the Liquidity Management Center, and the International Islamic Rating Agency.

A number of countries and institutions have adopted accounting standards developed by the AAOIFI, which complement the International Financial Reporting Standards. The IFSB aims to promote the development of a prudent and transparent Islamic financial services industry and provides guidance on the effective supervision and regulation of institutions offering Islamic financial products. The IFSB has recently finalized standards on capital adequacy and risk management, and has made progress in developing standards on corporate governance. Once developed and accepted, these international standards will assist supervisors in pursuing soundness, stability, and integrity in the world of Islamic finance.

1.18 Summary

The Islamic financial industry is one of the most thriving sectors of the financial world. As a result, it has received support and involvement from the conventional banking and financial institutions. In order to survive in today's highly competitive financial marketplace, the Islamic banking and finance industry is in the process of tackling a number of important challenges at this stage of its growth. Islamic banks and financial institutions must now look at developing innovative products and services and consolidating their operations. Aligning the architecture of Islamic finance to the evolving industry needs is an essential step in order to maximize the growth and potential for Islamic financial services worldwide.

References

www.rhbislamicbank.com.my, www.muamalat.com.my, www.bankislam.com.my, www.bankinginfo.com.my

http://biz.thestar.com.my/news/story.asp?file=/2006/5/15/business/14058846&sec=business

http://cief.wordpress.com/2006/02/06/contract-of-al-Ijarah/

http://english.webislam.com/?idt=168

http://infad.kuim.edu.my/modules.php?op=modload&name=News&file=article&sid=9346&mode=thread&order=0&thold=0

http://islamic-finance.net/Journals/Journal14/vol4no2art1.pdf

http://islamic-world.net/economics/salam_n_istisna.htm

http://muamalat.com.my

http://news.bbc.co.uk/1/hi/world/middle_east/5064058.stm

http://news.bbc.co.uk/2/hi/business/4264939.stm

http://news.bbc.co.uk/2/hi/middle_east/5064058.stm
http://www.1stethical.com/publications.asp
http://www.aaoifi.com/
http://www.accountancy.com.pk/docs/islam_modes_of_finance.pdf
http://www.al-baraka.com/istisnaa.html
http://www.asiafinanceblog.com/asiafinanceblog/islamic_finance/index.html
http://www.bankerme.com/bme/2005/sep/venture_capital.asp
http://www.bankerme.com/bme/2005/sep/venture_capital.asp
http://www.bankinginfo.com.my/index.php?ch=24&pg=36#
http://www.bankrakyat.com.my/index.php?ch=6&pg=26&ac=13&lang=en
http://www.bernama.com.my/bernama/v3/news_business.php?id=234905
http://www.bnm.gov.my/index.php?ch=174&pg=469&ac=383
http://www.bnm.gov.my/index.php?ch=174&pg=469&ac=387
http://www.businessweek.com/magazine/content/05_32/b3946141_mz035.htm
http://www.darululoomkhi.edu.pk/fiqh/islamicfinance/Ijarah.html#commencement
http://www.darululoomkhi.edu.pk/fiqh/islamicfinance/musharakah.html
http://www.freemuslims.org/document.php?id=84
http://www.halaljournal.com/artman/publish_php/article_1005.php
http://www.ibb.com.bn/bank_concept.htm
http://www.islamibankbd.com/
http://www.islamibankbd.com/
http://www.islamicbank.com.ph/products.html#p4
http://www.islamic-finance.com/item_ijara_f.htm
http://www.islamicfinancenews.com/glossary.php
http://www.islamicmortgages.co.uk/shariah_debate_08.html
http://www.islamic-world.net/economics/financial_system_02.htm
http://www.islamic-world.net/economics/word/b.htm
http://www.kaau.edu.sa/CENTERS/SPC/page-091.htm
http://www.khaleejtimes.com/DisplayArticle.asp?xfile=data/business/2005/August/business_August104.xml&section=business&col=
http://www.lariba.com/fatwas/usmani.htm
http://www.meezanbank.com/knowledgecenter/knowledge-islam-guide-intro.asp
http://www.rhbislamicbank.com.my/articles/2006/09-21.htm
http://www.salaam.co.uk/themeofthemonth/november02_index.php?l=2

http://www.theedgedaily.com/cms/content.jsp?id=com.tms.cms.article.Article_124addd6-cb73c03a-11087270-22652ee9
http://www.utusan.com.my/utusan/content.asp?y=2004&dt=1013&pub=Utusan_Express&sec=Front_Page&pg=fp_03.htm
http://www.westga.edu/~bquest/2004/musharaka.htm#change
http://www.worldbank.org/fandd/english/0697/articles/0140697.htm
http://www.zawya.com/special/islamic/insight/insight_page_three.cfm

Abdul Halim Umar, M. Comparison between Salam and other similar techniques in Islamic jurisprudence and contemporary thinking. Retrieved from http://islamic-finance.net

Abdul Halim Umar, M. Shari'ah framework of Salam. Retrieved from http://islamic-finance.net

Abdullah, Mazni. *Leasing and Ijarah: A comparison between the requirements in conventional and Islamic accounting standards.* 3rd International Islamic Banking and Finance Conference, Monash.

Abod, Sheikh Ghazali Sheikh, Agil, Syed Omar Syed, & Ghazali, Aidit Hj. (2005, November). *An introduction to Islamic economics & finance.* CERT Publications Sdn Bhd.

Agil, Syed Omar Syed, & Ghazali, Aidit Hj. (2005, November). *Readings in the concept and methodology of Islamic economics.* CERT Publications Sdn Bhd.

Al Jassar, Jassar. Islamic finance successes, prospects, and neglected areas. Retrieved from http://islamic-finance.net

Baharum, Mohd Ali.. *Ar-Rahnu: A new era in microfinance in Malaysia.* National Co-operative Organisation of Malaysia (ANGKASA).

Bank Negara Malaysia. *Money and banking in Malaysia.* Silver anniversary edition 1959–1984.

Chiu, Shirley, & Newberger, Robin. Islamic finance: Meeting financial needs with faith based products. *Profitwise News and Views.* Retrieved from http://www.chicagofed.org/community_development/files/02_2006_islamic_finance.pdf

Chowdhry, Sajjad. (2004, October 1). Islamic finance 101. Retrieved from http://www.dinarstandard.com/finance/finance_review100104.htm#key

Euromoney Books and AAOIFI. Islamic finance innovation & growth.

Haron, S., & Shanmugam, B. (2001). *Islamic banking system—Concept & applications.* Selangor, Malaysia: Pelanduk Publications.

Hassan, M., & De Belder, R. (1993, November). The changing face of Islamic banking. *International Financial Law Review, London, 12*(11), 5.

Hossain, Mohammad Delwar. *Al-Qard al-Hasan: A practical approach.* Retrieved from www.witness-pioneer.org

Husain, Ahmad Sansui. *Islamic pawning as a tool of enhancing socio economic development.* Presented at Workshop on Islamic Trading Contracts organized by IBFIM.

Iqbal, Munawar, & Molyneux, Philip. *Thirty years of Islamic banking: History, performance and prospects.*

Islamic Financial Services., Scientific Publishing Centre, King Abdulaziz University, Jeddah. 2005.

Kadir, Abdul Rashid Abdul. *Application of Islamic trading contracts from local and international perspective.* Presented at Workshop on Islamic Trading Contracts organized by IBFIM.

Kameel Mydin Meera, Ahamed, & Abdul Razak, Dzuljastri. Islamic home financing through Musharakah Mutanaqisah and al-Bay' Bithaman Ajil contracts: A comparative analysis. Retrieved from http://www.ahamedkameel.com/

Mirakhor, Abbas. (1997). Progress and challenges of Islamic banking international monetary fund. Retrieved from www.financeinislam.com

Moghul, Umar F., Esq. Introduction to Islamic finance. Retrieved from http://www.bos.frb.org/commdev/c&b/2006/summer/islamicfinance.pdf

New Horizon. The definition and legal nature of Istisna. Retrieved from http://islamic-finance.net

Pang, Johnson, & Savarimuthu, Nathaniel G. (1985). *Banking in Malaysia.* Heinemann Malaysia Sdn Bhd.

Rahman, Mohamed Nazim Abdul. *Practices of Islamic pawn broking operators in Malaysia.* 3rd International Islamic Banking and Finance Conference, Monash.

Razak, Dzuljastri Abdul. Islamic home financing through Musharakah Mutanaqisah and Al-Bay' Bithaman Ajil contracts: A comparative analysis.

Rosly, Saiful Azhar, Sanusi, Mahmood, & Yasin, Norhashimah Mohd. The role of Khiyar Al-'Ayb In Al-Bay' Bithaman Ajil financing. *International Journal of Islamic Financial Services, 2*(3).

Shanmugam, Bala, Perumal, Vignesen, & Ridzwa, Alfieya Hanuum. *Islamic banking: An international perspective.*

Skully, Michael. *Islamic pawn broking: The Malaysian experience.* 3rd International Islamic Banking and Finance Conference, Monash.

Tahir, Sayyid. Challenges facing Islamic finance: Research areas. Retrieved from http://www.sbp.org.pk.

Usmani, Mufti Taqi. Forward sales and manufacturing contracts: Salam and Istisna. Retrieved from http://islamic-finance.net

Usmani, M. I. A. (2002a). *Meezanbank's guide to Islamic banking*. Karachi, Pakistan: Darul-Ishaat Urdu Bazar.

Usmani, M. T. (2002b). *An introduction to Islamic finance*. Karachi: Maktaba Ma'ariful Quran.

Zarqa, Muhammad Anas. Istisna' financing of infrastructure projects. Retrieved from http://islamic-finance.net

7

Comparative Analysis: Islamic Banking Products and Services in Different Countries

1 Introduction

As explained in the previous chapters, Islamic financial products are aimed at investors who want to comply with the Islamic laws (Syariah) that govern a Muslim's daily life. These laws forbid the giving or the receiving of interests because earning a profit from an exchange of money for money is considered immoral. It also mandates financial transactions be based on real economic activity and prohibit investment in sectors such as tobacco, alcohol, gambling, and armaments. IFIs are providing an increasingly broad range of many financial services, such as fund mobilization, asset allocation, payment and exchange settlement services, and risk transformation and mitigation. These specialized financial intermediaries perform transactions using financial instruments compliant with Syariah principles.

In the last few years, Islamic banking has made extraordinary progress on the global front, in terms of growth in the number of IFIs and their asset base. The leading countries in this area are Malaysia and Bahrain. However, in terms of total assets, the Islamic banks of Iran and Saudi Arabia are the largest. Indonesia, Kuwait, Sudan, UAE, Thailand, and

Australia have also made considerable advances in the field of Islamic finance. The products being offered by these banks range from consumer credit to long-term finance for big investment projects using Islamic modes of financing such as Murabahah, Ijarah, salam, Musharakah, and mudarabah.

The successful operation of Islamic banks in several parts of the world has led to a growing interest in Islamic financing techniques. Being at an infancy stage has resulted in the Islamic banking industry being chaotic with respect to financial products administration. Each nation appears to have its own opinion on how to administer the financial products. This is hampering efforts for the globalization of Islamic banks. The common question generally raised regarding Islamic banking is on the similarities or differences with respect to these activities among Islamic banks themselves.

There are several reasons for these differences. The main reason is that the application of the theoretical aspects of Islamic banking systems differs from country to country and under different economic conditions and social environments. Another reason for the differences is due to the different madhabs or 'Schools of Religious Law'. There are four main madhabs, namely, Hanafi, Maliki, Shafii, and Hanbali. These madhabs play an important role in developing Islamic jurisprudence.

2 Comparison of Islamic Financial Institution by Country

The IFIs' main function is to mobilize savings and idle funds in the economy and to make them available to those who can optimize them. The statutory requirement is to ensure that any activities performed by IFIs are in compliance with Syariah. Islam prohibits interest in any forms therefore; IFIs have to look for permissible rewards and business relationship between those who provide funds and those who use the same. This basic principle is applicable to all IFIs worldwide. The following section will compare the various aspects of IFIs in specific countries.

2.1 Islamic Banking Evolution

There was a significant development in the area of Islamic banking in the 1970s and 1980s toward reviving the glory of Islam and the implementation of Syariah in all aspects of life. The effort to establish Islamic banking is one outcome of this movement. The Muslim countries began to rediscover Islam and wanted to mold their economic and financial activities in accordance with Islamic values. The nature of business for all IFIs is to facilitate financial intermediation in an Islamic way. The pace of evolution of Islamic banking in different countries is different. Therefore, we can find that the nature of business is not similar across the globe. This section will explain the evolution of Islamic banking in different countries.

1. Malaysia

Malaysia is considered as the center for Islamic financial services and is popular worldwide. The earliest form of Islamic banking in Malaysia can be traced back to September 1963 when Perbadanan Wang Simpanan Bakal-Bakal Haji (PWSBH) was set up as an institution for Muslims to save for their Haj (pilgrimage to Mecca) expenses. In 1969, PWSBH merged with Pejabat Urusan Haji to form Lembaga Urusan dan Tabung Haji (now known as Lembaga Tabung Haji).

The first Islamic bank, Bank Islam Malaysia Berhad (BIMB) was established under the Islamic Banking Act (IBA) 1983. The bank commenced its operations on July 1, 1983. On March 4, 1993, Bank Negara Malaysia introduced a scheme known as 'Skim Perbankan Tanpa Faedah' (Interest-free Banking Scheme) or SPTF in short. Under this scheme in 1993, conventional commercial banks, merchant banks, and finance companies were also allowed to offer Islamic banking products and services under the Islamic Banking Scheme (IBS). These institutions, however, are required to separate the funds and activities of Islamic banking transactions from that of the conventional banking business to ensure that there would not be any comingling of funds. By the end of 1993, there were 21 conventional banks with Islamic windows.

Currently, Malaysia has a 16 Islamic Banks, which account for USD170 billion in banking assets or 24% of the total banking assets of the country. In 2016, Islamic financing accounted for a third of all bank financing at USD125 billion. The same is true for the market share of Islamic deposits and investment accounts, which stood at USD137 billion, or 31.8%. Bank Negara Malaysia (BNM) is expecting Syariah-compliant financing to account for 40% of total financing in Malaysia by 2020, with the reality that this figure could reach 50% before the following decade.

To ensure the continued safety and soundness of financial institutions and to promote overall financial and payment systems stability, the BNM as a central regulator has undertaken a yearly assessment of risks and challenges faced by the financial system under the Financial Sector Assessment Program (FSAP) conducted by the International Monetary Fund and World Bank. As a result of the Financial Stability and Payment Systems Report 2012, the 'Islamic Financial Services Act' (IFSA) 2013 was enacted to reinforce the BNM's mandate to safeguard Islamic financial system.

The IFSA, which was implemented on March 22, 2013, has consolidated the Islamic Banking Act 1983 and the Takaful Act 1984. The new Act provides a comprehensive regulation and supervision of Islamic financial institutions, payment systems, and other relevant entities. It also covers the oversight of the Islamic money market and Islamic foreign exchange market to promote financial stability and compliance with Syariah. Some of the key features of the new legislation include:

- Greater transparency and accountability of the BNM in carrying out its principal object to safeguard financial stability through a more risk-focused and integrated approach to the regulation of financial institutions;
- A comprehensive or end-to-end Syariah-compliant legal framework with respect to regulation and supervision (from licensing to winding-up);
- Strengthened business conduct and consumer protection requirements to promote consumer confidence in the use of financial services and products;

- Strengthened provisions for effective enforcement and supervisory intervention through imposition of higher penalties to act as a credible deterrent. BNM can also issue directions of compliance or accept legally enforceable undertakings that commit financial institutions to take specific actions to address identified risks.

2. Indonesia

Indonesia, with the world's largest population of Muslims, came to Islamic banking late in comparison to other Muslim countries. The development of Islamic banking in Indonesia started before a formal legal structure for Syariah banking came into force. Before 1992, there have been several non-bank financial institutions such as Bait Maal Wat Tamwil (Islamic savings and loan co-operatives) offering Islamic financing to the rural sector. To meet the demand for interest-free banking system, the government allowed Syariah banking operations in the Act No. 7 of 1992 concerning banking under Government Decree No. 72 of 1992, stating the implementation of Syariah principles for banking. This has served as a legal foundation for Syariah banking operations.

Bank Muamalat was the first Syariah bank established in Indonesia and commenced operation in 1992. In 1998, the Act No. 10 of 1998 on the amendment of the Act No. 7 of 1992 concerning banking came into force to give a stronger legal foundation for the existence of the Syariah banking system. The new Act No. 23 of 1999 concerning Bank Indonesia gives authority to Bank Indonesia to also conduct its task according to Syariah principles. Since then, the Syariah banking industry has been growing more rapidly.

Bank Indonesia took a major step in the development of Islamic financial services in September 2002 when it issued a blueprint for Islamic banking and set regulation 4/1/2002 on the establishment and operation of commercial banks and bank offices based on Syariah principles. Bank Indonesia is also an active member of international organizations set up to standardize global Islamic banking rules and practices. In a bid to promote growth of Islamic banking in Indonesia, Bank Indonesia, since January 2006, has allowed conventional branches with Syariah banking units to offer Syariah's products and services. Like Malaysia, Indonesia has also implemented a dual banking system comprising both Islamic and conventional banking systems.

The enactment of Act no. 21 of 2008 issued on July 16, 2008, has provided a more adequate legal base to the development of Islamic banking in Indonesia and consequently accelerated the growth of the industry. As of 2016, there are 12 full-fledged Islamic banks, 22 Islamic banking units (special unit in conventional banks serving Sharia banking operations), and 163 Islamic rural banks (BPRS) accounting for total asset of 340 trillion Indonesian rupiah (USD25.5 billion), equal to just over 5% of the country's total banking assets.

Unlike other countries, the Islamic finance industry in Indonesia has largely been built on community-based initiatives. This has led to the development of unique features such as the presence of rural Islamic banks, retail Sukuk, haj funds, and various innovative social finance initiatives. With the government making the development of the Islamic finance industry a key pillar in their overall economic growth strategy, it is expected that the market share of Islamic banking will grow from 5% in 2016 to 11% by 2020.

3. Thailand

Although Thailand is predominantly a Buddhist country, the region bordering the north of Malaysia has a large Muslim population. Muslims are mainly concentrated in the provinces of Yala, Pattani, Songkhla, Satun, and Narathiwas. While only about 4% of the countries are Muslims, it is a wealthy and influential community. The earliest form of Islamic banking can be traced back in 1987 when the Pattani Islamic Savings Cooperative was established. The objective was to create a separate Islamic fund for the benefit of the poorer sections of the Muslim ummah. Following this, other four Islamic Institutes were established, that is, Ibnu Affan Savings Co-operative, As-Siddiq Savings Co-operative, Saqaffah Islam Savings Co-operative, and Al-Islamiyah Savings Co-operative. These institutions were co-operative societies.

The idea of establishing the full-fledged Islamic bank in Thailand was initiated in 1994 when the Thai government signed the Indonesia-Malaysia-Thailand Growth Triangle Project (IMT-GT Project) with a view to promote banking services specific to the needs of Muslim consumers, in particular those in the four southern provinces. Islamic banking services in accordance with Islamic precepts (Syariah) were first provided by a commercial bank in late 1997, but closed down because of the financial crisis. The next major step in the progress of Islamic banking in Thailand was the setting up of a fully fledged Islamic branch by state-owned Krung Thai Bank in 2002. Krung Thai Bank (Krung Thai Syariah Services is now under the Islamic Bank of Thailand), a major player in the Thai financial system, continued serving Muslims with more Islamic branches in Muslim-dominated areas.

Subsequently, to meet the demands of a full-fledged Islamic Bank, in 2002, the Islamic Bank of Thailand (IBank) was established under the Islamic Bank of Thailand Act B.E. 2545. The IBank is a full-fledged Islamic bank under the supervision of the Ministry of Finance. The IBank offers banking services that conform to Islamic principles to both Muslim and non-Muslim consumers. It thus operates its business in a way that does not involve profit making from interest margins, with part of the profit set aside for charitable social work. Apart from IBank, other banks and co-operatives such as Islamic window of the Government Savings Bank, Bank for Agriculture and Agriculture Cooperatives, and Ibnu Affan Saving Cooperative also offer Islamic banking services. The total Islamic banking asset in the country is not more than USD5 billion as of 2014 which represents less than 1% of the total banking assets in Thailand.

As early as 2010, the Thai government stated that a regulatory framework regarding tax issues for a sovereign Sukuk, called the Trust Act, would be put in place; however, this has not materialized, and the regulations for Islamic finance as a whole still remain fragmented. Currently, the country's only Islamic bank, the IBank, is prohibited from investing abroad, limiting its scope to Syariah-compliant investment options within Thailand.

In Thailand, Islamic banking is not restricted to Muslims and the growing viability of the sector would attract non-Muslims to participate in its activities. Despite a minority Muslim population, the Thai government has embarked on a brave scheme to introduce Islamic banking in the country. This is in line with the government's secular objectives of catering for all religious communities.

4. Brunei

Banking in Brunei also follows the dual banking system, whereby conventional banks operate in parallel to Islamic Banks. In Brunei, Islamic banking started in 1991 with the establishment of Perbadanan Tabung Amanah Islam Brunei or more commonly known as TAIB. The creation of TAIB came by virtue of the Constitution of Brunei Darussalam (Order under section 83[3]) Emergency (Perbadanan Tabung Amanah Islam Brunei) Order, 1991. TAIB is government owned and its main objective is to offer Islamic financial services and raise the socio-economic status of the population. Islamic Bank of Brunei was the second full-fledged Islamic Bank in Brunei. Established in 1993, when it replaced the International Bank of Brunei, the Islamic Bank of Brunei conducts its savings and financing operations in accordance with Islamic law.

Banks in Brunei until 2010 were regulated under the Banking Act and Finance Companies Act through the Ministry of Finance since there was no Central bank in Brunei. In 2010, his Majesty the Sultan and Yang Di-Pertuan Negara of Brunei Darussalam consented to the Authority Monetary Brunei Darussalam Order, which commenced on January 1, 2011. The Authority Monetary Brunei Darussalam Order, 2010, among other things, provides for the establishment of Authority Monetary Brunei Darussalam (AMBD). Four divisions previously under the Ministry of Finance merged to form AMBD, namely, (1) the Financial Institutions Division or FID, (2) the Brunei Currency and Monetary Board or BCMB, (3) the Brunei International Financial Center or BIFC, and (4) Part of the Research and International Division or RID.

Brunei has a dual legal system, one part of which is common law based and the other Syariah based. The regulatory framework for finance is quite comprehensive. It includes the Banking Order 2006, the Insurance Order 2006, and their respective 2008 Islamic banking/Takaful counterparts, that is, the Islamic Banking Order, 2008, and the Takaful Order, 2008. The Securities Markets Order 2013 covers both conventional and Islamic securities business. These Orders provide Brunei Darussalam with a generally adequate legal framework for the conduct of the banking, insurance, and securities business.

In 2015, Islamic banking held a significant role in Brunei's banking industry with total assets of BND 8.94 billion and deposits totaling BND 7.34 billion which accounted for 52.4% and 51.5% of the total market share. The operations of the licensed banks are governed by the provisions of the Banking Order, 2006, and the Islamic Banking Order, 2008. All fully licensed banks and finance companies operating in Brunei are mandatory members of the Brunei Darussalam Deposit Protection Corporation which was established in January 2011. Current banking system of Brunei consists of eight banks comprising one Islamic Bank and seven conventional banks, as well as an Islamic Trust Fund which is set up under its own statute. Out of the eight banks, three are international, three regional, and two domestic. In addition, there are three licensed finance companies, of which two are conventional and one is Islamic. The three finance companies are wholly owned subsidiaries of three licensed banks in Brunei Darussalam. According to ICD Thomson Reuters Islamic Finance Development Indicator 2014, Brunei ranked tenth out of 92 countries that practice Islamic finance.

The above statistics reflect bright prospects for Islamic banking and finance in Brunei Darussalam, in line with Brunei Darussalam's aspiration to contribute to the development of the Islamic financial industry. This demonstrates the government's seriousness to promote and boost Islamic banking. It is expected that with more government involvement and incentives, Islamic banking is set to move to the greater heights in Brunei

5. Australia

Muslims are one of the many minorities in Australia. Islamic banking in Australia was introduced quite successfully through a co-operative formed a decade ago by a small group of young Australian Muslims in the face of growing demands for interest-free banking from the community. The MCCA or the Muslim Community Co-operative (Australia) Ltd. was established in February 1989. MCCA was the first financial service provider that operated on Syariah principles in Australia. A capital of AUD22,000 was initially contributed to begin the institution.

The MCCA operates as a co-operative and specifically deals with investment accounts, where withdrawals are restricted. The services offered by

MCCA are personal and business finance, halal investments, Qard Hassan, and zakat collections and distributions. In its 1999 Annual Report, the MCCA wrote: 'The Co-operatives operation is based on the principles and ideals of Islamic finance based on the undisputed Islamic references, namely the Quran and the Sunnah (the authentic traditions of Prophet Muhammad). Under Islamic law, riba may neither be earned nor paid'.

The MCCA offered a limited range of halal financial services, and as the need for services grew, the Muslim Community Credit Union Ltd. (MCCU) was launched, whereby the MCCA was registered as a credit union. The MCCU is now governed by the provisions of the Australian Banking Act of 1959, the Australian Prudential Regulation Authority (APRA) Prudential Standards, the Consumer Credit (NSW) Code of 1996, and the Credit Union Code of Practice. The MCCU operates primarily a retail banking service where accounts are serviced on a day-to-day basis. MCCA is also a member of the Accounting and Auditing Organization of Islamic Financial Institutions (AAOIFI). In a nutshell, there is a growth in Islamic banking in Australia but challenges remain.

Other dominant financial service firms in Australia that offer Syariah-compliant services such as Islamic home finance, car loans and insurance, as well as halal investments are Crescent Wealth, an Islamic fund manager that exceeded $100mn in assets under management in 2015. Others are Islamic home financing specialist Amanah Islamic Finance, which has its own board of Syariah scholars, Islamic Cooperative Finance Australia, specializing on home and vehicle finance and on fund investments, home financing specialist Iskan Finance, fully fledged Islamic banking institutions such as Arab Bank Australia, as well as the Islamic window of Westpac Bank, in addition to industry associations such as the Australian Center for Islamic Finance and a number of law firms and consultancies specialized on Syariah-compliant financial services.

One of the latest entrants in the market was Sydney-based Equitable Financial Solutions (Efsol), specialized in Islamic savings structures, home and car financing, and halal investment products. Efsol turned out to become the most expansive Australian Islamic finance firm. In addition to its Sydney headquarters, it has offices in Brisbane, Melbourne, Adelaide, and Perth and one overseas office each in Karachi and Singapore (opened in April 2016).

According to Crescent Wealth's MD, Islamic finance in Australia has the potential to double from the 11 billion Australian dollars under management in 2013 to A$22 billion ($16.5bn) by 2020 owing to a combination of growing domestic demand and foreign capital inflows seeking halal investment opportunities.

Furthermore, Islamic finance is expected to be bolstered significantly in Australia when newly proposed tax changes eventually will come into effect. Currently, uncertainty surrounding the tax treatment of Islamic investments is hampering the development of the market as Islamic investors are technically subject to a multitude of obligations such as capital gains tax, withholding tax, land tax, and stamp duty. But a new law proposed in Australia's 2016–17 budget and expected to become effective on July 1, 2018, will eventually remove or at least drastically reduce tax barriers for Islamic investment structures such as asset-backed deferred payment contracts and hire-purchase arrangements.

6. Pakistan

Steps for Islamization of banking and financial system of Pakistan were started in 1977–78. Pakistan was among the three countries in the world that had been trying to implement interest-free banking at comprehensive/national level. But as it was a mammoth task, the switchover plan was implemented in phases. The Islamization measures included the elimination of interest from the operations of specialized financial institutions including HBFC, ICP, and NIT in July 1979 and that of the commercial banks from January 1981 to June 1985. The legal framework of Pakistan's financial and corporate system was amended on June 26, 1980, to permit issuance of a new interest-free instrument of corporate financing named Participation Term Certificate (PTC). An ordinance was promulgated to allow the establishment of mudharaba companies and floatation of mudharaba certificates for raising risk-based capital. Amendments were also made in the Banking Companies Ordinance 1962 (The BCO, 1962) and related laws to include provision of bank finance through PLS, mark-up in prices, leasing, and hire purchase.

Separate interest-free counters started operating in all the nationalized commercial banks, and one foreign bank (Bank of Oman) on January 1, 1981, to mobilize deposits on profit- and loss-sharing basis. Regarding investment of these funds, bankers were instructed to provide financial accommodation for government commodity operations based on sale on deferred payment with a mark-up on purchase price. Export bills were to be accommodated on exchange rate differential basis. In March 1981, financing of import and inland bills and that of the then Rice Export Corporation of Pakistan, Cotton Export Corporation, and the Trading Corporation of Pakistan were shifted to mark-up basis. Simultaneously, necessary amendments were made in the related laws permitting the State Bank to provide finance against Participation Term Certificates and also extend advances against promissory notes supported by PTCs and mudharaba certificates. From July 1, 1982, banks were allowed to provide finance for meeting the working capital needs of trade and industry on a selective basis under the technique of Musharakah.

As from April 1, 1985, all finances to all entities including individuals began to be made in one of the specified interest-free modes. From July 1, 1985, all commercial banking in Pak rupees was made interest-free. From that date, no bank in Pakistan was allowed to accept any interest-bearing deposits, and all existing deposits in a bank were treated to be based on profit- and loss-sharing. Deposits in current accounts continued to be accepted, but no interest or share in profit or loss was allowed to these accounts. However, foreign currency deposits in Pakistan and on-lending of foreign loans continued as before. The State Bank of Pakistan had specified 12 modes of non-interest financing classified in three broad categories. However, in any case, the mode of financing to be adopted was left to the mutual option of the banks and their clients.

The procedure adopted by banks in Pakistan since July 1, 1985, based largely on 'mark-up' technique with or without 'buy-back arrangement' was, however, declared un-Islamic by the Federal Shariat Court (FSC) in November 1991. However, appeals were made in the Shariat Appellate Bench (SAB) of the Supreme Court of Pakistan. The SAB delivered its judgment on December 23, 1999, rejecting the appeals and directing that laws involving interest would cease to have effect finally by June 30, 2001. In the judgment, the Court concluded that the present financial system had to be subjected to radical changes to bring it into conformity with the Syariah. It also directed the government to set up, within specified time frame, a commission for transformation of the financial system and two task forces to plan and implement the process of the transformation.

The Commission for Transformation of Financial System (CTFS) was constituted in January 2000 in the State Bank of Pakistan under the Chairmanship of Mr. I.A. Hanfi, a former Governor State Bank of Pakistan. A Task Force was set up in the Ministry of Finance to suggest the ways to eliminate interest from government financial transactions. The CTFS constituted a Committee for Development of Financial Instruments and Standardized Documents in the State Bank to prepare model agreements and financial instruments for new system.

The CTFS in its report identified several prior actions, which were needed to be taken to prepare the ground for transformation of the financial system. It also identified major Syariah-compliant modes of financing, their essentials, draft seminal law captioned 'Islamization of Financial Transactions Ordinance, 2001', model agreements for major modes of financing, and guidelines for conversion of products and services of banks and financial institutions. The Commission also dealt with major products of banks and financial institutions, both for assets and liabilities side, like letters of credit or guarantee, bills of exchange, term finance certificates (TFCs), State Bank's refinance schemes, credit cards, interbank transactions, underwriting, foreign currency forward cover, and various kinds of bank accounts. The Commission observed that all deposits, except current accounts, would be accepted on mudharaba principle. Current accounts would not carry any return and the banks would be at liberty to levy service charge as fee for their handling. The Commission also approved the concept of Daily Product and Weightage System for distribution of profit among various kinds of liabilities/deposits. The Report also contained recommendation for forestalling willful default and safeguarding interest of the banks, depositors, and the clients.

According to the Commission, prior/preparatory works for introduction of Syariah-compliant financial system briefly included creating legal infrastructure conducive for working of Islamic financial system, launching a massive education and training program for bankers and their clients, and an effective campaign through media for the general public to create awareness about the Islamic financial system.

The House Building Finance Corporation (HBFC) had shifted its rent-sharing operations to interest-based system in 1989. The Task Force of the M/O Law proposed amendments in the HBFC Act to make it Syariah compliant. Having vetted by the CTFS, the amended law has been promulgated by the government. Accordingly, the HBFC launched in 2001 Asaan Ghar Scheme in the light of amended ordinance based on the diminishing Musharakah concept. A committee was constituted in the Institute of Chartered Accountants, Pakistan (ICAP), wherein the SBP was also represented, for development of accounting and auditing standards for Islamic modes of financing. The committee is reviewing the standards prepared by the Bahrain-based Accounting and Auditing Organization for Islamic Financial Institutions (AAOIFI) with a view to adapt them to our circumstances and if considered necessary, to propose new accounting standards.

It was decided in September 2001 that the shift to interest-free economy would be made in a gradual and phased manner and without causing any disruptions. It was also agreed that State Bank of Pakistan would consider for:

1. Setting up subsidiaries by the commercial banks for conducting Syariah-compliant transactions;
2. Specifying branches by the commercial banks exclusively dealing in Islamic products; and
3. Setting up new full-fledged commercial banks to carry out exclusively banking business based on proposed Islamic products.

Accordingly, the State Bank issued detailed criteria in December 2001 for establishment of full-fledged Islamic commercial banks in the private sector. Al Meezan Investment Bank received the first Islamic commercial banking license from SBP in January 2002 and the Meezan Bank Limited (MBL) commenced full-fledged commercial banking operation from March 20, 2002. Further, all formalities relating to the acquisition of Societe Generale, Pakistan, by the MBL were completed, and by June 2002 it had a network of five branches all over the country: three in Karachi, one in Islamabad, and one in Lahore. The MBL now maintains a long-term rating of A+ and short-term rating of A1+, assessed by JCR VIS Credit Rating Company Ltd., signifying a consistent satisfactory performance.

The government and the State Bank are mainly concerned with stability and efficiency of the banking system and safeguarding the interests, particularly of small depositors. With this concern in mind it has been decided to operate Islamic banking side by side with traditional banking. The approach is to institute best practice legal, regulatory, and accounting frameworks to support Islamic banks and investors alike. The year 2002–2003 witnessed strengthening measures taken in the areas of banking, non-bank financial companies, and the capital markets.

Assets and deposits of Islamic Banking Industry (IBI) were recorded at Rs. 1885 billion and Rs. 1564 billion, respectively, by end of March 2017. Market share of Islamic banking assets and deposits in overall banking industry stood at 11.7% and 13.2%, respectively, by end of March 2017. The network of IBI consisted of 21 Islamic banking institutions: 5 full-fledged Islamic banks (IBs) and 16 conventional banks having standalone Islamic banking branches (IBBs) by end of March 2017. Branch network of IBI was recorded at 2317 branches (spread across 116 districts) by end of March 2017.

2.2 Functions and Principles

The primary function of Islamic institutions is to follow strictly to the Syariah principles in relation to financial contracts, effective resource allocation, investment in development projects, profitable placement of surplus funds, Syariah-compliant products/services, and so on. All the above functions have underlying Syariah principles. This section will focus on the comparison of application of principles by financial institutes in selected countries.

Muslim jurists have suggested a number of Syariah principles to be adopted by Islamic banks in delivering their products and services. Among the most widely used Syariah principles recommended by these scholars are Mudharabah, Musharakah, Murabahah, bai-mua'zzal, Ijarah, Ijarah wa-iqtina, Qard Hassan, wadiah, and rahnu. Basically, these principles can be broadly classified into four categories as below:

1. **Profit- and Loss-Sharing Principles**

    (a) Mudharabah (profit-sharing or trust finance)
    (b) Musharakah (partnership)

2. **Profit- and Loss-Sharing Principles**

    (a) Murabahah (cost-plus financing)
    (b) Bai Bithaman Ajil (deferred payment sale)
    (c) Ijarah (leasing finance)
    (d) Ijarah wa-iktina (lease-purchase financing)

3. **Free Service Principles**

    (a) Qard Hassan (benevolent loan)

4. **Ancillary Principles**

    (a) Wadiah (trusteeship)
    (b) Rahnu (pledge or pawn)

Generally, IFIs all over the world follow the above principles. The only difference is that the implementation of the above principles, business process, and other operational procedures vary from country to country, and among the different IFIs within the country.

2.2.1 The Use of Terminology

There is no universally followed terminology for Islamic financing. Malaysia is the only country where Arabic terms are used to describe all the Syariah principles governing its Islamic banking operations. Other countries, however, retain Arabic terms and principles and use vernacular terms for others. Some of the Arabic terms commonly used by almost all IBs are the principles of Mudharabah, Musharakah, Murabahah, Ijarah, and Qard Hassan. The slight differences in spelling are due to the different pronunciation of words in various countries (Table 7.1).

Table 7.1 Terminologies in practice for Islamic banking in ASEAN region

Terminology in Malaysia	Terminology definition	Terminology in Indonesia	Terminology in Thailand	Terminology in Brunei	Terminology in Australia
Wadiah yad dhamanah (savings with guarantee)	Refers to goods or deposits, which have been deposited with another person, who is not the owner, for safekeeping. As wadiah is a trust, the depository becomes the guarantor and, therefore guarantees repayment of the whole amount of the deposits, or any part thereof, outstanding in the account of depositors, when demanded. The depositors are not entitled to any share of the profits, but the depository may provide returns to the depositors as a token of appreciation.	Wadiah yad dhamanah	Al-wadiah	Al-wadiah	Not in practice

(continued)

Table 7.1 (continued)

Terminology in Malaysia	Terminology definition	Terminology in Indonesia	Terminology in Thailand	Terminology in Brunei	Terminology in Australia
Mudharabah (profit-sharing)	Refers to an agreement made between a capital provider and another party (entrepreneur), to enable the entrepreneur to carry out business projects, based on a profit-sharing basis, of a pre-agreed ratio. In the case of losses, the losses are borne by the provider of the funds	Mudharaba muthlaqah	Al-Mudharabah	Al-Mudharabah	Not in practice
Musharakah (joint venture)	Refers to a partnership or joint venture for a specific business, whereby the distribution of profits will be apportioned according to an agreed ratio. In the event of losses, both parties will share the losses on the basis of their equity participation	Musharakah	Not in practice	Al-Musharakah	Musharakah or shirkat al-mul

(continued)

Table 7.1 (continued)

Terminology in Malaysia	Terminology definition	Terminology in Indonesia	Terminology in Thailand	Terminology in Brunei	Terminology in Australia
Murabahah (cost plus)	Refers to the sale of goods at a price, which includes a profit margin as agreed to by both parties. Such sales contract is valid on the condition that the price, other costs, and the profit margin of the seller are stated at the time of the agreement of sale	Murabahah	Al-Murabahah	Al-Murabahah	Not in practice
Bai' Bithaman Ajil (deferred payment sale)	Refers to the sale of goods on a deferred payment basis at a price, which includes a profit margin agreed to by both parties	Deferred Murabahah or Bai' Bithaman Ajil	Deferred Murabahah	Al-Bai' Bithaman ajil	Ijarah wa iqtina
Bai' al-dayn (debt trading)	Refers to debt financing, that is, the provision of financial resources required for production, commerce, and services by way of sale/purchase of trade documents and papers. Only documents evidencing real debts arising from bona fide merchant transactions can be traded	Not in practice	Terminology used by Islamic Bank of Thailand is not explicitly defined	Not in practice	Not in practice

(continued)

Table 7.1 (continued)

Terminology in Malaysia	Terminology definition	Terminology in Indonesia	Terminology in Thailand	Terminology in Brunei	Terminology in Australia
Bai' al-inah	The financier sells an asset to the customer on a deferred payment, and then the financier immediately repurchases the asset for cash at a discount	Not in practice	Not in practice	Not in practice	Not in practice
Al-Ijarah Thumma Al-Bai' (leasing and subsequently purchase)	Refers to a Al-Ijarah (leasing/renting) contract to be followed by Al-bai (purchase) contract. Under the first contract, the hirer leases the goods from the owner at an agreed rental over a specified period. Upon expiry of the leasing period, the hirer enters into a second contract to purchase the goods from the owner at an agreed price	Ijarah bai ut takjiri or Ijarah muntahia bittamliik or Ijarah wa iqtina	Al Ijarah	Not in practice	Ijarah muntahia bittamleek

(continued)

Table 7.1 (continued)

Terminology in Malaysia	Terminology definition	Terminology in Indonesia	Terminology in Thailand	Terminology in Brunei	Terminology in Australia
Ijarah (leasing)	Refers to an arrangement under which the lessor leases equipment, building, or other facility to a client at an agreed rental against a fixed charge, as agreed by both parties	Ijarah	Al Ijarah	Al Ijarah	Not in practice
Qardhul Hassan (benevolent loan)	Refers to an interest-free loan. The borrower is only required to repay the principal amount borrowed, but he may pay an extra amount at his absolute discretion, as a token of appreciation	Qardh	Not in practice	Not in practice	Qard Hassan
Bai' as-salam (future delivery)	Refers to an agreement whereby payment is made in advance for delivery of specified goods in the future	Salam	Not in practice	Not in practice	Not in practice

(continued)

Table 7.1 (continued)

Terminology in Malaysia	Terminology definition	Terminology in Indonesia	Terminology in Thailand	Terminology in Brunei	Terminology in Australia
Bai' al-istijrar (supply contract)	Refers to an agreement between the client and the supplier, whereby the supplier agrees to supply a particular product on an ongoing basis, for example, monthly, at an agreed price and on the basis of an agreed mode of payment	Not in practice	Not in practice	Not in practice	Not in practice
Kafalah (guarantee)	Refers to a contract of guarantee by the contracting party or any third party to guarantee the performance of the contract terms by contracting parties	Kafalah	Terminology used by Islamic Bank of Thailand is not explicitly defined	Al-kafalah	Not in practice
Rahnu (collateralized borrowing)	Refers to an arrangement whereby a valuable asset is placed as collateral for debt. The collateral may be disposed in the event of default	Ar-rahnu or rahn	Not in practice	Ar-rahnu	Not in practice

(continued)

Table 7.1 (continued)

Terminology in Malaysia	Terminology definition	Terminology in Indonesia	Terminology in Thailand	Terminology in Brunei	Terminology in Australia
Wakalah (nominating another person to act)	Refers to a situation, where a person nominates another person to act on his behalf	Wakalah or wikalah	Not in practice	Al-Wakalah	Not in practice
Hiwalah (remittance)	Refers to a transfer of funds/debt from the depositor's/debtor's account to the receiver's/creditor's account whereby a commission may be charged for such service	Hiwalah	Terminology used by Islamic Bank of Thailand is not explicitly defined	Terminology used is not explicitly defined	Not in practice
Sarf (foreign exchange)	Refers to the buying and selling of foreign currencies	Terminology used is not explicitly defined	Terminology used by Islamic Bank of Thailand is not explicitly defined	Terminology used is not explicitly defined	Not in practice
Ujr (fee)	Refers to commissions or fees charged for services	Terminology used is not explicitly defined	Terminology used by Islamic Bank of Thailand is not explicitly defined	Terminology used is not explicitly defined	Terminology used is not explicitly defined

(continued)

Table 7.1 (continued)

Terminology in Malaysia	Terminology definition	Terminology in Indonesia	Terminology in Thailand	Terminology in Brunei	Terminology in Australia
Hibah (gift)	Refers to gifts award voluntarily in return for deposit kept with the bank	Hibah or bonus	Not in practice	Dividend. (Islamic terminology used is not explicitly defined)	Not in practice
Istisna	Sale and purchase of goods by order based on period, criteria, terms, and conditions earlier agreed, which payment can be made in instalment by the customer as the buyer to the bank as the seller upon receipt of the goods by the customer	Istisna	Al istisna	Not in practice	Not in practice

Source: www.bnm.gov.my, wwww.muamalat.com.my, www.bankislam.com.my, www.bni.co.id, www.muamalatbank.com, www.danamon.co.id, www.syariahmandiri.co.id, www.bi.go.id, www.isbt.co.th, www.ibb.com.bn, www.mcca.com.au

From the table, we can surmise that besides the common principles, countries also have specific Syariah principles for their Islamic banks. Although these principles are country specific, they do not necessarily mean that other countries are not familiar with these principles. This is because each Muslim country has its own independent religious body. It is the prerogative of the religious body within each country to establish its own principles. A particular principle adopted by one country is not necessarily regarded as a distinct principle by other countries.

Upon comparison with other Muslim and Middle East countries, it is noted that the principle of bai salam (purchase with deferred delivery) is used under the same name in Bangladesh (Islamic Bank of Bangladesh Limited) and Indonesia (Bank Muamalat) but is called salaf (forward delivery) by the Islamic banks in Iran. Similarly, rahn (Collateral Agreement) is an arrangement whereby a valuable asset is placed as collateral for a debt. The collateral may be disposed of in the event of a default. It is a popular tool for financing based on collateral in countries like Bahrain, Kuwait, UAE, and Indonesia, but not in Malaysia.

In the case of Iran, for example, other principles such as mozaraah and mosaghat, which are methods in agricultural financing, have been introduced. In mozaraah, banks may provide agricultural lands that they own or are in their possession (e.g. as trust) to farmers for cultivation for a specific period and a predetermined share of the harvest. In mosaghat, banks may also provide orchards or trees that they own or that are in their possession (e.g. as trust) to farmers for a specific period and a predetermined share of the harvest. Iran also has a product named Joaalah (service charge) where there is a small charge applicable to the customer for using the products and services of the banks. This is similar to al-kafalah, al-hawalah, and al-wakalah principles used in Malaysian banks.

As noted in a study by Haron (1998), there is no standardized Syariah principle used by Islamic banks in delivering deposit facilities. In the case of current accounts, for example, Iran and Kuwait use the principle of qard-al-hassan, whereas other countries such as Bangladesh, Jordan, Bahrain, and Turkey use the principle of wadiah. For Saving Account, Iran uses the principle of qard-al-hassan, whereas in Kuwait, the principles of qard-al-hassan and mudarabah are applicable for these accounts. The principle of qard-al-hassan is applied to the un-invested portion of funds in the Saving Account and the principle of mudarabah is for the invested portion. In Malaysia, Saving Account are controlled by the principle of wadiah yad dhamanah (guaranteed custody).

There is an interesting feature in the Dubai Islamic Bank in that it offers a special banking channel exclusively for women under the name of Johara Banking, which offers all the products being offered in commercial banking. This is in contrast to Kuwait, where women are not allowed to open bank accounts, and Saudi Arabia, where Saudi women cannot open an account without the permission of the husband or guardian.

The Syariah principles adopted by Islamic banks can be divided into four categories (Table 7.2):

1. Profit- and loss-sharing;
2. Fees based;
3. Free services; and
4. Ancillary principles.

3 Products and Services

Islamic banks perform a socially useful function in transferring financial resources from surplus units (households) to deficit units (business firms). Conventional banks perform these functions on the basis of interest. Islamic banks carry out the same functions by trading assets, that is, buying and selling. This section will cover the different products and services offered by different IFIs and the differences in the products and services offered in Malaysia, Middle East, Pakistan, and other Muslim countries.

3.1 Current Account

All Islamic banks operate current accounts on behalf of their clients, individuals, and business firms. These accounts are operated for the safe custody of deposits and for the convenience of customers. These accounts govern what is known as demand deposits given to the bank. The bank guarantees full return of these deposits on demand. The depositor authorizes the bank to use the funds, and hence, any profit or loss is owned by

Table 7.2 Comparison of functions and principles

Category	Malaysia	Indonesia	Thailand	Brunei	Bahrain	Dubai	Bangladesh	Iran	Kuwait	Pakistan
Profit- and loss-sharing principles	*Mudarabah *Musharakah	*Mudarabah *Muthalaqah *Musharakah	*Al-Mudarabah	Al-Mudarabah Al Musharakah	*Mudarabah, *Musharakah	*Mudarabah, *Musharakah	Al-mudaraba musharaka	*Musharakah, *lease-purchase	Mudaraba musharaka	*Musharakah
Fee- or charge-based principles	*Murabahah *Bai-bithman ajil *Bai-al dayn *Bai-al inah *Al-ijarah *Ijarah *Bai-al-salaam *Kafalah *Wakalah *Ujr *Istina	*Murabahah *Deferred Murabahah *Ijarah bai Ut takjiri *Ijarah *Salam *Wakalah *Hiwalah *Istina	*Al-Murabahah *Deferred Murabahah *Al Ijarah *Al-istina	*Al-Murabahah *Al-bai-bithmal ajil *Al Ijarah *Al-wakalah	*Ijarah, *Istina.	*Murabahah *Istina, *Ijarah *Salaam *Parallel Salaam *Manzil *Sakan *Salaf	Bai-mua'zaal Bai-salam Hire-purchase Ijarah Murabahah Commission	*Mozaraah, *Mosaghat, *Joaalah *Salaf	Murabahah commission service charges istisna leasing	*Ijarah *Istina
Free service principles	*Qurd-al-hassan	*Qardh			*Qurd al hassan	*	Qard-e-hassan	*Qurd-al-hassan	Qard hassan	*Qurd-al-Hassan
Ancillary principles	*Wadiah yad dhamanah *Rahn	*Wadiah yad dhamanah *Ar-rahnu	*Al-wadiah	*Al-wadiah	*Al shefa *Rahn,*education account	Al-qard-ul-hassan *Rahn	Wadiah	*Rahn		

Source: www.bnm.gov.my, www.muamalat.com.my, www.bankislam.com.my, www.bni.co.id, www.muamalatbank.com, www.danamon.co.id, www.syariahmandiri.co.id, www.bi.go.id, www.isbt.co.th, www.ibb.com.bn, www.anb.com.sa, www.bahisl.com.bh, www.bmi.ir, www.bnm.gov.my, www.bank-saderat-iran.com, http://www.alislami.co.ae/, www.mcb.com.pk, www.sbp.org.pk

the bank. Normally, there are no conditions imposed on the account holder with respect to the number of deposits and withdrawals. In addition, a check book is given to the account holder to draw check on their account.

There are two dominant views about current account. One is to treat demand deposits as wadiah yad dhamanah. Under this principle, the account is treated as a trust account instead of a current account. A trust deposit is defined as 'cash deposits received by the bank where the bank is authorized to use the deposits at its own risk and responsibility in respect to profit or loss and which are not subject to any conditions for withdrawals or depositing'. Thus, these deposits are handed over to the bank by depositors as a Trust, and the bank does not have the authority to use them without first obtaining the specific permission of the owner of the funds. In Malaysia, Bank Muamalat and RHB Bank offer Wadiah Current Account-i using wadiah as an underlying contract. Normally, the hibah is given to the customer on monthly basis at the bank's discretion. In Brunei, al-wadiah principle is used for current account and likewise in Thailand but no profit is shared with the depositor.

The other view is to treat current account deposits under the Mudharabah principle. Under this concept, a customer provides funds to the bank to invest in permissible activities in accordance with Syariah principles. The profits earned from the investment will be shared between customer and the bank, based on mutually agreed profit-sharing ratios. In Malaysia, RHB Bank offers Mudharabah Current Account-i (MudhCA-i), using Mudharabah as the underlying contract. In Australia, current accounts based on Islamic principles are currently not offered.

Islamic current account holders are provided with check books and other common facilities such as ATM cards, Internet banking, bill payment facilities, bank drafts, bill of exchange, and travelers' checks. These facilities differ from country to country. Table 7.3 provides a summary of facilities offered to Islamic current account holders in selected countries.

3.2 Saving Account

Islamic banks also accept savings deposits from individuals, but again the practice varies. Bank Islam Malaysia's (BIM) Saving Account product Wadiah Saving Account-i is based on the wadiah principle whereby the

Table 7.3 Comparison of Islamic current account facilities

Country	Islamic current account offered	Underlying principle	Hibab (gift/bonus)	Facilities provided
Malaysia	Yes	• 'Wadiah yad-dhamanah' • Mudharabah	Yes, based on bank's discretion	• Cheque book • ATM • Internet banking • Remittance • Bill of exchange • Traveler's check • Phone banking • Zakat
Indonesia	Yes	• 'Wadiah yad-dhamanah'	Yes, based on bank's discretion	• Cheque book • ATM • Internet banking • Remittance • Bill of exchange • Traveler's check
Brunei	Yes	• Al-wadiah	Yes, based on bank's discretion	• Cheque book • ATM • Remittance • Traveller's cheque
Thailand	Yes	• Al-wadiah	No	• Cheque book • ATM • Remittance • Traveler's cheque
Australia	No	Not applicable	Not applicable	Not applicable

Source: www.rhbislamicbank.com.my, www.muamalat.com.my, www.bankislam.com.my, www.bni.co.id, www.syariahmandiri.co.id, www.muamalatbank.com, www.ibb.com.bn, www.isbt.co.th, www.mcca.com.au

Note: Please note that the 'Facilities Offered' in the above tables differs from Bank to Bank within the country.

bank accepts deposits from its customers as a safe custodian. The bank gets the permission from the depositors to use his funds and in return may offer him hibah (gift) as a token of appreciation. In addition, the bank also guarantees the refund of deposit anytime to offer a convenience to the depositor. The underlying principle is that the depositor is not participating in a business risk, due to the right to withdraw the amount anytime and hence is not entitled for any returns.

BIM has also introduced a Saving Account based on Mudharabah principle known as Mudharabah Saving Account-i whereby the bank will use the funds for investment. Any profits gained by bank from the investment will be shared with the depositor as per the agreed profit-sharing ratio. The unique facility offered by Bank Islam Malaysia to Saving Account holders is the free Takaful. This is an extra value-added service to the customer (Table 7.4).

Table 7.4 Comparison of Islamic Saving Account facilities

Country	Islamic Saving Account offered	Underlying principle	Hibah (gift/bonus)/dividend	Facilities provided
Malaysia	Yes	• 'Wadiah yad-dhamanah' • Mudharabah	• Yes, based on bank's discretion • Yes	• Passbook • ATM • Internet banking • Remittance • Bill of exchange • Traveler's cheque • Takaful • Phone banking • Zakat
Indonesia	Yes	• 'Wadiah yad-dhamanah' • Mudharabah	• Yes, based on bank's discretion • Yes	• Passbook • ATM • Internet banking • Remittance • Bill of exchange • Traveler's cheque
Brunei	Yes	• Al-wadiah • Al-Mudharabah	• Yes, based on bank's discretion • Yes	• Passbook • ATM • Remittance • Traveler's cheque
Thailand	Yes	• Al-wadiah	• Not explicitly defined	• Passbook • ATM • Remittance • Traveler's cheque
Australia	No	Not applicable	Not applicable	Not applicable

Source: www.rhbislamicbank.com.my, www.muamalat.com.my, www.bankislam.com.my, www.bni.co.id, www.syariahmandiri.co.id, www.muamalatbank.com, www.ibb.com.bn, www.isbt.co.th, www.mcca.com.au

Note: Please note that the 'Facilities Offered' in the above tables differ from bank to bank with in the country.

Likewise, in Indonesia and Brunei, wadiah and Mudharabah principles are used as underlying contracts for the Islamic Saving Account. In Thailand, only the wadiah principle is used for Saving Account, and in Australia currently, MMCA is not offering the Islamic Saving Account facility. Islamic current account holders are provided with passbooks and other common facilities such as ATM cards, Internet banking, bill payment facilities, bank drafts, bill of exchange, and travelers' cheque and these facilities differs from country to country. The Table 7.4 above provides a summary of facilities offered to Islamic Saving Account holder in different countries.

Although it is not promised but in Malaysia, Indonesia, and Brunei, banks provide returns to their Saving Account customers. These rewards, however, are solely based on the discretion of the banks, and the customers will have no prior knowledge of the reward. Examples of the rewards are non-fixed prizes of bonuses in cash or in kind such as air tickets to holy shrines, carpets, gold coins or even cars, and an exemption or reduction from payment of commission for banking services. In Malaysia, the rewards for Saving Account holders are usually in the form of rate of profit announced by the bank on a monthly basis.

Bahrain Islamic Bank calls these accounts Saving Account with authorization to invest. Depositors provide the bank with an authorization to invest their money. Depositors have the right of withdrawal, but profits are calculated on the basis of the minimum balance maintained for a month. The Saving Account at the Dubai Islamic Bank also request from depositors, the authorization to invest and give them the right to deposit and withdraw funds. The profits in the Saving Account are calculated on the minimum balance maintained during the month. Depositors participate in the profits of Saving Account with effect from the beginning of the month following the month in which the deposits are made. Profits are not calculated with effect from the beginning of the month in which a withdrawal is made from the account. This account comes with a restriction, whereby depositor must maintain a minimum balance to qualify for a share in profits.

The Iranian Islamic banks include Saving Account in qard hasan accounts and call them qard hasan deposits. The operation of these accounts is similar to that of Saving Account in the conventional system as far as the deposit and withdrawal of money by means of a Saving Account passbook is concerned. Although no dividends are due in the case of qard hasan deposits, Iranian banks use different promotional methods to attract and mobilize deposits. These include incentives to depositors such as non-fixed bonus either in cash or in kind, discount on commission or service charge, and so on.

In addition, there are, however, some differences in the treatment of Saving Account facility among these banks. Islamic banks in Iran, BIMB of Malaysia, El Gharb of Sudan, and DIB of United Arab Emirates, for example, regard Saving Account as a facility by itself. IBB of Bahrain, IBBL of Bangladesh, JIB of Jordan, KFH of Kuwait, and BEST of Tunisia consider Saving Account as one of the facilities within the category of investment accounts.

3.3 Investment Deposits

Investment deposits under Islamic banks are called profit- and loss-sharing or participatory accounts. These accounts could be opened either by individuals or companies for any specified period, such as six months, one year, or even longer. The depositors do not receive any interest. Instead, they are entitled to a share in actual profit accrued from the investment operations of the bank. The profits are shared based on a pre-agreed sharing ratio. In the event of premature withdrawal, the depositor will have to forego his share of profit, which will depend on the tenure for utilization of deposit by the bank. In Malaysia, Bank Islam offers the investment account facility under 'Investment Account-i' using Mudharabah as the underlying principle for customer to gain maximum profit through investment. Under this facility, the customer is the provider of capital and the bank acts as an entrepreneur. Profit gained from the investment will be shared between both parties according to a predetermined ratio.

The duration for investment ranges from one month to a maximum of 60 months. The funds collected from the depositors are put into an investment pool, that is, a general investment account. Usually it is not tied to any specific investment project, but is utilized in financing different operations of the bank. The profits are accounted and distributed at the end of the period on a *pro rata* basis. The deposit amount ranges from RM500 to RM1000 based on the investment period and again differs from bank to bank. The bank also selectively accepts deposits from the government and corporate customers in the form of special investment accounts which are also operated on the Mudharabah principle; but the modes of investment of the funds and the ratios of distribution of profits may differ for each client.

Similarly, Bank Muamalat and RHB Islamic Bank in Malaysia not only offer Mudharabah General Investment Account-i (similar to Bank Islam) but also offer Mudharabah Special Investment Account-i. Under this investment deposit scheme, depositors provide specific authorization to the bank to invest in a project or trade. In this case, only the profits of this project are distributed between the bank and its customers according to mutually agreed terms and conditions. In the case of special investment accounts, Islamic banks function as an agent on behalf of depositors, and the minimum deposit amount is very high (e.g. RM500,000 as per the RHB Islamic Bank website).

In Indonesia, banks mainly use the Syariah principle of mudharaba muthalaqah. Unlike Malaysia, the maximum duration of investment is limited to 12 months only. A monthly profit share is automatically credited either to mudharaba/wadiah Saving Account or is cleared and circulated by the bank. In Brunei, the principle used for Islamic fixed deposits is Al-Bai' Bithaman Ajil (ABBA) and al-Mudharabah. The maximum duration for investment period is 60 months. Upon maturity, the contract will be automatically terminated; however, rollover is allowed for investment on the same tenure. The profit payment will be made at the end of the tenure period. In Australia, currently Islamic fixed deposits are not offered. The Table 7.5 provides the summary of facilities offered to Islamic investment holder in different countries:

In Iran, the duration of short-term investment deposits is three months and long-term deposits are of one year or more. According to prevailing practices, short-term deposits are left with the banks for an initial period of three months which can subsequently be extended by one month. The duration of long-term investment deposits is extendable by a multiple of three months. A minimum balance of Iranian riyal 2000 and 50000 is required for short- and long-term investment deposits, respectively.

Investment deposits are used by Iranian banks in any one of the following ways:

1. Banks can combine their own resources, that is, their capital, with investment deposits to finance an investment project. In this case, the resulting profits are shared between the depositors and the banks. In calculating the returns to depositors, the required reserves are subtracted from the base amount. The banks announce their profit rates every six months. The share of profits to depositors is also distributed accordingly. No profits are earned by depositors if the amount is either withdrawn before the required time or falls below the required minimum (Table 7.5).
2. Iranian banks are only allowed to invest their depositors' funds, that is, without mixing these funds with their own resources. In this case, the bank acts only as an agent on behalf of the depositors, and the profits earned as a result of the bank's investment of such funds are distributed among the depositors after the deduction of the bank's fees for acting as an agent. Furthermore, the return on the principal of these deposits is guaranteed by the bank.

In Pakistan, deposits, other than current accounts, are classified into three categories: special notice deposits, savings deposits, and fixed-term deposits. Under the Islamic banking system adopted in the country since 1985, all deposits are accepted only on a profit- and sharing-basis. Special notice deposits are further classified into two types: those requiring a notice of 7 to 29 days and those requiring a notice of 30 days or more. Savings deposits also comprise two types: with cheque facilities and without cheque facilities. As such, investment account facilities can be divided primarily into three categories:

(a) Deposits based on time, for example, for three months, six months, nine months, and so on;
(b) Deposits based on notice, that is, notice must be given by customers prior to any withdrawal; and
(c) Deposits for specified projects or purposes.

Table 7.5 Comparison of Islamic investment facilities

Country	Islamic investment facility offered	Underlying principle	Tenure	Profit payment
Malaysia	Yes	Mudharabah—General/special investment account	Period of 1 month and a multiple of 1 month thereof up to a period of 60 months	The profits are calculated and distributed at the end of the accounting period that may vary from one month to a year
Indonesia	Yes	Mudharaba mutlaqah	Period ranging from 1, 3, 6, to 12	A monthly profit share is automatically credited either to mudharaba/wadiah Saving Account or is cleared and circulated by the bank
Brunei	Yes	• Al-Bai' Bithaman Ajil (ABBA) and • Al-Mudharabah	Period ranging from 1 month to 60 months	Profit payment will be made at the end of the tenure period
Thailand	Yes	Al-Mudharabah	Not explicitly defined	Dividends are credited to Saving Account (Al-wadiah) and can be withdrawn only upon maturity
Australia	No	Not applicable	Not applicable	Not applicable

Source: www.rhbislamicbank.com.my, www.muamalat.com.my, www.bankislam.com.my, www.bni.co.id, www.syariahmandiri.co.id, www.muamalatbank.com, www.ibb.com.bn, www.isbt.co.th, www.mcca.com.au

Note: Please note that the 'Facilities Offered' in the above tables differ from bank to bank within the country.

Investment account facilities based on time are available at all Islamic banks in all countries. Investment deposit facilities based on notice, however, are only available at IBBL of Bangladesh and JIB of Jordan. Customers of IBBL must give 7 days' notice prior to any withdrawal and 90 days' notice at JIB. Specific investment facility is available in most countries except in Iran, Kuwait, Pakistan, and Turkey. In Tunisia, the investment account is divided into two categories, namely, participating deposit account and committed participating deposit. Participating deposit account comprises tawfir or Saving Account and time deposit. The operations of these two accounts are similar to the savings and ordinary investment accounts of other Islamic banks. In the case of committed participating deposits, its operations are similar to special or specific investment account facility of other banks.

The studies also show that the profit-sharing ratios and the modes of payment vary from place to place and from time to time. Thus, for example, profits are provisionally declared on a monthly basis in Malaysia, on a quarterly basis in Egypt, on a half-yearly basis in Bangladesh and Pakistan, and on an annual basis in Sudan.

3.4 Murabahah Financing

Murabahah is one of several Islamically permissible contracts of sale and purchase, which are increasingly being used in the financial sector by various Islamic banks. Islamic banks use the concept of Murabahah sale to satisfy the requirements of various types of financing, such as the financing of raw materials, machinery, equipment, and consumer durables as well as short-term trade.

In Malaysia, Murabahah financing is currently utilized for financing of working capital and for the issuance of letters of credit. Normally, the financing is for a short term and the duration ranges from 30 days, 60 days, 90 days, or any other period as the case may be. The customer may make the lump sum payment at the end of the financing term. The working capital financing is mainly for SME/corporate clients to purchase stock and inventories, spares and replacements of raw materials, and semi-finished goods.

In Indonesia, Murabahah financing is for a long-term duration. This financing method is used for business (financial capital and investment: purchasing product, machinery, tools equipment, etc.) or personal needs (vehicle and car). In Brunei, the Murabahah concept is mainly utilized for letter of credit financing. A customer engaging either in trading or manufacturing may require purchasing merchandise or raw materials in the course of his business. In this case, the customer requires LC together with financing over a certain period of time. The bank would offer him a LC facility under the al-Murabahah contract. The customer must initially inform the bank of the requirements of his LC and request the bank to purchase/import the goods. The customer as the purchasing agent for the bank must agree to purchase the required goods from the bank upon due arrival. Upon compliance of all LC requirements, the bank delivers the shipping documents and the bill of lading to the remitting or negotiating bank, from the bank's own funds. The bank then sells back the goods to the customer at an agreed marked-up price for settlement by cash on deferred basis. In addition, the Murabahah principle is also used in Brunei for working capital financing. It allows the customers to pay for their purchase on sight or on a deferred payment term of either 30, 60, or 90 days, or any other term as agreed by both parties.

In Thailand, al-Murabahah financing is mainly used for consumer financing and buying material financing. This facility caters for the purchase of commercial goods and raw material to be used in the production process under commercial financing. The duration of repayment is not more than one year. In addition, the Murabahah contract is also used for investment financing, whereby the existing entrepreneurs who wish to increase their production, enlarge the factory, or even invest in new project in the areas of land and building, land and construction, heavy machinery, and so on. The maximum financing is not more than 80% of appraisal value. The buyer is required to mortgage any of his property or equivalent for the purposes of value of collateral. The repayment period is up to five years. In Australia, Murabahah concept is used for financing of capital goods, motor vehicles, and other durables.

Table 7.6 provides the summary of various products offered using Murabahah principle in different countries:

Table 7.6 Comparison of Murabahah financing product

Country	Underlying principle	Product name	Tenure	Purpose
Malaysia	Murabahah	• Working capital financing • Issuance of letter of credit	Duration ranges from 30 days, 60 days, 90 days, or any other period as the case may be	Trade finance: Purchase stock and inventories, spares, and replacements of arrow materials and semi-finished goods
Indonesia	Murabahah	• Murabahah financing	Long-term and can be up to ten years	Business: Financial capital and investment (purchasing product, machinery, tools equipment, etc.) or personal needs (vehicle and car)
Brunei	Al-Murabahah	• Letter of credit • Working capital trade financing	Duration ranges from 30 days, 60 days, 90 days, or any other period as the case may be	Purchase of merchandise or raw materials, and so on
Thailand	Al-Murabahah	• Consumer financing • Investment financing • Buying material financing	• Maximum one year • Maximum five years • Maximum one year	• Consumer goods and household appliances • Commercial goods and raw material • New projects in the area of land and building, land and construction, heavy machinery, and so on

(continued)

Table 7.6 (continued)

Country	Underlying principle	Product name	Tenure	Purpose
Australia	Murabahah	Murabahah scheme	Not restricted	Capital goods, motor vehicles, and other durables

Source: www.rhbislamicbank.com.my, www.muamalat.com.my, www.bankislam.com.my, www.bni.co.id, www.syariahmandiri.co.id, www.muamalatbank.com, www.ibb.com.bn, www.isbt.co.th, www.mcca.com.au

Note: Please note that the 'Facilities Offered' in the above tables differ from bank to bank within the country.

Al Barakah Bank of Sudan also utilizes Murabahah concept for financing. Under this contract, the client requests the bank to purchase a commodity as per his specifications and to resell it to him at a marked-up price based on the agreed margin of profit. At the Jordan Islamic Bank, a Murabahah sale is used to finance the purchase of goods, such as cars, that are subject to mortgage and to purchase goods which are not subject to mortgage, such as household equipment, electrical appliances, and so on. The method is essentially the same with the difference being that in the case of goods which cannot be mortgaged, payment by the purchaser is deferred on the strength of a promissory note which is regulated by the bank in accordance with the conditions of the Murabahah contract. The merchandise is delivered to the client by the bank.

In Murabahah, payments have often been held up because of late payments and cannot be penalized, in contrast to the interest system in which delayed payments would automatically mean increased interest payments. In Malaysia, if the customer is not able to meet his payment schedule then the bank can charge 1% on the outstanding instalment to recover the administration fees, and this has been endorsed by Bank Negara Malaysia. 'Mark-down' amounts to giving rebates as incentives for early payments. But the legitimacy of this 'mark-down' practice is questionable on Syariah grounds, since it is time-based and, therefore, smacks of interest.

3.5 Bai Bithaman Ajil Financing

In Malaysia, Bai Bithaman Ajil (BBA) is widely practiced and is also known as deferred Murabahah or deferred sale. Under this facility, the bank shall first purchase the asset concerned. The bank then sells the relevant asset to the customer at a selling price which comprises the actual cost of the asset to the bank and the bank's profit margin. BBA facility is used for term financing and working capital financing. The prime difference between Bai Bithaman Ajil and Murabahah is that the cost of asset and percentage margin profit is not disclosed to client under BBA, whereas in Murabahah it is a mandatory condition. Murabahah is mainly used for short-term financing and usually the payment by the client is a lump sum, for example, Accepted Bills-i offered by Hong Leong Islamic Bank (www.hlib.com.my) is an Islamic version of banker acceptance and is based on the Murabahah principle.

BBA is also known as bai muajjal (sale on deferred payment basis) and is actively used in Pakistan and Bangladesh for asset financing such as houses, cars, and so on. Some Islamic economic authors make no reference to BBA as it is incorporated into Murabahah. However, in Malaysia, BBA is used separately and distinctly from Murabahah for its specific purpose, that is, long- versus short-term financing. BBA is for the acquisition of assets such as building and machines for a longer period of time (e.g. 10 to 30 years), while Murabahah is for financing working capital, that is, within 30 to 180 days. Secondly, one lump sum versus instalments. BBA is a deferred payment by instalments, while Murabahah is also deferred payment but in a lump sum. The BBA is currently practiced for medium- and long-term financing to acquire an asset, which may include the following:

1. Residential houses/building/shop houses/apartments/office space, and so on;
2. Plant and equipment;
3. Other appropriate assets;
4. Motor vehicles;
5. Shares;
6. Land; and
7. Refinancing of assets owned by the customers.

In addition, clients can utilize the facility as working capital requirement for halal business activities/operations by issuing cheques from the customer's designated current account. The naqad facility currently offered by Bank Islam Malaysia is a refinancing of an asset owned by the customer under a BBA contract. The facility proceeds are credited into the customer's designated current account and the customer is provided with a cheque book to withdraw the proceeds. Amount in drawn will earn income, which will be credited from time to time. The instalment payment is usually made monthly. However, other payment terms can be negotiated.

In Indonesia, financing based on Bai' Bithaman Ajil (purchase with instalments) is only offered by Bank Danamon and is mainly for house purchase, house renovation, jewelry, valuable products, working capital, and so on. with a flexible repayment terms, which differ based on the product and financing amount. In Brunei, Al-Bai' Bithaman Ajil (ABBA) is utilized by the banks to provide the customers with medium- and long-term financing to acquire assets or for any personal/trade financing. This facility is also used for financing of personal needs, education, computers, and other household appliances. For corporate clients, this facility is also used for real estate and corporate financing. Like Indonesia, the payment terms in Brunei differ for each product. Currently, this principle is not used explicitly in Thailand and Australia, but both countries currently offer deferred Murabahah, which is similar to the Bai Bithaman Ajil principle. Table 7.7 provides the summary of various products offered using the Bai Bithaman Ajil principle in different countries:

3.6 Musharakah Financing

Under this method, the bank and the would-be customer agree to join in a partnership for effecting certain operations within an agreed period of time. Both parties contribute to the capital of the project and agree to divide the net profit in proportions determined in advance. There is no fixed formula for profit-sharing and each case is dealt with on its own merit. Such operations, in practice, vary in duration from a few weeks to a few months, or if need be, for years. In the case of medium- and

Table 7.7 Comparison of BBA financing products

Country	Underlying principle	Product name	Tenure	Purpose
Malaysia	Bai Bithaman Ajil	• Consumer financing • Home financing • Education financing • Vehicle financing • Umrah and tour financing • Wahdah-debt consolidation plan • NAQAD • Fixed asset financing • Corporate financing • Share financing package	Duration ranges up to maximum of 30 years	Both personal and commercial financing
Indonesia	Bai Bithaman Ajil	• BBA-Rumah • BBA-Renovasi • BBA-Mobil • BBA-Sepeda Motor • BBA-Multiguna • BBA-Profesi • BBA-Modal Kerja • BBA-Investasi	Long term and can be up to 15 years	Both personal and commercial financing
Brunei	Al-Bai Bithaman Ajil (ABBA)	• ABBA personal financing • ABBA Al-Falah education financing • ABBA computer financing • ABBA personal household financing • ABBA real estate financing • ABBA corporate financing	Short term and long term	Personal and commercial working capital, operating expenses, ad-hoc financing and financing of fixed asset/ machinery

(continued)

Table 7.7 (continued)

Country	Underlying principle	Product name	Tenure	Purpose
Thailand	Not in practice	Not applicable	Not applicable	Not applicable
Australia	Not in practice	Not applicable	Not applicable	Not applicable

Source: www.rhbislamicbank.com.my, www.muamalat.com.my, www.bankislam.com.my, www.bni.co.id, www.syariahmandiri.co.id, www.muamalatbank.com, www.ibb.com.bn, www.isbt.co.th, www.mcca.com.au

Note: Please note that the 'Facilities Offered' in the above tables differ from bank to bank within the country.

long-term operations, a 'decreasing' form of participation is usually agreed on whereby the ownership of the whole project passes to the client after an agreed period of time during which the bank is expected to have retrieved its principle plus a suitable share of profits. The bank screens the client, appraises the project, monitors implementation, and if necessary takes part in actual management in order to make sure that the anticipated results are achieved. It is the bank's policy, however, to entrust management to its partners in the different joint ventures. A percentage of the net profit is left to the partner in consideration of his role as manager. The rest of the profit is distributed between the bank and partner according to their respective shares in the capital of the venture. The value of the fixed assets owned by the partner is estimated in monetary terms and included in his share of capital.

Bank Islam Malaysia issues Letters of Credit (LC) under the principle of Musharakah. The method adopted is as follows: The customer is required to inform the bank of his letter of credit requirements and negotiate the terms of reference for Musharakah financing. The customer places with the bank a deposit for his share of the cost of goods imported which the bank accepts under the principle of al-wadiah. The bank then issues the LC and pays the proceeds to the negotiating bank utilizing the customer's deposit as well as its own finances and subsequently releases the documents to the customer. The customer takes possession of the goods and disposes of them in the manner stipulated in the agreement. Profits derived from this operation are shared as agreed. The Musharakah principle is also followed for project financing. Musharakah financing is not that popular in Malaysia compared to the Middle East. Currently, Bank Islam in Malaysia only offers the products based on Musharakah principles; Bank Muamalat and other banks are currently in the process of implementation.

In Indonesia, Musharakah financing is mainly used for project funding and venture capital financing. Under project funding, Musharakah is generally used for funding a project where both the customer and bank provide funds to finance the project. Upon completion of the project, the customer returns the fund and gives a profit share to the bank as what has been pre-agreed by the two parties at the beginning of the contract. Likewise, under venture capital financing, the banks will do a capital investment and is carried out for a certain period and after that the bank will divest shortly or gradually. Type of businesses that are funded by the bank under Musharakah financing are trade, industry, manufacturing, contract-based business, and so on. The underlying principles used by Bank Danamon for Musharakah financing are as below:

1. *Al Inan*: Al Inan is a contract between two persons or more; each person contributes a portion of the whole fund and participates in a co-operative work. Both parties share profits and losses, which are based on a mutual consent. The portion of the fund contribution, responsibility for loss, and profit share are not necessarily the same for each person; they are based on the mutual agreement. Such cooperation is justified by all major Islamic scholars.
2. *Musharakah Mufawadha*: This is a contract between two persons or more, where each party contributes a portion of fund to the total amount of capital and takes part in a co-operative work. All parties share profits and losses of the enterprise. The main requirement of this Musharakah is that the fund, the work, and the responsibility of liability are shared at the same portions by each party. Scholars Hanafi and Maliki justify this Musharakah but make many limitations on its implementation.
3. *Musharakah A'maal*: In the Syariah system, two persons agree to carry out a work and share profit from the work. For example, two persons of the same profession and have the same expertise are willing to cooperate and share profit from the work. Both sides should agree on the

obtained profit-sharing as well as the work. This Musharakah is also known as Musharakah abdan or sanaa'i. Musharakah a'maal is justified by scholars Hanafi, Maliki, and Hanbali. This method is considered valid if the profession of both persons is the same. The justification is based on strong evidence, including an agreement by the Prophet Muhammad. This Musharakah has been in effect for many years and nobody ever disagrees with it.

4. *Musharakah Wujuh*: This is a partnership contract between two businessmen or more who have sharp expertise as well as good reputation and prestige. The persons involved in the contract buy an item from a company by credit, the process of which depends on their reputation. Then they sell the item in cash. They share profits as well as losses from the transaction, the portion of which is based on the guarantee provided by each partner to the supplier. In short, this Musharakah does not need capital, because it is based on a credit supported by a guarantee. Therefore, such partnership contract is also called 'credit Musharakah'.

In Brunei, Musharakah financing is also mainly for funding of projects similar to Indonesia. In Australia, for MCCA/MCCU, the Musharakah scheme is the primary source of business finance. It is an investment agreement between MCCA/MCCU and the business manager (the applying member) in which all terms and conditions, including the ratio of profit-sharing and security in a recovery situation, are pre-agreed. The co-operative/union, apart from the stringent criteria for the release of funds to the member, does not get involved or exercise any control or influence over the operations of the member's commercial activities. There are basically two types of Musharakah contracts, namely, for commercial investment schemes and shared equity and rental schemes currently practiced in Australia.

This method of diminishing partnership has been successfully applied by both the MCCA and MCCU mainly to finance the purchase of owner-occupied residential or commercial properties. Under this diminishing Musharakah partnership arrangement, MCCA/MCCU and the occupant (the buying member) agree jointly to purchase the property. Based on the share of each party's beneficial ownership, both parties agree to a fixed rental, which is divided proportionally between the parties on the basis of such an ownership. The occupant also agrees to purchase co-operatives beneficial ownership in the property over a deferred period. As the co-operative share declines, its share of rental income also declines. This process continues until the property is solely owned by the occupant. As a means of rationing supply, members have to serve a six-month qualifying period and must have at least 20% of the property purchase price invested with the co-operative/union prior to being eligible to apply (MCCA/MCCU will not invest more than 80% of the purchase price).

Thailand is currently not offering any financing products based on the Musharakah principle. The Table 7.8 provides the summary of various products offered using Musharakah principle in different countries.

This method of diminishing partnership has been successfully applied by the Jordan Islamic Bank mainly to finance real estate projects. The projects are financed by the bank, fully or partially, on the basis that the bank obtains a proportion of the net profits as a partner and receive another payment toward the final payment of the principal advanced. When the original amount is fully repaid, the ownership is fully transferred to the partner and the bank has no claim whatsoever. The Jordan Islamic Bank has financed the construction of a commercial market in Irbid, a community college in Jerash, and a hospital in Zerqa using this method of financing (Table 7.8).

Islamic banks in Sudan, especially the Sudanese Islamic Bank (SIB), have evolved yet another application of Musharakah which has tremendous potential for rural and agricultural development in the Islamic countries. Sudanese Islamic Bank has been experimenting in providing finance to farmers under Musharakah arrangements. The Al Barakah Islamic Bank of Sudan is using the technique of Musharakah to finance the sale and purchase of goods in the local market and also applies the same technique to finance the import of goods.

3.7 Mudharabah Financing

Mudharabah financing is a contract between two parties whereby one party, the rabbul-maal (beneficial owner or sleeping partner), entrusts money to the other party called the mudarib (managing trustee or labor partner). The mudarib is to utilize it in an agreed manner and then return to the rabbul-maal, the principal and the pre-agreed share of the profit.

Table 7.8 Comparison of Musharakah financing products

Country	Underlying principle	Product name	Tenure	Purpose
Malaysia	Musharakah	• Letter of credit	Duration ranges up to maximum of 30 years	• Purchase/import and sale/export of goods and machinery • Acquisition and holding of stock and inventories • Spares and replacements • Raw materials and semi-finished goods
Indonesia	Musharakah	• Project funding • Venture capital	Medium term and long term	Trade industry, manufacturing, and contract-based business
Brunei	Musharakah	• Project funding	Medium term and long term	Trade, industry, manufacturing, and contract-based business
Thailand	Not in practice	Not applicable	Not applicable	Not applicable
Australia	Not in practice	• Commercial investment scheme • Shared equity and rental scheme	Medium term and long term	Trade, residence, and commercial property

Source: www.rhbislamicbank.com.my, www.muamalat.com.my, www.bankislam.com.my, www.bni.co.id, www.syariahmandiri.co.id, www.muamalatbank.com, www.ibb.com.bn, www.isbt.co.th, www.mcca.com.au

Note: Please note that the 'Facilities Offered' in the above tables differ from bank to bank within the country.

The mudarib (bank) keeps for itself what remains of such profits. The division of profits between the two parties must necessarily be on a proportional basis and cannot be a lump sum or guaranteed return. The investor is not liable for losses beyond the capital he has contributed. The mudarib does not share in the losses except for the loss of time and effort.

In Malaysia, Mudharabah financing is applied for project financing and in special case for term financing. However, Mudharabah as a financing technique is not often used in Malaysia. In Indonesia, Mudharabah financing facility is used to support and help the customer's business, based on the pre-arranged agreement on profit-sharing. The bank carries the responsibility if the business suffers from financial losses except when the losses are caused by mismanagement and fraud from the customer himself. The common uses for this type of financing facility are for trading, industry, manufacturing, contract business, working capital, investment, and so on. However, this principle is not used for any financing products in Brunei, Australia, and Thailand.

In Iran, Mudharabah is considered a short-term commercial partnership between a bank and an entrepreneur. All of the financial requirements of the project are provided by the bank and the managerial input is provided by the entrepreneur. Both parties of the Mudharabah agreement share in the net profits of the project in an agreed proportion. Iranian banks are directed by the monetary authorities to give priority in their Mudharabah activities to co-operatives. Furthermore, commercial banks in Iran are not allowed to engage in the Mudharabah financing of imports by the private sector. In view of the limited relevant information, it is not easy to identify the comparison in practice of Mudharabah financing.

3.8 Ijarah Financing

Leasing is also one of the approved methods of earning income according to Islamic law. In this method, a real asset such as a machine, a car a ship, a house, and so on can be leased by the lessor to the lessee for a specified period against a specified price. The benefit and cost of each party should be clearly spelt out in the contract so as to avoid any element of uncertainty (gharar) with respect to their irresponsibility.

Bank Islam Malaysia also uses lease-purchase contracts. The procedure adopted is the same as that described earlier except that the client and the bank enter into an agreement at the time of the lease, that the client will purchase the equipment at an agreed price with the provision that the lease rentals previously paid shall constitute part of the price. In Malaysia, Ijarah is practiced for rental contracts and AITAB (Al Ijarah Thumma Al Bai) for hire purchase and sale contract. This financing amalgamates two concepts: the leasing contract and the trading contract. Leasing contract requires the customer to agree to rent/lease according to the mutually agreed period. Once the lease rental period has ended, the hirer agrees to purchase the goods from the lessor (owner) at the mutually agreed price. Under this concept, the bank makes available to the customer the use of service or assets/equipment such as plant, office automation, and motor vehicle, for a fixed period and price. The banks basically provide customers with short- to medium-term financing by way of leasing and finally acquiring items such as:

1. Plant and machinery;
2. Property;
3. Computers and information technology equipment;
4. Motor vehicles and heavy machinery; and
5. Other fixed assets.

In Malaysia, Ijarah thumma al bai contracts are also used to meet working capital requirements for customers who already own the assets. In this case, the customer will first sell the asset to the bank which constitutes the financing amount, with the understanding that the bank will lease it back to the customer. This is also known as a sale and leaseback transaction.

In Indonesia, Ijarah bai ut takjiri is widely practiced. This product is a contract of rent, which terminates at a transfer of ownership. This service is offered to customers who need to reinforce their assets through rental, but in the end they can own the assets. The other name for this kind of Ijarah is Ijarah muntahia bittamliik or Ijarah wa iqtina. Essentially, this product applies the rent-and-buy principle, where price of the rent and purchase is determined at the beginning of the agreement or contract. In addition, Ijarah Musharakah muntanaqisah is also a unique and popular product practiced in Indonesia. This product enables customers to own an asset by paying in instalments. The customer only has some part of the fund and the bank will supply the rest of the fund in this Musharakah method. Under this concept, bank and customer contribute to a joint fund for buying an asset. The asset is lent to the customer at a pre-agreed price. Since the customer intends to own the asset at the end of the rental period, the customer will not take any part of the rent money. All monies are submitted to the bank to complete the customer's fund contribution for the asset.

Therefore, the more the instalment fund is paid by the customer to the bank, the bigger the capital which is submitted for the asset ownership. In the end, the bank has no share of fund in the asset, and the asset belongs to the customer completely. This method is suitable for financing a house purchase and an alternative way to replace the conventional house ownership credit.

In Brunei, both al-Ijarah and Al-Ijarah Thumma al-Bai products are offered and the process is similar to Malaysia. In Brunei, al-Ijarah is also popular for leasing. Under this product, the lessee can also negotiate for a lease-purchase of the product, where each payment includes a portion that goes toward the final purchase and transfer of ownership of the asset. In this type of contract, the capital owner is responsible for all the risks attached to the life of the asset. This is mainly practiced for retail and commercial financing. Currently, Ijarah is not practiced in Malaysia.

The lease-purchase arrangement is also used by the Islamic banks in Iran, which purchase the required machinery, equipment, or immovable property and lease it to firms. At the time of the contract, the firms guarantee to take possession of the leased assets if the terms of the contract are fulfilled. The terms of the lease cannot exceed the useful life of the asset which is determined by the Central Bank of Iran. Banks in Iran are not allowed to lease assets with a useful life of less than two years.

3.9 Qard Hassan Financing

Many Islamic banks also provide interest-free financing (Qard Hassan) to their customers. However, practices differ in this respect. Some banks provide the privilege of interest-free loans to the holders of investment accounts at the bank. Other banks have a provision to provide interest-free loans to the economically weaker sections of the society. Yet some other banks provide interest-free loans to small producers, farmers, and entrepreneurs who are not qualified to get financing from other sources. The purpose of these interest-free loans is to assist them in financing their business ventures or to raise their income and standard of living.

In Malaysia, Qard Hassan is normally used for extra financing Islamic charge card and for few premium corporate clients. The bank offers qardh financing facility to staff of selected corporate clients, whereby the corporation will act as a guarantor. In Australia, the Qard Hassan fund is maintained solely as a benevolent function for the social advancement of members and non-members alike. The fund consists solely of donations and temporary placements. It is made available to those experiencing genuine and emergency financial crisis under an interest/cost-free loan agreement. In Indonesia, it is mainly practiced for the financing of charitable activities.

In Pakistan, a distinction is made between ordinary loans which are granted with a service charge and Qard Hassan loans which are granted without any service charge. The Faisal Islamic Bank of Egypt provides interest-free benevolent loans to the holders of investment and current accounts, in accordance with the conditions laid down by its board of directors. The bank also grants benevolent loans to other individuals under conditions decreed by its board. On the other hand, the Jordan Islamic Bank Law authorizes the bank to give benevolent loans for productive purposes in various fields to enable the beneficiaries to start independent lives or to raise their incomes and standard of living.

Iranian banks are required to set aside a portion of their resources out of which interest-free loans can be given to:

1. Small producers, entrepreneurs, and farmers who are not able to secure financing for investment or working capital from other alternative sources, and
2. Needy customers. It should also be noted that Iranian banks are permitted to charge a minimum service fee to cover the cost of administering these funds.

3.10 Bai Inah

Bai inah is a financing facility involving two separate contracts. In the first contract, a financier sells an asset to a customer on deferred payment terms. Immediately after, the financier repurchases the same asset from the customer on cash terms at a price lower than that of the deferred payment sale. It can also be applied vise versa where a financier buys an asset from a customer on cash terms. Immediately after, the financier sells back the same asset to the customer on deferred payment terms at a price higher than that of the cash sale.

The concept of bai inah is practiced for the Islamic charge card, working capital financing, and cash line financing in Malaysia. However, this concept is not permitted in the Middle East, Pakistan, Bangladesh, and Indonesia. The reason is that the contract is ethically flimsy when applied in this manner. The transacted sale is a fake sale and thus just a means of masking riba. Currently, this product is also not offered in Thailand, Brunei, and Australia.

3.11 Islamic Charge Card

The Islamic charge card is the substitute for conventional interest-based credit cards. In 2001, AmBank Malaysia launched the Al Taslif Credit Card in Malaysia. The underlying Syariah principle for financing is bai inah that covers instalment repayments over a fixed period. Cardholders are charged 1.25% per month or 15% per annum on the outstanding balance, with nothing to pay if the minimum payment requested is made on time. The bai inah contract works based on two 'aqad' agreements. The first is the bank's agreement to sell an item to the customer at an agreed price, with the second agreement covering the customer selling back to the bank at a lower price. The difference is the bank's profit on the transaction and is a predetermined amount. There is no penalty charged to the customer, and for the unutilized financing amount, the customer is eligible for rebate.

Similarly, Bank Islam Malaysia launched its Bank Islam Card (BIC) on July 23, 2002. This card works off a combination of three Syariah contracts: bai inah (as for AmBank's Al Taslif card), wadiah, and Qard Hassan. Once an initial bai inah transaction has taken place, the item nominally transacted being 'a piece of land' according to the bank, the proceeds of the second transaction are transferred into the customer's wadiah BIC account at the bank. The customer can then use the BIC card to make payments with the collateral all coming from the funds in the wadiah account. Finally, the Qard Hassan contract is activated if the cardholder wants to spend more than the funds available in the wadiah account and the bank agrees to make more funds available on an interest-free basis. Same as Al Taslif, cardholder is eligible for rebate, Takaful, and no compounding of profit.

Brunei also has an Islamic charge card issued by Islamic Bank of Brunei under the name of An-Naim card and is based on ABBA (Al-Bai Bithaman Ajil) principle. In Indonesia, charge cards have been issued by Syariah using a kafalah and Ijarah agreements. In the implementation of Islamic credit cards in Indonesia, there are two mandatory conditions, which also serve as the differentiating factor from the practice of conventional credit card. Firstly, there must be a cash saving and the amount must be equal to the ceiling (limit) of the Islamic credit card; secondly, there must not be any interest imposed on the debt incurred. The existence of liquid guarantee on the issue of Islamic credit cards is an effective effort in order to meet the following requirements. From the Islamic aspect, it is considered that providing a guarantee will satisfy the Islamic norms because it conforms to the Sunnah (meritorious deeds). The proposition by Central Bank Indonesia is to use qardh (loan) and/or kafalah (guarantee) contract for Islamic credit cards. In addition, as per the central bank, the naming of the Islamic credit card is important and the terms that can be used are 'Islamic Liquidity Card' to reflect the essence of being in debt in Islam as a need for liquid instrument or 'Islamic Qardh Card' to reflect that being in debt in Islam does not allow interest. This product is currently not offered in Australia and Thailand.

The critics from the Middle East region are not in favor of using the bai inah concept used as an underlying principle for credit cards. Their reasoning is that the contract is ethically flimsy when applied in this manner, and the sale transacted is a fake sale and thus just a means of masking riba. As is the case with matters of Syariah-compliance, judgments are based on the Syariah board of each financial institution and so what may be acceptable to one board may yet be haram for another. For many Middle East bankers, the solutions found by the Asian banks are simply not stringent enough in their interpretation of Quranic rules.

Hence, in the Middle East region, Islamic credit cards are known as charge cards. One such example is Al Rubban MasterCard, available in Bahraini dinars, Saudi riyals, or US dollars. The approach followed is that no wadiah deposit is required as the collateral comes from a direct salary transfer rather than a balance. The payment system works by treating total card spend during any given month as being payable over 12 monthly instalments. So, for a balance generated of BD100, 12 equal monthly instalments of BD8.34 will be due. The revenue comes from a 5% fee for the provision of the guarantee and administrative costs that is levied on the first statement containing the transaction. This fee must be settled by the due date on that statement and there is a fixed fee for cash advances that must also be repaid in full on the due date of that first statement. The repayment period is set at 12 months for ease and convenience while the card is still being tested in the market and that the instalment period can be extended. The key point is that there is no link between the fees charged and the repayment period as in the case of conventional card repayments.

3.12 Istisna

Istisna means sale by order of goods/property, which is to be constructed/manufactured and delivered at a specified future date for an agreed price. Istisna is the best form of contract to finance customers who wish to acquire assets under construction. It is suitable in terms of payment and rules of sale. Under this facility, the bank will purchase the ownership to the asset being constructed from the customers by innovating the construction contract between the customer and his contractor. Subsequently, the bank will sell back the asset to the customer at a selling price which will be made up of the original purchase price and the bank's profit margin. Upon completion, the contractor will hand over the property to the bank, or the bank will authorize the contractor to deliver the property directly to the customer. The payment of instalments may start during or after the construction of the property. The ownership of the property purchased will be under the bank's claim and will be handed over to the customer upon full payment.

In Malaysia, the istisna principle is used by Bank Muamalat and Bank Islam to offer financing for construction of housing projects, construction of industrial/commercial building, and commercial projects. In Indonesia, it is a financing facility offered by Bank Muamalat to purchase products based on customer orders. In Thailand, istisna financing is used for real estate financing and housing financing. The bank offers 80% of the appraisal value to the customers and caters for the following purchases:

1. To purchase of vacant land;
2. To purchase of land and building;
3. To purchase house of residence;
4. To renovate/expand residence house; and
5. To refinance from other financial institutions.

4 Financial Reporting

Since Islamic banks are expected to perform the role of achieving equitable distribution of wealth in society (ummah), it is necessary for Islamic banks to provide information, which clearly shows the revenue generated from its different modes of activities. From a thorough investigation of the latest financial statements of selected Islamic banks in various countries, it is noted that there are many differences in their annual reports. It is worth noting that none of the selected Islamic banks surveyed, provided details of their investment activities in their annual report. The investments were only classified as Islamic investment or non-Islamic investment.

Under the mudarabah principles, there is a need for disclosure by IFIs to investors on how the funds are being managed so as to provide the assurance that the underlying business operations, the risk profile, and the risk control mechanisms are in place. In Malaysia, this has been addressed through the establishment of an effective rate of return framework, which provides a standard methodology for deriving the rate of return on deposits. The Profit Equalization Reserve has been provided in the rate of return framework for IFIs, which serves as a mechanism to mitigate the impact of the fluctuations in the rates of return. The reserve is appropriated from the gross income and is shared by both the depositors and the banking institution.

From the survey of the annual reports, it is noted that Islamic banks from Pakistan, Iran, Bangladesh, and Kuwait avoid making any mention of non-performing financing assets or the basis on which they make provision for uncertain receivables, particularly the specific provision. This is in contrast to the growing practice among conventional banks to give a breakdown of their overdue or non-performing loans so as to help the shareholders in analyzing the relative level of credit risk.

Another contention is whether using historical cost or current valuation is appropriate in preparing financial statements. The financial statements of The Bahrain Islamic Bank (BIB) financial statements are prepared under the historical convention fair value of the investments. These are stated on the investments in real estate and non-trading investment available for sale. Thus, the BIB's financial statements are prepared based on the combination of historical cost and current valuation. On the other hand, the BIMB financial statements are prepared under historical convention. It is stated in the report that the BIMB will treat the investment securities on the basis of cost or market whichever is lower. If the market is lower than the cost, the investments must be valued based on the market value.

It has been noted by Hameed and Yahya (2003) that Islamic banks are not only obliged to report their economic performance but also the banks' achievements in fulfilling their social and environmental objectives. They proposed that Islamic banks should not prepare the same type of financial reports as conventional ones do. Instead their reports should consist of several principle elements to attain the ultimate objectives of Syariah laws. Shahul et al. further proposed several elements that the Islamic banks should report, such as information which identify clearly the Islamic investments, and the non-Islamic investments, information about the halal and haram revenues, information which provide the statement of changes in restricted investments, proper disclosure of the sources and uses of funds in zakat and Sadaqah (charity), information about sources and uses of Qard Hassan funds, and information which clearly identify the sources of revenue. But it can be seen from the table 7.9 that except for Bahrain Islamic Bank, none of the banks reviewed, disclosed their sources of income, details of expense, usage of zakat, sources, and usage of Qard Hassan (Table 7.9).

5 Summary

The comparisons of these financing techniques in various institutions and countries have been noted. It may be observed that Islamic banking is far more complex than conventional banking as far as the financing techniques are concerned. Even in the case of deposit mobilization, Islamic banking has been able to offer various kinds of financial products. However, it is in the area of assets rather than liabilities that the practices of Islamic banks are more diverse and complex than those of conventional banks.

The major issue is that so far there is no standard law or practice for Islamic finance and banking. Standardization is urgently needed in the following respects:

1. *Vocabulary of Islamic Banking*: There is no universally followed terminology for Islamic financing. One finds interbank differences in the use of terms. This may cause the hurdle in communication among Syariah scholars and may also hinder popularization of Islamic banking.
2. *Financial Instruments and Documentation*: It is difficult to think of identical documentation for all IFIs in lieu of a given Islamic financial instrument. This is because practical concerns may vary from institution to institution, practical needs may not always be the same, and, finally, the door for financial innovation in emergent situations will always remain open. Nevertheless, there has to be some measure of standardization in financial instruments for speedy migration to an Islamic financial system in the Muslim world. This is almost a must for regulatory purposes.

Table 7.9 Financial disclosure of Islamic banks of different countries

Category	Malaysia	Indonesia	Thailand	Brunei	Bahrain	Dubai	Iran	Pakistan
Income sources	Yes	Yes	Yes	Yes	Yes. Figure in detail in the forms of Murabahah, mudarabah, and Musharakah	Yes. Figure in detail in the form murabahat	Yes	Yes
Expenses details	Yes	Yes	Yes	Yes	Yes. In detail in the form of Ijarah	Yes	Yes	Yes
Sources of Qurd-Al-Hassan	No	No	No	No	Yes. Sources are other banks or donations	No	No	No
Uses of Qurd-Al-Hassan	No	No	No	No	Yes. For marriages, medicals, and others	No	No	No
Use of Zakat/ Charity	No	No	No	No	Yes	No	No	No
EPS	Yes	Yes	Yes	Yes	Yes	Yes	Yes	Yes
Details of Islamic / non-Islamic investments	No	No	No	No	No	No	No	No

Source: www.anb.com.sa, www.bahisl.com.bh, www.bankislam.com.my, www.bmi.ir, www.bnm.gov.my, www.bank-saderat-iran.com, http://www.alislami.co.ae/, www.mcb.com.pk, www.sbp.org.pk, www.bni.co.id, www.bi.go.id, www.ibb.com.bn

3. *Pricing and Structure of Islamic Products*: Standard pricing formulas, in the light of Syariah principles, are needed for efficient working of the Islamic financing model across countries. Their development will also help promotion of Islamic financing in academic and professional circles.

Islamic banking requires consolidation in the area of product standardization and Syariah rulings to have a greater force in the market, and standardization will make the Islamic financial system more efficient. It is a common understanding that without greater standardization in certain core products and markets, Islamic banks will struggle to develop the necessary volumes of their conventional banking counterparts. To achieve the standardization, few non-profit institutions have been established. The Accounting and Auditing Organization for Islamic Financial Institutions (AAOIFI) prepares accounting, auditing, governance, ethics, and Syariah standards for IFIs. Likewise, the Islamic Financial Services Board (IFSB) was established in Malaysia in November 2002 to serve as an international standard setting body for the regulatory and supervisory agencies.

Harmonization of all disagreements is not straightforward. However, it is not impossible given the appropriate prerequisites and accommodative regulatory framework. The idea of trying to harmonize different concepts and applications is already in action. Here AAOIFI and IFSB play a pivotal role in standardization. This represents 'diversity in standardization' as the Islamic law itself reflects unity in diversity.

References

www.ibb.com.bn
www.taib.com.bn
http://asia.news.yahoo.com/060201/3/2f2tf.html (Islamic bank merger creates top Brunei lender).
http://biz.thestar.com.my/news/story.asp?file=/2006/8/11/business/15112945&sec=business
http://en.wikipedia.org/wiki/Talk:Islamic_banking
http://store.eiu.com/index.asp?layout=show_sample&product_id=280000228&country_id=ID (Country Finance Indonesia 2003 Main Report).
http://www.arabicnews.com/ansub/Daily/Day/020308/2002030825.html

http://www.asosai.org/R_P_financial_accountability/chapter_12_brunei_darulsalam.htm
http://www.bnm.gov.my/index.php?ch=174&pg=467&ac=367
http://www.bot.or.th/bothomepage/BankAtWork/Bond/bond_e.htm
http://www.brudirect.com/DailyInfo/News/Archive/Dec05/181205/nite02.htm (Brunei Islamic Financial Planning Week Launched).
http://www.brudirect.com/DailyInfo/News/Archive/June05/120605/nite02.htm (Brunei Stamps Mark in Global Islamic Banking).
http://www.financeinislam.com/article/35/1/190
http://www.hwwa.de/Projekte/IuD_Schwerpunkte/IDSPs/Asia_Gateway/Islamic%20Banking%20in%20Asia.htm
http://www.iiff.com/upl_images/pressrelease/IIFFDubai2005Issue4.pdf
http://www.iifm.net/news069.php?PHPSESSID=da7299be261067e4b82c8b03e759e8e0
http://www.imf.org/external/pubs/ft/fandd/2005/12/qorchi.htm
http://www.indianmuslims.info/news/2006/july/01/muslim_world_news/islamic_bank_of_thailands_fund_to_reach_more_than_10_billion_baht.html
http://www.isbt.co.th/en/about_ibt/history.htm
http://www.islamic-banking.com/news/archives_country/thailand_news.php
http://www.islamicfinancetraining.com/glossary.php
http://www.islamicity.com/finance/IslamicBanking_Evolution.asp
http://www.islamonline.net/English/News/2003-10/10/article04.shtml (Diverse Fortunes for Islamic Banking in Indonesia).
http://www.kaau.edu.sa/CENTERS/SPC/page-092.htm
http://www.mcca.com.au/page.php?id=AAOIFI&product_id=104
http://www.menafn.com/qn_news_story_s.asp?storyid=117909
http://www.mui.or.id/mui_en/news.php?id=50
http://www.nationsencyclopedia.com/Asia-and-Oceania/Malaysia-BANKING-AND-SECURITIES.html
http://www.onebrunei.com/news_item.php?nid=6239 (Two-day Islamic Banking Workshop opens).
http://www.profitera.com/article.php?story=20060317101316201 (Indonesia: Islamic banking faces skills shortage).
http://www.sultanate.com/news_server/2006/1_feb_3.html (Islamic banks merge).
http://www.thai2arab.com/eng/content.php?page=content&category=&subcat=&id=19
http://www.tmcnet.com/usubmit/-brunei-brunei-islamic-financial-planning-week-launched-/2006/02/21/1395252.htm (Brunei: Brunei Islamic Financial Planning Week launched).

http://www.usc.edu/dept/MSA/economics/islamic_banking.html
http://www.usc.edu/dept/MSA/economics/nbank3.html
http://www.usc.edu/dept/MSA/economics/nbank3.html
Bank Negara Malaysia. *Money and banking in Malaysia*. Silver anniversary edition 1959–1984.
El Qorchi, Mohammed. (2005, December). Islamic finance gears up. 42(4). Retrieved from http://www.imf.org/external/pubs/ft/fandd/2005/12/qorchi.htm
Archer, Simon and Abdel Karim, R. A. (Eds.). (2002). Islamic finance: innovation and growth. London: Euromoney Books and AAOIFI.
Hameed, S. M. I., & Yahya, R. (2003). *The future of Islamic corporate reporting: Lessons from alternative western accounting report*. Paper presented in the International Conference on Quality Financial Reporting and Corporate Governance, Kuala Lumpur.
Haron, S. (1995). The framework and concept of Islamic interest-free banking. *Journal of Asian Business, 11*, 26–39.
Haron, S. (1997). Islamic Banking Rules & Regulations. Pelanduk Publication, Kuala Lumpur.
Haron, S, Alam, N and Shanmugam, B (2007), Islamic Financial System: A Comprehensive Guide, Insight Network, Kuala Lumpur.
Hassan, T. (1991, April–June). Islamic banking: The need for uniform regulation. *Journal of Islamic Banking and Finance, 8*(2), 15–30.
Iqbal, M. and Molyneux, P. (2005), Thirty Years of Islamic Banking: History, Performance and Prospects, Palgrave Macmillan, New York, NY.
Islamic Bank Bangladesh Limited, Bangladesh. www.islamibankbd.com
Jordan Islamic Bank, Jordan. www.jordanislamicbank.com
Karim, R. A. A. (1995). The nature and rationale of a conceptual framework for financial reporting by Islamic banks. *Accounting and Business Research, 25*(100), 285–300.
Kuwait Finance House. www.kfh.com
Mirza, A. M., & Halabi, A.-K. (2003). Islamic banking in Australia: Challenges and opportunities. *Journal of Muslim Minority Affairs, 23*(2), 347–359.
Muslim Commercial Bank, Pakistan. www.mcb.com.pk
Shanmugam, B., Perumal, V. & Ridzwa, A.H. (2004), Islamic Banking: An International Perspective, Universiti Putra Malaysia Press, Selangor Darul Ehsan.
Toutounchian, I. (1995). Resource mobilization for government expenditures through Islamic modes of contract: The case of Iran. *Islamic Economic Studies, 2*(2), 35–58.

8

IT in Islamic Banks

1 Introduction

Information technology (IT) has become one of the most crucial competitive differentiators in the banking industry of the twenty-first century. Today's banking business cannot exist without IT. This is mainly due to the need to handle large volumes of transactions, implementing cost-saving measures, effective delivery channels, and for better information-based decision-making.

IBM had published a report on the future of banking, stating that technology will become even more critical to success and a central component of strategic decision-making. Banks now use IT to differentiate themselves from competitors and to seize market opportunities more quickly and effectively. IT also enables banks to serve customers better by offering more personalized products and banking experiences. Banks are now moving toward an 'on demand' environment, and technology is the key enabler in achieving this. With the advancement in IT, banking has become more integrated. IT provides new ways of collaboration. It also eases business integration and helps banks better manage rising complexities.

Islamic banking is young in comparison to conventional banking. IT plays an important role in the advancement of Islamic banking. Although Islamic banking is expanding rapidly, it is facing major competition from conventional banking. The need to provide more innovative processes and to be more dynamic in offering banking services has been acknowledged by Islamic banks. This offering of innovative products and services through reduced time to market product development, online services, and improved customer service is enabled by IT. This chapter will throw light on the evolution and usage of IT by Islamic banks.

1.1 Evolution of Technology in Islamic Banking

In the early days of Islamic banking, most of the Islamic financial institutions (IFIs) relied on manual processes for a small range of products and services. However, the need for automation comes with the increase in sophistication, data volumes, complexity, and cost benefits in the range of products and services.

The IT solutions for conventional banks are more developed than for Islamic banking. Conventional banks enjoy a variety of competing IT solutions to meet their needs. Islamic banking being relatively young lacks such luxury. There have been two main sources of supporting IT applications for Islamic banks.

1. *Pure Islamic IT Banking System*: There are a few systems that have been built from the ground upward to meet Syariah-specific requirements. The suppliers of these IT solutions are typically small and localized. Due to the niche market, their market segment is relatively small (e.g. projects for specific Islamic banks). However, they can claim the moral ground by using 100% Syariah-compliant IT solutions as their unique selling point. Their results are often turned into commercial offerings.

   Today, these IT solutions are in great demand as the IFIs believe that these applications and services are in compliance with Syariah. This is especially true in the event conventional banks migrating into Islamic banking or offering specific Islamic products. Hence, many financial institutions are opting for pure Islamic IT banking system.

2. *Customized Islamic IT Banking System*: The second source has been the standard conventional banking package that is customized to meet Islamic banking requirements. At present, most of the systems available in the market fall into this category. This is in the interest of suppliers as their market segment is not limited to only Islamic banks but also conventional banks. These suppliers enjoy the benefit of market presence having been in the industry for some time. This has also provided them lead time to invest in research and development. There is a debate on whether customized Islamic banking solutions are in compliance with Syariah requirements. The general perception is that these solutions are tweaked by replacing the 'Interest' label with 'Profit' and the rearranging of the profit, rebate, and penalty computation part to adapt the underlying processes or the addition of modules for Islam-specific products and services.

   The key issue is that Islamic banking is not a marketing tag or label. It differs in fundamental issues underlying the nature of the contract, transaction processing, documentation, and fiscal relations that need to be recorded in accordance to Syariah. Therefore, due to the underlying nature of Islamic finance and the methods of handling fund sources and usage, mere tweaking will not make the system fully compatible to Syariah requirements. These attributes are apparent as there are insufficient disclosure and transparency in the financial statements of Islamic banks. However, despite the ongoing debate, the majority of Islamic banking IT solutions fall into this category.
3. *Hybrid Islamic Banking System*: Banks use a combination of pure Islamic banking system and customized Islamic banking system to automate their financial products and services. Under this category, banks use a standard package such as a conventional customer relationship management (CRM) solution integrated with Islamic financing and deposit solutions. This provides an overall view of customer relationship, which enables the bank's customer care center to cross-sell products and services and address their queries.

Despite having a number of Islamic banking solution providers, finding a modern architecture capable of servicing the needs of Syariah compliance remains a challenging task for banks. To fill this gap, many software development companies, especially from the Middle East and India, are joining the race to meet the unique requirements of Islamic banking.

1.2　Islamic Core Banking System

The core banking system (CBS) refers to the application suite that manages a bank's entire banking operations and facilitates the business lines to provide fast and effective banking services. Core banking systems are the heart of a bank. All day-to-day banking transactions are processed real time through the CBS. CBS also refers to the main customer accounting applications responsible for processing and posting transactions; performing deposit accounting; maintaining financing accounts, multi-currency accounting, and collateral management; and clearing payments. It automates and integrates business operations, satisfying both operational and administrative data processing needs for a financial institution. The capability of the system to perform real-time processing of transactions offers banks' speed, accuracy, control, and efficiency at the operational level. The functionality of the system might differ for each bank as it is dependent on their strategic needs and operational requirements.

CBS is a critical system for banks and plays a vital role in improving customer service. IT helps in rolling out new products quickly and complying with regulations. Islamic banks are categorized as universal banks. Therefore, the system should address retail banking, corporate banking, investment banking, and treasury functions. It also enables the standardized connection to ensure the necessary communication (Online real time and/or batch) with other software products. It also enables the simple integration of third-party systems via open interfaces. The advanced and new generation solution supports end-to-end integration of business operations across the bank.

The core banking system comprises various key subsystems as illustrated in figure (Fig. 8.1):

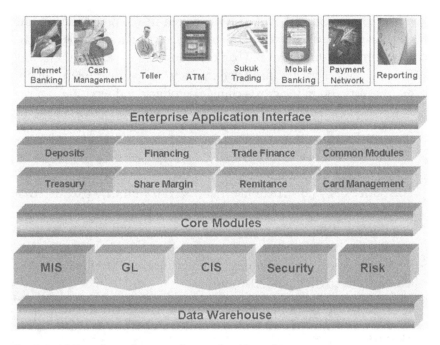

Fig. 8.1 Various key subsystems in core banking system

1.2.1 Customer Information System

The customer information system (CIS) is the nucleus of the CBS, where all information related to individuals and legal entities is managed. CIS is the first contact point of the customer. It is a one-step relationship management process. It enables the bank to capture the client's personal, demographic, and financial details. Customers are categorized as individuals and companies. This is further subcategorized for ease in marketing and positioning. This distinction helps the bank to better define the relationship between an individual or a company (a customer or prospective customer) and the financial institution to calculate profitability, risk, and to set the ground for customer relationship management (CRM).

Customer management is critical and banks recognize the need for a holistic and dynamic approach to customer management in the financial services industry. Customer-centric service strategies are a necessity in the quest for organic growth as institutions seek new revenue sources and fiercely defend existing revenue streams. CIS facilitates a single view on customer relationships with the bank. It consolidates information about a customer for the various financial products and services offered by the bank. It assists also in the cross-selling of products and services.

System Features

1. Classification of customer types into depositors, borrowers, guarantors, directors, and shareholders, and so on, with easy parameterization of customer categories;
2. Supports a complete view of their customers and facilitates cross-selling of other products;
3. Supports blacklisted customer maintenance and facilitates online check while starting new relationships;
4. Stores all the clients' personal, professional, financial, and statistical data and a wide range of other information such as transaction history records;
5. Flexible customer account search with multiple search options (name or part thereof, ID number, ID type, business registration, etc.);
6. Maintenance of both business and personal addresses and telephone numbers of the customer for contact management;
7. Inbuilt processes to avoid customer record duplication. This process ensures that the same customer is not duplicated in the system; and
8. Ready interfaces with other subsystems to provide a single view of relationships and should be capable to interface with other third-party systems.

1.2.2 Financing Information

This system manages investment transactions according to the bank's standards and conditions, including investment period, profit ratio, grace period, settlement period, central bank classifications, and mutual insurance. The core banking financing module address banking services demand adhering to Syariah rules. The system should efficiently automate and integrate operations, satisfying both operational and administrative data processing needs for a financial institution. The Islamic financing module supports a comprehensive range of features and functions that meet the needs of financing department based on the various Islamic financing concepts and principles as follows:

1. *Product Definition*: Product definition is one of the most powerful features of the system. It offers the bank the flexibility to easily and quickly set up and modify the product to reduce time to market. This is critical as Islamic banking is evolving and the range of innovative Islamic products introduced by Islamic banks must be sufficient to compete with their counterpart.

    The system should provide flexibility to define the product category, Islamic concept, product description, product life and validity, product eligibility criteria, financing duration, instalment computation, rebate, financing limits, general ledger (GL) account definition, and so on. As such, banks can easily customize and create the products to suit their requirements.

2. *Collateral Management*: The system contains information related to security or collateral that is tagged to financing facilities. List of securities supported should include landed property, stock and share, investment certificate, letter of guarantee, letter of credit, contracts, marginal deposit, life insurance, miscellaneous collateral, vehicles, financial guarantee, and so on.

3. *Financing Origination System*: This system will usually come with the financing origination module to capture financing requests and route them through a user-defined workflow for approval and processing based on the client's creditability. The module gives the user the control, flexibility, and dynamic workflow necessary to give the quick turnaround on financing approval.

4. *Account Management*: This module keeps detailed control of each of the different financing packages offered by the bank to its customers, as well as to configure and define the products available to the customers. The key features include:

(a) The system supports different types of Islamic financing with their own features such as different types of purchase price, selling price, grace period, profit, payment amounts, principal amount, penalties, fees, multiple types of payments, and so on;
(b) Storage of collateral/guarantees received and the bank users can record, modify, and assign it to financing transactions and transfers;
(c) Profit margin calculation for financing amount based on the rules maintained during product creation:

   (i) Flat rate (fixed rate to be charged to the customer for the whole financing period);
   (ii) Variable/multi-tier rate (rate will be charged based on the financing duration);
   (iii) Rule of 78.

(d) Supports multiple income recognition methods (monthly/daily/annual rest, Rule of 78, flat rate);
(e) Powerful calculation tools for all branch personnel to simulate the payment plan based on the client's request;
(f) Supports early settlement and redemption;
(g) Computation of penalty based on pre-defined rate on outstanding instalments;
(h) Provision for grace period computation;
(i) The system supports multiple repayment types and frequencies;
(j) Flexible financing disbursement method such as lump sum, multiple, against available and approved balance, and so on;
(k) Management of default accounts;
(l) Autogeneration of statutory notices and reminders;
(m) System supports GP3 (Garis Panduan 3) guidelines for non-performing loans/performing classification;
(n) Complete reporting, accounting, and finance tracking to help Islamic banks in better management of financing.

1.2.3 Deposits

The deposit system supports all types of commercial and consumer deposit products based on the principle of wadiah, Mudharabah, and so on. It automates all functions related to the operations of savings and current account. The bank will be able to create products, open accounts, and perform day-to-day banking transactions such as deposits, withdrawals, remittance, and so on, either in cash or clearing.

System Features

1. Online real-time transaction processing and access for all types of deposit accounts (savings/current);
2. Supports Islamic concept products such as wadiah yad amanah, wadiah yad dhamanah, Mudharabah (restricted/unrestricted);
3. Provides multiple methods of hibah calculation such as flat rate, multi-rate, multi-tier. The computation can be based on daily balance, monthly minimum balance, monthly average balance, or daily average balance;
4. Handling of cheque book management, cheque tracking, passbook printing, account statement generation, vouchers printing, certificate of deposits generation, and so on;
5. Generation of account statement on request basis;
6. Inventory control for the cheque books, passbooks, and so on;
7. Tagging of cash line facility for current account holder. Normally cash line account is opened under financing module but is linked to the client's current account;
8. Provide auto-sweep and standing instruction facilities for recurring and non-recurring transactions;
9. Classification of accounts such as dormant, active, closed, and no debit status;
10. Defining signatures of authorized clients, accounts' handling privileges, and ensuring the same automatically;

11. Integrated with online channels such as Internet banking, ATM, mobile banking, and other online channels for online transaction processing with anywhere branch banking facility to the customer.

1.2.4 Investment

The investment system supports complete processing of investment deposits from the stage of deposit placement until maturity. It maintains records of clients' participation in various investments and allotment of clients' profits based on the agreed profit-sharing ratio and the tenure of investment. It supports different types of investment types such as restricted (Mudharabah muqayyadah) or unrestricted (Mudharabah mutalaqah) with multiple placement transaction types such as placements made by cash, cheque, deposit, or account transfer.

System Features

1. Fixed-term deposits can be for different periods based upon clients' requests and the profit-sharing ratio that can differ for each client;
2. Automatic generations of fixed deposit certificate number and printing of certificate;
3. Issuance and maintenance of Mudharabah investment certificates such as pledges, lost, withdrawn, renewed, and frozen;
4. Provide multiple methods of dividend calculation such as flat rate, multi-rate, multi-tier. The computation can be based on daily balance, monthly minimum balance, monthly average balance, or daily average balance;
5. Automatic upliftment of matured or premature investment certificate with zakat deduction option;
6. Provide auto-renewal facilities for investment under Mudharabah with/without dividend compounded;
7. Inventory control for the investment certificates;
8. Users can perform maintenance, enquiry, signature verification, housekeeping, and the printing of relevant reports;

9. Under restricted Mudharabah, the system maintains all data of investment and participants, in relation to specific investment operations, carried out by the bank in favor of clients and automatic allotment of profits based on the agreed revenue sharing; and
10. Integrated with online channels such as Internet banking, ATM, and mobile banking for online deposit placement.

1.2.5 Treasury

This system supports dealing in Islamic money market instruments such as profit-sharing (Mudharabah) instruments, cost plus (Murabahah) instruments, and repurchase (bai inah) instruments for banks and on behalf of its customers. It automates and streamlines treasury operations with enhanced functionality and process integration that allow an integrated flow of trades, exceptions management, and maintaining the data integrity via straight-through processing (STP) of deals. It enables a centralized management of treasury operations and functionalities supported are as following:

1. Single-point entry for the dealers and operation staff for every trade;
2. Centralized risk control;
3. Online processing across whole treasury—Management process, prices, positions, profit, and loss;
4. Centralized information in a global data repository;
5. Flexibility to incorporate new processes and external data flows;
6. Wide range and user definable inquiries via screen or hardcopy;
7. Supports transactions for foreign exchange and other instruments based on Mudharabah, Murabahah, Bai Bithaman Ajil, Qard Hassan, and ujr (fees) principles;
8. Assist dealers in deal capturing, position maintenance/revaluation, and profitability analysis;
9. Multi-clients, portfolio of funds, multi-currency, multi-region, and trading markets;
10. Quantify and reduce the impact of market volatility through a comprehensive risk management framework;

11. Allow external solution integration with dealing and payment systems to improve straight through processing (STP);
12. Real-time integration with core systems for positions, cash management, settlement, and reconciliation.

1.2.6 Trade Finance

The trade finance system automates the operations involved in issuance and processing of inward and outward letters of credit, letters of guarantee, inward and outward bills for collection, and so on. In Malaysia, most of the trade finance instruments are based on Murabahah (mark up), al kafalah (guarantee), and al Wakalah (agency). The system handles end-to-end processing from the point of initiation where the customer submits the relevant document to avail LC service until it is reviewed, processed, and issued by the bank. Islamic trade finance system facilitates more sophisticated and automated trade finance facilities by following the Islamic banking framework. The key function of the system is to process the documents electronically and straight through processing by interfacing with external payment networks. It enables the centralization of the management of trade finance operations, and other key features are as below:

1. Processing of imports and exports instruments such as letter of credit, banker's acceptance, bankers and shipping guarantee, import purchase services, import purchase financing, export sale financing and agency function for Islamic foreign/domestic inward bill for collection, and Islamic foreign/domestic outward bill for collection;
2. Automation of various stages involved in letter of credit processing such as LC amendment, LC extension, expiry, cancelation, confirmation, acceptance, revocation, and so on;
3. Customer grading based on credit worthiness and collateral management processing;
4. Computation of charges, profit, and commission based on pre-defined parameters;

5. Assigning and monitoring of limits such as permanent limit, temporary limit, and one off limit; and
6. Interface with payment network such as SWIFT (Society for the Worldwide Interbank Financial Telecommunication), RENTAS (Real-Time Electronic Transfer of Funds and Securities), and Treasury Module for NOSTRO/VOSTRO Reconciliation.

1.2.7   Share Margin System

This system automates the Syariah-structured financing vehicle to leverage the share trading portfolio of the client. A facility will be granted for the sole purpose of trading halal shares (in compliance with Syariah) against pledge of shares/collateral owned by the client. Under this program, the facility will be financed on an agreed percentage (e.g. 50/50) shared between the client and the bank. It comprises front-end (order placement, portfolio, viewing of price feed, etc.) and back-end (order settlement, profit computation, reporting, check on trading of stock type, etc.) components.

System Features

1. The system addresses all regulatory reporting and complies with the regulated security standard and guidelines;
2. The system supports financing for trading based on the Islamic concepts such as bai inah, Mudharabah, and so on;
3. User-defined business rules for processing of brokerages, charges, settlement, profit computation, and so on;
4. The system provides connectivity to the retail banking system by linking the client's bank account to the client's trading account and is seamlessly integrated to the trading module;
5. User-defined parameterization for dealing in halal stocks such as price feed view limited to halal stocks, and so on;
6. Flexible interfaces with broker's system for online trading and other third-party systems;

7. Capping of share price and negative counter-list maintenance based on the bank's business policy;
8. Daily computations of buying and selling limit for brokers to perform a fund availability check prior to order placement;
9. Process of normal buy, sell, contra trade, and auto force sell in the event customer defaults on the settlement day; and
10. The products are normally categorized into share margin financing, share trading (no financing limit offered to the client), and ESOS (employee stock option scheme).

1.2.8 Remittance

The system supports processing of financial transactions, non-financial transactions, and standing orders. It facilitates online financial transaction processing for demand draft, intra-bank fund transfers, telegraphic transfers, travelers' cheque, banker's cheque, inter-bank fund transfers via Interbank Giro (IBG), and so on. This system serves clients by handling their outgoing and incoming transfers, and also returning a transfer in case of non-delivery. It automates the day-to-day remittance transactions. The functions supported are listed below:

1. Maintaining all outgoing and incoming transfers data;
2. Processing transfers, calculation, and settlement of commissions;
3. Returning outgoing and incoming transfers;
4. Supports online or batch processing of transactions initiated from deposit accounts or incoming clearing files and generates messages for the domestic clearing;
5. Processing of standing order by generating financial (payment order) or non-financial (direct debit or collection requests), based on the specified frequency period and other conditions;
6. Direct debit mandate for collection of funds from specified account based on the collected limit, number of collection, and frequency;
7. Earmarking of funds for specified purpose or transaction based on the pre-defined frequency, amount, and other set criteria;

8. Interface with payment network such as IBG, SWIFT (Society for the Worldwide Interbank Financial Telecommunication), and RENTAS; and
9. Auto computations of charges and inventory management for physical instruments such as demand draft, travelers' cheque, bankers cheque, and so on.

1.2.9 Card Management System

Card management system is a full-function credit, debit, and charge card management system supporting VISA, MasterCard, Diners Club, debit, and other commercial finance cards. It supports the issuing of card management, PIN (Personal Identification Number) management, as well as chargeback, settlement, risk management, dispute processing and authorization, and the online real-time processing of transactions. It assists the bank in personalization of cards for cardholders with all the cardholder account and finance details.

1. Card Type

   (a) *Debit Card*: It is a plastic card, which can be magnetic strip-based or chip-based, issued by a bank, which allows its customers to withdraw cash or pay for goods and services electronically. This removes the need for bank clients to go to the bank to withdraw cash from the account as they can now just go to an ATM or pay electronically at merchants' location via an EDC (electronic data capturing) terminal. This type of card, as a form of payment, also removes the need for cheques as the debit card immediately transfers money from the client's account to the business account.
   (b) *Credit Card*: A plastic card having a magnetic strip, issued by a bank or business authorizing the holder to buy goods or services on credit and is also known as charge card. It allows consumers to purchase products or services without cash and to pay for them at a later date. Islam permits the use of credit cards as long as they do not involve the element of interest. As an example, if withdrawing

cash advance from the card account will result in payment of an interest, it is strictly prohibited. Similarly, additional interest charges due to delay in payment are also prohibited. On the other hand, if the credit card serves as a charge card, where customer only pays the principal amount and the service charges, then it is permitted.

2. Other Features

   (a) *Processing of applications for cards*: initiating generation of PINs, PIN mailers, other card security numbers, and card carriers; generating personalization files; maintaining customer and card records; managing replacement of damaged, lost, and stolen cards; and managing the card renewal cycle;
   (b) Operating of accounts for prepaid, credit, charge, and deferred debit cards, as well as setting customer and account credit limits and charging interest and fees;
   (c) Link multiple account and other necessary details into a single card;
   (d) Processing of card transactions acquired through merchant outlets and ATMs; maintaining merchant and account details; charging merchant service fees, and generating payments to settle with merchants; and
   (e) Processing of incoming and generating outgoing transaction files for international, local, and internal interchanges and managing dispute transactions such as retrieval requests and acknowledgments, charge-backs, and re-presentments.

1.2.10 General Ledger

The General Ledger (GL) maintains a multi-currency enterprise and client accounting system. It supports multi-company, multi-branch, and multi-profit center facilities and facilitates consolidation and reporting of accounts information maintained within the Nostro/Vostro module. The system enables the user to process all kinds of transactions at both on and off balance sheet levels. Some examples are standard journal voucher processing, adjustments, allocations, reversals, cheque payments, bank reconciliation, budgeting, and forecasting. It also comes with a flexible report formatter for the bank user to define layouts for selected financial reports such as the balance sheet, profit/loss statement, and subsidiary statements for the financial institutions and the clients.

System Features

1. Defining chart of accounts, by means of defining main, subsidiary, and detailed accounts;
2. Multi-currency accounting;
3. Carrying out and reversal of accounting transactions, according to dual-entry concept;
4. User-defined GL chart definitions, cost centers, attributes, profit accrual and crediting, statement parameters, and so on;
5. Accounting rules in general are definable on the basis of product, customer types, amount types, balance sheet and off-balance sheet accounting, and accounting events;
6. Provides report formatter tools for users to perform financial analysis with slice and dice capabilities;
7. Provides online cash flow updates to enable the bank to plan their funding activities into the future;
8. Automatic ends of day, month, and year procedures, as per specific accounting periods;
9. Auto monthly and yearly closing, and generation of necessary entries;
10. Generation of profit and loss, balance sheet, and other account statements;
11. Compliance with AAOIFI (The Accounting and Auditing Organization for Islamic Financial Institutions) and MASB (Malaysian Accounting Standards Board) guidelines on Islamic accounting.

1.2.11 Internet Banking

Electronic banking is an umbrella term for the various processes by which a customer may perform banking transactions electronically without visiting the bank. The following terms refer to one form or another of electronic banking:

1. Personal computer (PC) banking;
2. Internet banking;
3. Virtual banking;
4. Online banking;
5. Home banking;
6. Remote electronic banking; and
7. Phone banking.

PC banking and Internet or online banking are the most frequently used designations. The terms used to describe the various types of electronic banking are often used interchangeably.

PC banking is the latest generation of electronic banking whereby the bank's customers' can perform banking transactions from a dedicated PC connected via a dial-up modem. Under PC banking, the bank offers the customer a proprietary financial software program installed on the customer's PC to perform financial and non-financial transactions. The customer uses a dial-up modem to connect to the bank's virtual private network. This technology still exists, but most of the banks are now moving on to Internet banking solution as it offers the flexibility to use general Internet connection to perform any transactions.

Internet banking, known also as online banking, is an outgrowth of PC banking. Internet banking uses the Internet as the delivery channel to conduct banking activities such as transferring funds, paying bills, viewing checking and Saving Account balances, paying mortgages, purchasing financial instruments and certificates of deposit. An Internet banking customer can access his or her accounts using the Internet browser such as Internet Explorer and Netscape Navigator. It offers bank's customers' instant access to account information, and it offers the flexibility to carry out financial and non-financial transactions anytime and anywhere. The system supports the following functionalities:

1. Account Information:

    (a) Account summary (wadiah savings/wadiah current/Mudharabah investment—General and special, etc.)
    (b) Account details (view account statement)

2. Funds Transfer

    (a) Intra-bank transfer between customer's own accounts
    (b) Intra-bank transfer to third-party (beneficiary) accounts
    (c) Inter-bank transfer to third-party (beneficiary) accounts with other bank
    (d) Transfer enquiries
    (e) Transfer can be immediate or scheduled (via standing order)

3. Bill Payments

    (a) Various payee categories (utility service providers such as electricity, water, telephone, and other third parties)
    (b) Online buying of prepaid mobile top up (talk value)
    (c) Direct debit from retail or financing accounts
    (d) Payment can be immediate or scheduled (via standing order)

4. Other Services

    (a) Request for card suspension (ATM and debit cards)
    (b) Cheque management (order cheque book, tracking of cheque, stop cheque payment instruction)
    (c) Online submission for account opening (retail accounts)
    (d) Online service application (ATM/debit card, housing financing, Islamic card, etc.)
    (e) Contact call center
    (f) Mudharabah investment placement and maturity instructions

(g) Cash order/Telegraphic transfer payment
(h) Standing instruction maintenance

5. Personalization by Bank's Customer

   (a) Customer can personalize the main page such as personalized account name for each account, preferred transaction display format, preferred currency exchange rate display, etc.
   (b) Change information (password, reminder question, contact address, set log off time).

6. Security

   The system is accessible via Internet, and banks normally use encryption technologies to provide a secure transaction environment. The security feature includes:

   (a) *Data Confidentiality and Integrity*: Using strong encryption and digital signature functions (128-bit symmetric cryptography and 1024-bit asymmetric cryptography) to ensure that sensitive data are not exposed or tampered with.
   (b) *Application Security*: Careful security architecture design to ensure that application security is observed (e.g. preventing unauthorized linking of bank accounts)
   (c) *Access Control*: Fine grain control of access to functions and bank accounts within a business.
   (d) *Token Authentication and Authorization*: Security token used for strong authentication and authorization to ensure second-factor authentication.

1.2.12 Branch Teller System

The branch teller system provides effective branch management. Its functionality is dependent on the functions that are supported by the core banking modules. It is a front-end system for the branch personnel to serve customers and to perform day-to-day banking transactions on their behalf. It enhances the efficiency of branch operations and improves customer service. Normally, it is catered to single- and multiple-entry transactions to expedite the transaction processing and reduce the waiting time. It automates the branch operations and supports the following functions:

1. *Transaction Processing*: The key transactions normally supported by branch teller system are as follows:

    (a) Financial and non-financial transactions, that is, deposits/domestic and international payments and transfers/withdrawals, and so on;
    (b) *Ad hoc* statements/cheque issuance/account restraints, and so on;
    (c) Foreign exchange and travelers' cheques;
    (d) Financing payments;
    (e) Fixed deposit account (renewals/roll over/redemption/pre-termination);
    (f) Customer relationship opening/maintenance and product enrolment;
    (g) Signature verification module for capturing and maintenance of customer's signature;
    (h) Passbook printing with a provision to print consolidated or detailed transactions;
    (i) Bills and utilities payments;
    (j) Foreign Exchange transactions;
    (k) Cheque deposits and maintenance for house cheques, local cheques, outstation cheques, post-dated cheques, and so on;
    (l) Electronic journaling for all the transactions processed;
    (m) Inter-branch transaction handling;
    (n) Local and remote override for transactions exceeding the teller limit or specific transactions for which dual verification is needed; and
    (o) Interface to biometrics and/or smart card devices for teller and customer authentication.

2. *Store and Forward Processing*: In the event that there is no connectivity between the branch and head office, the system will still allow transactions to continue. Normally, there is a mini database at each individual branch for their customer to perform a limited number of transactions and enquiries during offline mode. The moment connectivity is established between the branch and head office system, all offline transactions will be uploaded to ensure synchronization of the data and accuracy. This function is to ensure that in the event of a network breakdown, the branch can still service customers;
3. *Cash Management*: Cash management is another key function of the system. It will keep records of cash given to an individual teller at the beginning of the day, and total collection and disbursement to compute the end of day balance, which has to be deposited by an individual teller. It ensures a tight control on the teller to mitigate the risk of frauds. It tracks cash-in and cash-out for each transaction performed by teller and cash position of each teller and the overall branch for ease in reconciliation. This enables total tracking and improves the branch supervision and reporting;
4. *Risk Management*: The system comes with a robust user access management to assign the role and access to each individual teller based on their job profile and function. In addition, the limit for cash collection, cash disbursement, maximum debit, and maximum credit is assigned for audit and security purposes. In the event that any transaction exceeds the limit, then the supervisor override is required to execute the transaction. Today, most of the banks prefer transaction authorizations that are based on events, transaction and account setup, limits, and strict audit trails to ensure the risk management features.

1.2.13 Cash Management

Cash management services refer to the mechanism created by banks to enable their corporate clients to facilitate efficient movement of money between internal units (e.g. company headquarters, manufacturing, sales divisions, etc.) and external bodies (e.g. suppliers, distribution channels, subsidiaries, regulatory authorities, etc.) within and across geographies. Receipts and disbursements could either be in the form of cash or through banking instruments like cheques, online remittance (domestic or international), demand drafts, and so on.

Cash management systems enable corporate clients to administer the company's daily financial activities to ensure that cash is used efficiently. In the finance department, cash managers are responsible for managing the collection, investment, borrowing, and disbursement of funds as well as for forecasting future funds flow and interacting with the company's financial institution(s) as necessary. To accomplish this, cash managers rely on cash management systems that facilitate communication between the business and the financial institution.

Banks are now moving on to business to increase the fee-based income, as revenue from financing is getting slimmer due to the increasing competition in the market. More and more banks are focusing on higher fee incomes from collections and payment transactions by using the cash management channel.

System Features

1. *Information Module*: This system provides access to online account balances and detailed transaction histories (current, previous day, and historical information) on all of the company's accounts (e.g. multiple accounts held by the financial institution). Normally, the system allows users to download the account statement and other relevant information for them to do reconciliation with their legacy system;
2. *Payment Module*: This module will handle the customers' requests for bulk payments of different types such as demand drafts, pay orders, funds transfers, and customer cheques. The entire process from customer instruction, inventory management, multi-location printing, dispatch, clearing, charging, correspondent banking process, and reconciliation with main accounting system would be carried out by the application. The key functions include:

(a) *Bulk Payments*: The most common type of payments offered by IT solutions are bulk payments, that is, payroll, claims, bonus, third-party payments, supplier payments, and statutory payments such as EPF (Employee Provident Fund), SOCSO (Social Security Fund), tax, zakat, and so on. Normally, these transactions are processed in batch mode based on the pre-defined payment processing window.

(b) *Fund Transfers*: This function is for initiating fund transfers, similar to Internet banking but with electronic approval workflow for review and authorization. The transactions supported are:

  (i) Intra-bank transfer between company's internal accounts;
  (ii) (ii) Intra-bank transfer to third-party (beneficiary) accounts;
  (iii) Inter-bank transfer to third-party (beneficiary) accounts with other bank;
  (iv) Transfer enquiries;
  (v) Transfers can be immediate or scheduled (via standing order)

(c) *Bill Payments*: The company can pay for utility bills, and any payment has to undergo electronic approval workflow for review and authorization. The transactions supported are:

  (i) Various payee categories (utility service providers such as electricity, water, telephone, and other third parties);
  (ii) Direct debit from retail or financing accounts; and
  (iii) Payment can be immediate or scheduled (via standing order)

(d) *Dividend Module*: It helps banks to manage large volume payments of dividends and interest warrant on behalf of their corporate customers. It enables corporates to outsource their dividend payments to the bank, which helps in cutting down the processing time and cost.

3. *Collection Module*: Most corporate clients outsource the cheque/cash collection facility to their bankers. The service involves collection and assuring a pre-defined day of credit to the client and managing the

entire fund flow on behalf of the client. It also enables speeding up of billing and collection processes to move cash into the client's accounts so that it can be used effectively. The key business drivers for cheque collections are the float income opportunities and fee opportunities for banks. The typical collection components are retail cheque collections (retail lockbox), wholesale cheque collections (wholesale lockbox), and electronic collections (direct debit).

The system is also able to track the credit exposure of the client by assuring the predetermined day of credit the bank is exposed, and the credit risk in case the cheque bounces or bank receives funds later than the assured date. It also enables tracking of post-dated cheques and other receivables to improve the prediction of cash inflow and helps them in managing their outflow accordingly.

4. *Trade Finance*: It enables the client to initiate a request for the issuance of a letter of credit or a bank guarantee. The client may modify, save, view, or authorize the letter of credit/bank guarantee and much more;

5. *Liquidity Module*: Liquidity module facilitates the corporate customer in sweeping funds from one to many and many to one account based on the pre-defined instructions. It enables collection of funds from decentralized entities of the corporate bodies and pools them into a concentration account for optimization of their working capital.

1.2.14 Online Security Trading Portal

This solution is to offer online trading to the bank's customers. It is a solution that caters to typical investment banks' requirements and brokers for online trading. It is an online web-based trading system that enables bank customers to perform stock trading using the Internet instead of visiting the branch or using phone to place an order. It offers flexibility to customers to perform their trading transactions anytime and anywhere, subject to the availability of funds. The features in these solutions are similar to dealing stations at a brokerage house with real-time price feed, orders tracking, stocks movements, and electronic processing capability and research news. These empower the clients with all necessary tools and functions to perform trading.

System Features

1. User defined real-time price feed viewing limited to halal Sukuk, Syariah Index, and other information;
2. Online display of portfolio summary, buying limit availability, and order status to the customer;
3. Special checks to ensure no short sell (customer cannot sell the stock, until or unless he owns it) is allowed;
4. The system offers the flexibility to limit the trading to halal counters only based on the bank's requirement;
5. Online calculations for clients to perform calculation on funds needed to execute a trade with profit and loss details in the event of selling;
6. Online order placement and execution of orders;
7. Customer will have access to transaction status and history;
8. The system can compute and manage service charges/fees/commission on stock trading;
9. The system interfaces online with share margin financing host and multiple brokers for processing of orders. Trading with multiple stockbroking house does not limit the customer to deal through single broker only; and
10. The solution is normally available to the bank's customers 24 hours a day and can be accessible from anywhere in the world in a highly secure environment, but the orders can be placed only as per stock exchange trading hours.

1.2.15 Risk Management

Risk management is one of the greatest challenges for Islamic and conventional banking. The system covers all risk management issues arising from the Islamic financial and investment products such as Bai Bithaman Ajil, Musharakah, Murabahah, Ijarah, Mudharabah, salam, istisna, and Sukuk. The risk management system supports the following functions:

1. *Market Risk Mitigation*: A complete market risk management solution to support enterprise-wide risk analysis offering market VaR (value at risk) based on parametric methodology, Monte Carlo simulation, and historical simulation. The market risk management solutions provide Islamic banks with a comprehensive view toward understanding the intricacies of market movements and help generate various scenarios for better understanding of the market;
2. *Credit Risk Mitigation*: The credit risk system offers a variety of tools to perform scenario/sensitivity analysis, credit exposure, credit VaR, and economic capital including expected and unexpected losses. In addition to assisting in pricing decisions like probability of default (PD) using ratings migration matrix or loss given default (LGD), it also has the ability to perform tasks integral to credit risk management like stress-testing and back-testing of results for better credit evaluation.
3. Other Functions:

    (a) Analysis for both sharing and non-sharing profit and loss financial models
    (b) Asset and liability management
    (c) Liquidity risk analysis
    (d) Regulatory reporting and capital adequacy
    (e) Compliance with Basel II and IFSB guidelines on risk management.

1.2.16 Security

The solution should offer flexible and secure user access management for the bank and to create the role and access definition based on the user type (branch staff/back office staff/other users). This makes possible the administration of individual user profiles as well as of authorized user groups. In addition, the system should record the different accesses defined for each of the users. The system security module should comply with the following key functions:

1. *User Authentication*: Authentication is defined as secured identification of the user by the system. Normally, application users are required to enter credentials such as a user name and password to prove their identity. Upon successful authentication, the user can enter into the system.
2. *User Authorization*: The system should have user access matrix to define the rights and privileges for each authenticated user. In simple terms, the authorization policy determines who can do what.
3. *Secure Data Transmission*: The communication between the tiers of the application is secured to avoid attacks in which data is 'sniffed' or tampered with while it is being transmitted or is being stored in a queue. Secure communications involve securing data transfers via encryption between remote components and services. Normally, banks utilize SSL (secured socket layer), proprietary challenge/response mechanism, file encryption, and use of check sum value to ensure that the data are not tampered while in transmission.
4. *Audit Trail*: The audit trail can capture any maintenance or new creation performed by operation staff to any settings, business parameters, tables in the database at the account, customer, administrative, GL, or at user levels. This will trace any activity performed at system level for any investigation or audit purpose.
5. Other Generic Features:

    (a) Creation of ID and password
    (b) ID and password management
    (c) Password expiry period definition
    (d) Access right definition matrix
    (e) Definition of user roles or groups
    (f) Detailed system log to observe user activities.

1.2.17 Management Information System (MIS)

The system should support the requirement for comprehensive reporting for the internal use and other related parties. The reports can be categorized into:

1. *Daily/Monthly Reports*: Reports for bank listing the daily transactions processed, end-of-day balances, financing disbursed, collection summary and monthly reports on finance releases, customer listing, nonperforming finance, financial statements like profit and loss, balance sheet, income statement, trial balance, ledgers and supplementary sheets, periodic bank position and branch position, daily GL activity report, and so on.
2. *Managerial/Operation/Statutory Reports*: Other MIS reports for analysis, decision-making, statutory regulation (Central Credit Reference Information System [CCRIS], Capital Adequacy Report, etc.), and daily operation purposes.
3. *Audit Trail*: Details the record of system level and user level activities performed by the various users.

Banks have extensive requirements for reporting. These days, bank relies more heavily on business intelligence components other than core banking modules to generate the reports on need basis. It facilitates 'self-service' reporting, whereby banks can extract reports by putting in specific variables. The reports generated can be further mined for micro-level information.

1.2.18 Enterprise Application Interface (EAI)

From the above, we can realize that the bank needs a good number of systems and subsystems to automate their business operations. This leads to a new challenge of integrating all these applications. Banks implement enterprise application interface (EAI) solutions to link all these applications and others in order to realize financial and operational competitive advantages. In the real scenario, bank procures solutions from various vendors and runs on different technology. In this heterogeneous environment, EAI connects these systems together and enables the bank to communicate at enterprise level.

1. *Integration with Delivery Channels*: EAI integrates a bank's delivery channels with back-office processing and other enterprise systems. It

manages transactions between customer touch points such as branch teller system, ATM, POS (point of sale), kiosks, Internet banking and cash management and back-end systems, and supports the single view of customer relationship and real-time transaction processing.
2. *Integration with Payment Network*: EAI is used by banks to integrate their delivery channel or back-end system to integrate with third-party payment networks to support real-time transaction processing. It performs message transformation, routing, authentication, and validation. It serves as a messaging hub from which any number of financial applications can share centralized message-processing services, especially services that provide centralized access to various financial networks such as VISA, MasterCard, SWIFT, MEPS (Malaysia Electronic Payment System), IBG (Inter Bank Giro), and so on.
3. *Messaging Interface*: Normally EAI can support the following messaging interface to connect multiple applications:

   (a) ISO 8583 (1987, 1993 version),
   (b) XML (Extensible Mark-up Language)
   (c) Proprietary Message Format
   (d) HTTP (Hypertext Transfer Protocol)
   (e) SWIFT
   (f) File-based interface and so on.

EAI ensures that the information in multiple systems is kept consistent via data integration and also performs process integration by linking business processes across applications. It enables bank to respond to the changing market demands, seize new market opportunities, improve customer service, and achieve business growth potential. Competitive pressure to lower costs and deliver universal information across an enterprise fuels the trend toward EAI. The ability to incorporate and exploit existing information systems, prior technology investments, independent legacy systems, and other established applications and databases depends very much on EAI.

1.2.19 Other Touch Points

Banks normally implement various touch point devices to facilitate self-service banking. The focus is to reduce the traffic at branches and to use technology to minimize the cost with better customer service via self-service machines as mentioned below:

1. *ATM*: Automatic teller machine (ATM) is a self-service computerized communications device that provides Islamic banks' customers a secure method of performing financial transactions without the need for a human bank teller. The transactions are performed by using chip or magnetic strip-based cards with a PIN (personal identification number) for authentication. The ATM is connected online to core banking host via EAI to authenticate the customer and balance verification for withdrawals. The transactions supported at ATM are:

   (a) Cash withdrawal;
   (b) Fast cash;
   (c) Balance enquiry;
   (d) Request for statement;
   (e) Request for cheque book;
   (f) Mini-statement request;
   (g) Information enquiry (interest rates, FX rates, etc.);
   (h) Cash deposit;
   (i) Cheque deposit;
   (j) PIN change;
   (k) Funds transfer; and
   (l) Bill payment.

2. *Cash Deposit Machine (CDM)*: It is a self-service computerized communications device that provides Islamic bank customers a secure method of performing cash deposits without the need for a bank teller. There is no card or PIN validation needed. The customer has to just enter the account number and feed the physical currency notes in. All

successful transactions are immediately credited, and customers are issued an advice slip confirming the transaction status.
3. *Cheque Deposit Machine*: It is a self-service computerized communications device that provides an Islamic bank's customers a secure method of performing cheque deposits without the need for a human clerk or bank teller. There is no card or PIN validation needed. Customers have to just fill up the cheque deposit slip, put the cheque(s) in the envelope, and deposit the envelope in the machine. Customers are issued an advice slip confirming the transaction status. Banks are now moving into cheque scanning for deposits. This technology scans the image of the cheque.

1.2.20 Mobile Banking

The mobile phone is increasingly being recognized by banks as a cost-effective channel to deliver banking and trading services. Banks believe that mobile banking is better than Internet banking as it enables 'Anywhere Banking' in real terms. Customers do not need access to a computer terminal with Internet connection to access their bank accounts; they can now do so on the go—when they are traveling, waiting for friends, anytime, anywhere.

Mobile banking is offered using various technologies such as SMS (short messaging service) and WAP (wireless application protocol). Normally, a Java application is installed on the customer's mobile device, through which he can access all the features of their bank accounts by simple interactions with forms, menus, and buttons. The transactions normally offered via mobile banking are:

1. *Account enquiry*: Savings and current accounts, fixed deposit and financing enquiry;
2. *Funds transfer*: own accounts, favorite third-party and inter-bank transfers;
3. *Bill payment*: Immediate or future payments, financing instalment payments, and so on; and
4. *Cheques*: Status enquiry and cheque book requests.

1.2.21 System Set Up

The most important feature for any banking automation system is the capability of the system to meet business/implementation specific requirements with minimum code change. This feature not only reduces the overall cost but also reduces implementation time. The other advantage is less effort on customization exercise, and hence a more stable and generic system. The 'Set Up' module provides a high degree of parameterization facility to meet the requirements without doing any code changes for most of the cases.

This module offers flexibility to financial institutions to manage all the configuration information needed to operate the system. This is where codes can be defined, configured, and managed across products such as country code, currency master, account type, ID type, state code, branch, account status, exchange rate, charges, collateral types, error messages, profit rate computation parameters, product definition, and so on.

Product definition is one of the most powerful features of the system. It gives the bank the flexibility to easily, quickly set up and modify the product without any additional programming in most of the cases. This functionality will facilitate in reducing the time to market, which is critical for the rapid product responses that are required in today's competitive market place.

The system should provide flexibility to define the product category, Islamic concept, product description, product life and validity, product eligibility criteria, financing duration, installment computation, rebate, financing limits, general ledger account definition, and so on. As such, banks can easily customize and create the products to suit their requirements.

1.3 Payment and Settlement Network

Payment and settlement systems form the backbone of the banking system. The payment system assumes importance in the context of domestic financial sector reforms and global financial integration. According to the Boston Consulting Group (BCG), the payments business is core to a bank's profitability, generating up to 35% of their revenues and up to 40% of their costs. If managed through a clear, coherent strategy, payments can be a real source of competitive advantage and consistent profitability. As a result, an efficient, reliable, and smooth functioning payment system contributes to the growth of the economy, soundness of the financial system, and smooth functioning of financial markets.

Bank Negara Malaysia also has taken various initiatives to ensure efficient and faster flow of funds among various constituents of the financial sector. Bank Negara Malaysia plays an important role in the area of payment systems in Malaysia, namely, as the operator and overseer of the payment systems and facilitator to the payment system services. The objective is to migrate from predominantly paper-based payment transactions to electronic payments. The recognized payment networks in Malaysia and worldwide are:

1.3.1 Bankcard Network

Bankcard is a 'Payment Multi-Purpose Card' managed by MEPS (Malaysian Electronic Payment System). The Bankcard uses smart card technology with multiple applications and can be recognized easily by its new look—the smart chip on the front side and the bankcard logo on the other. MEPS is also the provider of the switching network for the shared ATM network between all local and development financial institutions in Malaysia. The Bankcard holder is able to perform online banking transactions such as cash withdrawals and account balance enquiries at any participating bank's ATM. This gives the customer a wider reach to use any bank ATM, and the charges are very nominal if the transaction is performed at the acquirer bank's ATM. MEPS also supports cross-border facilities via PT Artajasa Pembayaran Elektronis (Artajasa), Indonesia, and National Electronic Transfers (Singapore) Pte Ltd. (NETS), and National ITMX (Thailand) network.

1.3.2 Interbank Giro (IBG)

MEPS Interbank Giro Payment System (MEPS IBG) is an inter-bank fund transfer system provided by Malaysian Electronic Payment System (MEPS) to facilitate payment and collection processes within Malaysia. It enables payments to be made without the need to raise physical supporting vouchers or documents such as cheques, bank drafts, and so on. MEPS IBG digitized transactions between banks, whereby individuals can initiate an instruction to his bank to perform debit to his or her account and credit the beneficiary's account in another bank without using any supporting vouchers such as cheques, bank drafts, and so on. Through this system, the duration taken to credit a certain amount of cash into a customer's account can be minimized, especially transactions to outstation accounts. Currently, the IBG facilitates bulk credit transfers between banks electronically on a T+0 or T+1 basis. The maximum limit per IBG transaction is RM50,000. The customer can perform IBG transactions through the bank's branch or via online channels such as Internet banking or cash management system.

1.3.3 Financial Processing Exchange (FPX)

Financial Processing Exchange (FPX) is operated by FPX Payment Gateway Sdn. Bhd, a subsidiary company of Malaysian Electronic Payment System (1997) Sdn Bhd (MEPS). It is an alternative payment channel for customers to make payment at e-market places such as websites and online stores as well as for corporations to collect bulk payment from their customers. It leverages on the Internet banking services of participating banks and provides fast, secure, reliable, real-time online payment processing. FPX provides a complete end to end business transaction, resourceful payment records, simplified reconciliation, and reduced risks as fund movements are between established financial institutions. This network is currently limited to Malaysia only.

1.3.4 SWIFT

SWIFT is a co-operative organization dedicated to the promotion and development of standardized global interactivity for financial transactions. The Society operates a messaging service for financial messages, such as letters of credit, payments, and securities transactions, between member banks worldwide. SWIFT's essential function is to deliver these messages quickly and securely — both of which are prime considerations for financial matters. Member organizations create formatted messages that are then forwarded to SWIFT for delivery to the recipient member organization. SWIFT's worldwide community includes banks, brokers/dealers, and investment managers, as well as their market infrastructures in payments, securities, treasury, and trade.

1.3.5 Western Union Money Transfer

The Western Union is the world's premier international consumer money transfer system with more than 245,000 locations in over 200 countries and is a reliable way to send money, person to person, country to country, online, within minutes. A Western Union money order is similar to a bank's online wire transfer; the difference here is that customer can send money to any Western Union location (even without having a bank account). Now the banks are also becoming agents of Western Union to earn fees based on revenue income.

1.3.6 VISA Payment Network

VISA is the leading payment brand, backed by the world's most reliable, secure, and scalable payments network. It offers a diversified portfolio of payment products and services via the largest electronic payments network. VISA products allow buyers and sellers to conduct commerce with ease and confidence in both the physical and virtual worlds. Islamic banks become members of VISA to offer credit card and debit card facilities to their customers, which allows them to transact globally. VISA has unsurpassed acceptance at more than 24 Million locations worldwide including one Million ATMs.

1.3.7 MasterCard Payment Network

Similar to VISA, it also provides a global communications network for interchange, that is, the electronic transfer of information and funds among its members. Islamic banks become members of MasterCard to offer credit card and debit card facilities to their customer, which allows them to transact globally. With more than one billion cards issued through its family of brands, including MasterCard, Maestro, and Cirrus, MasterCard serves consumers and businesses in more than 210 countries and territories, and is a partner to 25,000 of the world's leading financial institutions.

1.3.8 National Cheque Image Clearing System (SPICK)

Sistem Penjelasan Imej Cek Kebangsaan or the national cheque image clearing system (SPICK) was introduced by the Bank Negara Malaysia in November 1997 to expedite the clearing of cheques. It is owned and operated by BNM. SPICK is available in the Central Region (Wilayah Persekutuan, Selangor, Perak, Pahang, Negeri Sembilan, and Melaka), Northern region (Pulau Pinang, Kedah, and Perlis), and Southern region (Johor). Ninety percent of the cheques cleared in the country use SPICK, while the remaining 10% are cleared manually. SPICK is an image-based cheque clearing system whereby inward cheque images are sent to the paying banks on a CD-ROM at the same time as the data is transmitted to the banks for verification of signatures, prior to receipt of physical cheques. SPICK is operated in the following manner:

1. Banks deliver cheques for clearing to SPICK by 18:00.
2. Cheques for clearing are processed, cheque images stored in a CD-ROM, and data is sent to banks through the Financial Institution Network (FINET).
3. At 9:00 on the following business day, the net clearing balance is settled through the accounts of member banks maintained at Bank Negara Malaysia with unpaid cheques cleared at 15:30 on the same day.

SPICK uses check truncation for faster clearing and settlement between SPICK regions. In addition to regular cheques, SPICK handles banker's acceptance bills, banker's cheques, demand drafts, interest warrants, pension warrants, and drawing vouchers.

1.3.9 Real-Time Transfer of Funds and Securities (RENTAS)

RENTAS is a nationwide, real-time gross settlement system for electronic domestic payments. It is the major wholesale payment system in Malaysia for settling funds and scriptless securities between participating institutions on a real-time basis. The minimum amount for payment is RM50,000. RENTAS also supports trading and settlement of scriptless commercial papers (CPs). It is conducted real-time on a delivery versus payment basis, to improve the efficiency and elimination of settlement risks. It enables payment instructions among participating banks and members to be processed and settled individually and continuously throughout the working day. All settled transactions are considered final and irrevocable. The receiver can use the funds immediately without being exposed to the risk of funds not being settled. RENTAS uses the COINS (Corporate Information Superhighway) network to effect transactions, which settles through member accounts with BNM. The RENTAS membership is restricted to licensed financial institutions.

1.4 Role of Technology for Regulatory Compliance

Demands for transparency from the market and supervisory pressures from regulators are increasing on Islamic banks. To comply with the ever-increasing set of regulatory requirements, banks need to effectively increase their effort and make investments in both skilled personnel and technology to reduce any potential risks that may arise because of non-compliance. They also need to develop mechanisms to assess and analyze compliance requirements to reduce their risk exposures and protect themselves from potential losses. Regulations are essential in today's world, and IT is a key enabler in facilitating transparency for the bank.

1. *Know Your Customer (KYC)*: The KYC norms requires a bank to analyze the background of every new customer acquired, such as nature of business, credit rating, customer's previous financial records, financial history, and relationship with existing customers in the bank. The core banking system, especially CIS, should be able to trigger alerts. It

should support customer identification, provide alerts for blacklisted customers and defaulting customers, and monitor customer accounts for abnormal behavior. This not only increases front office revenues, but at the same time reduces back-office processing time and efforts. It automates the compliance and due diligence practice in the front office and back-office.
2. *Anti-Money Laundering (AML)*: Technology has a major role to play when it comes to addressing the requirements of anti-money laundering (AML) and preventing terrorist financing. The systems should be able to analyze and report all suspicious transactions and can record and analyze the payment patterns, which is most important in identifying suspicious transactions. It helps the banks in filtering the transactions as per the rules and reports the same to the bank's compliance department with a flexibility to create, modify, and delete rules, to detect and prevent such transactions. The system should be able to detect and report on a continuous basis so that the banks can take corrective actions accordingly.
3. *Risk Management*: Areas such as credit risk and default risk can be effectively managed by technology solutions that monitor and track all borrowed accounts. These systems should provide support for online and real-time monitoring of funds utilization and the real-time valuation of collateral along with reporting. The system should also support automatic classification of assets based on the bank guidelines. Once classified as non-performing, the system should keep track of all transactions in that account, and support prudent income recognition norms prescribed by the regulatory authorities.
4. *Asset-Liability Management (ALM)*: ALM has developed quickly over the past five years in part because of the requirements of accords such Basel II and IAS 39. Although it is considered as one of the risk management tool, many central banks have placed greater importance for an effective asset-liability management (ALM) system within banks. However, not many banks have realized the importance of an ALM system. It is impossible to manually keep track of all the inflows and outflows in any bank; the size also adds to the complexity, which necessitates a proper system to be in place for managing liquidity risks, interest rate risks. Technology has proved very effective in this area

since banks are thrown with many choices. Today, ALM systems not only handle the required cash flows, but are also capable of analyzing the trends in such flows, alerts on mismatch, and triggers on stressed buckets, among others. It not only helps in increasing the efficiency of assets and liabilities and risk management but also helps in enhancing the controls. It also provides a platform for adding additional components in the future; this becomes particularly important with the adoption of Basel II.

5. *Operational Risk Management*: Technology solutions help banks in ensuring operational risk management and are an essential part of their system in any banks today. There are many instances to show how organizations have collapsed due to the absence of better operational risk management tools. Operational risk management takes on greater significance since banks deal with public money. To control operational risk, banks maintain a system of comprehensive policies and a control framework designed to provide a sound and well-controlled operational environment. The technology solution is based on a recognized and approved internal controls framework and helps in tracking important risk management metrics.

1.5 Islamic Core Banking Solution Provider

Major IT providers have begun to look at the growing Syariah-compliant finance business. Currently, the Islamic banking software space in Malaysia is divided among three companies, namely, Silverlake, Infopro, and Microlink. Microlink has the largest market share of Malaysian companies, with seven installed sites locally and two in Southeast Asia. The software companies that are currently providing Islamic banking solutions are as shown in Table 8.1:

1.6 Fintech and Islamic Finance

Fintech is the buzz word in today's financial industry landscape. In simple terms, it is a combination of word finance and technology to provide a better and innovative financial technology infrastructure for offering

Table 8.1 Software companies currently providing Islamic banking solutions

Solution provider	Product
Fidelity Information Systems (www.fidelityinfoservices.com) USA-based, Fidelity inherited a number of systems from companies it has acquired. Two of these, systematics and AllProfits, which both of came from Alltel, are applicable for Islamic banking and are live at a number of Islamic sites. Citibank uses the systematics solution for its operations in Bahrain, Oman, Turkey, and UAE	Systematics AllProfits
Tata Consultancy Services (www.tcs.com or ww.fns.com.au) TCS is an Indian-based company and is a leading information technology consulting, services, and business process outsourcing organization. TCS has acquired an Australian-based Financial Network Services Pty Ltd (FNS) known for its solution, 'BANCS'. The Islamic banking functionality has been developed on client to client basis, and National Bank of Dubai, Bank of Kuwait and Middle East, and Gulf Bank are some of their key customers	Bancs
Harland Financial Solutions, Inc (www.harlandfinancialsolutions.com) USA-based Harland acquired the Phoenix Banking System in 2004 from London Bridge Software via Fair Isaac. It has a reasonably impressive client list, with a clutch of these, gained via Kuwait-based International Turnkey Systems, using the system for Islamic banking	Phoenix
I-flex Solutions (www.iflexsolutions.com) It is an India-based company and known worldwide for its flagship FLEXCUBE system. FLEXCUBE is a complete product suite for retail, consumer, corporate, investment, and Internet banking, asset management, investor servicing, and enabled for Islamic banking practices. Their key reference site for Islamic banking is Shamil Bank of Bahrain	FLEXCUBE
Infopro Sdn Bhd (http://www.infopro.com.my/) Malaysia-based, Infopro's ICBA solution delivers full front office to back-office functionality and covers retail, wholesale, GL, and electronic banking, servicing both conventional and Islamic banking fields. The key clients using the Islamic ICBA are RHB Bank and KFH bank	ICBA

(*continued*)

Table 8.1 (continued)

Solution provider	Product
Infosys Technologies (www.infosys.com) India-based, Infosys has a retail banking system 'Finacle' and has been positioned in the leader quadrant in the recently released 'Magic Quadrant for International Retail Core Banking (IRCB) 2006' report. Saudi Arabia's 'Arab National Bank' is their first customer for the Islamic banking solution that is currently under development. The full-fledged Islamic banking solution is part of the Finacle core banking solution and will be ready in early 2008	Finacle
LEADS Corporation Limited (www.leads-bd.com) It is a software house from Bangladesh, and their flagship product is PcBANK2000. It is a window-based application and targeted to serve a high-volume, multiple branch bank networks. Its key Islamic banking clientele includes Al-Arafa Bank, Al-Shamal Islamic Bank, and so on	PcBANK2000
Microlink Systems Sdn Bhd (www.microlink.com.my) Microlink Solutions Bhd (MSB) is an IT solutions provider to the financial services sector with a niche in Islamic banking. Their flagship application is MiBS Islamic core-banking solution. Their key Islamic banking customers are Commerce Tijari, Bank Rakyat, Bank Muamalat, Amanah Raya, Bank Pertanian, Bank Pembangunan, SME Bank, Islamic Bank of Brunei, Capital Bank of Sudan, and Islamic Bank of Thailand	MiBS
Millennium Info. Solution (www.mislbd.com) It is a Bangladesh-based software house and their flagship product is 'Ababil'. The solution is strictly based on Islamic Syariah principles and is developed using latest tools, technology, and methodology. ABABIL is a complete Islamic Syariah-based banking application with anywhere branch banking facility. Their key Islamic banking customers are commerce Tijari, Bank Rakyat, Bank Muamalat, Amanah Raya, Bank Pertanian, Bank Pembangunan, SME Bank, Islamic Bank of Brunei, Capital Bank of Sudan, and Islamic Bank of Thailand. Their key Islamic banking clients are Al Arafah Islami Bank Ltd, Islami Bank Bangladesh Ltd, and City Bank Limited	Ababil

(*continued*)

Table 8.1 (continued)

Solution provider	Product
Misys Plc (www.misysbanking.com) Misys is based in UK and is mainly into banking, healthcare, and financial consulting. Misys banking systems is a division of Misys Plc and carries a flagship product 'equation'. The solution has been enhanced to specifically meet the needs of Sharia-compliant banking practices. Their key Islamic banking customers are Islamic Bank of Britain, Arab National Bank, National Bank of Sharjah, and so on	Equation
Nucleus Software (www.nucleussoftware.com) It is an India-based software house and is known for their FinnOne—core banking solution. It provides a solution for both the asset side as well as the liability side of business, core financial accounting and customer service. Their key Islamic banking customer includes UAE's RAKBANK, Arab bank (Jordan), and so on	FinnOne
Path Solutions (www.path-solutions.com) It has been established in 1992, with headquarters in Kuwait and subsidiaries in Lebanon and Bahrain. Its flagship products are iMal (full-fledged Islamic Banking and Investment System) and iFinance (Islamic retail and consumer finance.). Their key Islamic banking customers are Arab Islamic Bank, First Islamic Inv. Bank, Boubyan Bank (Kuwait), Kuwait Finance House (Kuwait, Bahrain), Kuwait Real Estate Bank, and Islamic International Arab Bank	iMal iFinance
Polaris Software Lab Limited (www.intellectsuite.com) It is headquartered in India and their flagship products are Intellect Suite, OrbiOne, BankWare, and BankNow. Intellect Suite is the global version of Polaris' successful OrbiOne suite of banking products. Their Islamic banking clientele includes National Bank of Abu Dhabi	Intellect Suite
Silverlake System Sdn Bhd (www.silverlakeaxis.com) Malaysia-based Silverlake also has a company, Kalix, to act as the marketing arm for the Middle East. Islamic support for its SIBS (Silverlake Axis Integrated Banking Solution) not only includes basic Islamic banking concepts but also more specialized products. The company has implemented its Islamic banking solution in Bank Islam Malaysia, Bank Mandiri (Indonesia), Affin Bank (Malaysia), Islamic Development Bank, Alliance Bank, Hong Leong Islamic Bank, and so on	SIBS

(*continued*)

Table 8.1 (continued)

Solution provider	Product
SunGard (www.sungard.com) SunGard has recently acquired System Access (www.systemaccess.com), which is a Singapore-based company. SYMBOLS (Core banking) and quantum (Treasury) are its flagship products, which serve the retail and wholesale banking, treasury, and trade requirements. Their key Islamic Bank customers includes ABC Islamic Bank (Egypt), Muslim Commercial Bank ltd. (Pakistan), First Dawood Islamic Bank ltd. (FDIBL-Pakistan), Faysal Bank (FBL-Pakistan), Bank Islam Malaysia, and so on	SYMBOLS Quantum
Temenos Systems SA (www.temenos.com) TEMENOS is a provider of integrated modular core banking systems to over 400 financial institutions worldwide in 110 countries worldwide. TEMENOS T24 is their product for Islamic banking and has also got the Arabic version. Their key Islamic banking clients are Al Salam Bank (Bahrain), Al-Rajhi Banking, and Investment Corp, and so on	Globus/T24
3i Infotech (www.3i-infotech.com) Headquartered in India, 3i Infotech has been known for its suite of applications that cater to the banking and insurance markets. It provides IT solutions through a range of software solutions for banking, finance, insurance, e-governance, manufacturing, retail, and distribution. Its flagship product is KASTLE and is covering both conventional and Islamic banking. They are yet to have any client for Islamic banking core banking solution but they have Hong Leong Bank and Bank Muamalat in Malaysia for selective modules	KASTLE

Note: This list is not exhaustive and has been adapted from www.ibspublishing.com and from the details provided on the individual solution provider's website

financial products and services. It is common to associate Fintech with mobile app-related solutions, but it is beyond that, that is, digitalization of financial services with innovation. It has revolutionized the offering of financial products and services by making it affordable, easier, and need friendly in comparison to traditional offerings. It provides an amazing platform and opportunity for the banks to promote financial inclusion by serving underbanked and unbanked community. Fintech is also associated with disrupting traditional models by creating services with or without intervention of financial intermediaries. In order to remain competitive, financial sectors, and especially banks, should be proactive in adopting Fintech. A recent Boston Consulting Group study showed that over the next five years, corporate banks that remain digital laggards could see profits drop by as much as 15–30% relative to their digitally fast-moving competitors.

Islamic finance, which is relatively new in comparison to conventional banking, also emphasizes on financial inclusion and social welfare. Islamic finance is demonstrating a double-digit growth and offers financial services in compliance with Syariah (Islamic Jurisprudence) to achieve social and financial objectives. Islamic finance is aspiring for growth but without compromising on Islamic principle, and this opens up an opportunity to join hands with Fintech to drive increase in adoption of Islamic finance products and services. In recent times, Islamic finance has been catching with the technological advancement across its service domains. A robo adviser called Wahed, supposedly the world's first automated Islamic investment platform, was launched by New York-based Wahed Invest Incorporation. Wahed is designed to analyze thousands of halal securities worldwide to create portfolio allocations with the highest growth potential for its clients. Abu Dhabi Islamic Bank, one of the largest Islamic banks in the GCC, partnered with Fidor Bank, an Internet-only direct bank licensed in Germany, to launch GCC's first 'community-based digital bank'.

Fintech's leveraging on mobile connectivity and digitally connecting Peer to Peer (P2P) with technology has opened up seamless business possibilities in the area of remittance, payments, crowdfunding, and so on. Fintech's presence in Islamic finance is still at a very early stage, but it means possibilities of many opportunities. Some segments of Islamic finance where Fintech can come in handy are discussed below:

P2P Crowdfunding: Crowdfunding allows easy access to funding online where borrower and lender can be from different geographical boundaries and would have never met. It is based on Peer to Peer (P2P) model embedded with Islamic finance principles such as Murabahah (mark up) for buying an asset and Musharakah or Mudharabah-based equity Financing model will provide an easier access of financing to individual and SMEs. The Mudharabah financing model will be based on venture capital model. Islamic Financial Institution (IFI) can collaborate with Fintech and can play a role of financier intermediary or can also own the debt created through financing. IFI can leverage on Fintech penetration using social media and can have cost saving on customer acquisition cost and same can be translated into cheaper financing products. IFI can target niche segments like asset financing and white goods financing based on Murabahah mark up financing for Syariah-compliant assets. P2P financing is based on risk-sharing concept and is in line with the Islamic principles. This will make the model appealing for both Muslims and non-Muslims looking for alternative financing options. There have been similar initiatives by IFIs in Malaysia by launching collaborative Investment Account Platform (IAP), where lenders, banks, and enterprises seeking funds are all connected together using common platform. Investors will have easy access to series of investment opportunities, and for IFIs, it will be a new channel to attract funding.

Remittance: Remittance for domestic and international remittance using P2P model is gearing up, and Fintech is providing creative way of remittance without moving the money cross border. It works by rerouting money domestically by connecting the senders from cross-border wanting to send money to their respective beneficiary. This provides a much cheaper option and saving on remittance charges, which matters a lot in case of migrant payment to their respective beneficiaries. There is an opportunity whereby Islamic Bank can connect with this Fintech's remittance platform, with their ATM network allowing them to withdraw funds based on the remittance amount and entering secured PIN and where no mandatory bank account is required. However, IFIs can encourage beneficiary to open bank account with minimum documentation based on financial inclusion policies.

Mobile Wallet: The latest trend in mobile money is offering of mobile wallets to mobile phone users who may not have regular bank accounts. These are now heavily being used for micro payment ranging from mobile top up, utility payment,and other day-to-day payments. This is also playing a major role in domestic and cross-border payments through instant messages without going through hassle of filling forms.

The rise of Fintech has opened up a world of possibilities for IFIs. It is a win-win for both parties whereby IFIs can leverage on their ATM network and branch infrastructure, and integrate with Fintech's platform to increase their offerings and services. IFIs will have to be at the forefront on the latest development in Fintech financial business models and collaborate with them to grow the products and services offerings. There is also a potential for IFIs to have their own venture capital funding initiatives under equity financing (Musharakah or Mudharabah) to potential Fintech and make them as part of their internal innovation team. On the other hand, Fintech also can leverage on ethical banking offered by IFI to scale up its offerings using collaboration approach and can tap on wider market including Muslims and non-Muslims.

Malaysia is leading the Fintech development for Islamic finance compared to other Islamic finance-focused economy. For example, the Middle East's banking sector has been relatively slow in adopting deep and transformative digitization compared to its global peers, according to a recent survey of corporate banking customers worldwide by the Boston Consulting Group (BCG). In Malaysia, the government also creating a start-up friendly business environment, whereby $47.8 Million (MYR200 Million) is the allocation for start-ups under Working Capital Guarantee Scheme (WCGS) Fund. In addition, Malaysian Central Bank and financial regulator Bank Negara Malaysia came out with regulatory sandbox framework to boost the Fintech sector in the country. 'Regulatory sandbox' is a concept where businesses can test innovative products, services, business models, and delivery mechanisms in a live environment without immediately incurring all the normal regulatory consequences of engaging in the related activities. The sandbox framework is applicable to all financial institutions licensed under Financial Services Act (FSA) 2013, Islamic Financial Services Act (IFSA) 2013, Money Services Business Act (MBSA) 2011, Development Financial Institutions Act (DFIA), and all Fintech companies intending to carry out businesses defined in all the acts stated above. In order to raise the P2P lending within the country, Securities Commission Malaysia has awarded six P2P licenses, one of which is the world's first license for Syariah-compliant P2P. This license was awarded to EthisKapital.com, which will be focused on funding small businesses, and real estate development projects. Above are some of the initiatives, which shows that government and regulatory bodies are Fintech-friendly. This will act as catalysis for Fintech to have innovative

Islamic finance ecosystem clubbed with technology, and social marketing network with ethical banking services will grain traction among the masses. Thus, the Islamic finance industry is well positioned to seize the opportunities to embrace new technological developments and pave the way for more Fintech growth.

1.7 Technology Challenges Ahead

Automation in the Islamic banking sector has started picking up lately. The achievements so far are only a modest beginning, and many more industry-wide projects are in the implementation process. Today, banks are depending on technology for their day-to-day business, and it is important to understand the complexity and risks of technology. The challenges faced by Islamic banking with respect to technology are listed below:

1. *Time to Market*: Syariah is interpreted differently in most countries, across most regions, and sometimes even within the country. The lack of standards that define a truly Syariah-compliant banking system affects the ability of the banks to implement Islamic products and services both at system and at operations levels. Although the core banking system provider claims that the solution is highly parameter driven due to the complex business process flow (documentation, computation, business rules, etc.) in Islamic banking, it does need some customization effort. In the event of standardization, the rules can be pre-built-in by the solution provider, and hence can increase the ability of Islamic banks to launch new products and faster service.
2. *Customer Demand*: Today, banks are in the race of offering sophisticated technology-based services to their customers. Customer demand will keep increasing, and banks could thereby end up in a technology war. For banks to win this war, they have to increase investments in technology and have to ensure proper utilization of these investments. This is essential for banks to ensure that the systems deployed are fully integrated with their operations. Islamic banks being relatively young,

find it difficult to invest heavily in technology, when compared with conventional banks, and are left out in the competition.
3. *Paucity of 100% Syariah-Compliant Solution*: There is a paucity of systems developed from scratch following the Islamic banking principles. The early adopters in Islamic banking were forced to cobble together systems and build the Islamic banking concepts into their processes in a manner that gave basic automation to allow a slow but painful growth path. There are only selective solutions providers with such products. As a result, Islamic banks have to fall back on a semi-manual approach for a few of their key operations to ensure that their processes are in compliance with Syariah with no loop holes.
4. *System Integration*: Most of the Islamic banks follow the hybrid system approach to fulfill their business requirements, as they find that not a single solution provider can meet their comprehensive requirement in different business areas. Hence, banks' IT solution inventory comprises various solutions running on different technologies and platforms; whereby the integration becomes a major challenge. Although various EAI solutions with a relatively easier plug and play route to connectivity and applications sharing are available, implementing them needs time and investment. The implementation timeline for such application is more than a year, and during that period, banks have to freeze changes on the legacy host, and it becomes a barrier in offering new products and services.
5. *Shortage of Resources*: Islamic banks lack specialized resources with relevant IT skills sets. The shortage of resources is also a major challenge for Islamic banking solution providers as well. Initiatives have been taken by International Centre for Education in Islamic Finance (INCEIF), Islamic Banking and Finance Institute Malaysia (IBFIM), and other local and international universities to develop expertise on Islamic banking.

To overcome the above challenges, some Islamic banks in Malaysia have considered the outsourcing model. In this model, the banks will focus exclusively on marketing and creation of innovative products. The other issues will be taken care of by the outsourcing party. The outsourcing model promises cost-saving, efficiency in processes, reduced processing time, and less cumbersome day-to-day coordination due to a single-point contact. In addition, banks need not incur heavy capital expenditure to automate their business operations. All they need is to pay the rental or per transaction charge, that is, operational expenditure. The outsourcing model is in the favor of Islamic banks and serious thought should be given into this area.

1.8 Summary

Though technology is a change agent, it is not a cure for all inefficiencies. The key area of attention for banks is going to be honing the skills set of the workforce, both in technology and non-technology areas. Another major area where reskilling is needed is in the area of customer service and customer focus such as managing customer expectation and feedback, attracting new profitable customers, packaging products and services to meet these needs, creating a suitable branch environment and other contact points. Another major need is to ensure consistent customer experience, irrespective of the channel used for interaction. Added to this is the security across all channels and distribution points for customer information and transactions to gain the customers' confidence.

While technology may not be a cure-all, it is definitely an enabler. The tool has to be used efficiently and effectively to derive maximum benefits. IT is expected to help banks provide a diversified range of high-quality banking products, services, and solutions to its customers with far greater speed, accuracy, and integrity through a wide range of distribution channels for greater customer comfort and convenience. This will definitely be a key differentiator in offering Islamic banking products and services and will assist in gaining a competitive edge in the market.

References

http://business.maktoob.com/bankingnew.asp?id=20061126015853
http://www.path-solutions.com/pathislamic.html
http://www.path-solutions.com/Bankermiddleeastnews.html

http://www.malaysianislamicfinance.com/monthly/archives/31October/page5.php
http://www.kishware.com/index_files/core.pdf
http://www.finsoftware.com/docs/Islamic_Money_Market_Support.pdf
http://www.iflexsolutions.com/iflex/media/mediadetails.aspx?PressRel_id=11417
http://www.open-solutions.gr/products1_L13.php
http://www.financial-technologies.com/bmaster_features_corebanking.htm
http://www.path-solutions.com
http://www.gtnews.com/article/5911.cfm
http://www.bobsguide.com/guide/prod/3-5516.html
http://rmbond.bnm.gov.my/RinggitBondMarket.nsf/DRBM?OpenForm
http://www.answers.com/topic/charge-card
http://aurionpro.com/new/html/downloads/iCashPro_way_ahead.pdf
http://www.iflexsolutions.com/iflex/pdf/website/islamic_banking.pdf
http://www.gtnews.com/article/5911.cfm
http://www3.sungard.com/financial/default.aspx?id=76
http://www.misysbanking.com/Misys_Banking_Family/Risk_Management/index.html
http://www.gtnews.com/article/5907.cfm
http://www.iris.ch/en/islamic_banking_factsheet.htm
http://www.sungard.com/software/news_5/kuwaitfinancehouseselectsbancwareforintegratedriskmanagement.htm
http://www.networkworld.com/news/2005/111605-oracle-thor-octetstring.html
http://www-306.ibm.com/software/info1/websphere/index.jsp?tab=solutions/appintegration&S_TACT=105AD02W&S_CMP=campaign
http://www.standardchartered.com.sg/cb/services/svc_cqdm.html
http://www.maybank2u.com.my/consumer/m2u_mobile/about_m2u_mobile.shtml#
http://www.bankislam.com.my/cms/default.asp?cms_articleID=22&languageID=0
http://www.webopedia.com/TERM/S/SWIFT.html
http://www.usa.visa.com/about_visa/press_resources/company_profile/index.html?it=h4|%2Fabout_visa%2Fpress_resources%2Fnews%2Fpress_releases_index%2Ehtml|Company%20Profile
http://www.corporate.visa.com/md/nr/press312.jsp?src=home
http://www.mastercard.com/us/business/en/welcome.html
http://www.dqindia.com/content/industrymarket/focus/2006/106103001.asp
http://www.bankcard.com.my/bankcardlogo.html

http://www.meps.com.my/products_services/meps_giro.html
http://www.meps.com.my/products_services/atm.html
http://www.meps.com.my/products_services/index.html
http://www.meps.com.my/products_services/meps_fpx.html
http://www.bnm.gov.my/files/publication/qb/2003/Payment.Systems.pdf
http://www.bankinginfo.com.my/index.php?ch=22&pg=34&ac=808#
http://www.hsbcnet.com/public/tcm/cibm/pcm/APH/pdf/cpmala.pdf
http://www.bnm.gov.my/files/publication/ar/en/2004/cp10.pdf
http://phoenixhecht.com/treasuryresources/PDF/myr.pdf
http://www.gtnews.com/article/5584.cfm
http://www.infosys.com/finacle/feb_01_07_news.htm
http://islamicbanking.blogsome.com/category/islamic-banking-news/
http://business.maktoob.com/news_briefs_inside.asp?id=20061003124154&h=1
http://www.ameinfo.com/51145.html
www.polaris.co.in
www.inntron.co.th
http://www.silverlakegroup.com/

Bidabad, Bijan, & Allahyarifard, Mahmoud. (2005, November 16–17). *IT role in fulfillment of profit & loss sharing (PLS) mechanism*. Paper prepared to be presented at the 3rd International Islamic Banking and Finance Conference, Monash University, Kuala Lumpur, Malaysia.

Bidabad, Bijan, & Allahyarifard, Mahmoud. (2006, Febraury 6). Implementing IT to fulfil the profit and loss sharing mechanism. *Islamic Finance News*, Industry Report.

IBS Publishing, Islamic Banking Supplement, International Banking Systems. www.ibspublishing.com

Microlink Systems. (2006, July 7). IT in Islamic banking—A Malaysian perspective. *Islamic Finance News*.

Othman, Zakariya. (2006, July 7). Interview with Naji Moukadam, President of path solutions. *Islamic Finance News*.

Singh, Surinder. (2005, November). *Asian corporate treasury yearbook 2005*. The evolution of cash management in Malaysia.

9

Corporate Governance in Islamic Banks

1 Introduction

Corporate governance (CG) refers to methods by which a corporation is directed, administered, or controlled. It includes the laws and customs affecting the direction and the goals toward which a firm moves. CG is important to all corporations, and especially to Islamic banks, as these institutions have a moral dimension to their commercial transactions. CG is recognized by Islamic banks and Islamic regulatory bodies, both regionally and globally.

Islamic banking is an ethical banking and operates on a profit-and-loss-sharing principle. The driving force for CG in Islamic banking is the concept of justice, moral obligation, solidarity, accountability, and equality, which are fundamental to Islam. The emphasis is for Islamic banks to follow a value-oriented approach and promote fairness and justice with respect to all stakeholders of a company. Through a transparent CG model, Islamic banks ensure effective monitoring and efficient use of funds by following Syariah principles.

CG reinforces sound regulation and supervision and contributes toward maintaining market confidence by strengthening transparency and accountability. Islamic CG is based on the principle of economic

© The Author(s) 2017
N. Alam et al., *Islamic Finance*,
https://doi.org/10.1007/978-3-319-66559-7_9

well-being of the ummah, universal solidarity, justice, accountability, and equitable distribution of income. The focus of this chapter is on the Islamic CG model, its components, and the challenges faced by Islamic financial institutions (IFIs) in its implementation.

1.1 Corporate Governance Definition

Business activities took center stage in the livelihood of early Muslims. Having encouraged and subsequently established a mercantile society, the scriptures went on to make righteousness within business a divine prerequisite. To assist the community on what constitutes good and bad, halal (allowed and praiseworthy) and haram (prohibited and blameworthy) codes were introduced to regulate all production and distribution. Business virtues were codified into positive values such as iqtisad (moderation), adl (justice), ibsan (kindness), amanah (honesty), infaq (meeting social obligation), and sabr (patience). Negative values were identified as zulm (tyranny), bukhl (miserliness), hirs (greed), iktinaz (hoarding), and israf (extravagance).

Business ethics and governance guidance came hand in hand with Islamic commercial activity, giving it the basic building blocks needed for today's (Western) notion of CG. Under the Western notion, a CG system consists of:

1. A set of rules that define the relationships between shareholders, managers, creditors, the government, and other stakeholders (i.e. their respective rights and responsibilities); and
2. A set of mechanisms that help directly or indirectly to enforce these rules.

Rules and the effectiveness of mechanisms that enforce them can vary greatly across countries. The variations arise from the interplay of political, economic, legal, cultural, and historical factors. Most discussions on CG and finance have focused on ownership structure, shareholder control and protection, creditor monitoring and protection, the market for corporate control, and the role of market competition.

CG can also be defined as the processes and structures to direct and manage the company toward enhancing business growth and realizing long-term shareholder value, while taking into account the interests of other stakeholders. Syariah scholars also share the same views, whereby the objective of CG is to ensure 'fairness' to all stakeholders be attained through greater transparency and accountability. Essentially, CG provides a sound framework for the resolution of issues and conflicts between the stakeholders of a financial institution. Today, corporations are required to exercise immense accountability to shareholders and the public and also monitor their management in running their businesses. CG is normally divided into two categories: self-regulation and statutory regulation. Self-regulation involves aspects of CG that are difficult to legislate. Issues in this category involve the human element such as the independence of the board of the directors, relationship with the management, and appraisal of directors' performance. Statutory regulation, on the other hand, is the framework of CG that can be explained in legal terms. The legislative and regulatory rules include:

1. Duties, obligations, rights, and liabilities of directors, controlling shareholders and company officers; and
2. Disclosure and transparency.

In Malaysia, statutory regulations covering CG are:

1. Islamic Financial Services Act 2013;
2. Companies Act 1965;
3. Securities Industry Act 1983;
4. Securities Commission Act 1993 and Securities Commission Policy and Guidelines; and
5. KLSE Listing Requirements.

CG is considered vital as it promotes morality, honesty, integrity, trust, openness, responsibility and accountability, mutual respect, and commitment to the organization from all stakeholders in an organization.

1.2 Corporate Governance in Banks

The governance model in banks differs from general CG primarily because banks have certain unique characteristics. Three main characteristics that lead to an independent discussion of CG of banks are, firstly, banks are generally more opaque than other financial institutions, which intensify the agency problem. Secondly, banks are exposed to extreme regulations, and thirdly, government ownership of banks makes the governance of banks different from other types of organizations.

In addition, banks also have to ensure that depositors' interest is recognized and safeguarded. Under conventional banking, banks normally undertake the following measures to protect the rights of depositors:

1. Promise of full guarantee of deposits;
2. Introduction of deposit insurance schemes; and
3. Rigorous enforcement of prudential regulations.

The above measures ensure that the depositor's interests are protected. However, for Islamic banking, CG is more complex due to the following reasons:

1. Syariah Compliance: Governance of conventional banks is based on best practices, which are secular in nature. In the Islamic system, it is based strictly on religious principles and in compliance with Syariah laws. Hence, it is mandatory for Islamic bank operations to meet a set of ethical and financing standards that are defined by the Syariah;
2. Social Cause: The source of all conventional activity emanates from the need for the preservation of rightful self-interest, while within the Islamic system the wider society (ummah) is just as important, if not more;
3. Profit-and-Loss-sharing (PLS) Business Model: Governance in the conventional banking system guarantee the deposits and the interest rates are pre-fixed based on the prevailing rate. However, under Islamic banking, interest rates are strictly prohibited and the returns are based on PLS model. In the event of loss, the depositor will not get the

deposit amount as well. This leads to difficulty in following the conventional CG due to the deposit protection scheme;
4. Trusteeship: Under the conventional governance model, the debate is largely on agency issue, whereas the Islamic view is one of stewardship or trusteeship. Wealth, in Islam, belongs to the Maker and everyone else—from the manager, shareholder, to the stakeholder—is the trustee of this wealth. It makes Islamic concepts of governance totally different from the West, as the central focus is on stewardship or trusteeship.
5. Dual Fiduciary Role: The scope for governance of conventional banks is primarily focused on defining the relationships between the shareholders (and the board representing the interests of shareholders) and bank management. However, for Islamic banks the governance structures would involve four parties: the shareholders (including the board), the bank management, the bank's Syariah board or consultant(s), and depositors. To protect the right of each party, a transparent and strong CG is needed for Islamic banks. The influence of Islamic religious and ethical standards leads to a sound CG model. As for the governance structure, teachings of Syariah enjoin fairness and honesty to the primary principles of any conduct including transactions. Prohibition of fraud, misstatement, misappropriation, and other forms of dealings that result in exploitation and deprive someone of her/his property without consent, complement the Syariah-compliant financial conduct.

1.3   Corporate Governance Model

An Islamic financial institution is an intermediary and trustee of other people's money and who shares profits and losses with its depositors. This concept means that IFIs should act as 'responsible' trustees to shareholders and investors. Responsible or amanah in this context means managing the business according to the principles of Syariah. Through this concept of amanah, fairness and justice is ensured and unethical behavior is avoided.

1.3.1 Stakeholder in Islamic Banks

The stakeholders in Islamic banks differ from conventional bank, as noted by Janachi (1995), and illustrated in the following diagram:

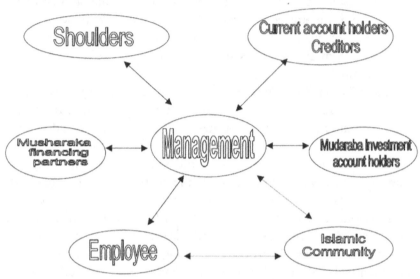

Source: Janachi, A.L. (1995)

In Islamic banking, the stakeholders are shareholders, account holders, Musharakah financing partners, Mudharabah investment account holders, its employees, and the Islamic community (ummah). Islamic banks operate on the concept of interest-free banking whereby shirkah or Musharakah (partnership) and Mudharabah (profit-sharing) are its basic products. Under this model, funds mobilization and utilization are based on profit-sharing. Islamic banks practice two-tier Mudharabah approach, whereby the funds collected from Mudharabah investment account holder (MIAH) is supplied to an entrepreneur on a profit-sharing basis and the profit earned from the venture is shared with MIAH. Mudharabah financing involves projects managed by a client and the bank shares the risk with the client. The bank acts as a partner and is entitled to monitor, supervise, and access books and records. Any loss under this financing is borne by the bank.

However, in a Musharakah financing setup, losses are borne proportional to the capital invested. Here, Islamic banks provide funds that are combined with funds of the enterprise. Profits are distributed in predetermined ratios among partners. Contributors have the option to be involved in the project management, but this is not compulsory.

As there is no clear definition of stakeholders, agency problems do arise from differences in economic interests between the agent (bank's management) and the principal (bank's investor). However, conscientious adherence to Syariah, which is replete with concepts of amanah, khilafah, tawhid, and so on. can counter the agency problems. This enables Islamic banks to maintain investors' confidence and assist in the establishing of a financial system, which is stable and secure.

1.3.2 Governance Structures

Governance operates within a particular environment immaterial to whether it is Islamic banking or conventional banking. It is underpinned and influenced by social institutions driving it into a particular direction with certain explicit or implicit goals. Suleiman in 'Governance Structure' sketches the conceptual framework of CG for Islamic banks in the chart below.

In the chart, internal regulatory systems comprise an independent, active, and engaged board of directors, which has the skill to properly oversee and direct management. The Syariah Supervisory Board (SSB) ensures that the products and services are Syariah-compliant. The internal regulatory system also guides the directors, managers, and employees in their daily administration of the bank. This in turn is translated into implementation of strong systems of internal controls. It ensures the bank's compliance with applicable legal and regulatory requirements.

The internal regulatory system leads to the adoption of international standards, practices, and dissemination of timely, accurate information to the external regulators and the public to ensure transparency.

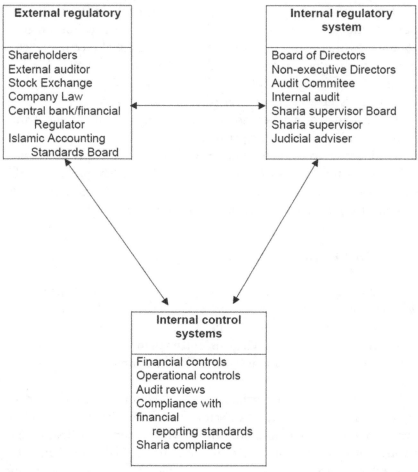

Source: Suleiman, Nasser M., (2000)

Islamic banks use the AAOFI (Accounting and Auditing Organisation for Islamic Financial Institutions) and IFSB (Islamic Financial Service Board) standards. All Islamic banks take account of risks, and this is where it is essential to have good CG and risk management.

This CG structure establishes and maintains an environment in which Syariah-compliant standards are followed. The CG structure is modeled by Syariah Supervisory Board, directors, senior management, and external regulators to provide a strong foundation for Islamic banks to meet the needs of its stakeholders.

Sound CG in Islamic banks also ensures addressing a number of legal issues, such as:

1. the protection of shareholder rights;
2. the enforceability of contracts, including those with service providers;
3. clarifying governance roles;
4. ensuring that corporations function in an environment that is Syariah-compliant and free from interest, corruption, and unethical elements; and
5. Laws/regulations (and other measures) aligning the interests of managers, employees, and shareholders.

All of these can help promote healthy business and legal environments that support sound CG and related supervisory initiatives.

1.4 Corporate Governance Components in Malaysia

CG principles and codes in Islamic banks have been developed in different countries and issued from various institutions such as stock exchanges, corporations, institutional investors, or associations (institutes) of directors and managers. Often these are done with the support of governments and international organizations. As a rule, compliance with these governance recommendations is not mandated by law, although the codes linked to stock exchange listing requirements may have a legal effect. There is, of course, no single recognized best model of CG.

At present, Islamic banks in most Islamic nations and Western countries—with the exception of Iran and Sudan—are operating under a dual banking system. Malaysia has a well-defined regulatory framework for both systems. This will ensure that there is no opportunity for regulatory arbitrage in banking practices that makes one system more advantageous to the other in terms of product pricing. The various components of the regulatory framework, which influence CG and currently practiced by Islamic banks in Malaysia, are described in the next section.

1.4.1 Formal and Codified Law

Malaysia has a comprehensive regulatory and supervisory framework that caters to the unique characteristics of Islamic finance. Islamic banks in Malaysia have to follow the following laws for their day-to-day business operation:

1. *Islamic Financial Services Act 2013*: The Parliament of Malaysia has enacted the Islamic Financial Services Act 2013 (IFSA). The Acts were published in the *Gazette* on March 22, 2013. The IFSA provides Bank Negara Malaysia with powers to supervise and regulate Islamic banks, similar to the case of other licensed banks. The Islamic Banking Act is a unique piece of legislation, which provides regulation for the setting up and licensing of 'Islamic banks' in Malaysia. It is unique in the sense that probably for the first time, an Act of Parliament has been enacted to deal specifically with Islamic banking.

    IFSA has been introduced to provide a stronger legal foundation to spur the growth of Islamic finance sector. The Act provides a legal platform for development of Islamic finance in Malaysia, which is reflected upon a comprehensive regulatory framework on specificities of the various Islamic financial contracts and supports on the effective application of Syariah financial contracts in the offering of Islamic financial products and services.

2. *Government Investment Act 1983*: The Government Investment Act 1983 now known as Government Funding Act (GFA) empowers the Government of Malaysia to issue Government Investment Certificates (GIC), which are government securities issued based on Syariah principles. The GFA provides for the raising of funds by the Government of Malaysia using instruments that adhere to Syariah principles as approved by the National Syariah Advisory Council. The Act grants the minister the authority to receive investment by creating and issuing instruments evidencing such investment, on behalf of the Government of Malaysia. Islamic banks could invest in the GIC to meet the prescribed liquidity requirements as well as to invest their surplus funds.

3. *The Companies Act 1965*: It governs all companies in Malaysia and deals with corporate matters such as pre-incorporation, incorporation, operations, and the duties and obligations of directors. It also deals with the rights of shareholders. Islamic banks in Malaysia are incorporated under the Companies Act 1965 and are subject to the provisions of IBA (1983) as well as to the provisions of this Act (Companies Act 1965), except when there is any conflict or inconsistency between the provisions of Companies Act and the provisions of IBA, the provisions of IBA shall prevail.
4. *Other Common Law*: The Islamic Banking Act and other Islamic laws are applied and implemented within the existing common law system and the regime of all other existing laws. An Islamic banking transaction has to comply with Islamic law (or in the words of the Act, it must 'not involve any elements which is not approved by the Religion of Islam') and also with all other applicable laws, for example, Contracts Act 1950, Bills of Exchange Act, 1949.
5. *Exchange Control Act 1953*: It governs dealings in gold and foreign currencies, payments to and from residents, issuance of securities outside Malaysia, imports and exports, and settlements.
6. *The Anti-Money Laundering Act 2001 (AMLA)*: It contains provisions for the offense of money laundering; the prevention, detection, and prosecution of money laundering; the forfeiture of property derived from, or involved in, money laundering; and the requirements of record keeping and reporting of suspicious transactions by reporting institutions. The Minister of Finance has appointed Bank Negara Malaysia as the competent authority for the purposes of administering the AMLA. The Houses of Parliament have passed the Anti-Money Laundering (Amendment) Bill 2003 to extend the scope of AMLA to include terrorism financing offenses and terrorist property.
7. *The Payment Systems Act 2003*: It came into force on November 1, 2003. The system provides for the regulation and supervision of payment systems and payment instruments. The objective of the act is to ensure the safety and efficiency of the payment-related infrastructure and to safeguard public interest. The act empowers Bank Negara Malaysia to designate a payment system and payment instrument. Operators of designated payment systems and issuers

of designated payment instruments are required to comply with specific regulatory requirements under the Payment Systems Act.
8. *The Securities Industry Act 1983 (SIA) and the Securities Commission Act 1993 (SCA)*: It makes up the legislative and regulatory framework of Malaysia's capital markets, under the authority of the Ministry of Finance. The Securities Commission (SC) has wide administrative powers, but does not have the judicial powers of a court. Islamic banks have to follow SIA and SCA guidelines for issuance of Sukuk.
9. *Bursa Listing Requirements*: In general, the Syariah-based principle of equity participation is essentially the same as that for conventional companies. However, from an Islamic perspective, corporate stocks can only be classified as Syariah-compliant if their business activities are not related to prohibited activities as outlined by Syariah scholars. In Malaysia, the screening of listed stocks for Syariah compliance is undertaken by a centralized body. The review and identification of stocks that are considered to be Syariah-compliant are undertaken by the Syariah Advisory Council (SAC) of the Securities Commission. The Securities Commission then compiles the decisions of the SAC and publishes the list of Syariah-compliant stocks twice a year. The Syariah-compliant stocks are listed at Bursa under FTSE Bursa Malaysia EMAS Syariah Index.

1.4.2 Regulation and Regulatory Authorities

Malaysia has a well-developed financial infrastructure. This well-developed financial infrastructure comprises an effective legal, regulatory, and supervisory framework, which would underpin the stability of the financial system. The regulatory and supervisory function is an indispensable and vital component of the financial infrastructure. They maintain a supervisory and regulatory environment that encourages innovation and efficient competition in financial services. The main objective is the promotion of systemic financial stability that ultimately ensures economic growth that increases the welfare of the people. The key regulators that govern the Islamic banks in Malaysia are listed below:

1. **Bank Negara Malaysia**

   Bank Negara Malaysia was established under the Central Bank of Malaysia Act 1958 (Revised 1994) on January 26, 1959. Bank Negara Malaysia (BNM) is the regulatory and supervisory authority for the banking industry. BNM's functions also include the regulation and supervision of the insurance industry, money changers, and development finance institutions. BNM is also responsible for the issuance of currency in Malaysia, to keep reserves, and to safeguard the value of the currency. BNM also acts as banker and financial advisor to the government. Furthermore, BNM plays an important role in promoting monetary stability and a sound financial structure.

   BNM promotes reliability, efficiency, and smooth operation of national payment and settlement systems, ensures that the national payment and settlement systems policies are directed to the advantage of Malaysia, and influences the credit situation to the advantage of the country.

   BNM is empowered to supervise and regulate Islamic banks, similar to the case of other licensed banks. Some of the key initiatives undertaken by BNM for growth and development of Islamic banking in Malaysia are:

   (a) BNM published the blueprint for country's Financial Sector Master Plan to strengthen the financial sector in Malaysia. The target set for the Islamic banking market share is to reach 40% by 2020.
   (b) In March 1993, BNM introduced a scheme known as Skim Perbankan Tanpa Faedah (Interest-free Banking Scheme) or SPTF in short. In terms of products and services, there are more than 40 Islamic financial products and services that may be offered by the banks using various Islamic concepts such as Mudharabah, Musharakah, Murabahah, Bai Bithaman Ajil (Bai Muajjal), Ijarah, Qard Hassan, istisna, and Ijarah thumma al-bai.
   (c) The Islamic Inter-bank Money Market (IIMM) was introduced on January 4, 1994, to link the institutions and the instruments.
   (d) In October 1996, BNM issued a model financial statement for the banking institutions participating in the SPTF requiring the banks to

disclose the Islamic banking operations (balance sheet and profit and loss account) as an additional item under the Notes to the Accounts.
(e) As part of the efforts to streamline and harmonize the Syariah interpretations among banks and Takaful companies, BNM established the National Syariah Advisory Council (NSAC) on Islamic Banking and Takaful on May 1, 1997, as the highest Syariah authority on Islamic banking and Takaful in Malaysia.
(f) Setting up of a Malaysian International Financial Centre (MIFC), which is collective initiative of Bank Negara, the Malaysian Securities Commission, the Labuan Offshore Financial Services Authority, and the Malaysian stock exchange Bursa Malaysia The central function of MIFC is to allow foreign currency denominated Islamic financial products to be conducted from anywhere in Malaysia.
(g) BNM has launched the International Centre for Education in Islamic Finance (INCEIF), an institute providing internationally recognized certification and programs, with the goal of strengthening the pool of specialists in Islamic finance. INCEIF offers an international professional certification program for Islamic financial practitioners that include a dedicated module on Takaful.

2. Securities Commission Malaysia

The Securities Commission (SC) established in 1993, encourages the development of the securities and futures markets in Malaysia. In addition, the SC regulates the capital market pursuant to the Securities Commission Act 1993, Securities Industry Act 1983, Futures Industry Act 1993, and Securities Industry (Central Depositories) Act 1991.

The SC is a self-funding statutory body with investigative and enforcement powers and reports to the Minister of Finance. The SC is the registering authority for the prospectus of corporations other than unlisted recreational clubs as well as the approving authority for corporate bond issues.

The SC regulates all matters relating to securities and futures contracts, takeovers, and mergers of companies and unit trust schemes. It is also responsible for licensing and supervising all licensed persons, exchanges, clearing houses and central depositories, besides encouraging self-regulation and ensuring proper conduct of market institutions and licensed persons.

The SC, unlike most other capital market regulators, has both a regulatory as well as a developmental role. The initiatives taken by SC in developing the Islamic capital market in Malaysia are as below:

(a) The Commission's early initiative toward establishing infrastructure support is reflected in the setting up of a dedicated Islamic Capital Market Department (ICMD) within its Market Policy and Development Division. The mandate of ICMD is to carry out research and development activities including formulating and facilitating a long-term plan to further strengthen the ICM in Malaysia.
(b) The SC published Capital Market Master Plan in 2001, a comprehensive plan for charting the strategic positioning and future direction of the Malaysian capital market for the next 10 years. One of the main objectives is to establish Malaysia as an international Islamic capital market center.

3. The Syariah Advisory Council (SAC)

The Syariah Advisory Council (SAC) was set up in SC. The terms of reference of the SAC are to advise the SC on all matters pertaining to the systematic development of a comprehensive Islamic capital market and to serve as the focal point of reference on all issues relating to the Islamic capital market and Syariah. As per the latest SAC release on October 27, 2006, a total of 886 securities or 86% of all listed securities on Bursa Malaysia are currently classified as Syariah-compliant. The SAC had undertaken the following to promote IFIs:

(a) Introduced guidelines to expand the range of products to cover real estate investment trusts (REITs), exchange-traded funds (ETFs), and structured warrants;
(b) Setting up of a strong Islamic capital market in Malaysia with 89 Islamic unit trust funds, 85% of Bursa Malaysia's counters are Syariah-approved counters and 46% of the corporate bond market is Islamic bonds or Sukuks.

Today, various capital market products are available for Muslims who only seek to invest and transact in the ICM. Such products include the list of the Commission's Syariah-compliant securities, Islamic bonds, Islamic unit trusts, Syariah indexes, warrants (TSR), call warrants, and crude palm oil futures contract. These have contributed significantly to the depth and breadth of the Islamic capital market.

4. Bursa Malaysia

The first formal stock exchange, the Malayan Stock Exchange, was set up in 1960 with two trading rooms, one in Singapore and the other in Kuala Lumpur. With the separation of Singapore from Malaysia in 1965, the Stock Exchange of Malaysia and Singapore (SEMS) was established. In 1973, SEMS was separated into the Kuala Lumpur Stock Exchange Berhad (KLSEB) and the Stock Exchange of Singapore. The Kuala Lumpur Stock Exchange (KLSE) took over the operations of KLSEB in 1976.

KLSE vested and transferred its exchange business to a wholly owned subsidiary, Bursa Malaysia Securities Berhad, while the de-mutualized KLSE became the exchange holding company known as Bursa Malaysia Berhad (Bursa Malaysia) with effect from April 20, 2004.

Bursa Malaysia is a frontline regulator and market operator for exchange-traded securities and derivatives which govern the conduct of its participating organizations and trading participants in securities and derivatives dealings. It is also responsible for the surveillance of the market place, and for the enforcement of its listing requirements, which spell out the criteria for listing, disclosure requirements, and standards to be maintained by listed companies.

Bursa Malaysia (Bursa) has also played an important role in the promotion of the ICM. Bursa offers a wide range of Syariah-compliant products, such as Syariah-compliant stocks and derivatives. As part of the efforts to offer foreign investors greater opportunity to invest in its products, Bursa is currently working with an international index provider to develop and launch a new set of Islamic indexes that will give investment access and provide benchmarks for international investors. The Labuan International Financial Exchange (LFX), an

Corporate Governance in Islamic Banks 375

offshore outfit of Bursa is providing a platform for the trading of global Islamic products, in particular for investors who wish to deal in non-ringgit instruments.

1.4.3 Malaysian Code on Corporate Governance

The 'Malaysian Code of Corporate Governance' was developed in March 2000 by the 'Working Group on Best Practices in Corporate Governance' and approved by the 'Finance Committee on Corporate Governance'. It was developed to initiate reforms of standards of CG in line with international standards to enable Malaysian companies whether based upon Islamic principles or not, to compete globally. One of the main aims of the Code is to encourage companies to have independent non-executive directors on the board.

The Code makes recommendations for an independent Board of Directors to be appointed. This requirement is to have a balance between executive and non-executive directors so that no one person or group can dominate the decision-making process (Part 1, A II). In addition, there should be transparent procedures for the appointment of new directors to the board, and all directors should submit themselves to re-elections at regular intervals (Part I, A IV and V). The Code also reiterates the importance of an Accountability and Audit Committee, whose role is not only specified within the Code but also by the Kuala Lumpur Stock Exchange.

The Code aims to lay out broad principles of good CG. Companies listed with the KLSE have to state how they have applied the recommendations within their company. This initiative should herald a new era where corporations, including banks, are more accountable to shareholders and to the public. The principles are certainly in place for this to occur.

Part 2 of the Code lays out the best practices, and among these is the recommendation that the position of Chief Executive Officer and Chairman is divided to ensure a balance of power and authority (Part 2, AA II). In addition, it states that independent non-executive directors should make up at least one-third of the Board's membership (Part 2, AA

III). Where there is a majority or significant shareholders in the company, there should be a sufficient number of non-executive directors to represent the other shareholders (Part 2, AA IV and V). More importantly, the board has to put in place a process to assess the effectiveness of the board as a whole (Part 2, AA X).

The Code provides for balanced and independent financial reporting, which is crucial to the management of companies. It recommends a system of internal control and states that there should be a formal and transparent arrangement to depict the relationship between the company and its auditors (Part 1, D). The board has to establish an audit committee of at least three directors, which is chaired by an independent non-executive director. The committee should have investigative powers. The board has to devise proper corporate strategies and then evaluate whether the management of the company is carrying out the strategies properly. In addition, the board has to identify principal risks and ensure the implementation of proper systems to manage these risks (Part 4, AA—4.17). With reference to Mudharabah accounts in Islamic banks, the risk management factor is of great importance to depositors and shareholders alike.

The Malaysian Code on Corporate Governance 2000 aims to introduce good CG in companies. The most crucial factor in the Code is the independence of the Board and the Chairman. The working group that drafted the Code has stated in the explanatory notes:

> One issue that surfaces in the Malaysian context in respect of the role of the Chairman is the almost 'too ready' acceptance of the views of the dominant voice at the meeting. There is a general unwillingness by boards to pursue debate and a perhaps an over-eager desire to find a consensual resolution to issues and problems. Achieving consensus more often than not is a compromise toward the most entrenched view on the board, of sometimes a single voice rather than that of the majority of board members. (Part 4 AA—4.21)

This is a very important acknowledgment by the working group as the general unwillingness to engage in debate and confrontations must be overcome if the board is ever to be independent and protect the interests of the company, shareholders, and creditors. The drawback though is in the definition of the term independence, which is 'independence from management and independence from a significant shareholder' (Part 4 AA—4.23). It is almost as if the working group shied away from addressing another serious problem with CG, which is independence from politics.

In 2005, additional guidelines on corporate governance for licensed institutions were issued by BNM. The primary objective of the revised guidelines is to promote the adoption of effective and high standards of CG practices by licensed institutions and bank/finance holding companies. The revised guidelines prescribe broad principles and minimum standards as well as specific requirements for sound CG, which licensed institutions and banks/financial-holding companies are expected to adopt.

The revised guidelines are formulated on the fundamental concepts of responsibility, accountability, and transparency, with greater emphasis on the role of the board and management. Among the key elements of the revised guidelines include the requirement on the separation between shareholders and management, a clear separation between the roles of Chairman and Chief Executive Officer, enhancement of the role and composition of independent directions, establishment of board committee (i.e. nominating committee, remuneration committee, and risk management committee), limited vetting for the appointment of Deputy Chief Executive Officer/Chief Finance Officer (or other key positions) of licensed institutions, and limitation on the number of executive directors on the board.

1.4.4 Recognized Global Standards

Islamic banking operations have to be governed by the national standards and best practices from the international standards. The international standards as such are not legally binding, but when national authorities approved them, the compliance with the standards can be enforced by regulators. The Islamic bodies currently known and recognized for publishing standards for best practices in strengthening Islamic financing practices are as follows:

1. The Malaysian Accounting Standards Board

   The Malaysian Accounting Standards Board (MASB) is established under the Financial Reporting Act 1997 as an independent authority to develop and issue accounting and financial reporting standards in Malaysia. The MASB's primary role is to develop accounting and financial reporting standards.

   MASB i-12004 (Presentation of Financial Statements of Islamic Financial Institutions) is the first Islamic accounting standard ever issued by MASB. This is to streamline the accounting procedures of Islamic financial institutions and to ensure comparability of financial performance of Islamic banks and conventional banks that participate in Islamic banking schemes. The Standard was later renamed as FRS i-12004 in January 2005. MASB has also issued guidance in the form of technical releases for those involved in Islamic products on how to apply MASB accounting standards to Islamic financial transactions in respect of zakat (one of the Islamic fundamental obligations) and Ijarah (Islamic leasing).

   The Financial Reporting Standards are developed in harmony with the International Accounting Standards (IASs) and The Accounting and Auditing Organization for Islamic Financial Institutions (AAOIFI) standards. The standards are developed specifically to meet the needs of Islamic financial practices and the regulatory as well as economic structures in Malaysia.

2. Rating Agency Malaysia

   Rating Agency Malaysia Berhad (RAM)—Malaysia's premier credit rating agency—was incorporated in November 1990. To promote transparency and instill confidence, the rating of corporate bonds was made mandatory by Bank Negara Malaysia in May 1991. RAM-rated issuers mainly comprise public-listed companies, with a steadily growing number of non-listed companies, statutory organizations, and subsidiaries of foreign multinationals. RAM's unique achievement is its experience in the rating of infrastructure project financing and, more recently, asset-backed securities and Islamic debt instruments. RAM's credit rating definition for Islamic bonds refers to the level of safety for timely payment of financial commitments under the Islamic Instrument.

3. The General Council for Islamic Banks and Financial Institutions (CIBAFI)

   The General Council for Islamic Banks and Financial Institutions (CIBAFI) is an international autonomous non-profit corporate body that represents Islamic banks and financial institutions and the Islamic financial services industry globally. The IDB and other Islamic financial institutions have jointly formed the CIBAFI. It was incorporated in the kingdom of Bahrain under an Amiri Decree on May 2001. CIBAFI promotes and supports Syariah-compliant banks and financial institutions of all sizes, especially on issues of international importance for these institutions and their customers. Major objectives of the CIBAFI are:

   (a) Dissemination of Islamic Syariah concepts, rules, and provisions related to them, and to develop the Islamic financial industry;
   (b) Enhance co-operation among its members;
   (c) Provide information related to Islamic financial institutions; and
   (d) To cater to the interests of its members and to confront the common difficulties and challenges.

4. Islamic Financial Services Board

   The Islamic Financial Services Board (IFSB) was established in Kuala Lumpur in the year 2002 to develop international prudential regulatory standards globally to enhance soundness and stability of Islamic financial system. BNM is the founding member of IFSB, together with 15 other full members that comprise central banks and monetary and supervisory authorities. It serves as an international standard-setting body of regulatory and supervisory agencies that have vested interest in ensuring the soundness and stability of the Islamic financial services industry, which is defined broadly to include banking, capital market, and insurance.

   In December 2005, the Council of the IFSB adopted two standards, the Guiding Principles of Risk Management and Capital Adequacy Standard for Institutions (other than insurance institutions) offering only Islamic financial services. BNM will be implementing these IFSB standards for adoption by Malaysian Islamic banking insti-

tutions with effect from year 2007. An exposure draft for Corporate Governance has recently been issued and is currently available for public comment. The IFSB is currently preparing standards on supervisory review process, transparency and market discipline, special issues in capital adequacy, and governance of investment funds.
5. The Accounting and Auditing Organization for Islamic Financial Institutions (AAOIFI)

   The Accounting and Auditing Organization for Islamic Financial Institutions (AAOIFI) is an international autonomous non-profit Islamic corporate body that prepares accounting, auditing, governance, ethics, and Syariah standards for Islamic financial institutions. The Bahrain-based AAOIFI was established in 1991 by several major Islamic financial institutions to regulate international accounting and auditing standards for the industry. The standards issued by AAOIFI also have helped to focus energies and elevate the level of discourse among bankers, policy-makers, and others about the imperative of standardization and harmonization for the Islamic financial services industry at large. AAOIFI worked closely with organizations like the International Accounting Standards Board to devise standards for reporting and accounting practices. Although it does not have the authority to enforce the standards it promulgates on Islamic financial institutions, it does work closely with respective central banks and governments. AAOIFI has now 140 registered members from 30 countries.

   The standards issued by AAOIFI have contributed toward improved quality of financial statements and reporting methodology of Islamic financial institutions. AAOIFI has also issued standards on the role of the Syariah committee as well as the code of ethics that should govern the accountants and auditors of Islamic financial institutions. Efforts by AAOIFI have also accelerated the pace of transparency and CG of Islamic financial institutions.
6. The International Islamic Financial Market

   The International Islamic Financial Market (IIFM) is one of the core infrastructure institutions of the Islamic banking and finance industry. The IIFM was established in April 2002 under a Royal Decree and headquartered in the Kingdom of Bahrain, the leading center for Islamic banking and finance in the Middle East region. The setting up of International Islamic Financial Market (IIFM) as a not-for-profit organization was founded by the joint efforts of the Central Banks/Monetary Agencies of Bahrain, Malaysia, Brunei, Indonesia, Sudan, and the Islamic Development Bank, Jeddah, upon the realization that Islamic financial institutions will have to develop the infrastructure necessary to support their activities to become a viable alternative to the conventional banking system.

The primary function of IIFM is to enhance cooperation among Islamic countries and financial institutions, specifically in the promotion of active secondary market trading in Syariah-compliant financial instruments. IIFM has strong relationship with other related infrastructure institutions that have been established to contribute positively toward the growing needs of the Islamic banking and finance industry, namely, General Council for Islamic Banks and Financial Institutions (GCIBIFI), Islamic Financial Services Board (IFSB), Accounting and Auditing Organization for Islamic Financial Institutions (AAOIFI), Liquidity Management Centre (LMC), and the International Islamic Rating Agency (IIRA).

Its role also includes the promotion of harmonization and convergence of Syariah interpretations in developing Islamic banking products and practices that are universally acceptable as well as the involvement of a large number of Islamic financial institutions in the market through the introduction of a wide range of Syariah-compliant products and the creation of an active secondary market.

7. The Islamic International Rating Agency

The Islamic International Rating Agency (IIRA) started operations in July 2005. Its aim is to assist in the development of the regional financial markets by providing an assessment of the risk profile of entities and instruments, which can be used as one of the basis for investment decisions. IIRA is sponsored by several multilateral finance institutions, leading banks, and other financial institutions and rating agencies from different countries.

As a leading credit rating agency, the Islamic International Rating Agency (IIRA) assists the Islamic financial services industry to gain recognition locally and internationally as strong and capable financial institutions, adhering to greater standards of disclosure and transparency. Its mission is to support the development of the regional capital market and to improve its functioning.

IIRA is a unique rating agency in that it provides a Syariah quality rating, credit rating, CG rating, and sovereign rating services. IIRA's credit rating services cover both Islamic banks and institutions and their products such as Sukuks, as well as conventional banks and financial institutions and their products such as bonds and commercial paper.

1.4.5 Internal Syariah Committee

The Internal Syariah Committee of an Islamic Banking Institution plays a pivotal role in a bank to ensure Syariah compliance. Their job is to ensure that the guidelines and procedures issued by the Bank Negara Syariah Advisory Council are implemented at the operational level.

The Syariah committee comprises experts in the interpretation of Islamic law and its application within modern-day financial institutions. The committee meets on a regular basis to review all contracts and agreements related to banking transactions and sanction any new services that we introduce. The committee certifies every product and service, and without their approval, the bank cannot introduce a new product or service.

To ensure compliance, procedures for decision-making by the Syariah committee of the Islamic banking institutions, therefore, need to be clear and transparent. The role and responsibility of the committee needs to reflect their responsibility and accountability to the management and the public. Their position is comparable to the auditors of the Islamic banking institutions. Hence, the financial reporting by an Islamic banking institution is required to provide the necessary disclosure to report on the conformity of its operations with Syariah principles. These will promote the foundations for building public confidence and assurance that the Islamic financial products are Syariah-compliant.

1.4.6 Syariah-Compliance Review

Daud Abdullah has suggested that a Syariah-compliance review (SCR) be undertaken on a regular basis in financial institutions that offer Syariah-compliant products to ensure greater transparency and improved CG. At this stage, these reviews are not mandatory but it is an initiative by individual banks to ensure that their products, services, and day-to-day business operations are in compliance with Syariah. The key driver to conduct this review is to ensure that the financial institution is not exposed to any unnecessary risk, particularly 'reputation risk'. SCR could be a means of gaining assurance that all services are in line with Syariah standards. The framework for SCR is illustrated below.

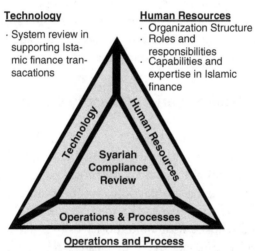

The above framework ensures that activities carried out by the Islamic Financial Institution (IFI), both at the operational and transactional levels, are Syariah-compliant. This would include a review of overall business operations. An integrated approach is used to conduct the SCR, where three main areas are assessed for Syariah compliance. These areas comprise the IFI's operations and processes, as well as its technology and human resource functions.

A review of the operational aspects such as product manuals, accounting policies, and contract conditions is conducted as part of the exercise. An assessment of the application systems and human resources supporting Islamic finance operations is also performed. A systems review of the organization structure, roles and responsibilities, together with the capabilities and expertise in Islamic finance, is also undertaken. For successful SCR, the bank has to address the few challenges as below:

1. Firstly, proper governance and structure, programs, and procedure need to be in place prior to undertaking an SCR;
2. Secondly, those conducting the review should possess adequate levels of knowledge and skills across the various disciplines; and
3. Thirdly, promote the involvement of the external auditors in order to enhance the independence and transparency of the industry.

1.5 Bank Negara Syariah Advisory Council

The Syariah Advisory Council (SAC) or the Syariah Supervisory Board (SSB) monitors the workings of the Islamic bank and all their products and services. The SSB also provides continued supervision and permanent checking of contracts, transactions, and procedures to ensure all the activities are Syariah-compliant. The members of SAC comprise trustworthy qualified scholars with an authority to issue fatwa (religious rulings) on financial transactions. They possess relevant knowledge and experience in modern financial dealings and transactions.

In Malaysia, the Syariah Advisory Council (SAC) of BNM was established on May 1, 1997, as the authority for the ascertainment of Islamic law for the purposes of Islamic banking, Takaful business, Islamic financial business, Islamic development financial business, or any other business which is based on Syariah principles and is supervised and regulated by BNM. The function of SAC is to perform check and balance to ensure that the management and operations of the Islamic banking institutions do not deviate from the Islamic principles in the formulation of their policies. The guidelines, fatwas, issued by the SAC are implemented by Islamic banks. In Malaysia, each Islamic bank has its own Syariah council or committee to supervise on Syariah matters and to ensure that SAC guidelines are being adhered to.

To enhance the Syariah framework in Malaysia, the Syariah Advisory Council at the Bank Negara acts as the sole authority on all Syariah matters pertaining to Islamic banking and finance. Being an apex body, the council standardizes Syariah ruling on similar issues to provide greater certainty and confidence to the financial institutions and to the investors and consumers. To strengthen the Syariah and legal framework, the Malaysian judiciary has set up a dedicated high court to adjudicate cases involving Islamic banking and Takaful in accordance with the existing Malaysian civil laws. Any dispute, within or outside the court system, that calls into question issues concerning Syariah is referred to the Syariah Advisory Council for guidance and clarification. Alternatively, disputes may also be referred to the arbitration center for resolution. In this connection, Malaysia will enhance the Regional Centre for Arbitration in Kuala Lumpur to serve as a platform to deal with dispute cases on Islamic banking and finance, and to extend these services beyond our borders.

1.6 Social Dimension of Corporate Governance

Humayon Dar conducted a study among stakeholders (customers, depositors, managers, employees, Syariah advisors, regulators, and local communities) of two leading Islamic banks in Malaysia. Based on his findings, patronage of Islamic banking is influenced in order of importance:

1. Reputation and service quality;
2. Corporate social responsibility (CSR) of Islamic banks; and
3. Convenience and price.

In deciding on reputation and service quality, the stakeholders of Islamic banks look at factors like knowledge and competence of personnel, Islamic reputation and image, friendliness of personnel, Islamic working environment, customer service quality, and professional reputation.

As such, the reputation and service delivery is the most important factor influencing patronage of Islamic banking in Malaysia. CSR of Islamic banks moderately affects the bank selection. A surprising result, however, is that of the role of convenience factor and pricing of the products offered by Islamic banks, which appears to be of the least concern of the stakeholders of Islamic banks.

The perception of CSR among the stakeholders of Islamic banks is quite a bit different from the conventional notion of CSR. The payment of zakat and sadaqa, for example, is considered as one of the most important indicators of CSR of Islamic banks. On the other hand, the stakeholders of Islamic banks are least concerned with environmental issues, an area of prime importance in conventional framework of CSR. Our analysis suggests that there are four important aspects of CSR, which are deemed relevant to Islamic banking. These are (in order of importance):

1. Religious and philanthropic activities;
2. Concern with social exclusion and human rights;
3. Environmental concerns; and
4. Human resource developments.

Among the religious and philanthropic activities, the stakeholders put heavy emphasis on:

1. Fostering Islamic values among customers;
2. Fostering Islamic values among staff;
3. Payment of zakat and sadaqa;
4. Support for charities and community projects;
5. Solving social problems;
6. Sensitivity to public causes, and
7. Granting interest-free loans.

The emphasis on social exclusion and human rights emanates from people's concern, in order of priority:

1. Financing of SMEs;
2. Financing of companies that do not violate human rights; and
3. Provision of affordable services to deprived areas.

CSR does not feature prominently in the minds of stakeholders of Islamic banking in Malaysia. The specific aspects of environmental friendly policies on recycling and energy and water conservation do not seem to influence those involved in Islamic banking in Malaysia. A plausible explanation of this is that since the banking industry is only indirectly related to the environmental issues, it is deemed as less important than other issues.

In years to come, Islamic banks will have to put more emphasis on social welfare and CSR-related issues if they want to fit the expectations of their stakeholders. While maximizing shareholders' equity is an important aspect of managing an Islamic bank, it is equally important to manage the stakeholders' expectations.

1.7 Challenges in Corporate Governance Implementation

The mandate is clear and the ethical underpinnings of Islamic CG principles are unequivocal. However, there are some important challenges in implementing this vision, most notably in terms of legal aspects, accounting, and general governance issues in Muslim countries. Shamshad Akhtar (Former Governor of the State Bank of Pakistan) has highlighted a few key challenges in implementing CG during the 'Annual Corporate Governance Conference' held in Dubai on November 27, 2006.

1. Reputational risk arising out of any uncertainty on Syariah compliance

    Success of an Islamic financial system is based on stakeholder's belief that the system is Syariah-compliant. This single factor intensifies the role of good CG to ensure that the faith of stakeholders is not compromised and the system sustains and grows smoothly. The reputational risk factor, that is, loss of faith, has to be managed right from

the inception of an IFI and the Syariah advisor/board assigned to perform their duties.
2. Commitment of dedicated, qualified directors who understand and can assess Syariah compliance

   This would facilitate effective oversight and protect the industry from overall reputation risks. Qualifications/experience of Syariah advisors is the key to judge and support the development of Syariah-compliant financial services. In absence of this, there is a risk that for short-term profits/gains, the shareholders/Board of Directors (BOD) may become willing to compromise on the Syariah principles. The presence of Syariah-literate directors would discourage precedence of profit motive over Syariah compliance. From the regulatory point of view, the licensing stage is of particular importance whereby the licensing authority should demand a clear demonstration of the sponsors' commitment to Islamic banking.
3. Demarcation of responsibility and accountability between Board, Management, and Syariah Advisor

   Similar to the demarcation issue in a conventional bank between BOD and the management is the demarcation between the role and functions of the Syariah advisor or a special Syariah board (as the case may be) as distinct from the Management/BOD. Due to the faith-based nature of the business, it is evident that the Syariah advisor will review most aspects of the businesses, but the involvement could vary and focus on approval of basic structure of products and other special activities rather than interfering in day-to-day operations of businesses. Notwithstanding, the Syariah advisor has to be more mainstream than an advisor in a conventional bank. To perform their functions effectively, there is a need to enhance the pool and capacities of Syariah scholars in financial businesses, as currently the most experienced Syariah scholars are represented on Syariah boards of different institutions.
4. Investment policies to comply with Syariah criteria

   An IFI cannot invest, whether through financing or share purchase, in the companies, which are engaged in non-halal businesses. This adds a new dimension to CG, which the Board and the management of the IFIs have to fulfill. The investment policy, which has to be consistent with Syariah, is part of the encompassing corporate strategy to be approved by the Board.

5. Investors' protection

Under the principle of Mudharabah, the Investment Account Holder (IAH) as rabbul maal bears the risk of capital invested by the IFI as mudharib. This equates the IAHs' investment risk with the shareholders of IFI who bears the risk of losing their capital as investors in the IFI. Given the IAH would be more risk-averse than owners of IFIs, the supervisory authorities should play a role in protecting the interests of the IAH *vis-à-vis* the shareholders of IFIs with regard to their rights and safeguarding against commingling of funds and/or conflict of interest of shareholders. The way for central banks offering deposit insurance schemes would be to devise Syariah-compliant deposit insurance schemes for depositors of IFIs to provide a safety net, while ensuring stability in the financial system.

On the financing side, if the funds are invested on Musharakah or Mudharabah basis, the safety of the funds invested would depend on the governance of the borrowing enterprise. The IFIs should be expected to conduct active monitoring of enterprises they invest in under Musharakah or Mudharabah. IFIs relationship with such enterprises ought to be of long-term nature with active involvement in governance in contrast to a short-term, transactional relationship. Among others, some expertise about business of such enterprises would be a prerequisite for IFIs to assess business risks appropriately and to effectively monitor their operations.

6. Disclosure and transparency

Transparency and disclosure of a structure of product and its strengths and weaknesses are critical, and IFIs should be mandated to this discipline. IFIs should further conform to the highest international standards and practices for financial and non-financial reporting and disclosure. Moreover, IFIs should be transparent in the adoption and application of Syariah rules and principles issued by its Syariah scholars. These should be made publicly available through appropriate channels. In line with the IAHs' rights of monitoring the performance of their investments, they should be entitled to be informed of the methods of profit calculation, asset allocation, investment strategies, and mechanics of smoothing the returns (if any) in respect to their investment accounts.

CG framework should ensure, in order to provide relevant information for investors' decisions, that the disclosure is timely and accurate on all material matters, is in accordance with high-quality standards of accounting and disclosure, and the audit and review of these disclosures by independent, competent, and qualified auditors is carried out. The external auditors of Islamic financial institutions also need to develop expertise to conduct Syariah-compliance audit and report on their findings to the shareholders and general public.
7. Harmonization of Syariah rulings
One of the issues faced by the Islamic financial industry is the lack of standardization of Syariah rulings within the same jurisdictions and among various regions. The diversity provided by different schools of thoughts on similar issues at times creates confusion in the minds of general public. However, if properly harmonized across the globe, it can become a great strength for the Islamic financial services industry. AAOIFI and IFSB have taken a lead by preparing Syariah standards approved by renowned Syariah scholars across the world. Some countries have recognized these standards in their regulatory framework. The adoption of these standards in other countries will pave the way not only for Syariah compliance but also product innovation. In addition, the central banks/regulatory agencies monitoring the performance of Islamic financial institutions also need to establish their own Syariah Board for guiding them in the formulation of policies and rules as well as for the resolution of conflicting Syariah opinions.

Adequate standards and best practices cannot be established without consensus on critical issues. Islamic banks need to arrive at a consensus among themselves with respect to a number of issues related to treatment of capital, risks, risk-management instruments, liquidity enhancing instruments, and contractual obligations.

1.8 Standardization through Corporate Governance

One of the biggest challenges today is developing a framework for governing, supervising, and regulating Islamic banks. There is no common approach among countries where Islamic banking exists. One of the two main views held by regulators in Malaysia and Yemen, for example, is that Islamic banks should be subjected to a supervisory and regulatory regime of central banks that is entirely different from that of conventional banks. The second main view recognizes the uniqueness of Islamic banks' activities, but favors putting them under the same central bank supervision and regulatory regime as that for conventional banks, with slight modifications and special guidelines that are usually formalized in occasional central bank circulars. Bahrain and Qatar are examples of countries that practice this latter form of central bank supervision and regulation.

The comparison of practices of CG models in various countries is illustrated below.

From the country wise Syariah Compliance Framework, it is clear that the regulatory framework for IFIs differs from country to country. In the absence of uniformity, financial markets and regulators alike are unable to make informed comparisons and decisions about the integrity and financial health of financial institutions across broadly similar markets.

Hence, there is an acute need to design a standardized regulatory framework for Islamic finance; regulators need to factor in the differences in these forms of finance and have at least minimal standards or benchmarks to gauge compliance and assess risks. There needs to be some level of consistency in regulatory treatment across the board, subject to the particular country's legal and regulatory regime. The Islamic Development Bank is playing a key role in developing internationally acceptable standards and procedures and strengthening the sector's architecture in different countries. Several other international institutions are working to set Syariah-compliant standards and harmonize them across countries. These include the Accounting and Auditing Organization for Islamic Financial Institutions (AAOIFI), the Islamic Finance Service Board (IFSB), the International Islamic Financial Market, the Liquidity Management Centre, and the International Islamic Rating Agency. Once fully developed and accepted, these international standards will assist regulators and supervisors in their respective regions to formulate better regulatory policies for supervising Islamic financial institutions (IFI). This in turn will promote soundness, stability, and integrity among IFIs.

Shariah Compliance Framework – Country wise

Country	Islamic Banking Law	Shariah Committee At Central Bank	Shariah Committee at bank Level	Fit & Proper Criteria for Shariah Advisor/Committee	Shariah Compliance Inspection	Shariah Standards	Accounting Standard
Malaysia	Islamic Banking Law 1983	Shariah Advisory Council	Shariah Committee	Approval by BNM	Governance through Shariah Committee	All Products approved by SAC. Role of Shariah Committee defined by BNM	Accounting Standards developed by MASB
Bahrain	Regulations for Islamic Banks	Shariah Supervisory Committee	Shariah Supervisory Board	N.A	Internal and External Shariah Audit as per AAOIFI standards	AAOIFI	AAOIFI
Indonesia	Laws for Islamic Banking Introduced in 1992 & Amended in 1999	National Shariah Board	Shariah Supervisory Board	NSB approves appointment of SSB members	Internal and External Shariah Audit	Fatwa on products issued by NSB	AAOIFI
Iran	Usury free Banking Act 1983	Council of Guardian	N.A	N.A	No	Guidelines provided by Council of Guardians	Not Known
Brunei	Islamic Banking Act Cap. 168	Shariah financial supervisory Board (SFSB)	Shariah Advisory Board	SFSB approves appointment of Shariah Advisory Board members	No	SFSB Approves Islamic products introduced by Financial Institutions	Not Known
Pakistan	Banking Companies Ordinance, 1962 and Policies for Islamic Banking in 2001 & 2003	Shariah Board	Shariah Advisor	Fit & Proper Criteria by SBP	Manual developed in 2004, now being implemented	Essentials for Islamic modes	AAOIFI standards are being adapted by a committee of ICAP

1.9 Summary

Financial information is the lifeblood of financial markets, and high standards become an essential ingredient for the efficient operation and continued health of both markets as a whole and their constituents. Enhanced governance and transparency require standards that promote the dissemination of financial information that are readily understandable to a wide range of information users. This is where the role of uniform accounting standards becomes paramount.

Appropriate regulations and supervision are critical to alleviate the risks involved with IFIs. The monitoring of the Islamic banking institutions through effective supervision by a regulatory authority is very much needed to ensure that prudential requirements are observed by IFIs. Inadequate supervision and control and over-exposure to risks are among the factors that could seriously weaken the Islamic financial system.

The need for good CG practice is vital in all banking sectors and even more so within the Islamic banking paradigm. It also has to be noted here that the question of governance issues is well placed in all aspects of Islamic banking operation. The Syariah council needs to play an even more crucial role in monitoring and ensuring a well-adapted governance practice in Islamic banking. Again, we have to remember that the responsibility of practicing ethical governance in Islamic banking does not only fall in the hands of the Syariah council, but also all other parties involved such as directors and shareholders.

References

http://english.peopledaily.com.cn/english/200102/19/eng20010219_62772.html

http://web.worldbank.org/WBSITE/EXTERNAL/TOPICS/EXTFINANCIALSECTOR/EXTISLAMF/0,,contentMDK:20639527~pagePK:210058~piPK:210062~theSitePK:399996,00.html

http://web.worldbank.org/WBSITE/EXTERNAL/TOPICS/EXTFINANCIALSECTOR/EXTISLAMF/0,,contentMDK:20639531~menuPK:2170857~pagePK:210058~piPK:210062~theSitePK:399996,00.html

http://www.bnm.gov.my/files/publication/ar/en/2005/cp09.pdf

http://www.bnm.gov.my/index.php?ch=14&pg=17&ac=16&full=1
http://www.bnm.gov.my/index.php?ch=14&pg=17&ac=18&full=1
http://www.bnm.gov.my/index.php?ch=174&pg=467&ac=367
http://www.bnm.gov.my/index.php?ch=174&pg=467&ac=367
http://www.bnm.gov.my/index.php?ch=18&pg=55&ac=420
http://www.bnm.gov.my/index.php?ch=9&pg=15&ac=151
http://www.bnm.gov.my/index.php?ch=9&pg=15&ac=226
http://www.bnm.gov.my/index.php?ch=9&pg=15&ac=229
http://www.bnm.gov.my/index.php?ch=9&pg=15&ac=234
http://www.erf.org.eg/tenthconf/Financial_Markets_Presented/Kabir_Bashir.pdf
http://www.fhlbboston.com/aboutus/thebank/08_01_10_corporate_governance_principles.jsp
http://www.ftse.com/Indices/FTSE_Bursa_Malaysia_Index_Series/Downloads/FTSE_Bursa_Malaysia_Index_Rules.pdf
http://www.iasplus.com/country/malaysia.htm
http://www.iirating.com/presentation/20061209_rating_of_islamic_banks_and_financial_institutions.pdf
http://www.imf.org/external/pubs/ft/fandd/2005/12/qorchi.htm
http://www.iosco.org/library/pubdocs/pdf/IOSCOPD170.pdf
http://www.islamic-bank.com/islamicbanklive/RoleofCommittee/1/Home/1/Home.jsp
http://www.islamic-banking.com/comment_sep05.htm
http://www.islamic-banking.com/comment_sep05.htm
http://www.khaleejtimes.com/malaysia/mt_bank_cnt1.html
http://www.khaleejtimes.com/malaysia/mt_bank_cnt3.html
http://www.lawandtax-news.com/asp/story.asp?storyname=24582
http://www.lofsa.gov.my/lofsa5/Eve/conf/ILIFC%202004/Day%20Two/D2(7)/D2(7)%20-%20Mr%20Suresh%20Menon.pdf
http://www.mida.gov.my/beta/view.php?cat=3&scat=30&pg=157
http://www.mida.gov.my/beta/view.php?cat=3&scat=30&pg=159
http://www.mngt.waikato.ac.nz/ejrot/cmsconference/2005/abstracts/postcolonialism/Lewis.pdf
http://www.pwc.com/extweb/indissue.nsf/docid/1d681d874f24fda7ca25720a00158bfd
http://www.rhbislamicbank.com.my/index.asp?fuseaction=general.article&aid=19

http://www.rhbislamicbank.com.my/index.asp?fuseaction=general. article&aid=19
http://www.ruf.rice.edu/~elgamal/files/IBCGR.pdf
http://www.sbp.org.pk/about/speech/governors/dr.shamshad/2006/Corporate-Governance-30-Dec-06.pdf
http://www.sc.com.my/eng/html/cg/imp_rep_1-3.html
http://www.sc.com.my/eng/html/cg/Legal.html
http://www.sc.com.my/eng/html/resources/inhouse/mccg.pdf
http://www.sc.com.my/eng/html/resources/press/1996/pr_19961031.pdf
http://www.sc.com.my/eng/html/resources/press/pr_20060314.html
http://www.sc.com.my/eng/html/resources/speech/sp_20040707.html
http://www.sc.com.my/eng/html/resources/speech/sp_20070112.html
http://www.seacen.org/bankwatch/malaysia.pdf
http://www.takaful-malaysia.com/page.php?file=Internet/profile/income.htm
http://www.theedgedaily.com/cms/content.jsp?id=com.tms.cms.article. Article_597e778b-cb73c03a-160c4b00-bbed3c69

Abdullah, D. (David Vicary). (2005, April 18). Syariah compliance reviews. *Islamic Finance News*, 2(8).

Akhtar, S. *Syariah compliant corporate governance*. Keynote address by Dr Shamshad Akhtar, Governor of the State Bank of Pakistan, at the Annual Corporate Governance Conference, Dubai, 27 November 2006.

Alam, N., & Shanmugam, B. (2007, February 2). Strong regulatory framework: A vital tool for Islamic banking. Retrieved from www.islamicfinancenews.com

Al-Omar, F. Supervison, regulation and adaptation of Islamic banks to the best standards: The way forward. Retrieved from www.islamic-finance.net

Capulong, M. V., Edwards, D., Webb, D., & Zhuang, J. (eds.). Corporate governance and finance in East Asia a study of Indonesia, Republic of Korea, Malaysia, Philippines, and Thailand: Volume one (A consolidated report). Retrieved from http://adb.org/Documents/Books/Corporate_Governance/Vol1/default.asp

Cunningham, Andrew. (2004, January). *Regulation and supervision: Challenges for Islamic finance in a riba-based global system*. Moody's Investor Service

Dar, H. (2005, June). Islamic banks: Are they really what their stakeholders intended them to be? *Islamic Finance News*, 2(13).

El Qorchi, M. (2005, December). Islamic finance gears up. 42(4). Retrieved from http://www.imf.org/external/pubs/ft/fandd/2005/12/qorchi.htm

Governor's speech at the IFSB Summit—Islamic Financial Services Industry and The Global Regulatory Environment—"Approaches to Regulation of Islamic Financial Services Industry". Retrieved from http://www.bnm.gov.my/index.php?ch=9&pg=15&ac=151

Ibrahim, A. A. Convergence of corporate governance and Islamic financial services industry: Toward Islamic financial services securities market. Georgetown law, Georgetown law graduate paper series, 2006. Retrieved from http://lsr.nellco.org/cgi/viewcontent.cgi?article=1002&context=georgetown/gps

Janachi, A. L. (1995). *Islamic banking, concept, practice and future* (2nd ed.). Manama: Bahrain Islamic Bank.

'Meet the head' Islamic finance news talks to leading players in the industry. (2006, August 11). *Islamic Finance News*, 3(27).

Meet the head, Islamic finance news talks to leading players in the industry. (2006, July 21). *Islamic Finance News*, 3(24).

Mohammed Shariff, M. I. B. (2002, February–March 3–6). The development of Islamic banking juridical and practical issues—Is the law equipped? No. 116. Retrieved from https://www.financeinislam.com/

Mohammed Shariff, M. I. B. The legal aspects of marketing for Islamic banking services. Retrieved from www.financeinislam.com/

Rowey, Kent, July, Charles, & Fèvre, Marc. (2006). *Islamic finance: Basic principles and structures: A focus on project finance*. Freshfields Bruckhaus Deringer.

Ruin, J. E. (2004, November 22). Instilling risk management culture for corporate governance in Islamic banking. *Islamic Finance News*, 1(2).

Securities Commission. (2006, November). Quarterly bulletin of Malaysian Islamic capital, 1(3). Retrieved from http://www.sc.com.my/eng/html/icm/ICMNews_Nov06.pdf

Shabsigh, G. Issues in Islamic banking governance. Retrieved from www.islamic-finance.net

Sheikh Ebrahim Bin Khalifa Al Khalifa, H. E. The need for regulation of Islamic banking. Retrieved from www.islamic-finance.net

Subbulakshmi, V. (Ed.). (2004). *Islamic finance regulatory perspectives*. Hyderabad: ICFAI University Press.

Suleiman, Nasser M., (2000) Corporate Governance in Islamic Bank, Islamic Banking, 1 (1) 99–116. Retrieved from http://www.nubank.com/islamic/governance.pdf

Sundararajan, V.. Remarks to the conference on the regulation of Islamic banks. Retrieved from www.islamic-finance.net

Wouters, P. (2005, November 7). Compliance and compliance function. *Islamic Finance News*, 2(22).

# 10

Islamic Capital Market

1 Introduction

The Islamic Capital Market (ICM) is an integral element of Islamic finance and one that complements Islamic banking and Islamic insurance. This chapter introduces the components of conventional capital markets and explains the role of the ICM, which closely follows the conventional markets in structure. This chapter will also introduce the components and features of the ICM, which make it distinct from both the banking and insurance industries followed by introduction to the development phases of the ICM.

1.1 Role of the ICM in Global Financial System

The ICM functions as a parallel market to the conventional capital market for capital seekers and providers. The recent decade has seen the accelerated development of this market and its significant role in strengthening the already established conventional capital market. The global development of this market is particularly important in more challenging and volatile global financial and economic environment. The financing requirements for economic development are huge, and the bond market plays a key role in meeting these funding needs for both the public and private sectors. The global experience has shown that the lack of well-developed bond markets brings with it vulnerabilities arising from over-reliance on financing from the banking sector. This has often resulted in funding mismatches with adverse implications on financial stability. The development of the Sukuk market (an important component of ICM) allows for access to funding with the appropriate maturities, thus avoiding the funding mismatches. It also allows for the diversification of risks by issuers and investors. The central merit of the Sukuk structure is that it is based on real underlying assets. This approach discourages overexposure of the financing facility beyond the value of the underlying asset, given that the issuer cannot leverage in excess of the asset value.

The emergence of ICM products has also promoted greater global financial integration. The bringing together of financial institutions and market players across continents to participate in this expansion of interregional investment flows has fostered financial linkages among the major regions especially among emerging economies. This will not only provide great synergies and opportunities but will contribute toward facilitating international financial stability.

ICM overall and particularly the encouraging development of the Sukuk market is playing an important role in enhancing the linkages between financial markets as it facilitates cross-border flows in the international financial system. The further development of the ICM will add to the depth and diversity of the overall global capital market as well as provide a significant contribution to the overall growth of the financial services industry. ICM intermediation therefore has the potential role of contributing toward financial stability in overall global financial system.

1.2 Essential Components of ICM

Generally speaking, the ICM provides three markets similar to the conventional capital markets such as the Islamic equity markets, the Islamic fixed-income instruments or Sukuk market, and Islamic derivatives or Islamic-structured products market. While the components are similar to those found in the conventional capital market, the features of the products underlying each respective component are different. For example, the main concern of Islamic equity does not relate to the structure of an ordinary share, but to the activities of the company that issues the share to the public. In other words, investors, particularly investors who are sensitive to Islamic investment guidelines, must examine whether the company undertakes its activities according to Syariah principles. As shares represent an ownership right in a company, shareholders should not invest their capital to support activities that are non-compliant. Non-compliant companies might offer, among other things, interest-based financial products, conventional insurance, gambling, and pornography or entertainment activities.

There is no Syariah requirement for a segregated stock exchange to make these shares compliant, and the ICM does not, at present, provide a separate stock exchange for Islamic-approved equities or stocks. Shares are compliant once they pass the screening criteria set by various providers according to Syariah principles (Fig. 10.1).

Islamic capital market instruments fall into three main categories.

(a) **The equity market and its related products:**

- Public listed companies
- Unit trusts and mutual funds
- Private equity funds
- Specialized funds

(b) **Islamic fixed-income instruments—Sukuk**
(c) **Islamic-structured products and derivatives**

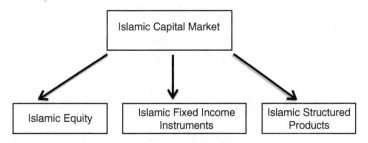

Fig. 10.1 Components of the ICM

1.2.1 The Islamic Equity Market—Public Listed Companies

As with the conventional equity market, the Islamic equity market provides a platform for deficit units to raise money through equity financing and for investors to invest in the shares of companies. It also facilitates collective investments through funds, whereby investors share the profit and loss proportionately, according to the performance of those funds. It should be noted that in this structure, although investment could be made in assets other than equities, for example, commodities or equipment, the main feature of equity investment is that all investors contribute capital in the form of shares or units for subsequent investment in underlying assets. In addition, the profit or loss is shared collectively and proportionately in the form of dividend. The key instruments linked to the equity market are shares in publicly listed companies, shares in privately owned companies, and Islamic unit trusts or mutual funds.

Islamic Shares

As with conventional shares, an Islamic share represents a proportionate ownership right or interest in a company. A shareholder, by subscribing to the shares of a company, is deemed to be the rightful owner of this company in proportion to their shareholding. A share, as defined in the Accounting and Auditing Organisation for Islamic Financial Institutions (AAOIFI) Syariah Standard No.21 Financial Paper (Shares and Bonds), is 'a share in the assets of a corporation and is represented by a certificate that can be negotiated. This applies to all shares, whether Syariah compliant or not. The term share is also applied to the certificate that represents such shares'. A share is known in Arabic as sahm or ashum (plural). A share in Islamic finance is essentially the same as a conventional share and used as capital-raising instruments, a means of sharing risk, a means of securing ownership. Shares are also transferable, negotiable, and liquid.

Shares in Syariah-Compliant Companies

From an investor's perspective, shares provide an opportunity to share in the profit of the company while assuming the risk of loss. Shareholders are not lenders but are equity providers who support companies' activities to promote productivity and generate higher expected levels of profits. As such, they also share a risk proportionate to their investment. In addition to the potential dividend to be paid by the company, a shareholder may dispose of their shares for capital gains, if the market value of the shares exceeds the cost of the original investment. A shareholder may also sell and liquidate their shares if the company underperformed, termed as cut-loss.

The main concern of Islamic equity does not relate to the structure of an ordinary share, but to the activities of the company that issues the share to the public. In other words, investors, particularly Muslim investors who are sensitive to Islamic investment guidelines, must examine whether the company undertakes its activities according to Syariah principles. As shares represent an ownership right in the company, Muslim shareholders should not invest their capital in companies whose activities are non-compliant. As stated earlier, non-compliant companies might offer interest-based financial products, conventional insurance, gambling, pornography, or entertainment activities.

Regulatory Framework for Islamic Equity and Indexes

Islamic equity market is supposed to perform all the functions of conventional equity markets but with justice and equitable distribution of benefits. The Quran and Hadith have given clear guidance on moral rules and obligations, prohibition of interest, and the prohibition of obtaining others' property by wrongful means. Based on these guidelines, an Islamic equity market should function without interest as well as without malpractices tantamount to grabbing others' property by wrongful means. In the conventional financial system, an ideal effective and efficient regulatory structure is said to promote financial markets that are: (1) liquid and efficient where there exist free flow of capital and it is allocated properly given the underlying risks and expected returns; (2) transparent and fair where information must be reliable and relevant and must flow in a timely and fair-handed manner to all market participants; and (3) ethical and sound where market participants must act with integrity and in accordance with principles of unassailable conduct as they make capital transactions and other related activities. The success of regulators in this case is seen in terms of the extent to which they can build investor confidence in the integrity and fairness of transactions in capital market and the extent to which they are able to develop the markets in the direction of better transparency, greater competition, and hence greater efficiency.

It should be noted that regulations cannot prevent investors from losses, nor should regulations attempt to do so. Furthermore, laws and regulations should not discourage risk-taking, but regulations should make sure that investors have reliable information on which to base their decisions. Hence, the role of the regulator is to ensure that strong investor protection is in place through effective surveillance and enforcement as well as enhance the level of competition in the marketplace and facilitating product innovation. Rather than slowing the development of the Islamic equity market, an optimal and efficient level of regulation will bolster investors demand for Islamic securities.

Hence, the growing significance of the Islamic equity market requires the development of an effective and efficient regulatory framework to provide the enabling environment to support the development of the Islamic financial services industry. It is also necessary to promote the efficient operation of the equity market and its institutions for accelerating the development of the Islamic equity market.

One of the key aspects of regulating Islamic equity market is related to guidelines on regulations of Syariah-compliant stock indexes. Syariah-compliant indexes differ from their conventional counterparts in at least three ways; Syariah supervisory boards establish investing guidelines and monitor the process; the guidelines are then applied to the universe of securities; and finally, purification rules are set to 'cleanse' any impure profits from securities-paying dividends.

(a) **Syariah Supervisory Boards**

One crucial aspect of index construction is Syariah law, with decision-making about compliance provided by well-respected and financially savvy Syariah scholars. In order to be included in an index, companies must meet Syariah guidelines for acceptable products, business activities, debt levels, and interest incomes and expenses. It is up to each index provider to develop its own screening methodology—however, Dow Jones Indexes took the critical extra step of establishing an internal Syariah Supervisory Board to provide qualified advice on compliance.

(b) Screening

One area in which there is little room for debate is screening. Syariah-compliant instruments and Syariah indexes generally prohibit investment in alcohol, pork, tobacco, weapons, gambling, pornography, certain leisure and entertainment businesses, as well as conventional financial systems. Each index provider, however, approaches screening in its own way:

- *The Dow Jones Islamic Market Indexes* do not include companies involved in alcohol, conventional financial services (banking and insurance), pork-related products entertainment, tobacco, weapons, and defense;
- *FTSE Syariah Global Equity Index Series* also prohibits alcohol, tobacco, conventional finance, pork-related products, and non-halal food production, packaging, or processing;
- *MSCI Islamic Index Series* prohibits distillers and vintners, banks and insurance companies, aerospace and defense companies, casinos and gaming, hotels resorts, cruise lines and restaurants, as well as broadcasting and satellite movies and tobacco;
- *S&P Syariah Indexes* prohibit alcohol, advertising and media (with the exception of newspapers), financials, gambling, pork, pornography, tobacco, and companies involved in the trading of gold and silver as cash on deferred basis; and
- *The Russell-Jadwa Index* goes one step further, prohibiting the inclusion of companies involved in stem cell/human embryos and genetic cloning.

However, this is only part of the picture. The Dow Jones Islamic market Indexes prohibit any involvement in the activities mentioned, while the FTSE Syariah Global Equity Index Series allows companies to be included if the income on their total interest and non-compliant activities does not exceed 5% of the company's total revenue. Similarly, the

MSCI Islamic Index Series only prohibits companies that derive more than 5% of their revenues (cumulatively) from any prohibited activities, as does S&P. Like Dow Jones Indexes, the Russell-Jadwa Syariah Index prohibits non-compliant companies from inclusion.

For Dow Jones Indexes, the exclusion of companies that are non-compliant is important. It is the only way, we believe, to ensure that an index is truly Islamic, and that the index remains pure. Screening is also not always a straightforward process. What happens when an index provider prohibits breweries from being represented in an index, but then approves a supermarket which sells alcohol, or prohibits non-halal meat producers, but then includes McDonald's? It is not enough to have quantitative screening of stocks. We believe it is necessary to include a qualitative function that goes deeper. For Dow Jones Indexes, this involves an in-house research team that looks qualitatively at company information on an ongoing basis. The team examines many sources and considers how each company's revenues are broken down. The real work is in looking closely at the so-called gray areas.

Rather than exclude all supermarkets, for example, Dow Jones Indexes will include certain Gulf Cooperation Council region supermarkets and hotels that do not serve or sell alcohol. Companies in the gray area undergo an internal review—they are also considered by the quarterly review group. The information is then forwarded to Dow Jones Indexes' Syariah Board for an opinion. Once a year, the group goes through each of the 65,000 securities that the indexes consider. On top of this, there are 'watch lists', on which are companies that have the potential to be of concern. Dow Jones Islamic Indexes also set up news filters to monitor company information on a daily basis to ensure that a company, which might be compliant one day but not compliant on another, is then prohibited.

Regular, qualitative scrutiny is particularly relevant when it comes to company debt. A stock may have a portion of Syariah-compliant debt, for example, which would not be apparent from information downloaded from a data vendor. This is often the case for companies in the Middle East.

Screening also applies for debt ratios. Dow Jones Indexes exclude companies with:

- More than 33% total debt divided by a 24-month average market capitalization, and
- Companies with more than 33% cash and interest-bearing securities divided by a trailing 24-month average market capitalization.

Accounts receivable must also be less than 33%. A debt-to-market capitalization ratio better captures the 'new economy' economies, service-orientated companies, or companies that rely on larger amounts of goodwill. Debt-to-market capitalization is also more dynamic: it captures market-sector rotations. As it is market-value based, it is subject less to manipulations, as debt-to-market assets is an accounting treatment. The methodology also provides a faster accuracy of the health of a company. For example, companies like Enron, WorldCom, Tyco, and Global Crossing were all in the Dow Jones Islamic market Index, but as their accounting issues came into the public domain; their market capitalizations were negatively impacted. Since they violated the debt-to-market-cap screen, they were removed from the indexes at the next quarterly review.

(c) Dividend Purification

Index providers also have different approaches to dividend purification, a ratio that has developed over time in which a certain proportion of the profits earned through dividends (which corresponds to the proportion of interest earned by the company) must be given to charity. Syariah scholars have different opinions about purification. For the Dow Jones Islamic market Indexes, dividend purification is not an issue because the indexes do not allow non-compliant companies to be included. For FTSE, appropriate ratios stand at 5%, while MSCI Barra applies a 'dividend adjustment factor' to all reinvested dividends.

1.2.2 Unit Trusts/Mutual Funds

Unit trusts are popular in Southeast Asia. They resemble mutual funds that are popular in the USA, Europe, and Japan. A unit trust or mutual fund is an investment scheme whereby a fund manager pools money from investors with similar investment objectives to invest in a portfolio of assets, such as shares and bonds. The pooled monies in the unit trust or mutual fund will then be invested in a variety of asset class in accordance with the unit trust fund's investment objectives. The unit price of a fund is its net asset value (NAV per unit). NAV is derived from its assets, less its liabilities, and divided by the total number of units or shares currently issued and outstanding. Unlike stocks, where prices are changed at each trade, a fund's NAV is based on the closing prices of the stocks in its portfolio on each trading day.

The portfolio is managed by a professional fund manager appointed by the investment management company. Unit trusts or mutual fund investments allow investors to tap into the expertise of professional fund managers to help them boost the return on their investment.

Mutual funds can be open-ended or close-ended funds. Close-ended funds have a fixed level of capital that is set when the fund is created, which does not change over the life of the fund. Open-ended funds arise where the capital of the unit trust is not fixed but grows or shrinks with the demand of the investor. The fund manager will issue more units for investment if there is more demand, thus expanding the capital base of the unit trust. On the other hand, the unit trust will shrink when investors redeem their investment from the fund management company.

Managers, Trustees, and Unit Holders or Investors

The investment scheme of a unit trust fund is a tripartite relationship between the manager, the trustee, and the unit holders or investors. The manager is responsible for the day-to-day management and operations of the unit trust fund, while the trustee holds all the assets of the unit trust fund in the interests of the unit holders. The obligations and rights of each of the three parties are specified in a deed called a trust deed. The deed regulates the duties and responsibilities of the manager and the trustee with regard to the operations of the unit trust fund and the protection of the unit holders' interests.

The Attraction of Unit Trusts/Mutual Funds

Unit trust funds/mutual funds provide investors with a simple, convenient, and less time-consuming method of investing in securities compared with investing directly in the stock market. Listed below are the benefits associated with unit trust funds/mutual funds.

(a) *Professional investment services*: All investments are managed by full-time professional fund managers. Investment decisions are backed by extensive research, market analysis, and vigilant monitoring of the economic and market environment. These are skills that may be beyond those of most individual investors.

(b) *Diversification opportunities and minimized risk*: Investment in such funds provides the opportunity to spread the investment over a diversified portfolio of assets that may not otherwise be possible for investors with limited resources.

(c) *Affordability*: Investment in such funds may be more affordable than a direct investment in a portfolio of securities since the minimum investment amount in such schemes is relatively low.

(d) *Liquidity*: Unlike an investment in fixed assets, such as land and properties, which may take a relatively long time to liquidate, investors in this scheme may sell all or part of their unit holdings to the manager on any business day.

Syariah Perspective

From a Syariah perspective, there are no major issues with regards to the structure or features of either unit trusts or mutual funds. Indeed, the Syariah perceives investors as one entity that pools its monies together for the same investment objectives. Investors in this scheme are Musharakah partners as each investor invests in the scheme. What is more relevant is the position of possible investment assets, for example, stocks, bonds, bank deposits, or short-term papers, or money market instruments. As a guiding principle, investment under Islamic unit trusts or mutual funds must be in assets that are compliant to Syariah principles. The typical working structure of Islamic trust funds/mutual funds is illustrated in Fig. 10.2.

From the above figure it can be seen that the fund manager must establish a Syariah board to advise on all issues related to the operations and investments of the fund. This is a factor that distinguishes Islamic funds from conventional unit trusts/mutual funds. All investment assets must receive Syariah approval from the Syariah advisory board of the fund management company.

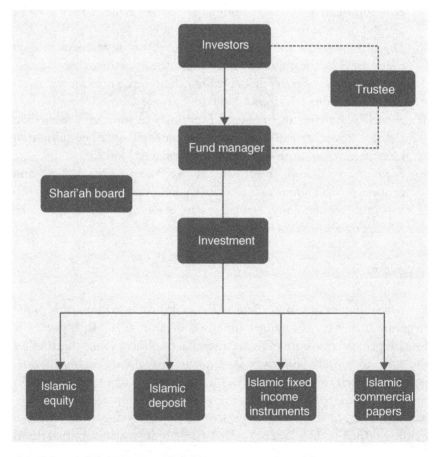

Fig. 10.2 Working structure of Islamic unit trusts/mutual funds

1.2.3 Islamic Private Equity Funds

Private equity is a broad term used to describe the equity of companies that are not listed on a public stock exchange. Not being listed means that any investor wishing to sell such securities must find a willing buyer in the absence of a market place. The main difference between Islamic and conventional private equity funds is the suitability of the target investment that is the investee companies. The Syariah board of an Islamic private equity fund must screen identified companies.

Investors invest in private equity funds, instead of stocks and unit trusts or mutual funds, in order to have an opportunity to gain from the increase in value of the investee company. This gain can be achieved either through the sale of the investee company to another interested investor at a price higher than the original investment value or through an initial public offering (IPO) by selling the shares in the company to the public, normally at a premium. There is always the risk that the investee company may not achieve the growth or success originally anticipated. The decision to invest in a private equity investment fund often comes down to the fund managers' ability in spotting successful investee companies.

Many private equity fund managers also find it appealing to own the majority of the shares in an investee company, thus giving the fund a management right. This can allow the investors to drive the company to either a sale or IPO through the services of the fund manager.

1.2.4 Islamic Specialized Funds

These are funds that invest neither in listed nor non-listed companies. The investment objective will be spelt out clearly in the investment prospectus. This is a dedicated fund for a specific purpose, and investors must pay more attention as the risk of investing may differ significantly from that of traditional forms of collective investment such as unit trusts/mutual funds and private equity funds. Islamic asset management companies have introduced, among others, Islamic leasing funds and Islamic Murabahah commodity funds, which are obviously not related to any equity investment.

Islamic Leasing Funds

An Islamic leasing fund is a collective investment scheme that pools investment money to purchase certain assets that could be leased out to operators/lessees. Examples are aircraft, vessels, and equipment. A typical example is aircraft leasing. An Islamic leasing fund may collect funds from investors, which are pooled and used to purchase, for example, passenger-carrying aircraft direct from the manufacturer. The fund may then lease the aircraft to one or more airline operators. The rental received is distributed proportionately as a dividend to all investors.

Islamic Exchange-Traded Funds (ETFs)

Islamic ETFs are essentially open-ended mutual funds that can be traded at any time through the stock market. ETFs are designed to mimic the performance of a particular stock market index, such as the S&P 500 or the Dow Jones Islamic Market Titan 100 (SM) Index, a specific market sector such as logistics or technology, or a commodity such as copper or petroleum. There is no structural difference between Islamic ETFs and conventional ETFs except that the underlying asset for Islamic ETFs, that is, the basket of shares that mirror the composition of a selected index, must be Syariah-compliant.

In Malaysia, there are two ETFs currently available. These are the FBM 30ETF which is a conventional ETF that tracks the FBM 30 Index. The FBM30 is an index of the 30 largest companies listed on Bursa Malaysia. The second available ETF is an Islamic ETF known as MyETF-DJIM Titan 25 (or simply MyETF). This is an ETF whose underlying is an index of 25 Syariah-compliant Malaysian companies listed within the Dow Jones Islamic Markets Index (DJIM). Introduced in January 2008, it is not only Malaysia's but also Asia's first Islamic ETF. What makes ETFs an interesting proposition to investors is the exposure they provide to an index or basket of stocks in the form of a single unit or share of the ETF. That is, buying a single share of an ETF is similar to taking a small position in each of the underlying index of stocks. This is made possible by the fact that an ETF is listed on an exchange and its shares traded like any other shares. Besides the trading flexibility that it allows, ETFs offer instant diversification (when investors purchase ETF, they invest in a fund that buys and holds multiple assets), access to diverse market segments, transparent pricing, and above all lower transaction costs. The lower transaction costs result from the fact that ETFs are passively managed. Like other listed shares, the value of an ETF share gets a price quote which is dependent on the ETF's NAV.

Islamic Real Estate Investment Trust (IREIT)

An Islamic REIT is an investor-owned company, trust, or association that sells shares to investors and invests in income-producing properties. An equity REIT owns and operates income-generating properties in the form of commercial, industrial, and residential properties or a combination of all of them. An Islamic REIT essentially represents a fund that investors contribute to in order to own a selection of properties. Thereafter, the investors are entitled to a proportionate share of the rental proceeds and capital gains. As with all Islamic products, the most relevant factor is that all the underlying income-producing properties must be compliant with Syariah principles to ensure that both the rental and capital gains are lawful. This means that the real estate assets must be leased out for compliant purposes only. For example, a property that was currently leased to a business that sold alcohol would not be an appropriate investment opportunity. Nor would it be appropriate for a property held within the portfolio to be subsequently leased to such a business.

When it comes to investment in new properties, the Islamic REIT must ensure that the activities of tenants currently renting the property are Syariah-compliant. In Malaysia, if a proportion of the rental is from existing tenants involved in non-Syariah compliant activities, the REIT must ensure that it does not exceed 20% of total rentals received from the property. In addition, the Syariah advisors of the fund must ensure that no new tenants, whose business activities may be non-Syariah compliant, are allowed. This applies, even if the inclusion of the new tenants' rentals results in a proportion below the 20% threshold.

In the case of appropriate insurance for the assets of the REIT, an Islamic REIT is only allowed to insure its properties using Takaful and not conventional insurance. Only if Takaful schemes are unable to provide coverage can the REIT use conventional insurance. A REIT receives rental income throughout the year, yet dividends are paid once or twice a year. Thus, at any point in time, a REIT would have surplus funds. Income from investing such funds is typically an important source of income for REITs. Where Islamic REITs are concerned, they can only invest surplus funds in Syariah-compliant investments.

From an operational viewpoint, an Islamic REIT is very similar to that of conventional ones. Malaysia's first Islamic REIT was the Al-Agar KPJ REIT, which was listed on Bursa Malaysia in August 2006. It was the result of KPJ, a healthcare provider, placing six of its hospitals into the REIT. Following this, a number of other Islamic REITs have also been listed, the most notable of which is the Al-Hadharah Boustead REIT. This is the world's first Islamic plantation REIT.

1.2.5 Islamic Fixed-Income Instruments—Sukuk

A bond is a debt instrument whereby the issuer owes the investor an amount of money consisting of both the principal and coupon payment. This form of structure is not acceptable under Syariah principles. Not only is the structure that contains the element of interest not permissible, but the trading of these bonds in the secondary market is equally prohibited. As the sale of Sukuk certificates to a third party at any price other than their face value is not permitted under Syariah, most Sukuk cannot be traded in the secondary market. Most Sukuk which have been issued to date tend to be privately placed, that is, the trust certificates are issued to institutional investors who will invest in trust certificates in large denominations, rather than to the general public. Some Sukuk such as Sukuk musharaka can be traded in the secondary market

The Islamic equivalent of a conventional bond is called a Sukuk. The origins of Sukuk can be traced back to the classical Islamic period (700–1300 AD) during which papers representing financial obligations originating from trade and other commercial activities were issued in conformity with verse 2:282 of the Holy Quran, which encourages fixing contracts in writing:

> *When ye deal with each other, in transactions involving future obligations in a fixed period of time, reduce them to writing... It is more just in the sight of God, more suitable as evidence and more convenient to prevent doubts among yourselves.*

During the classical Islamic period, a sakk (singular of Sukuk and literally meaning 'deed' or 'instrument') was used to describe any document representing financial liability. The Organisation of the Islamic Conference International Islamic Fiqh Academy (the Fiqh Academy), an academy for the advanced study of Islam based in Jeddah, Saudi Arabia, laid the basis for the development of the Sukuk market through the issuance of a statement in 1988, holding that 'Any combination of assets (or the usufruct of such assets) can be represented in the form of written financial instruments which can be sold at a market price provided that the composition of the groups of assets represented by the Sukuk consist of a majority of tangible assets'.

The Fiqh Academy's decisions are highly influential on most Syariah-compliant financial institutions and their Syariah committees. This statement in particular, which was seen to approve Sukuk trading, was a milestone in the evolution of Islamic finance, paving the way for the introduction of Sukuk as capital market instruments. AAOIFI, established in 1991, also plays an important role in harmonizing Syariah standards relating to finance. AAOIFI's Syariah Board consists of scholars representing various Muslim countries and it is therefore considered as an industry-level representative body of Syariah scholars.

The first Sukuk followed shortly after the Fiqh Academy issued the statement referred to above, with Shell MDS Sdn Bhd 125 Million Malaysian ringgit Bai Bithaman Ajil Sukuk issued in 1990. Another 11 years passed before the issue of the first international US dollar Sukuk—the Malaysian plantation company Kumpulan Guthrie Bhd's US$150 Million Sukuk in 2001. The Bahrain Monetary Authority (now the Central Bank of Bahrain) was the first GRE to issue Sukuk in 2001. Several sovereign Sukuk followed Malaysia, the State of Qatar, the

Republic of Pakistan, and the Emirate of Dubai, which garnered international attention for Sukuk and set the stage for unprecedented international growth.

The Sukuk market faltered slightly between late 2007 and early 2009, mainly as a result of two distinct and separate events: the debate surrounding the Syariah compliance of some Sukuk structures and the global credit crisis, the latter of which resulted in increased borrowing costs and a lack of investor commitment to, and confidence in, capital market securities. In late 2007, Sheikh Muhammad Taqi Usmani, chairman of AAOIFI, issued a divisive statement questioning whether the majority of Sukuk instruments existing in the market were in fact compliant with Syariah principles. The ensuing market uncertainty caused by Sheikh Usmani's statement led AAOIFI's scholars to hold meetings in early 2008, following which AAOIFI issued an official statement (the AAOIFI statement), which sought to provide some guidance in relation to Sukuk structures.

The global Sukuk market has since recovered, growing rapidly since the global financial crisis with global Sukuk issuances reaching US$116.4 billion in 2014. The Sukuk market is now a significant source of capital for many companies, sovereigns, and Government Related Entities (GREs) in Southeast Asia, the Middle East, and North Africa—regions that are each home to fast-growing Muslim populations. Malaysia currently continues to dominate the sovereign Sukuk issuance market, accounting for approximately 60% of Sukuk issuances globally.

In the past, the difficulties of structuring Sukuk transactions caused many entities that might have otherwise been logical Sukuk issuers to continue to raising funds either through the bond market or through conventional bank loans provided by European and US banks. In addition, Sukuk pricing was generally less favorable than that available in the conventional loan and bond markets. However, the credit crunch in Europe and the USA, along with the Eurozone crisis, changed the landscape and caused many companies to increasingly turn to the liquid Sukuk market.

In recent years, the United Arab Emirates (UAE), particularly Dubai, have relied heavily on international funding. Dubai will spend an estimated US$8.1 billion on roads, an airport, hotels, and an extension to its rail network in preparation for the World Expo 2020, which is likely to result in a surge of Sukuk issuances in the Emirate. Even countries like Qatar, which historically financed much of its growth from gas revenues, are expected to require significant external funding to finance the air-conditioned stadiums and substantial infrastructure needed to stage the 2022 FIFA World Cup. The retreat of European and US banks will create a significant funding gap in this expanding regional economy.

As European and US lending markets contracted, companies in the Middle East looked closer to home at the considerable liquidity in the region, which was, at least until late 2014, being driven by high oil prices and strong regional economic growth. In 2014, the economies of Saudi Arabia and the UAE grew by an estimated 4.4% and 4.2%, respectively. As a result of this strong regional economic growth, the liquidity of local and regional banks increased, with greater than anticipated deposits and low loan-to-deposit ratios. Banks and financial institutions in the region have therefore become important investors in the growing Sukuk market in the Middle East. Additionally, increasing numbers of family-owned businesses in the Middle East, after suffering considerable losses on their investments in European and US markets, now prefer to keep their investments closer to home and, where possible, to invest in Syariah-compliant instruments.

The continued liquidity within the overall Islamic investor base (in particular from Islamic banks), both in the Middle East and Asia, will likely be a key driver of global Sukuk issuances. Sukuk has also typically been purchased by investors intending to hold the Sukuk certificates to maturity, so the secondary market performance of Sukuk has generally been more stable, despite the wider economic instability. Importantly, as the Sukuk market has developed, most prospective issuers of Sukuk are able to achieve more favorable pricing in the Sukuk market as compared to an equivalent issue in the conventional bond market. These factors, among others, have led to a number of market participants predicting that the global issuances of Sukuk will reach over US$250 billion by 2020.

Regulatory Framework for Sukuk Issuance

The world's capital markets are governed primarily by the conventional finance system. Accordingly, it was inevitable that Sukuk or Islamic debt market would be governed by the same laws and regulations that govern conventional finance. To make matters worse, most existing laws in different countries do not favor Islamic finance.

Securitization is 'a process of pooling/repackaging the nonmarketable and illiquid assets into tradable certificates of investment'. In addition, Sukuk could be understood in a same line of general securitization, as it makes underlying assets tradable by giving undivided ownership to many Sukuk holders. However, it is necessary to understand the things that make difference between conventional securitization and Sukuk. First, theoretically, Islamic securitization should be on Islamic principles; therefore, anything that contradicts Syariah is not allowed in Sukuk contracts and securitization. Second, Islamic securitization must involve the funding or the production of real assets rather than financial securities.

The problem, however, is that most countries do not have Islamic securitization law, and due to the different nature of the Islamic and conventional securitization concepts, conflicts and obstacles in the application of Islamic securitization exist in many countries. The first conflict involves interest payments. Islamic principles prohibit the payment of interest in finance, whereas conventional securitization includes loans, bonds, and other receivables. Even though some portfolios or pools of assets with a combination of physical assets and financial claims (such as receivables) are allowed, these types of vehicles should include a majority of their pooled assets (at least 51%) as physical assets. Second, conventional securitization does not care about prohibited items in Islam (haram) such as alcohol, pork, and gambling, which means that under conventional securitization any assets could be securitized without legal restriction. Third, credit enhancement in conventional financing is accompanied by a fee, which is related to the issue of riba in Islam. Islamic banking, on the other hand, allows credit guarantees that are called 'kafala' (without fee). The fourth is that limitations exist in Islamic finance with respect to liquidity enhancement, as this is set in conventional banking with interest-based loans. The

Islamic banking system has short-term qard hasan or interest-free loans, meaning that Islamic securitization only occurs when there is no financial reward for the provider. Therefore, Islamic liquidity is supported by bai inah and tawarruq in some countries; however, these two ideas are quite controversial among Muslim scholars.

The high-tax problem with respect to Sukuk is one of the most significant challenges and is pertinent in Islamic finance developed countries under their conventional tax systems. The most significant tax problem related to Sukuk stems from the taxation of the underlying assets. Because Islamic finance should be based on underlying assets, whenever assets are transferred between parties additional tax could be attached (as compared with conventional finance).

Bankruptcy or insolvency law becomes very important when originator is failed to fulfill their obligations, in order to protect the Sukuk holder. For an efficient capital market, effective insolvency and creditor rights systems are vital to stability in commercial relationships and financial systems, and effective framework for insolvency regimes of Islamic financial institutions is important to ensure stability of the Islamic financial markets, as well as for sustainable development and growth.

Features, Types, and Mechanisms of Islamic Sukuk

Sukuk refers to the process of aggregating tangible assets or usufruct, or an interest in a project into pieces or securities that reflect proportionate ownership. Sukuk does not deal with receivables or financial assets. Sukuk holders each have an undivided beneficial ownership interest in the underlying assets. Consequently, Sukuk holders are entitled to share in the revenues generated by the relevant assets in the case of Sukuk mudarabah and Sukuk Musharakah. As for Sukuk Ijarah, the revenues are generated by the lease rental payment paid by the obligor/lessee to the issuer/SPV to be proportionately distributed to Sukuk Ijarah investors.

It is important to understand that Sukuk, unlike bonds, are not debt certificates or 'IOU' instruments. Sukuk, by and large, are certificates that provide evidence of an investment in either an asset or a project, which is typically an income-generating asset or a project. The return to investors is not fixed or guaranteed but is subject to the performance of this underlying asset. The issuing of Islamic bonds or notes, particularly by the Malaysian market prior to the development of Sukuk Ijarah, was contentious mainly because the trading of these securities was based on the sale of debt concept. This is because these Islamic bonds are essentially based on the receivables securitization and any trading of these securities must be based on par value to avoid riba transaction. Receivables have been perceived by the majority of scholars as representing monetary assets. Therefore, the trading of those securities must be based on face value to avoid the element of riba, which requires an equal amount in the exchange of money.

(a) Sukuk Ijarah

The first Islamic fixed-income instrument or Islamic security accepted by the global market was the Sukuk Ijarah, which is based on a sale and leaseback concept. The development of Sukuk Ijarah through the Malaysian Global Sukuk Ijarah in 2002 introduced the concept of asset-based securitization. Securities or Sukuk, which are issued out of these leased assets, represent an undivided and proportionate beneficial ownership of the leased asset, which are tradable based on there being a willing buyer and a willing seller.

The development of Sukuk Ijarah was a ground-breaking innovation in offering Islamic fixed-income instruments to investors. Sukuk are tradable in the secondary market without any Syariah constraint as they represent the ownership right of the leased asset instead of pure receivables in the case of Islamic bonds or notes. Figure 10.3 illustrates the structure of the Malaysian Global Sukuk Ijarah.

The diagrammatic structure of Sukuk Ijarah shows that the process of its issue begins with the originator who is the owner of an asset. The originator sells the asset at 'x' amount and leases it back from the SPV at 'x + y', which represents the principal and rental payment to the investors.

The investors are deemed to be the owners of this asset because they provided the money to purchase the asset from the originator through an SPV/issuer. An asset-based securitization has now taken place in the sense that the asset has been packaged and transformed into units. Investors

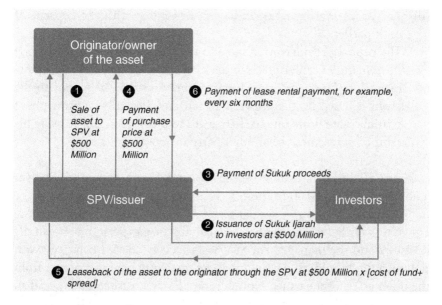

Fig. 10.3 Structure of Sukuk Ijarah

who subscribed to these units are purchasing a share in the asset along with all ownership rights. Once this asset is leased back to the originator, the investors are equally entitled to receive the rental payment since they are the owners and lessors of the asset.

(b) Sukuk Mudarabah

Mudarabah is a partnership contract whereby one party provides the capital and the other provides the management and entrepreneurship skills. For a Sukuk structure to raise the necessary capital, the capital providers will be the investors, the issuer will be the company, and the manager (mudarib) who will manage the business venture. The other features of a mudarabah contract include:

(i) Neither the capital nor the profit is guaranteed.
(ii) The manager (mudarib) will not be liable for the loss, unless it is caused by his negligence and misconduct.

(iii) The profit-sharing ratio (PSR) can be revised with the consent of both parties.
(iv) The capital providers may agree to limit the rate of return whereby the remainder can be given to the manager as an incentive or performance fee; the decision of the investors to waive their right to the profit is based on the principle of tanazul; Tanazul is a principle of Syariah that allows one of the parties to a contract to give away his right or entitlement to another party for no consideration.

Figure 10.4 illustrates how a company can issue a Sukuk mudarabah at a nominal value of $100 Million. In practice, the company may issue the Sukuk directly or set up a special purpose vehicle (SPV), being a remote entity, to issue Sukuk mudarabah to facilitate the partnership between the investors and the manager. An SPV is a specially created company with the purpose of holding the Sukuk assets so that they are separated from the other assets of the issuer. Normally an SPV is a trust company, and all the assets it holds are for the benefit of the Sukuk investors. The creditors of the issuer cannot serve any liquidation order on this entity. The incorporation of the SPV is to protect the interest of the Sukuk holders.

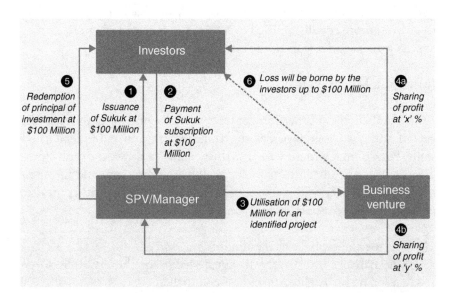

Fig. 10.4 Illustration of a Sukuk mudarabah

The proceeds of a Sukuk mudarabah subscription will be used to finance the business activities in the identified venture. The venture could be in the area of construction, manufacturing, trading, services, mining, or oil production. The profit, if any, will be paid to the investors based on an agreed PSR. As mentioned, although the profit is based on a ratio or percentage, such as 1/3:2/3 or 30%:70%, investors may agree to cap their profit to, for example, 10% of the capital. The remainder will be waived and given to the manager as a performance fee.

(c) Sukuk Musharakah

Sukuk Musharakah is similar to Sukuk mudarabah as both are equity-based contracts. However, some features are unique to a Musharakah contract. These include:

(i) Both parties to a Musharakah contract must contribute the capital into the business venture.
(ii) While a PSR can be negotiated, loss sharing must be proportionate to capital contribution.
(iii) Both parties have the right to participate in the management of the business venture.

A typical structure of Sukuk Musharakah is depicted in Fig. 10.5.

The above diagram illustrates a typical Sukuk Musharakah structure. Both the company and investors contribute their respective capital in an identified business venture, such as upgrading an airport's facilities. The capital could be in the form of cash or kind, such as forklift trucks, and so on. The profit, if any, will be distributed between the investors and the company according to an agreed PSR. To waive some profit in favor of the company is also permissible under the principle of waiver or tanazul. Investors would expect to receive the estimated periodic profit distribution, say biannually, as Sukuk are deemed to behave like fixed-income instruments. Neither mudarabah nor Musharakah is a debt-based financing contract. There is no obligation on any party to pay a fixed amount by way of income or profit and there is no guarantee on the capital invested.

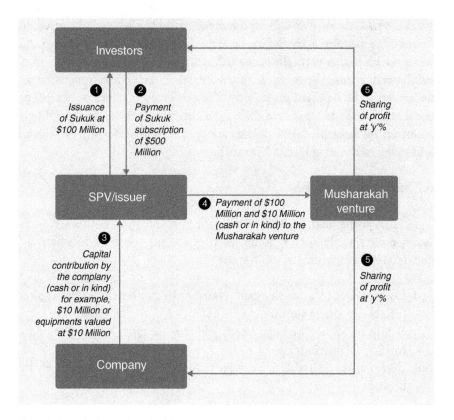

Fig. 10.5 Sukuk Musharakah

Recent Trends in Sukuk

(a) **Hybrid Sukuk**

Hybrid Sukuk combine the securitization of receivables and tangible assets in one issue. As mentioned, full receivables-based or financial-asset securitization results in securities that can only be traded at par value since they are deemed to be monetary assets. With the exception of Malaysia, where receivables have been securitized and traded as bonds, this renders most Islamic receivables incapable of being securitized. As such, accounts receivable cannot be converted into liquid assets and the financier must hold the receivables until maturity. In order to address this problem, the Islamic Development Bank (IDB) issued the first and second Sukuk istithmar by combining assets that are financial, Islamic receivables, and assets that are physical or tangible in a proportion acceptable to the bank's Syariah board. In these two issues, the Syariah board allowed the composition of the financial asset to be up to 70% vis-à-vis the tangible asset, which cannot be less than 30%. Prior to this fatwa, the acceptable ratio of receivables to asset was 45/55 or 49/51, respectively, which is endorsed by many Syariah Boards including the Dow Jones Islamic Market Index (DJIM).

Given the nature of financing undertaken by the IDB, which consists mainly of project financing in the form of istisna and asset financing in the form of Murabahah, this fatwa suits the need to securitize this financial asset because a large portion of the bank's assets are in the form of account receivables. A combination of Ijarah assets (not less than 30%) and receivables (not more than 70%) make this Sukuk unique and tradable. In this arrangement, the IDB bundles certain Ijarah assets (minimum 30%), as well as istisna and Murabahah receivables that it owns (assets) and sells to the SPV for the SPV to issue Sukuk istithmar. The investors will have a claim on these assets and the proceeds of their sale will be used by the IDB for its working capital. This line of argument was later endorsed by the Accounting and Auditing Organization for Islamic Financial Institutions' (AAOIFI) Syariah Standard on Financial Papers (No.21). This has paved the way for the future structuring of Islamic securities using this hybrid approach.

(b) Exchangeable and convertible Sukuk

As investors become more sophisticated, they require more value-added features within the Sukuk structure. One feature is the exchangeability or convertibility of the Sukuk into shares of certain companies. This gives them an opportunity to convert their Sukuk into shares. Essentially, an exchangeable security is a straight bond or security issue, which also gives the investor the right (but not the obligation) to convert or exchange the bond or security into a predetermined number of shares of a company at a predetermined exchange price. Both exchangeable and convertible securities have this option, but they differ from each other with respect to the shares to be exchanged with or converted into. While convertible securities give the right to the holders of securities to convert to ordinary shares of the issuer company, the holders of securities under exchangeable securities can convert their securities to ordinary shares of other companies.

What is important in this structure of Sukuk is the conversion price, which is fixed at the time the securities are issued, and is based on the par value of the bond. When this par value of the securities is divided by the price of the share, then a conversion ratio is calculated upon which the security will be converted or exchanged into ordinary shares of the respective companies.

This development obviously benefits the holders of securities. If the Sukuk holder decides to convert or exchange their Sukuk, they will be become shareholders of a company with all the respective rights and liabilities. They will also be eligible to receive dividends and/or capital gains as the case may be. The dividend, or the capital gain, is not limited to any rate because this will be eventually determined by the market. If holders do not convert or exchange their Sukuk, they will continue to receive the fixed income or the expected periodic distribution of profit. They are also entitled to the redemption of their principal at the maturity period. In addition, being Sukuk investors, they have a preference over ordinary shareholders of the issuing company in the case of liquidation.

Box 10.1 Case Study: Projek Lebuhraya Usahasama Berhad (PLUS Berhad) Musharakah Based Sukuk 2012

Projek Lebuhraya Usahasama Berhad (PLUS Berhad), a company that provides expressway operation services in Malaysia, issued Sukuk al-Musharakah structure-based Sukuk worth Malaysian ringgit (MYR) 30.6 billion (US $ 9.7billion) in January 2012. It is the largest global Sukuk and Malaysia's single largest bond issuance to date, following the privatization exercise. This Sukuk provides an excellent case study for long-term Syariah-compliant fund-raising exercise using readily available infrastructure assets which generate stable returns. It is a case of matching long-term and stable revenue streams against long-term financing obligations.

Sukuk al-Musharakah

They are certificates of equal value issued with the aim of using the mobilized funds for establishing a new project, financing a business activity, and so on on the basis of any of partnership contract so that the certificate holders become the owners of the project. (Musharakah Sukuk is an investment partnership between two or more entities which together provide the capital of the Musharakah and share in its profits and losses in pre-agreed ratios.)

PLUS Berhad Musharakah-based Sukuk
PLUS Berhad issued MYR 30.6 billion (US $9.7 billion) Musharakah-based structured Sukuk on January 12, 2012. The Sukuk proceeds were utilized to partly finance the purchase of assets, liabilities, businesses, undertakings, and rights of five toll concessions—Projek Lebuhraya Utara-Selatan Berhad, Expressway Lingkaran Tengah Sdn Bhd, Konsortium Lebuhraya Butterworth-Kulim Sdn Bhd, Linkedua (Malaysia) Berhad, and Penang Bridge Sdn Bhd. The proceeds were also used for capital expenditure, working capital, and other general funding requirement. PLUS Berhad acquired all the assets and liabilities of the respective concession companies, through MYR 11 billion of government guaranteed (GG) and MYR 19.6 billion of non-government guaranteed AAA-rated (AAA) Sukuk issuances of varying tenors, sizes, and expected returns and yields to maturity (YTMs). The issuances were distributed on a direct placement basis. The Sukuk repayment period ranges from 5 to 27 years. CIMB Investment Bank was the financial adviser, sole principal adviser, sole lead arranger, and joint lead manager for the deal. AmInvestment Bank, Maybank, and RHB Investment Bank were the other joint lead managers. The principal transaction documents consist of Musharakah Agreement(s), Management Agreement, Purchase Undertaking, and Sale Agreement.

Sukuk Structure and Transaction Flows

1. *SPV*: The Sukuk was issued by PLUS Berhad which is a wholly owned subsidiary of Plus Malaysia, a special purpose company setup to acquire business interests of PLUS Expressways Berhad.
2. *Trustee*: Maybank Trustees Berhad was the trustee for the certificates.
3. *Use of Sukuk Proceeds*: In respect of each issue of Sukuk al-Musharakah under the Sukuk program, PLUS Berhad will identify its business comprising of rights under the respective toll-road concessions granted by the Government of Malaysia or part thereof which will be used as the underlying asset for that particular Musharakah transaction.

   Sukuk holders shall via the trustee, from time to time, form a Musharakah among themselves, which is a partnership among the Sukuk holders, to invest in the underlying asset ('Musharakah Venture') via the subscription of the Sukuk. There will be at least two Sukuk holders forming the Musharakah through a *Musharakah Agreement* at each issuance. The Sukuk al-Musharakah shall represent, among others, undivided proportionate interest of the

Sukuk holders in the Musharakah Venture. A declaration shall be made by Plus Berhad that it holds on trust, the underlying asset for the benefit of the Sukuk holders. PLUS Berhad shall receive Musharakah capital arising from the subscription of the Sukuk.
4. *Management of Musharakah Venture*: Pursuant to the *Management Agreement* to be entered into between PLUS Berhad and the Trustee (acting on behalf of the Sukuk holders), the trustee shall appoint PLUS Berhad as the manager of the Musharakah Venture.
5. *Periodic Distribution Payments*: The expected return of the Sukuk holders from the Musharakah Venture shall be the yield for the Sukuk al-Musharakah up to the maturity date of the Sukuk al-Musharakah or the date of declaration of an event of default/dissolution event, whichever is the earlier. In respect of Sukuk al-Musharakah with periodic distribution, income from the Musharakah Venture of up to an amount equal to a certain percentage of the face value of the Sukuk al-Musharakah per annum ('expected periodic distribution') shall be distributed periodically in the form of periodic distribution to the Sukuk holders. The periodic distribution shall be made semi-annually or on such period to be determined prior to each issuance. In the event of any shortfall between the periodic distribution and the Expected Periodic Distribution for such relevant period, PLUS Berhad shall make top-up payments to compensate for the shortfall. The top-up payments will be set-off against the Exercise Price defined under dissolution payments. Any income in excess of the expected periodic distribution shall be retained by PLUS Berhad as an incentive fee. In respect of Sukuk al-Musharakah without periodic distribution, income from the Musharakah Venture of up to the expected return shall be distributed on a one-off basis upon the maturity date of the Sukuk al-Musharakah or the dissolution date, whichever is the earlier. In the event of any shortfall between the one-off distribution and the expected return for such relevant period, PLUS Berhad shall make top-up payment

to make good the difference. The top-up payment will be set off against the exercise price. Any income in excess of the expected return shall be retained by PLUS Berhad as an incentive fee.

6. *Dissolution Payments*: Pursuant to a *Purchase Undertaking* granted by PLUS Berhad (as 'obligor') in favor of the trustee (acting on behalf of the Sukuk holders), PLUS Berhad shall undertake to purchase the Sukuk holders' interest in the Musharakah Venture by entering into a *Sale Agreement* and pay the exercise price on either the maturity date of the Sukuk al-Musharakah or on the dissolution date, whichever is the earlier. PLUS Berhad shall be entitled to set off the exercise price with any top-up payment(s) made. In the case of Sukuk al-Musharakah with periodic distribution, the exercise price for the Sukuk al-Musharakah shall be equivalent to the Musharakah capital plus the expected return less total periodic distributions. In the case of Sukuk al-Musharakah without periodic distribution, the exercise price shall be equivalent to the Musharakah capital plus the expected return less any one-off distribution.

1.2.6 Islamic Derivatives or Structured Products

Islamic derivatives and structured products are equally important in the ICM as they aim to manage financial risk in a more effective way and, at the same time, are compliant with Syariah principles. Risk management is an important aspect of most Islamic financial products, which are based on contracts such as sale, lease, and partnership. Due to its inherent features and characteristics and the fact that it is essentially exposed to different risks to those of conventional finance, the need for effective risk management in Islamic finance is highly important. While conventional finance's main exposure is to credit risk, Islamic finance products may be exposed to market risk, operational risks, rate of return risk, and equity investment risk. Due to unique nature of different underlying contracts (profit- or loss-sharing mechanism and asset-based structure) of Islamic capital market instruments, Islamic finance risk exposure is somewhat different from conventional finance.

(a) Islamic forward forex

An Islamic forward forex is used to hedge the exchange rate risk of foreign currencies. Without this instrument, an international importer or exporter would be exposed to currency exchange rate fluctuations.

(b) Islamic options

It is usual in the stock market that the value of a share exhibits volatility. A person may have purchased a share today at $100 per unit. This unit of share may be traded in the future either at a higher or lower price or alternatively known as upside profit potential and downside loss exposure, respectively. Both of these possibilities are unlimited, and if the share price decreases to zero, the investor will lose all their investment. Islamic options or 'Arbun' (down payment, also known as 'earnest money') instruments are used to protect the downside of any investment in stock or commodities and to provide an opportunity to benefit from the market upside. The option gives the holder the right to purchase underlying instrument in the future, but at a fixed price.

The downside risk is limited to the premium or 'Arbun' if the option holder decides not to proceed with the purchase of the underlying stock in the case where its value has decreased significantly. However, if the value of the stock increases, the profit potential is unlimited. This can be achieved through an 'Arbun' contract, which is a down payment scheme paid by the purchaser to ensure the seller delivers the asset upon full payment at maturity. If the purchaser fails or declines to pay the remaining amount, the down payment paid will be forfeited to the seller. This mechanism shares the same economic benefit of an option.

(c) Islamic forward and future contracts

Islamic forward and future contracts, under the basis of a Salam sale, are used to lock-in the price of the commodities in the future. Although a Salam contract cannot fully replicate the functions and benefits of conventional forward and future contracts, it may help to reduce both the producer's and the manufacturer's market risk.

(d) Islamic profit rate swap

Islamic profit rate swaps are used to hedge the asset-liability mismatch of Islamic Financial Institutions (IFIs). Profit or interest rate swaps, as practiced in conventional finance, seek to ensure that the liability of a financial institution always matches or corresponds to its assets. It essentially aims to match fixed liabilities with fixed assets and floating liabilities with floating assets, in order to avoid a potential mismatch of asset-liability in an IFI.

References

Adam, J. N., & Thomas, A. (2004). *Islamic bonds—Your guide to issuing, structuring and investing in Sukuk*. London: Euromoney Books.

Ayub, M. (2007). *Understanding Islamic finance*. West Sussex, UK: John Wiley & Son Ltd.

Haroon, A. (2008). Globalization in Islamic capital market instruments. *Islamic Financial Services Board*. Retrieved from http://www.oicexchanges.org/presentations/Abdullah%20Haron.pdf

IIFM—International Islamic Financial Market. (2009). *Sukuk report–A comprehensive study of the international Sukuk market*. Retrieved from http://www.iifm.net/default.asp?action=category&id=66

IOSCO. (2005). *Islamic capital markets: Fact finding report*. Retrieved from http://www.sc.com.my/wp-content/uploads/eng/html/icm/ICM-IOSCOFact%20finding%20Report.pdf

Khan, T., & Ahmed, H. (2001). *Risk management—An analysis of issues in Islamic financial industry*. Occasional Paper No. 5, Islamic Development Bank/Islamic Research and Training Institute, Jeddah.

Obiyathulla, I. B. (2007). *Financial derivatives: Market and applications in Malaysia* (2nd ed.). Shah Alam, Malaysia: McGraw Hill.

Sardehi, N. (2008). *Islamic capital markets—Developments and challenges*. Germany: VDM Verlag Publishers.

Securities Commission. (2001). The capital market master plan—Malaysia.

11

Takaful

1 Introduction

Takaful is an insurance concept in Syariah, which literally means shared responsibility, shared guarantee, collective assurance, and mutual undertakings. The Takaful industry is relatively a new industry compared to its conventional counterpart; even then it has shown impressive growth rate of about 20% in recent years. The first Takaful company was established in 1979, which rose to 250 Takaful providers globally in 2016. As per the Islamic Financial Services Industry Stability Report 2016, the gross contributions in the global Takaful industry are estimated to have increased 5% year on year to $23.2 billion in 2015, and the global Takaful sector is expected to continue and reach $20 billion by 2017 (Source: http://gulfnews.com/business/sectors/banking/global-takaful-premium-to-reach-20-billion-by-2017-1.1491084).

The remarkable growth in Takaful industry is because conventional insurance contains elements of maisir (gambling), gharar (uncertainty), and riba (usury/interest) that conflicts with Syariah and is unacceptable. Further to that, the 1985 Fiqh Academy ruling declared that conventional commercial insurance was haram (forbidden), and insurance based on the application of shared responsibility, Syariah compliance, joint indemnity, common interest, and charitable donations was halal (permissible). Hence, in the past 20 years, Takaful industry has spread not only into Muslim countries but also into Asian and Western countries with sizable Muslim population. The returns are lucrative, growth rate is in double digit more, and more players including Westerners are entering into the Takaful industry to capture the market.

This chapter is to provide an insight into the Takaful industry with a focus on Malaysian market. It also covers the current practices, growth, and challenges faced by the players and recent advancement in the industry.

1.1 Takaful Definition

Takaful comes from the Arabic root word 'kafala', meaning 'guaranteeing each other' or joint guarantee. Takaful, the Islamic alternative to insurance, is based on the concept of social solidarity, cooperation, and mutual indemnification of losses of members. Under this concept, a group of participants mutually agree among themselves to guarantee each other against defined loss or damage that may inflict upon any of them by contributing donation in the Takaful fund. Each member of the group pools resources and efforts to support the needy participants within the group. This is how the fortunate many assist the unfortunate few. The essence of Takaful is to bring equity among all the participants involved in an operation based on helping each other from risks and misfortunes, whereby earning profit is not the sole objective.

Takaful is based on the principle of 'taawun' (brotherhood or mutual assistance) and Tabarru (donation, gift, or contribution) where the risk is shared collectively by the group voluntarily. Following this contract, participant agrees to donate a predetermined percentage of his contribution to a Takaful fund, to assist fellow participants. In this way participants fulfill their obligation of joint guarantee and mutual help, in the event any fellow participant suffers a loss. This concept eliminates the element of gharar from the Takaful contract. Hence, participants are both the insurer and the insured at the same time and make Takaful as a unique insurance model.

1.2 History and Crucial Elements of Takaful System

The foundation of Takaful can be traced more than 1,400 years ago in the pre-Islamic era and after the rise of Islam. During that era, a common practice among ancient Arab tribal known as the system of 'aquila' resembles insurance practices. It was a mutual agreement or joint guarantee given between Arab tribes to protect the individual or families from any financial liability arising from the situation, whereby any tribe member was killed or injured by a member of another tribe. When such an event occurred, blood money (*'diyah'*) would be payable to the heirs of the victim from the paternal relatives of the accused. In order to mitigate such financial liability, all the members of the accused's tribe who were participants in the scheme would contribute until the diyah had been satisfied. The tribes would hence collectively share responsibility for sums individually owed.

The traces of Takaful can also be found in business transactions as well. Muslim Arabs were expanding trade into Asia and used to follow 'aquilla' practice, whereby they mutually agreed to contribute to a fund to cover anyone in the group that incurred mishaps or robberies along the numerous sea voyages. The obligation to make regular financial payments to the fund is similar to premiums paid for conventional insurance, and the compensation amount in the event of any mishap is similar to the indemnity or sum insured in the present insurance practices.

Since Takaful is based on divine principles, there are mandatory key elements that must co-exist to establish a proper framework for Takaful system as listed below:

- All activities should comply with Syariah conditions, that is, risk-sharing under Taawun and Tabarru principles, coincidence of ownership, participation in management by policyholders, avoidance of riba and prohibited investments, and inclusion of al mudharaba and/or al-wakalah principles for management practices.
- Practice utmost sincerity (Neaa) by following the guidance and strictly adhering to the purpose and principles of Takaful, that is, to enable cooperative risk-sharing and mutual assistance.

- Follow ethics, moral value, and social objective, whereby business is conducted in accordance with utmost good faith, honesty, transparency, truthfulness, and fairness in all dealings.
- No existence of forbidden (haram) element that contravenes Syariah and all commercial contract should have necessary elements and conditions such as:
    - Parties have legal capacity and are mentally fit
    - Insurable interest
    - Principle of indemnity prevails
    - Payment of premium is consideration (offer and acceptance)
    - Mutual consent which includes voluntary purification
    - Specific time period of policy and underlying agreement
- Appointment of Sharia Advisory Council or Committee to oversee the development and Islamic auditing of the Takaful operation

1.3 Comparison Between Takaful and Conventional Insurance System

Takaful distinguishes itself from conventional insurance in several different ways; the key issues are listed in Fig. 11.1.

1.4 Mudharabah Model in Practice

This refers to the co-operative risk-sharing where participants and Takaful operator has profit- and loss-sharing arrangement. The nature of *Mudharabah* (profit and loss sharing) practices is that it is a financial contract whereby one party called *rabbu al-mal(participant)* provides fund to the other party called mud*arib(Takaful operator)* who undertakes to manage the fund through investment or trade and generates profits. The Takaful operator shares the surplus on underwriting and a share of profit from the investments. No loss is borne by the Takaful operator as he puts only his labor at risk.

Under this model the contributions are given on trust ('amanah') to the Takaful operator and so are repayable to the participants in due course, minus the operator's costs. The contribution is split into two separate

Issues	Conventional Insurance	Takaful
Governing Principles	Functions and operating modes are based on Syariah law, derived from the Quran, Hadith & Sunnah	Functions and operating modes are based on manmade principles and not based on any religious laws or guidelines.
Concept	Insurance provides the means for people to transfer the burden of uncertainty (of financial loss) to the insurer, for an agreed financial consideration called the "premium". In exchange, the insurer promises to provide financial compensation to the insured should a specified loss occur.	Takaful follows principles of contract for mutual co-operation (Taawun) and Tabarru. The premium in Takaful is paid on the basis of Tabarru'. Following this principle, participants themselves are carrying the risk and not the insurance company. The Takaful operator act as a custodian and cannot use the contributions except as intended by the donors i.e. for mutual help.
Uncertainty (Gharar)	Policyholders are not aware of how profits are distributed and in what the funds are invested in.	Takaful is based on Mudharabah (Profit Sharing) concept and the distribution of profits to the Takaful operator and the participants are clearly outlined in the contract
Gambling (Maisir)	Policyholders stand to loose all the premiums paid if the risk does not occur. On the contrary, he stands to get more should a misfortune happens, while paying small amount of premium.	In the event risk does not occur, the participant is entitle to get back the contribution that he has paid. In the event risk occurs, premium amount along with the funds from Takaful fund (Pool of Funds) from the donations made by other fellow participants.
Riba (Interest)	Insurance companies invest their funds in interest based avenues and without any consideration to Syariah principles.	Takaful companies undertake investment only into Syariah compliant equity investment scheme, where returns are not derived from unethical commercial activities.
Funds Ownership	Funds belong to the Insurance company and not to the policy holders.	Risk sharing Takaful funds belong to the participants on a collective basis and are managed by the Takaful operator for a legitimate consideration (fee)

Fig. 11.1 Comparison between Takaful and conventional insurance system

Regulations	Regulations are governed by statutes, case laws and judicial precedents, legal literature and customs	Regulation in Takaful is undertaken through Syariah justified statutory provisions, juristic opinions (Fatwa), decisions undertaken through Syariah supervisor bodies and other relevant Syariah based cases.
Syariah Supervisory Council	There is no such requirement for Conventional Insurance companies..	Takaful companies must have Syariah Supervisory Council to monitor their operation to make sure they do not engage in forbidden practices such riba;
Initial Capital	Initial capital supplied by the Shareholders	Initial capital supplied by Rabbu Al Mal or paid in via premium from Participant
Motive	Profit motive and maximization of returns to Shareholders	Social objective to serve community well being and offer affordable risk protection to s as well fair profits for the Takaful Operators
Profit Sharing	Profit and bonus units to be shared with policyholders are decided by management.	Takaful contract specifies in advance how and when profits/surplus and/or bonus units will be distributed.

Fig. 11.1 (Continued)

account, that is, 'Tabarru' and the 'investment fund'. There must be a clear segregation of funds to ensure that the participants are mutually insuring and bearing the risk of each other rather than any third party doing it on their behalf.

- **Tabarru**
 The Tabarru element, also called as 'risk premium', is reserved for compensation to be paid to participants who suffered a defined loss. This contribution acknowledges that participant has agreed to pay and enables him to fulfill his obligation of mutual help and joint guarantee. It is similar to a donation with charitable intention and with a

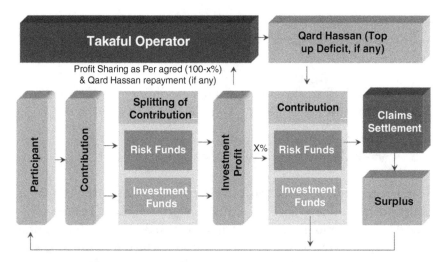

Fig. 11.2 Mudharabah model

condition of compensation to those in need of it, as opposed to 'premium', to avoid any concern over riba and so that gharar is forgiven (it is never eliminated).

- **Investment Premium**
  Part of the total premium will go into the investment fund, which is invested by the operator in Syariah-compliant investments for the generation of profits. Any returns on the investment are distributed on the mudaraba principle between the participants and the operator in pre-agreed proportions as 'investment profit'. However, in the event of loss, it is entirely borne by the participants and not by the Takaful operator.

- **Surplus from Tabarru**
  After payments have been made from the Tabarru funds to those participants requiring them, the amount of capital remaining net of expenses is labeled the 'surplus'. The surplus (or any loss, which may have arisen) is shared collectively upon maturity in a pre-agreed ratio between the participants (and sometimes with the operator too, varies from country to country). In the event of any losses in the risk pool, the Takaful operator normally offers an interest-free financing based

on Qard Hassan (benevolent loan) principle. This has to be repaid when the risk pool returns to profitability and prior to distribution of future surplus.

Figure 11.2 illustrates the simplified form of Takaful based on Mudharabah model.

1.5 Wakalah Model in Practice

Wakalah model is a fee-driven Islamic contract. Since Mudharabah is under question, due to sharing of surplus with the Takaful operator, this model is gaining more popularity. Under this model the Takaful operator acts on behalf of the participants for a fee, whereby the Takaful operator manages the Takaful fund on behalf of the participant for a fixed fee called a 'Wakalah fee'. This fee can be a percentage of the contribution (total premium) or an absolute amount.

- **Wakalah Agreement**
  Wakalah is an Arabic word for delegation or representation. It is a contract between the participants and the Takaful operator. The participants delegate all related activities with respect to fund management to the Takaful operator. Takaful operator is entitled for ujr (fee) in return, which is transparent and agreed to at the time of participation. The fee payments could be from a general fund or investment returns from the general fund. The latter is preferred by Syariah Advisory Board. Under this agreement, the Takaful operator as an agent does not share any annual surplus or loss from the investment of funds.
- **Tabarru Agreement**
  Tabarru is essential part of Takaful, whereby participants contribute to the Takaful funds without expecting any profit and with pure intention of cooperation.
- **Modus Operandi**
  The premium paid by the participant is split into 'Tabarru' contribution and 'ujr' (fee). The 'Tabarru' funds will be further split into

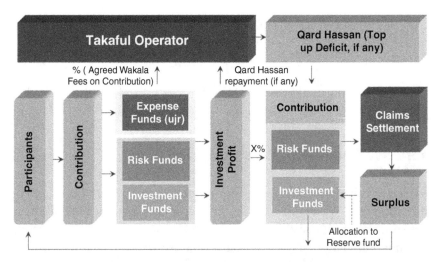

Fig. 11.3 Wakalah model. Note: The surplus can also be shared with Takaful operators, as it depends on how the model is structured. The Wakalah model is the most recognized and accepted in the international Takaful market comprising 30 countries

'risk funds' and 'investment funds' for transparency in funds management. The portion of the contribution that goes into the 'investment funds' is for savings and the other portion into 'risk funds' is for donation and the rest portion is for the fee payment. All underwriting costs such as claims and re-Takaful contributions will be paid from 'risk funds'. In the event of any deficit, the Takaful operator would top up by extending a financing following interest-free Qard Hassan (benevolent loan) to be repaid before any future surplus distribution.

- The surplus made from 'Tabarru' funds can be utilized in three different ways. The first option is to keep the whole surplus in the 'Tabarru' fund. The second option is to keep a certain portion of the surplus within the fund as a contingency reserve and distribute the rest to participants. The third option is similar to the second, except that the balance after contingency reserve is distributed among participants and the Takaful operator. The structure for surplus distribution is transparent and agreed to at the time of participation to both participant and the Takaful operator.

Figure 11.3 illustrates the simplified form of Takaful based on Wakalah model.

1.6 Wakalah with Waqf Model in Practice

Wakalah with Waqf, a hybrid model, is refinement of the earlier Wakalah model. It is a Wakalah model with a separate legal entity of Waqf in between. Waqf, in contrast to al-wakalah and al-mudarabah, operates as a public foundation, and the Takaful fund is owned by members in the first two models, in Waqf it belongs to nobody in particular.

Waqf is a gift of land or property made by a Muslim, intended for religious, educational, or charitable purpose. Waqf is practiced in most Muslim countries. Waqf may be set up as a separate Syariah entity, which has the ability to accept ownership or make someone the owner of any asset. The objectives of the Waqf fund are to provide relief to participants against defined losses, as per the rules of the Waqf fund. A fund manager or administrator appointed for this purpose may manage the fund on a commercial basis for a fee and returns may be used for social benefits.

- **Shareholder's Donation**
  The shareholders of the Takaful operator initially will make a donation to establish the Waqf fund. Upon creation of the Waqf fund, the shareholders will lose their ownership rights of the Waqf fund. However, they will have the right to administer and develop rules and regulations for the fund. This fund will be invested in Syariah-compliant investment and returns will be used for the benefit of participants.
- **Participant's Contribution**
  The contribution (Tabarru) received from the participants seeking Takaful protection is also part of Waqf fund. In this modified Wakalah

model with Waqf, the relationship of the participants and the operator is directly with the Waqf fund. The Takaful operator is the wakeel of the Waqf fund and the participants pay one-sided donations to the Waqf fund (not conditional) and become members.

The consolidated amount is used for investment, and the profits earned are deposited into the same fund. As per Waqf principles, a member (donor) can also benefit from the Waqf fund. The company takes this donation on behalf of the Waqf fund as an administrator of the fund and deposits it in the fund. The participants loose the ownership of contribution upon payment, and then onwards it becomes the property of the Waqf fund.

- **Sharing of Surplus**
The Waqf fund rules define the basis for compensation of losses to its members and may define the sharing of surplus and other rules under which it would operate, but there is no obligation to distribute surplus. All operational costs incurred for providing Takaful services, for example, re-Takaful costs, claims investigations, and so on, will be met from the same fund.

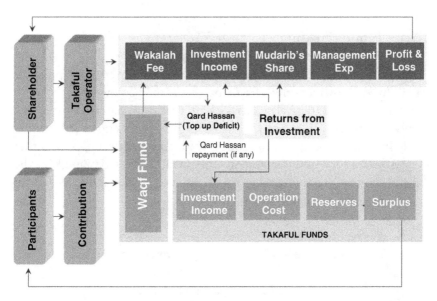

Fig. 11.4 Wakalah with Waqf model

Further, in the event of any deficit, the Takaful operator would top up by extending a financing following interest-free Qard Hassan (benevolent loan) to be repaid before any future surplus distribution. The Qard Hassan will be given by the shareholders to the Waqf entity and not to individuals, as in the typical Wakalah model.

Under this model, the Takaful operator earns from various sources. The first and foremost is remuneration for performing services, which would be deducted from the Waqf fund. The second source could be sharing in the investment profits or service charges for acting as an agent for investment. The third source would be earning profit by investing the shareholders' money.

Figure 11.4 illustrates the simplified form of Takaful based on wakala with Waqf model.

1.7 Types of Takaful

The Takaful currently practiced by Takaful operators can be broadly divided into family Takaful insurance and general Takaful insurance.

1.7.1 Family Takaful

A family Takaful plan is a long-term savings and investment program with a fixed maturity period. Participants not only enjoy the investment profit but the program also provides mutual financial assistance. The family Takaful plan is a financial program that pools efforts to help the needy in times of need due to sudden death and other mishaps resulting in personal injury or disablement. The Takaful plans designed by the Takaful company would enable participants to participate in a Takaful scheme with the following aims:

(a) To save regularly;
(b) To invest with a view of earning profits which are Sharia-compliant; and
(c) To avail of cover in the form of payment of Takaful benefits to heir(s) should a participant die before the maturity date of his Takaful plan.

Some examples for family Takaful currently practiced are Individual Family Takaful Plan, Takaful Mortgage Plans, Health/Medical Takaful, and so on.

Family Takaful Benefits

In the event that a participant dies before the maturity of his family Takaful plan, his family members is entitled for the following Takaful benefits:

- The total contribution paid until date, that is, the due date of the installment payment prior to his death and his share of profits from the investment of the contribution, which has been credited into the participant's account.
- The outstanding Takaful installments which would have been paid by the deceased participant should he survive. This outstanding amount is calculated from the date of his death to the date of maturity of his Takaful plan, which shall be paid from the participant's special account as agreed upon by all the participants in accordance with the Takaful contract.

If a participant survives until the date of maturity of his Takaful plan, the following Takaful benefits shall be paid to him:

- The total amount of contribution paid by the participant and his share of profits from the investment of the Takaful installments credited into his participant's accounts.
- The net surplus allocated to his participant's special account as shown in the last valuation of the participant's special accounts.

In the event that a participant is compelled to surrender or withdraw from the Takaful plan before the maturity of his Takaful plan, he shall be entitled to the surrender benefits. The participant is entitled to receive the proportion of his Takaful installments that have been credited into the participant's account including his share of investment profits. However, the amount that has been relinquished as Tabarru will not be refunded to him (BNM n.d.).

1.7.2 General Takaful

General Takaful schemes are contracts of joint guarantee, on a short-term basis (normally one year), between groups of participants to provide mutual compensation in the event of a defined loss. The schemes are designed to meet the needs for protection of individuals and corporate bodies in relation to material loss or damage resulting from a catastrophe or disaster inflicted upon properties, assets, or belongings of participants.

In the event of a catastrophe or disaster resulting in a loss or damage to a property or bodily injuries or other physical disability to a person, the owner of the property or the person concerned may suffer substantial financial losses. For instance, if a house is destroyed or damaged by fire, the owner would certainly require a sufficient sum of money to repair the house, or rebuild a new one, as well as enough money to replace the damaged furniture, fixtures, and fitting.

The general Takaful scheme is for short-term basis, that is, 12 months. The contribution paid by participant is credited into 'General Takaful Fund' with no further splitting of funds. This fund is utilized for settlement of claims and operating expenses, and so on. If at the end of the Takaful period there is a surplus, then it will be shared between the Takaful operator and participants (or among participants only, varies based on the model followed), if the participant has not incurred any claim or has not received any other benefit (BNM n.d.).

Some examples for general Takaful currently practiced are Fire Takaful Scheme, Motor Takaful Scheme, Marine Takaful Scheme, and so on.

1.8 Global Outlook of Takaful

Around year-end 2014, the Takaful assets were estimated to be around USD 33 billion. Gross Takaful contribution was estimated to be around USD 14 billion by the end of 2014. Takaful market is highly concentrated in the GCC and Southeast Asia with Saudi Arabia and Malaysia predominating these markets. Out of total 308 Takaful companies, 93 are Takaful windows. However, these Takaful windows own only 2.5% of the total Takaful assets, although still in its nascent stage and with a smaller asset base and more varied performance. Although Takaful mar-

Table 11.1 Number of Takaful operators/Takaful windows globally by category (2014)

Category	Number
Life	57
General	107
Composite	116
Re-Takaful	25

kets have not grown in tandem with the Sukuk and Islamic banking markets, it is estimated to reach the USD20 billion mark by 2017 (ICD Thomson Reuters 2014). Up until 2012, the industry grew at a CAGR of 10–12% in various key Islamic finance jurisdictions, and a slowdown has been witnessed ever since (Table 11.1).

The gross Takaful contributions in the GCC region were estimated at USD8.9 billion showing a Y-o-Y growth of 12%. Malaysia leads the Takaful industry in the Southeast Asian region. It is home to 12 registered Takaful operators. The growth prospects of Takaful in Malaysia are bright as the industry has the support of the government support in all aspects in addition to favorable demographical breakdown. Wider product innovation and distribution coverage is likely to drive sector growth as public acceptance of the model increases. Malaysia's Takaful industry grew faster than conventional insurance, with general and family Takaful recording 8.3% and 9.7% growth, respectively, at the end of June 2015, compared with conventional general and life insurance growth of 6.6% and −0.4%, respectively. In Indonesia, Takaful has expanded to account for 6.2% of Indonesia's insurance market by gross written contributions as of the end of 2015, from 2.6% as of the end of 2010. The sector's contributions expanded by around 4.1% to around USD757 Million (IDR10.5trn) in 2015, slower than the previous year amid a slowdown in the country's real GDP growth but outperforming the conventional insurance product segment that had more modest growth of 1.6%.

1.9 Takaful in Malaysia

Malaysia's Takaful industry started out modestly in 1985, and due to the increasing demand for Islamic financial products, it has grown from strength to strength over the years. The first Takaful operator was established in Malaysia in 1985 to meet demand from insurance buyers for Syariah-compliant products. To provide the legal basis for Takaful operations, the Takaful Act came into effect in 1984. Takaful operations are regulated and supervised by Bank Negara Malaysia (BNM), the country's regulator. The Malaysian Takaful market is expanding at a good clip. There are 11 registered Takaful operators in the country, accounting for 64,200 agents. The industry continues to exhibit good financial results each year, as reflected in the 60% increase in total assets to RM26.8 billion (US$ 6.2 billion) in December 2016, compared to RM17 billion (US$4.5 billion) five years ago and accounted for 12.1% of the total assets of the insurance industry. The Takaful industry grew strongly, with combined Takaful contribution income increasing to RM7.5 billion in December 2016. While sustaining the current pace of development, there still exist high growth prospects for the Takaful sector in view of the large untapped potential.

1.10 Challenges in Takaful

Despite a remarkable breakthrough and a dynamic and sustained growth, there are challenges facing the Takaful industry

- Takaful is a fairly young industry and is still developing, so is the Corporate Governance policies. Regulatory bodies have to implement sound policies and standards to ensure Syariah compliance and to avoid conflict of interest between the operator, shareholder, and policyholder.
- Rating model for Takaful operators on the basis of Syariah compliance, financial strength, and solvability will strengthen the confidence of shareholder and participants. Currently only the International Islamic Rating Agency (IIRA) provides such ratings and Moody has also joined the race, but more established rating bodies should enter this space.
- Lack of awareness about Takaful/insurance at both individual and corporate levels. There should be a joint effort from insurance companies, insurance associations, and the different governments to educate the customers.

- Takaful companies are not innovative yet to offer new products, and serious efforts need to be put in the following key areas:

  (a) Product Structuring: Differentiate Takaful from conventional insurance with innovative Syariah-compliant financial structuring to make products more attractive to the mass.
  (b) Customer Service: Better service level to be offered by Takaful operators to increase their market share.
  (c) Technology: Takaful operators can invest in cost-effective technology to reach more clients using new distribution channels (Internet) without relying on physical outlets.
  (d) Strategic Alliances: Tie up with Islamic banks to tap their customer base and infrastructure to have better market coverage.

- Shortage of talented resource is another stumbling block for Takaful operators. Although few institutions are offering specialization degrees in the area of Takaful, demand is overwhelming the supply. More universities have to offer to specialized Takaful courses to meet the demand.
- Slow pace in development of technical, legal, tax, Syariah, and accounting framework in countries like Indonesia is becoming a challenge for global players to expand into country like Indonesia with a great potential.
- The existence of several Takaful business models—Mudharabah (profit- and loss-sharing), wakala (agency contract with a performance fee element to replace surplus sharing), and the Waqf model—creates confusion among the customers and leads to doubts on Syariah compliance as well. The regional Takaful institutions and organizations need to come together internationally in order to promote and standardize best practices within the industry.

1.11 Summary

The demand for Takaful exists, although the penetration rate is low. On the other hand, GDP of economies such as Malaysia, Middle East, and Indonesia is growing; hence, the supply should also be able to draw the sleeping demand. The coming evolution depends on Takaful operators' strategy and ability to differentiate them by innovation and not merely by Islamizing conventional insurance.

References

http://eynotrading.blogspot.com/2007/10/takaful-concept-in-family-takaful.html
http://www.bnm.gov.my/index.php?ch=174&pg=469&ac=386
http://www.insuranceinfo.com.my/_system/media/downloadables/family_takaful.pdf
http://www.mifc.com/060201_tka_overview.htm
http://www.mondovisione.com/media-and-resources/news/dubai-international-financial-centre-joinsworlds-most-influential-global-takaf-1/
https://www.reorient.co.uk/pdfs/takaful_retakaful_companies.pdf
http://www.zawya.com/marketing.cfm?zp&p=/story.cfm/sidZAWYA20060402070937
https://ceif.iba.edu.pk/pdf/ThomsonReuters-IslamicFinanceDevelopmentReport2015GlobalTransformation.pdf
Al-Jarhi, M. A. Islamic finance: An efficient & equitable option. The Islamic Research and Training Institute, P. O. Box 9201 Jeddah, Saudi Arabia. Retrieved from www.irti.org.sa
Bank Negara Malaysia. 20 years experience of Malaysian Takaful industry, Malaysian Takaful industry 1984–2004. Islamic Banking and Takaful Department.
Family Takaful: Case for "window" operations. (2006, September 15). Retrieved from http://www.secp.gov.pk/Events/pdf/FamilyTakaful_MohammedAli.pdf
Fisher, O., & Taylor, D. Y. (2000, April). Prospects for evolution of Takaful in the 21st century. Copyright and reserved by Fellows and President of Harvard University, MA, USA. Retrieved from http://www.takaful.com.sa/m4sub3.asp
Islamic insurance firm to begin working soon. (2006, December 13). Retrieved from http://www.dailytimes.com.pk/default.asp?page=2006%5C12%5C13%5Cstory_13-12-2006_pg5_7
Jamil Akhtar Khan, M. Takaful an emerging niche market presentation. Takaful Pakistan.

Kassim, Z. A. M. (2006). *The Islamic way of insurance*. Malaysia: Mercer Zainal Consulting Sdn. Bhd.

Pirani, A. (2007, July 13). *Introduction to Takaful presentation*. Karachi: Pak-Qatar Family Takaful.

Shahid Ebrahim, M., & Joo, T. K. (2001). Islamic banking in Brunei Darussalam. *International Journal of Social Economics, 28*(4).

Shanmugam, Bala, & Gupta, Lokesh. (2007, November). Islamic banking: A technical perspective, *77*(10), 62–65 (Asia edition).

Takaful: A market with great potential special to Gulf news. (2006, September 16). Retrieved from http://archive.gulfnews.com/articles/06/09/16/10067709.html

Taylor, D., & Aljazira, B. (2007, December). Brief overview of Takaful Ta'awuni brief. Retrieved from http://www.newhorizon-islamicbanking.com/index.cfm?section=lectures&action=view&id=10577

The Oxford Business Group. (2007, March 1). Abu Dhabi sees potential in Islamic insurance. Retrieved from http://www.arabianbusiness.com/10037-dhabi-sees-potential-in-islamic-insurance

12

Islamic Wealth Management

1 Introduction

There is an upward trend in Islamic banking demand, and indeed, a large number of Muslims who were previously customers of conventional banks have shifted their assets and portfolio to Islamic banks. As a result, the Islamic Wealth Management industry has grown tremendously in recent years. With the economic landscape in the region, increasing wealth and strengthening demand for Syariah-complaint investments indicates immense potential for further growth of the industry. Lately the global and major regional players are focusing on this fastest growing niche segment. The attempt is to capture the estimated US$ 1 trillion worth of wealth from the Muslims in the GCC, UAE, and Southeast Asia. The figures are dynamic and change with the fluctuation in oil prices. As per the latest statistic published under *Global Islamic Economy Report 2015/2016*, Muslim consumer spending on food and lifestyle is projected to reach $2.6 trillion in 2020. Global assets of Islamic banks exceed $1.3 trillion, and are set to double by 2020 (http://www.dinarstandard.com/state-of-the-global-islamic-economy-report-2015/).

Islamic Wealth Management (IWM) is seen as a service that caters to the need of investment of surplus funds of Muslims in a manner which is Syariah-compliant and yet bestows good returns. It is offered as a part of private banking services. It is normally associated with the very exclusive and catered for the high net worth individuals to offer tailored service in the area of wealth management, savings, inheritance, and tax planning. A high-level form of private banking is often regarded as wealth management.

Islamic Wealth Management has a very comprehensive meaning. The scope is much wider than investment management, as it also includes liabilities management and risk management. The wealth management should be according to the principles of Syariah, the person's intention (niah), how the wealth is earned, how it is grown (invested), how it is spent, and the right of the poor and needy must all be determined. It is unique in nature; whereby religious principles are followed in determining the financial needs of their clients. This chapter will focus on the various aspects of Islamic Wealth Management in the following sections.

1.1 Wealth in Islam

Wealth can be simply defined as all things having an economic value, such as money, property, or goods—assets, capital, fortune, and resource. Essentially, these are merely material possessions. It is also defined as surplus income, that is, beyond the daily and basic requirements of a family. Here it is important to note that income and wealth are two different things, which are related but not the same. Wealth is a stock as opposed to income which represents a flow. Hence, wealth is considered as reservoir of all past net savings invested in those enduring objects or skills that make it more productive and fulfilled. Wealth increases with production and decreases with consumption.

Islam has a unique dispensation on the theme of wealth, its ownership, distribution, and social relationship. In Islam wealth belongs to Allah and a person has no right to satisfy his fancies, as extravagance and wastage are scorned. Muslims are taught that money should be earned, invested, and spent in approved (halal) avenues. Only then will he, his family, and the society (ummah) obtain rewards for this life and also for thereafter (Salim 2006). Islam also recognizes that a Muslim should not forego wealth. Neither should he be avaricious in the pursuit of wealth. Syariah does not discourage the acquiring of wealth, but it must be earned and spent in compliance with Islamic principles. The only caution Islam put forward is the danger of obsessive preoccupation in accumulating and conglomerating wealth either in the individual or in the societal and governmental level to the extent sidelining the most essential parts of his self, his spirituality. Without sufficient spiritual defense, man will easily be deluded by the deception of wealth (ZAKARIA 2007).

Wealth can be obtained through effort or through inheritance. It must be reiterated that since all wealth (maal) belongs to God, man is only considered as a trustee of this wealth.

Hence, wealth owned by individuals or groups is a result of their work or inheritance. This kind of wealth is also governed by Syariah guidelines. Although Islam did not take a negative stand regarding personal property, it hindered its accumulation in the hands of few people. It was concerned through its tax (Zakat) system and inheritance to ensure that the wealth is distributed among the biggest number of people.

In a capitalistic economy, wealth is almost anything of monetary value that one accumulates in sufficient quantity. Rights to wealth determine the relative power and rank of a person. The concept of wealth from various perspectives is illustrated below:

Concept	Capitalism	Islam	Socialism
Wealth /resources	Scarcity of resources	Bounties of God and no scarcity	Scarcity of resources
Ownership	Individual freedom	A trust	The source for the exploitation of labor
Lifestyle goals	Personal satisfaction (needs and wants)	Al-Falah (prosperity)	Equal welfare among the workers

In other economies, people may have enduring but not endearing wealth. However, Islam requires Muslims to have both enduring and endearing wealth. Islam not only encourages every Muslim to work and earn a legitimate income to sustain him and his family, but also encourages every Muslim to work hard to achieve perfection and excellence in his chosen profession. Hence, Islamic Wealth Management can be translated into wealth creation, enhancement, protection, distribution, and purification of wealth. Islamic Wealth Management is concerned with providing end-to-end solutions using products and services throughout the wealth management cycle in compliance with Syariah.

1.2 Wealth Management from Islamic Perspective

Wealth management according to the Syariah serves many purposes. Not only does it motivate a person to work hard and earn his wealth, but it gives hope to the poor and needy. Managing wealth disciplines a person to save in order to help himself, his family, and his society financially. By saving even a small part of his income or profits earned, instead of wasteful spending on impulse, a Muslim can fight consumerism, thus keep inflation down (Salim 2006). Islamic Wealth Management is explained by a system of interrelationships between the tenets of justice, equitable distribution and fairness, and limits of ownership, all governed by the tenets of the moral law, as illustrated in the following picture:

Wealth Creation
From business, savings in bank, investment in first property, etc.

Wealth Enhancement
Enhancing total returns from capital gains and income, including via use of leverage

Wealth Distribution
Passing on assets through wills and trusts

Wealth Protection
Capital preservations, risk management, insurance, trusts

- *Wealth Creation in Islam*: In Islam, God owns the wealth and that wealth has been bestowed by Him. Since God is the absolute owner, man is just a trustee. Wealth creation is more than possessing a wealth and is a form of increasing wealth. All actions of individual and corporate have certain steps involved in attaining its financial goal. For example, as relating to income, besides ensuring the permissibility of the income, there must also be some planning involved in terms of increasing income via other permissible activities. Earning extra income should not, however, make a person abandon his responsibilities as a husband or a father and other social responsibilities toward society. Wealth must be earned and created in an Islamically permissible way. This means that it is not generated from prohibited business activities. Spending money is also a responsibility of every Muslim. Money should not be spent on unlawful products and services. Nor should money be spent to show off wealth, or spent in vain.
- *Wealth Enhancement in Islam*: Wealth enhancement is done through investment process. Muslims have to do investment in those products that are Syariah compliant. The objective is to achieve a reasonable capital growth with the objective of preserving accumulated wealth. This also involves asset allocation strategies, investment policy, and others. The channels of investment must be Syariah compliant—free from elements of gharar (uncertainty), riba (usury), and maisir (gambling) and free from haram products such as pork, alcohol, and so on. Currently there are various products offered by Islamic banks for wealth enhancements such as Sukuks, private equity funds, family Takaful plans, shares, property, wadiah and Mudharabah saving plans, and so on.
- *Wealth Protection in Islam*: The objective here is that investment should be made in an appropriate financial solution to meet his financial goals. A proper analysis of risk-return should be performed prior to the investment. Risk is directly related to returns; the logic is to diversify the investments into various asset classes. Assets with low returns (under 10%) are generally not likely to make losses, while assets with high returns (above 100%) are likely to fall by a similar quantum, or even bigger (Salim 2006). The protection of wealth has to be against every conceivable financial risks and threats through sound wealth management instruments. For an individual who has accumulated a

reasonable size of wealth, a bad investment can cause some major discomfort but still poor investment performance is not debilitating. Hence, proper liability containment planning, business shareholding and succession planning and debt management is needed. This can be done through Takaful and Sukuk and so on. to balance the risk.
- *Wealth Cleansing and Distribution in Islam*: Cleanliness in Islam covers both physical and spiritual cleanliness. This involves cleanliness of the mind from bad intentions, or committing unlawful acts, and cleanliness of the heart from jealousy, hypocrisy, and evil desires. A person must also indicate hope, truthfulness, forgiveness, compassion, and other such qualities.

Islam instituted the zakat tax system as a way to wealth purification. It is mandatory for every Muslim whose wealth has reached more than a certain amount to pay zakat at a fixed rate, equivalent to 2.5% of his holdings of money or tradable goods. Zakat is also a means of narrowing the gap between the rich and the poor and to make sure that everyone's needs are met in society.

Another form of wealth distribution takes the form of faraid, a law that stipulates estate distribution of a deceased Muslim after his death to his heirs (minus burial costs, debts, rights of the spouse to mutually acquired properties, incomplete lifetime gifts (hibah), and after-death legacies limited to one-third and non-heirs (wasiyat or will).

From above we can see that two of the five pillars of Islam (faith, prayers, fasting, zakat, Hajj) are related to wealth. The fourth pillar states that it is mandatory for every Muslim to pay zakat. The fifth pillar relates the performance of the Hajj or pilgrimage for Muslims with financial ability. This demonstrates that managing wealth is of prime importance in order to uphold the pillars of Islam. Thus, the attainment of wealth forms one of the five basic needs in Islam.

1.3 Key Growth Drivers for Islamic Wealth Management

There is always demand for Islamic Wealth Management as there are high net worth individuals and corporates in GGC and globally for diversification of investment to balance the risk of equity swings. Syariah-compliant investment products offer an avenue for Muslims and non-Muslims to invest in ethical responsible funds with an underlying asset. The increase in awareness of customer has created a demand for products in the area of Takaful, Sukuk, and Islamic funds. There are various growth drivers for the expansion of Islamic Wealth Management industry and are listed below:

- Macro-economic growth in the region has been robust on the back of strong oil prices and diversification. This is expected to continue to drive growth for the development of Islamic Wealth Management products, for example, Middle East region seeks appropriate avenues and tailored products for diversifying economic, business, and financial holdings.
- High oil prices have benefited oil-producing countries, mostly emerging economies of Asia (Malaysia, Indonesia, and Vietnam) and GCC. Robust oil earnings contributed to combined fiscal surpluses, which in turn contributed to massive wealth accumulation in the region. High commodity prices have also led to increased interest in foreign investments (in emerging Asia, South Africa, South America, Eastern Europe), particularly in real estate, plantation, mining, and exploration sectors.
- There has been a recent finding whereby it is estimated that only a fraction of US$11.5 trillion worth of wealth owned by Muslim individuals, institutions, and government is managed by Islamic banks and financial institutions. About US$9.5 trillion remain outside the global Islamic financial services industry that has US$2 trillion asset under management (Zawya 2016).
- The major investments are generally driven by sovereign wealth funds and government investment corporations another key segment looking for investment opportunities are high net worth individuals (HNWI).
- The diversity of Islamic finance products and experienced Islamic capital market players such as Malaysia, are working towards to be at the forefront of capturing the anticipated net capital outflows of oil-producing nations. Malaysia recognizes the market potential in Islamic

Wealth Management and has launched a five-year Islamic Fund and Wealth Management Blueprint to further strengthen the country's position as a global hub for Islamic funds by 2021 (Star Online 2017).
- Supported by a facilitative and comprehensive regulatory framework, and global acceptance of Islamic finance has come to the stage where development in wealth management services will drive future growth.

1.4 Islamic Will Writing

A will is an important tool of estate planning for it can be used to enable meeting one's established goals or objectives of wealth distribution. Although the law of inheritance (faraid) has specific heirs identified, which comprises of spouse, parents, and children, they are automatically included in the faraid. However, grandchildren, adopted children, illegitimate children, foster parents, non-Muslim parents, non-Muslim children, and non-Muslim family members are not included in the law of inheritance. In the event a Muslim wishes to bequest his wealth to the parties mentioned, he could do so via a will because he has the right to give away up to one-third of his wealth according to his desire.

Writing a will is a religious obligation on all Muslims. If they fail to do so, they have all reasons to fear that their estate/treasure may not be distributed in accordance with the Islamic laws (www.islamicwill.com). The Islamic will includes both bequests and legacies, instructions and admonishments, and assignments of rights. No specific wording is necessary for making a will. In Islamic law the will (wasiyya) can be oral or written, and the intention of the testator must be clear that the wasiyya is to be executed after his death. Any expression which signifies the intention of the testator is sufficient for the purpose of constituting a bequest.

There should be two witnesses to the declaration of the wasiyya. A written wasiyya where there are no witnesses to an oral declaration is valid if it is written in the known handwriting/signature of the testator according to Maliki and Hanbali fiqh. The wasiyya is executed after payment of debts and funeral expenses. The majority view is that debts to Allah (SWT) such as zakah, obligatory expiation, and so on should be paid whether mentioned in the will or not. However, there is difference of opinion on this matter among the Muslim jurists.

The difference between the Muslim will and non-Muslim will is mentioned below:

Muslim will	Non-Muslim will
The assets to be distributed are permissible as defined by the Islamic law	Every asset can be included in the will
No one can make a bequest (write a will for inheritance) to any of his or her Quranic heirs as distribution of inheritance to Quranic heirs will fall under the law of faraid	The will can be made to anyone whether kin or not to the person who writes the will
The bequest of a will can only be made of up to one-third of the entire property, and the rest will be distributed to the Quranic heirs under the law of faraid. Consent is required from Quranic heirs after the demise of the testator, if the bequest is made to the non-Quranic heirs more than one-third of the entire estate or to the Quranic heirs more than two-third of the entire estate	The will can amount to 100% of the total assets

Source: www.hlib.com.my/wm/ww_faq.htm

Based on the recent statistics of Star Online (2016), estates of the deceased worth RM60 billion of cash and non-cash assets in Malaysia have been left by the deceased and remained unclaimed by the heirs since independence in Malaysia. In the event when someone dies without a will (intestate condition), all the assets will be frozen (including bank accounts). In Malaysia, the beneficiaries must obtain the letter of administration (LA), including Muslims, and then go to court for distribution of the assets. This indicates there is a good potential waiting to be tapped although this requires educating the consumers about will-writing.

1.5 Islamic Investment Funds

Islamic investment equity funds market is one of the fastest growing sectors within the Islamic financial system. This can be termed as a shared pool wherein the investors contribute their excess money for earning Halal profits. The funds collected from the investors will be invested into a variety of assets classes, which has to strictly comply with the precepts of Islamic Syariah. The subscribers of the fund may receive a document certifying their subscription and entitling them to the prorated profits accrued to the fund (Taqi Usmani, undated). Each fund has its own mechanism, capital, subscription, maturity, and expected returns and risks. The investors represent the owners of the capital and the company (bank) represents the speculator who runs the operations. There are many Islamic funds which differ according to type of investment and financing methods (Murabahah, Musharakah, salam, istisnah, Ijarah), field of investment (public, real estate, leasing), period of investment (short, medium, or long term), risk involved (low, medium, or high), and, finally, whether they are open or closed funds (Tayar 2006).

Investment funds achieve many privileges:

- Specialized administration where high caliber fund managers perform studies and undertake research important to taking investment decisions.
- Geographical- and sector-based distribution investment decisions for these funds are very flexible, covering industry and trade to minimize the risk involved.
- Flexibility to withdraw where an investor can enjoy low value shares that suit most investors, with strict dates for withdrawing shares.

- Clear legal terms—each fund has clear terms and conditions which the founder of the fund abides to.
- The investment will in Syariah Syariah-compliant businesses and the returns will be based on agreed profit-sharing ratio and no fixed returns are promised by the fund manager to the investors.

Islamic investment fund sector has witnessed an exciting growth path globally. Islamic funds are also known as sustainable and responsible investments (SRI), as it is governed by Syariah principles, whereby the objective is to have positive social outcomes along with commercial returns in the form of profit. At the end of 1Q2017, the total global Islamic assets under management (AUM) were USD70.8 billion and the number of Islamic funds stood at 15,351. It is estimated that Islamic investment fund sector is projected to register an annual growth of 5.05% per annum for the next five years and estimated to reach USD77 billion by 2019 (MIFC 2017).

The various modes of Islamic investment funds such as listed Islamic equities and fixed-income instruments currently practiced by Islamic banks are explained in the following section.

1.5.1 Equity Funds

An equity fund is simply an investment into the shares of a joint stock companies. The profits are mainly achieved through the capital gains by stock trading and the dividends distributed by companies. This investment vehicle allows investors to diversify risk by investing in multiple stocks based on the risk and returns. It also offers the opportunity to participate in the long-term performance of the stock market.

Islamic funds, however, add two other elements to these well-known stock market funds. They add a screening process to remove stocks of companies deemed to be inappropriate for Muslim investors (Hanware 2006).

- *Screening of Sector*: By way of guidance, stocks whose core activities are or are related to the following are excluded:
    - Banking, insurance, or any other interest-related activity
    - Trading in alcohol, tobacco, and gambling

- Any activity related to pork
- Activities deemed impermissible (haram) in Islam
- Sectors/companies significantly affected by the above—based on a threshold of 5% of operating income

- *Debt Ratio Screening*: In the event a company's interest-bearing debt divided by assets is equal to or greater than 33.33%, it is excluded (<33.33% is acceptable).
- *Dividend Cleansing or Purification*: 'Tainted dividend' receipts relate to the portion, if any, of a dividend paid by a company that has been determined to be attributable to activities that are not in accordance with Islamic Syariah principles and therefore should be donated to a proper charity or charities (Rifai 2003). Normally the percent share of the offending item(s) is deducted from the funds' gross annual revenues and donated in zakat, sadaqah, that is, to charities.

Based on the recent statistics, funds invested in the GCC market represent more than half of the entire Islamic equity fund industry. Saudi Arabian funds and fund managers dominate the industry, accounting for nearly 75 funds out of around 300 Islamic equity funds worldwide. Bahrain has now become the favored center for fund registrations in the Gulf, with institutions such as Kuwait's Global Investment House and Saudi Arabia's National Commercial Bank having established fund management operations there recently.

1.5.2 Ijarah Funds or REITs

The Securities Commission of Malaysia defines REIT as 'an investment vehicle that proposes to invest at least 50% of its total assets in real estate, whether through direct ownership or through a single purpose company whose principal asset comprise real asset' (Securities Commission 2005). Thus, REIT is an entity that accumulates a pool of fund from investors, which is then used to buy, manage, and sell assets in real estate industry. The objective of REITs is to obtain reasonable returns on investment. Returns are generated from rental income plus any capital appreciation that comes from holding the real estate assets over an investment period.

Unit holders will receive their returns in the form of dividends or distribution and capital gains for the holding period.

Islamic REITs are managed by professional managers who have specialized knowledge of real estate and real estate-related assets. Islamic REITs are liquid assets, which can be listed and traded on Bursa Securities (Malaysia Stock Exchange). This makes REITS attractive to investors, who are able to invest and diversify their real estate investments without large capital, while meeting their needs for Syariah-compliant investment (Islamic Finance News 2006).

The structure of Islamic REITs is illustrated in the following diagram:

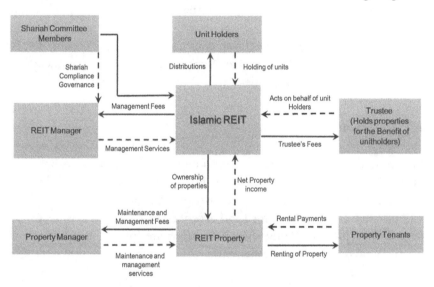

Properties under an Islamic REIT must generate rental income from permissible activities. A benchmark of up to 20% of rentals can be derived from non-permissible activities, under the 'Islamic REITs Guidelines' issued by Security Commission Malaysia. In addition, the manager of an Islamic REIT has to ensure that all forms of investment, deposit, and financing instruments comply with the Syariah principles. Also, it has to use the Takaful scheme to insure its real estate. Islamic REITs investment must be reviewed, monitored, and approved by the appointed Syariah committee/adviser.

The key benefits of REITs to investor are listed below:

- Higher dividend yield as REITs are required to distribute at least 90% of its net cash flow (income). This is significantly on average higher than other equities and provides a stable income returns to the investors.
- Transparent investment policy for investors as it is governed by Syariah Board and regulated by governing body such as Securities Commission.
- Lower transaction costs and greater liquidity as listed REITs are traded like stock at stock exchange. This makes buying and selling easier in comparison with buying and selling of actual property.
- Scalable investment vehicle in comparison to property investment companies.
- Diversification of risk as portfolio comprises of different types of properties with different lease lengths, tenants, and geographical locations compared to single properties.

1.5.3 Islamic Commodity Funds

In commodity funds, the subscription amounts from investors are used in purchasing different commodities for the purpose of the resale. The profits generated from the sale are distributed prorated among the subscribers. In order to make this fund acceptable to Syariah, it is necessary that all the rules governing the transactions are fully complied with as listed below ((Taqi Usmani undated).

- The commodity must be owned by the seller at the time of sale; therefore, short sales where a person sells a commodity before he owns it are not allowed in Syariah. Forward sales are not allowed except in the case of salam and istisna.
- The commodities must be halal; therefore, it is not allowed to deal in wines, pork, or other prohibited materials.
- The seller must have physical or constructive possession or the commodity he wants to sell.
- The price of the commodity must be fixed and known to the parties.
- Any price which is uncertain or is tied up with an uncertain event renders the sale invalid.

The performance of commodity prices in recent years has attributed to favorable demand conditions for raw materials and, in most cases, inelastic supply responses due to years of under-investment in production capacity. The advantage of commodity fund is that it is not highly correlated to equity and fixed-income asset classes. Hence, it acts as a diversification factor particularly in volatile markets for balanced investment portfolios. The fund aims to provide investors with regular income over the tenure of the fund linked to the performance of commodities through investments that conform with Syariah principles.

CIMB-Principal Asset Management Berhad has launched the CIMB Islamic Commodities Structured Fund 1 and 2, Syariah-compliant funds, which offer investment access to commodities such as energy, agriculture products, and metals. The funds invest in structured products. The structured products are principal protected when held to maturity, making them ideal for investors seeking refuge from market volatility. These funds also offer investors an exposure to potential appreciation in commodity prices. The CIMB Islamic Commodities Structured Fund 1 is a close-ended fund which will invest at least 95% of its net asset value (NAV) in a three-year Islamic Dynamic Best of Commodity Structured Product to be issued by CIMB Investment Bank and up to 5% of its NAV in liquid assets. The CIMB Islamic Commodities Structured Fund 2 is similar in structure, but invests in a five-year Islamic Dynamic Best of Commodity Structured Product making it ideal for investors who desire stable investment returns via potential annual distributions over the fund's tenure (www.cimbislamic.com).

1.6   Islamic Investment Funds Statistics

The requirement for Syariah-compliant investment products among Muslims and non-Muslims has led to the expansion of Global Islamic Funds Industry. According to data from Bank Negara Malaysia (BNM), as of Mar 2017, Islamic unit trust and investment funds in the world reached 1535, while total Islamic assets under management (AUM) were estimated at US$70.8 billion. This shows tremendous growth in two digits, year on year basis as in 2008; there were only 802 funds with AUM of USD47 billion. Malaysia and Saudi Arabia were the top two markets for Islamic funds in the world with the most number of funds and biggest fund sizes in terms of AUM. Both countries hold more than 67% of the total Syariah-compliant AUM and are leading the global Islamic funds industry. The statistics are illustrated in Figs. 12.1 and 12.2.

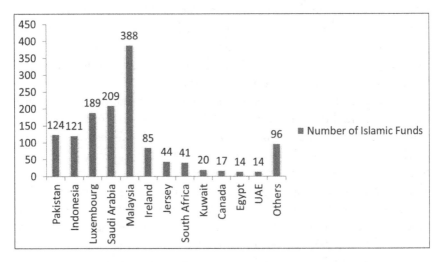

Fig. 12.1 Number of Islamic funds domiciled by country as on March 2017

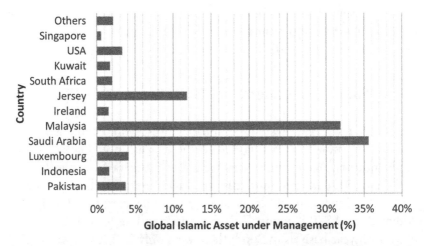

Fig. 12.2 Global Islamic assets under management (AUM) by domicile as of Mar 2017. Source: www.mifc.com

Country	Number of Islamic Funds	Global Islamic AUM
Pakistan	124	4%
Indonesia	121	2%
Luxembourg	189	4%
Saudi Arabia	209	36%
Malaysia	388	32%
Ireland	85	2%
Jersey	44	12%
South Africa	41	2%
Kuwait	20	2%

From the fig 12.2, it is clear that the Islamic fund industry is dominated by Saudi Arabia (36%), followed by Malaysia (32%). In terms of fund size, the two countries held close to three-quarters of market share. They were the earliest to develop Islamic funds—Malaysia offered the first one in 1968, while Saudi Arabia started offering funds in the 1980s.

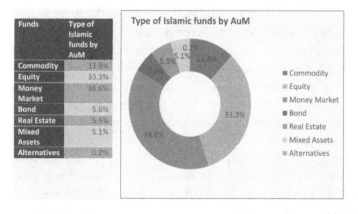

Funds	Type of Islamic funds by AuM
Commodity	11.8%
Equity	33.3%
Money Market	38.6%
Bond	5.6%
Real Estate	5.5%
Mixed Assets	5.1%
Alternatives	0.2%

From the fig 12.1, it can be seen that as of March 2017, Malaysia has the largest number of Islamic funds with 388 for a total AUM of USD22.6 billion. Compared to Saudi, they are largely in money market fund with a share of 76% of the total AUM. For Malaysia, there are several of funds which are equity funds (45% of total AUM), money market funds (32% of total AUM) and others (23%). For Malaysia and Saudi, the portfolio of Islamic funds dominates by money market and equity funds. The number of Islamic funds for Luxembourg is high compared to Jersey which is 189 and 44 of funds respectively. But, the global AUM for Jersey ranked as third (11.8%) compared to Luxembourg ranked fourth (4.1%).

The above statistics shows that the Islamic funds are growing at a fast pace, not only in numbers but also in variety to meet the appetite of high net worth individuals. The supply and demand for such funds will increase significantly as the target is not only limited to Islamic investors but it also to non-Islamic investors. The government is also offering tax incentives to attract more investors. Fund management based on Islamic precepts is gaining ground as financial authorities and banks consider its impact on the economy and customers. Management of Islamic funds seems to be the priority goal.

1.7 Islamic Wealth Management—The Way Ahead

There is a growing demand for Islamic Wealth Management products and services, and studies show that a number of Muslim high net worth individuals (HNWIs), who were using conventional banks before and now begin to take advantage of using Islamic banks' offerings.

Almost 70% of Middle Eastern wealth is transferred overseas. To attract this wealth into Islamic funds, Islamic wealth managers need to manage different assets from real estate to short-term money market instruments. Islamic investment opportunities are now accessible to institutional investors as well as non-Muslim investors to diversify their investments through Syariah-compliant funds. Eyeing on the broader prospects, globally, high net worth individuals (HNWI) wealth is projected to nearly triple in size from 2006–2025 to surpass USD100 trillion by 2025, propelled by strong Asia-Pacific growth. It is reported HNWIs hold less than one third of their global wealth with wealth managers, underscoring the potentials to amass HNWIs total investable wealth.

Islamic asset management industry can offer a wide range of Syariah-compliant products, and services under Islamic Wealth Management, crowdfunding, socially responsible investments, private equity, and environmental, social, and governance funds, and so on are gaining traction globally. Sukuk, REITs, and equities are the most popular type of investments under Islamic Wealth Management suite. The catch here is for Islamic financial institutions to provide better yields and customized product with better service quality. Technology-enabled digital investment services over the Internet could be a channel to attract the investors by providing data and analytics services. It is also known as 'Robo-advisors' and is becoming prominent in digital investment management. This will enable to attract the tech-savvy investors including new young-generation customer base, who prefer to transact online.

Muslim and non-Muslim investors are increasingly interested to invest surplus funds in a Syariah-compliant manner due to the ethical guidelines underpinning Islamic Wealth Management products. The increased transparency of customer terms and conditions, pricing structure, regular monitoring for compliance by the relevant Syariah boards, and adequate disclosure of material aspects; such offerings have tended to attract both the Muslim and non-Muslim customers. The acceptance of Islamic investment, Sukuk, private equity, and structured products is gradually growing among the affluent customer base regardless of the religion and race. Hence, looking into the tremendous potential, both the global and major regional players have focused on this fast-growing market segment and invested in professional resources and technology to meet and, in some cases, exceed their customer expectations in the area of Islamic Wealth Management.

1.8 Challenges

Islamic Wealth Management is still at its early stages. Today, players in the industry face a lack of information and academic research, as available market data is often incomplete and inconsistent. Additionally, there are only a limited number of professionals who are well-trained in the principles of Syariah law and their application, especially when it comes to the development of new products and structures.

What is needed to accelerate the Islamic Wealth Management industry's development in particular is skilled and educated human capital, as well as a higher level of standardization across countries, disciplines, and products of the entire Islamic finance space. Critical success factors on the micro-level include product development expertise, client relationship management, and competitiveness, both in terms of quality and pricing, among others. In this context, innovation is the key, as it enables individual players and the industry as a whole to draw the link between conventional and Islamic financial products by structuring the former in adherence to Syariah principles.

Another challenge is some disagreement as to the level of compliance of some of the structures with Islamic principles, but the reality is that most stakeholders in the industry realize that in order for the industry to develop, structures will need to be devised and improved upon as the scope of Islamic jurisprudence (fiqh al-muamalat) is applied to a wider range of investment products.

Islamic private equity promises to be one of the fastest-growing areas both within the private equity and the Islamic finance space over the coming years. To date, there are only a few Islamic private equity funds in the market. However, the popularity of these funds is growing tremendously and demonstrating a strong and yet unmet investor demand.

1.9 Summary

The potential of the Islamic Wealth Management industry is clearly present. This is the time for financial institutions to rise up and challenge themselves. High net worth individuals are on the rise in the region and this is time to capitalize on the change. More and more people are prospering in the Middle East following a successful past few years.

Soaring oil markets and booming economies in the Middle and Far East are multiplying the numbers of Muslim HNW individuals worldwide and boosting private client demand for Sharia-compliant investments. The growing investment demand by HNW Muslims is tapping into a raft of innovations well beyond the plain-vanilla bond market where Sharia-compliant investment originated. There are now compliant-structured products, real estate funds, secured equity funds, and even hedge funds (Wilson 2008). Islamic Wealth Management is the way forward. For it to move forward, Islamic investment banks need to challenge the culture of ignorance and educate its clientele. The coming years will be testing times for wealth managers as clients learn to accept these new practices and embrace them. The benefits are not just limited to short-term gains, but make for a long-lasting value-added relationship.

References

http://biz.thestar.com.my/news/story.asp?file=/2008/5/20/business/21299725&sec=business
http://books.google.com.my/books?id=S6AUNVo4eHAC&pg=PA99&lpg=PA99&dq=islamic+commodity+funds&source=web&ots=oMP30ndv9x&sig=AOImlKPmycwYwR4U17catyLppx0&hl=en&sa=X&oi=book_result&resnum=5&ct=result#PPA98,M1
http://findarticles.com/p/articles/mi_m2742/is_345/ai_n25094793/print?tag=artBody;col1
https://opzaney.wordpress.com/2007/07/03/the-philosophy-of-wealth-in-islam/
http://www.ameinfo.com/157605.html
http://www.ameinfo.com/159020.html
http://www.bnm.gov.my/microsites/giff2007/pdf/iif/Session3_c.pdf
http://www.bnm.gov.my/microsites/giff2007/pdf/iif/Session4_d2.pdf
http://www.cimbislamic.com/index.php?ch=islam_about_news&pg=islam_about_news_oview&ac=1285&tpt=islamic
http://www.cpifinancial.net/v2/print.aspx?pg=magazine&aid=912
http://www.failaka.com/downloads/Johnson_BeyondtheThobe103107.pdf
http://www.failaka.com/downloads/Nov06_BME%20islamic%20funds.pdf
http://www.islamicarchitecture.org/islam/zakat.html
http://www.islamic-banking.com/ibanking/ief.php
http://www.lexpress.mu/display_article.php?news_id=91917
http://www.mifc.com/060401_icap_products.htm#ireits
http://www.mifmonthly.com/article9.php

http://www.nst.com.my/Weekly/PropertyTimes/News/News/20051219100744/Article/
http://www.pwmnet.com/news/fullstory.php/aid/2241/Growing_appetite_for_Islamic_wealth_.html
http://www.ringgittune.com/fund/cicsf.pdf
http://www.theedgedaily.com/cms/content.jsp?id=com.tms.cms.article.Article_bf464b9b-cb73c03a-9fdee000-e30a89a3
http://www.theedgedaily.com/cms/content.jsp?id=com.tms.cms.article.Article_bf464b9b-cb73c03a-9fdee000-e30a89a3

Al-Hadharah. (2008, January 11). The real McCoy of I-REITs. *Islamic Finance News*, 5(1).

Al-Rifai, T. (2003, October 6). *Islamic equity funds: Workshop, an overview of Islamic finance and the growth of Islamic funds*. Presented to Islamic Funds World 2003.

Bahrain report 2007 Islamic real estate investment trusts (REITs). (2007, August 31). *Islamic Finance News*.

Banerjee, A. (2008, May 9). Pessimism persists in global property and REITs. 5(18).

Bescht, C. -S. (2007, June 15). Islamic private equity outgrowing conventional. *Islamic Finance News*, 4(24).

Hanware, K. (2006, February 6). How have Islamic funds performed? *Arab News*. Retrieved from http://www.arabnews.com/?page=6&section=0&article=77400&d=6&m=2&y=2006

Hussain, A. The Islamic law of wills. Retrieved from http://www.islaam.com/Article.aspx?id=527

Islamic Capital Market Review. (2005). *Securities Commission Annual Report 2004*. Malaysia Securities Commission. Retrieved from www.sc.com.my/eng/html/resources/annual/ar2004_eng/pdf/pt2_icm.pdf

Juma, Y. A. (2007, February 1). Islamic finance news guide 2007 Islamic wealth management.

Lim, M. W. (2008). Malaysia as a hub for Islamic wealth management. Retrieved from https://www.islamicbanker.com/publications/malaysia-as-a-hub-for-islamic-wealth-management

Merhi, S. (2008, July 1). Asset & wealth management guide 2008 comparison of REITs and I-REITs. *Islamic Finance News*.

MIFC. (2017). Islamic funds: Gearing up. Retrieved from http://www.mifc.com/index.php?ch=28&pg=72&ac=180&bb=uploadpdf

Miller, N. D., Naumowicz, D., & Atta, A. (2008, March 21). Investing in Islamic structured products. *Islamic Finance News*, 5(11).

Mokhtar, S. (2008, June 20). Will writing: A new retail product in Malaysia. *Islamic Finance News*, 5(24).

Shariff, M. I. M. (2007, November 23). Legal and legislative issues in I-REITs. *Islamic Finance News*, 4(47).

Stanton, D. (2008, February 18). Islamic equity funds see rapid growth. Retrieved from http://www.arabianbusiness.com/511518-islamic-equity-funds-see-rapid-growth

Star Online. (2016). Estates worth RM 60bil left unclaimed. Retrieved from http://www.thestar.com.my/metro/community/2016/02/03/estates-worth-rm60bil-left-unclaimed/#Os5sQPf49EBkYduQ.99

Star Online. (2017). Malaysia launches Islamic fund and wealth management blueprint. Retrieved from http://www.thestar.com.my/business/business-news/2017/01/12/malaysia-launches-islamic-fund-and-wealth-management-blueprint/#doo6jpQp4Z23gsT3.99)

Salim, N. (2006, November 24). Wealth management. *Islamic Finance News*, 3(42).

Tapping global high net worth individuals KFH research. (2008, May 30). *Islamic Finance News*, 5(21).

Tayar, E. A. (2006). Islamic investment funds and their role in developing savings. *Islamic Finance News Guide 2006*, 70–71.

Wilson, R. (2008, March 14). Islamic finance in Europe. *Islamic Finance News*, 5(10).

Zawya. (2016). USD95_trillion of Muslims wealth remain outside the global Islamic financial industry. Retrieved from https://www.zawya.com/story/US95_trillion_of_Muslims_Wealth_Remain_Outside_the_Global_Islamic_Financial_Industry-ZAWYA20160210072608/

Index

A

AAOIFI, *see* Accounting and Auditing Organisation for Islamic Financial Institutions (AAOIFI)
Absolute ownership, 10
Accounting and Auditing Organisation for Islamic Financial Institutions (AAOIFI), 187, 236, 239, 254, 258, 303, 323, 366, 378, 380, 381, 390, 391, 400, 413, 414, 423
Account types, 88–91, 113
Accumulating wealth, 20
AITAB, *see* Al-Ijarah Thumma Al-Bai (AITAB)
Akhlaq, 17
Al-Ijarah Thumma Al-Bai (AITAB), 175–190, 293
Ancillary principles, 260, 270, 271
Aqidah, 17–19

B

Bai Bithaman Ajil (BBA), 68, 75, 80, 133–154, 159, 165–167, 206, 217, 223, 260, 263, 284, 285, 287, 317, 332, 371, 413
Bai inah, 75, 231–234, 296, 297, 317, 319, 417
Bai muajjal, 284
Bai salam, 75, 206–222, 225, 269
Bank Islam Malaysia Berhad (BIMB), 7, 178, 247, 276, 300
Bank Muamalat, 228, 249, 269, 272, 277, 288, 299, 348, 350
Bank Negara Malaysia (BNM), 8, 13, 97, 98, 126, 152, 228,

Bank Negara Malaysia (*cont.*)
247–249, 283, 340, 343, 344,
353, 368, 369, 371, 372, 377,
379, 384, 446, 465
Bank Rakyat, 228, 348
Benevolent loan, 5, 77, 80, 92, 226,
227, 265, 295, 438, 442
Bonds, 32, 373, 374, 378, 382, 400,
406, 407, 412, 416–418, 422
Bursa Malaysia, 370, 372–374, 410,
412

C

Capacity, 27, 59, 63, 98, 114, 115,
143, 159, 434, 465
Capital, 5, 6, 12, 36, 46, 76, 77, 80,
85, 87, 93, 94, 102–104, 113,
121, 132, 143, 153, 157, 159,
160, 166, 170, 174, 188, 190,
192–197, 200–205, 221, 222,
225, 227–229, 234, 235, 238,
240, 253, 255, 259, 262, 276,
280–285, 287, 288, 291–296,
331, 333, 335, 352, 353, 356,
365, 370, 372–374, 379, 382,
389, 390, 397–429, 437, 452,
455, 457, 460, 462, 463, 470
Capital Bank, 348
Capital market, 234, 259, 370,
372–374, 379, 382, 397–429,
457
Classification based on nature,
60–62
Classification of riba, 37
Collateral, 109, 144, 227, 229, 230,
232, 266, 269, 281, 297, 298,
310, 313, 314, 318, 319, 339,
345

Commercial banks, 7, 79, 126,
127, 247, 249, 255, 256,
258, 292
Company accounts, 120, 127, 128
Conventional banking, 1, 5, 11, 12,
14, 80, 141, 151, 163, 238,
240, 247, 250, 301, 303, 308,
309, 332, 351, 362, 365, 381,
416
Co-operative societies, 126, 250
Corporate social responsibility
(CSR), 385–387
Current account, 2, 80, 86, 92–97,
99–103, 107, 114, 117–119,
121, 125–129, 256, 257, 269,
270, 275, 278, 285, 295, 315,
338
Customer information system (CIS),
311, 344

D

Deferred payment, 68, 75, 133, 137,
141, 143, 151, 217, 231, 232,
255, 256, 263, 264, 281, 284,
296
Deferred payment scale, 68, 75, 143,
151, 263, 296
Deferred price, 159, 191
Depositors, 2, 4, 15, 48, 76, 79, 82,
83, 85–90, 92, 93, 96, 98,
104, 105, 112, 113, 151, 152,
238, 257, 259, 261, 267, 270,
272–278, 300, 312, 362, 363,
376, 385, 389
Diminishing musharakah, 200–218,
258
Dubai Islamic Bank, 7, 270,
275

E

Essential elements, 56–60, 63, 68, 134, 135, 154, 155, 159, 170–172, 180, 181, 192–194, 197, 218–220
Executor's and administrators' accounts, 122

F

Faisal Islamic Bank of Egypt, 7, 295
Faisal Islamic Bank of Sudan Fasting, 7
Financial reporting, 239, 299, 301, 376, 378, 382
Financing concept, 131, 151, 313
Fiqh-al-muamalat, 55, 470
Foreign exchange, 96, 248, 267, 317, 327

G

General Council for Islamic Banks and Financial Institutions (GCIBFI), 381
General investment account, 102, 104–107, 276, 279
Gharar, 3, 6, 13, 35, 51, 56, 66, 144, 292, 431, 432, 437, 455
Gharar Fahish, 50, 51
Gharar Yasir, 52
Governance, 167, 185, 240, 303, 350, 359–393, 446, 469
Government accounts, 126, 127
Government Investment Act 1983, 368
Government Investment Certificates (GIC), 368

H

Hadith, 19, 47, 234, 401
Halal, 3, 46, 58, 84, 102, 188, 196, 203, 254, 255, 285, 300, 319, 332, 351, 360, 432, 453, 460, 464
Haram, 5, 6, 9, 30, 31, 46, 47, 145, 298, 300, 360, 416, 431, 434, 455, 462
Harmonization, 77, 239, 303, 372, 380, 390, 391, 413
Hawalah, 269
Hoarding, 6, 10, 360
Hukum, 234

I

Ibadat, 20
IFSB, *see* Islamic Finance Service Boarding (IFSB)
Ijarah, 75, 131, 165, 177, 178, 180, 186, 189, 201, 217, 259, 260, 263–265, 292–294, 297, 332, 371, 378, 417, 418, 423, 460, 462, 464
Ijma, 26, 27
Ijtihad, 27, 178
Individual accounts, 88, 96, 105, 114–116, 143, 160, 174
Interest, 1–7, 9, 12–14, 27, 28, 31, 32, 35, 36, 46–49, 56, 112, 113, 126, 134, 137, 143, 145, 153, 162, 168, 176, 186, 189, 192, 198, 200, 201, 221, 225, 226, 229, 235, 237, 245, 246, 251, 255–257, 259, 270, 276, 283, 297, 309, 321, 322, 337, 343, 345, 361–363, 365, 367,

Interest (*cont.*)
  369, 376, 379, 389, 400–403,
  405, 406, 412, 416, 417, 420,
  425, 427, 431, 432, 434, 446,
  457
Interest-free Banking Scheme, 247,
  371
Interest warrants, 330, 343
Internal Syariah committee, 413,
  463
International trade, 163
Investment account, 2, 80, 85, 101,
  102, 104–107, 109, 110, 113,
  124, 125, 128, 129, 144, 234,
  248, 253, 276–280, 294, 352,
  364, 389, 390
Islamic Banking Act 1983, 2, 248
Islamic banking evolution, 7, 8,
  247–259
Islamic banking system, 1, 12, 13,
  82, 84, 113, 151, 246, 278,
  309, 417
Islamic charge card, 295, 296, 298
Islamic Finance Service Boarding
  (IFSB), 239, 240, 303, 333,
  366, 379, 381, 390, 391
Islamic Inter-bank Money Market
  (IIMM), 371
Islamic International Rating Agency
  (IIRA), 381, 382, 446
Islamization, 77, 255, 257
Istihsan, 27
Istisna, 66, 75, 80, 222–225, 268,
  298, 299, 332, 371, 423, 464

J
Jinayat, 20
Joint accounts, 88, 105, 115, 116,
  128, 143, 160, 174

Jordan Islamic Bank, 283, 290, 295
Justice, 3, 9, 14, 19, 20, 23, 40, 56,
  113, 237, 238, 359, 360, 363,
  401, 454

K
Kafalah, 77, 266, 271, 297, 318
Kuala Lumpur Stock Exchange
  (KLSE), 361, 374, 375
Kuwait Finance House, 349

L
Laws, 3, 12, 17, 19, 23, 24, 26, 28,
  33, 50, 56, 114, 116, 134,
  245, 255, 256, 300, 359,
  362, 367–369, 385, 402,
  416, 459
Leasing, 75, 133, 165, 168, 170,
  173–178, 186, 188, 201, 204,
  217, 237, 255, 260, 264, 271,
  292–294, 378, 409, 410, 460
Legal consequences, 62–65, 232
Letters of credit (LC), 257, 280, 287,
  341

M
Makrooh, 30, 31
Mandoob, 30, 31
Maruf, 28
Maslaha, 56
Maslahat, 28
Mecca, 7, 23, 47, 141, 247
Medina, 7
Modus operandi, 93, 137, 139, 140,
  142, 156–159, 168–170, 178,
  180, 194, 195, 201, 202, 220,
  232, 438

Muamalat, 20, 49, 74, 83, 228, 249, 269, 272, 277, 288, 299, 348, 350
Mubaah, 30, 31
Mudharabah, 94, 99, 101, 102, 129, 131, 237, 272, 290, 292, 317, 364, 417
Mudharabah Current Account, 94, 98, 99
Mudharabah muqayyadah, 86, 109–111, 316
Mudharabah muthalaqah, 85, 102, 104
Munakahat, 20
Murabahah, 67, 75, 80, 131, 153–157, 159, 160, 162–165, 170, 259, 260, 263, 271, 280–285, 318, 332, 351, 352, 371, 409, 423, 460
Murabahah ijarah, 246, 260, 332
Musharakah, 4, 76, 80, 131, 188–218, 237, 246, 256, 262, 285, 289, 290, 293, 302, 351, 364, 365, 389, 407, 417, 421, 424–427, 460
Muslim jurists, 5, 198, 259, 459
Muslim scholars, 36, 132, 417

N

Normal practice, 106, 107

P

Partnership accounts, 117, 119, 128
Pawn, 229, 230, 260
Payment Systems Act 2003 (PSA), 369
Pilgrimage, 7, 21, 23, 141, 247, 456
Pillars, 10, 21–23, 250, 456

Pledge, 49, 55, 77, 260, 316, 319
Potential capital, 5, 6
Professionals' accounts, 119
Profit-and loss-sharing, 3, 4, 10, 14, 76, 194, 197, 199, 236, 256, 260, 270, 276
Profit computation, 88, 89, 92, 94, 95, 99, 319
Profit motive, 388
Profit-sharing, 4, 5, 14, 35, 67, 85, 93, 99, 102, 104–106, 110, 117, 118, 193–195, 200, 202, 234, 235, 237, 272, 274, 280, 285, 289, 292, 316, 317, 364, 461
Prohibition of riba, 1, 5, 12, 35–53, 59, 163

Q

Qardh hassan, 77, 92, 93, 225–227, 231, 254, 259, 260, 294, 295, 297, 301, 317, 371
Qiyas, 27
Qualified legal scholars, 27
Quran, 8, 19, 25–27, 30, 38, 47, 55, 56, 163, 198, 254, 298, 401

R

Rahnu, 77, 227–230, 259, 260, 266
Rating Agency Malaysia (RAM), 378
Religious bodies accounts, 125, 128
Reserve requirement, 235
RHB Islamic Bank, 277
Riba
   definition, 36, 163
   element, 82

Riba buyun, 40–41
Riba duyun, 38–39
Riba fadhl, 40
Riba jahiliyyah, 39
Riba nasiah, 41
Riba Qardh, 38–39
Ribawi, 36, 40, 41
Righteous, 360
Risk, 3, 5, 6, 11, 14, 49, 50, 53, 73, 82, 87, 92, 93, 113, 137, 144, 151, 153, 154, 158, 159, 168, 188, 191, 192, 197, 218, 221, 238, 240, 245, 248, 272, 273, 294, 299, 300, 317, 321, 328, 331, 332, 341, 344–346, 354, 364, 366, 376, 377, 379, 381, 383, 387–389, 391, 393, 398, 400, 401, 407, 409, 427, 428, 432, 434, 437, 439, 452, 455, 456, 460, 461, 464

S

Sadaqah, 301, 462
Salam, 75, 80, 131, 206–222, 225, 246, 265, 332, 350, 428, 460, 464
Savings account, 2, 80, 85, 87–92, 114, 118, 128, 144, 269, 272–277, 280, 324
Schools of thought, 188, 237, 390
Securities Commission Malaysia, 353, 372
Securities Industry Act 1983 (SIA), 361, 370, 372
Social dimension, 385, 386
Sole Proprietorship Accounts, 116–117

Special investment account, 109, 110, 116, 129, 277, 279
Standardization, 354
State Bank of Pakistan (SBP), 256–258, 387
Sudanese Islamic Bank (SIB), 290
Sukuk, 32, 102, 250, 251, 332, 370, 373, 382, 398, 399, 412–427, 445, 455–457, 469
Sunnah, 26, 27, 30, 163, 198, 254
Suppliers of funds, 5
Supporting contracts, 77, 78
Syariah
  objectives, 28, 29, 300
  principles, 1, 3, 5, 11, 15, 20, 33, 88, 98, 245, 249, 253, 259, 260, 269, 270, 272, 303, 399, 401, 408, 411, 412, 414, 427, 462, 463, 465
Syariah Advisory Council, 234, 368, 370, 373, 382, 384, 434
Syariah Compliance Review, 383, 384
Syariah Supervisory Board, 7, 13, 402

T

Takaful, 32, 136, 144, 160, 248, 252, 274, 297, 372, 384, 412, 431–448, 455–457, 463
Takaful Act 1984, 248
Technology challenges, 354, 356
Trade finance, 96, 160, 237, 282, 318, 331
Transformation, 245, 257, 336
Transparency, 14, 32, 56, 248, 309, 344, 359, 361, 365, 377, 378, 380, 382–384, 389, 393, 402, 434, 439, 469

Treasury, 20, 126, 310, 317, 319, 342, 350
Trustee account, 124
Trusteeship, 9, 10, 260, 363

Trust finance, 253, 373, 406–408
Trustworthy, 384
Two-tier mudharabah, 234, 235, 364

CPSIA information can be obtained
at www.ICGtesting.com
Printed in the USA
LVHW081932090619
620633LV00012B/312/P